APPROACH MARCH

The author in 1943: a portrait by Olive Snell.

JULIAN AMERY

APPROACH MARCH

a venture in autobiography

HUTCHINSON OF LONDON

312464

HUTCHINSON & CO (*Publishers*) LTD
3 Fitzroy Square, London W1

London Melbourne Sydney Auckland
Wellington Johannesburg Cape Town
and agencies throughout the world

First published 1973

DA
591
.A6 A32
1973

*This book has been set in Times type, printed in Great Britain
on antique wove paper by Anchor Press, and
bound by Wm. Brendon, both of Tiptree, Essex*
ISBN 0 09 113270 3

Mon cher, qu'ils étaient beaux ces jours où
nous chevauchions avec l'Armée d'Italie dans
la fleur et le printemps de notre jeunesse!
Que de souvenirs, que de regrets!

Those were days when we rode with the
Army of Italy—the flower and springtime of
our youth!
What memories, what regrets!

MARSHAL MARMONT

To Catherine,
this story of the years before we met

Contents

Illustrations

Acknowledgements

I would first express my thanks to the Prime Minister, Mr. Edward Heath, for permission to publish this book while a member of his Administration. I should, however, dispel any idea that it was written during my time in Office. The typescript, indeed, was finished by the beginning of 1970; but in the interest of accuracy and for my general guidance, I submitted part or all of the book to friends who were familiar with the events described in it or whose judgement I value. To collate and digest their comments and to read the proofs necessarily took some time.

In this connection I am particularly indebted to Colonel Neil McLean, Head of the British Military Mission to the North Albanian Resistance; Colonel Bill Bailey, head of the British Military Mission to General Mihailovitch, and the late Mr. John Bennett, a close friend and colleague in S.O.E., who checked those chapters dealing with the Balkans from their own recollections and papers.

I should also like to acknowledge my gratitude to Miss Katie Guest, Miss Nicola Blundell Brown and Miss Anne Walker who typed and re-typed the text.

In accordance with the provisions of the Official Secrets Act, my manuscript was submitted to the competent authorities before publication. I am alone responsible, however, for the opinions I have expressed and for the accuracy of the statements I have made.

Preface

The General Elections of 1964 and 1966 deprived me in turn of Office and of a seat in Parliament. I found myself without a job and, virtually, without an income.

Presently Hutchinson, who had published my father's autobiography, enquired if I would write my political memoirs. The chance to vindicate nearly twenty years of public life was tempting. But, if I wrote with discretion, the book would be a bore; while, if I wrote with candour, I must offend friends and colleagues in Parliament whose ranks I hoped soon to rejoin.

Hutchinson understood my difficulty and asked if I would tell the story of my early life instead. There were, they pointed out, distinguished precedents; my pre-political memoirs were unlikely to give offence; the work, moreover, could always serve as a first volume of any subsequent autobiography. These powerful arguments, seconded by a study of my bank account, decided me to write this book.

Its theme is simple enough. It is the story of how a young Englishman, born at the end of the First World War, received a conventional education and, after rather less conventional experiences as a war correspondent, a secret agent, and a guerrilla, fulfilled his boyhood ambition to enter public life.

Memory apart, my main sources have been letters, diaries and diary notes. I had preserved almost all the letters sent to me during the years to which this book relates. My parents had done the same with mine to them. I had kept a diary of my visits to Spain during the Civil War and, though in breach of regulations, had done the same during my mission to the Albanian Resistance. I had also made notes, as leisure and security allowed, but usually within days or at most weeks of any talks or experiences that seemed of interest. For further accuracy I have submitted the main chapters to school friends or wartime comrades with whom I lived and worked. I have sought throughout to record my opinions as I held them at the time, trusting that the reader will be generous enough to relate them to the age and standpoint at which they were formed.

The Britain of my boyhood and the World at War of my youth seem very far removed from the present age. Our material environment has been transformed. Our social and even our personal values have undergone deep changes. Our role and influence in the world has sadly, though perhaps only temporarily, declined.

The British Commonwealth and Empire of these pages ranked as a great power in its own right. Our influence in India, the Middle East and Africa was still unchallenged. We alone had been in the struggle against Germany from the beginning; and this gave our statesmen and soldiers a moral ascendancy among the Allies. Nor did our Military power seem so much inferior to theirs. Our contribution in terms of ships, aircraft and men, indeed, was only surpassed by the United States in the last year of the conflict.

But the view from a secret agent's window or a guerrilla's hideout is starker than most. Survival, let alone success, depends on piercing through the fog of propaganda, the hopes of friends and the wiles of foes. My wartime work thus left me with few illusions about the dangers ahead for Britain.

Already, at the outbreak of war, I had accepted that we should have to pay a heavy price for the complacency, selfishness and cowardice which had brought us from the pinnacle of victory in 1918 to the abyss of 1939. Later, working in neutral and in occupied countries, I saw the war for the European Civil War which it was and recognised that it must lead, for a long time, to a major shift in the balance of power away from Europe to the United States and the Soviet Union. Then, as the tide of war turned in our favour, experience of the rival Resistance movements of the Balkans and the Far East helped me to discern the outlines of the 'cold wars' between the wartime allies that would grow out of the defeat of Germany and Japan.

To these external dangers was added another: the failure of British officialdom to adjust to the realities of a fast changing scene. I saw in the Balkans how, even after Churchill had taken power and France had fallen, the tradition of appeasement made us pathetically slow to adjust our policies and methods to the exigencies of total war. Later on, when victory was no longer in doubt, we proved equally slow to escape from the illusions of our own propaganda and to recognise the dangers which Soviet Imperialism and American 'anti-Colonialism' presented to our interests.

Nevertheless, I believed that much could be saved from the past and still more won in the future, if our leaders had keen enough eyes to size up the realities of our situation and strong enough nerves to seize our opportunities in time. If they gave a strong enough lead, our people would respond.

I had heard the call of politics when still only a child, and the ambition to serve in Parliament and Government had filled many of my youthful dreams. But it was wartime experience of the dangers from without and of complacency within which finally decided me to enter the lists in 1945.

Thus, as well as a record of youthful adventures, these pages are also the log book of my approach march to public life.

J.A.

112 Eaton Square
London S.W.1

Author's Note

In the spelling of names and place names I have sought to render the spoken word as nearly as possible to the way in which it is pronounced. I have thus disregarded the conventions of modern Albanian, Serbo Croat (*latinitsa*) and Turkish spelling. These may be logical enough but they give a wholly false impression to an Englishman of the sounds they are intended to convey. In modern Albanian, for instance, the name of the President of Albania is spelt *Hoxha* but pronounced *Hodja*. Likewise, in Serbo-Croat the name of the wartime Yugoslav Monarchist leader is written *Mihailovic* but pronounced *Mihailovitch*.

I have accordingly applied the phonetic system of English consonants and Italian vowels recommended by Sir Ronald Storrs in his book *Orientations*. I have followed the same general system in the transliteration of Greek, Cyrillic, Arabic and Chinese names.

My sole object has been to convey to my readers the strange sounds of what may be to some of them strange lands in the belief that these will help to evoke—for sounds have a magic of their own—something of the atmosphere of the places and countries which form the background to this story.

I

A CONVENTIONAL EDUCATION

1919–1938

'I call, therefore, a complete and generous education that which fits a man to perform justly, skilfully and magnanimously all the offices both private and public of peace and war.'

JOHN MILTON

1

Childhood

The summer of 1918 saw the supreme crisis of the First World War. General Ludendorff had launched his greatest and last offensive. The Allies responded by placing all their forces in the West under the command of Marshal Foch. My father, then a Conservative Member of Parliament but also one of the Secretaries to the War Cabinet, was involved in the setting up of the new command. He spent most of his time between Whitehall and Paris. But at the end of June he escaped for a few days with my mother to a cottage they had taken near Woldingham in Surrey. It was then that I was first thought of.

I was born at 3 Embankment Gardens at about five o'clock in the afternoon of 27 March 1919. By this time the guns were silent and the statesmen were assembling at Versailles.

I weighed 8 lbs. 2 oz. at birth and was brought into the world by Dr. Gilliat and Nurse Carter. There was a heavy fall of snow on my birthday. But two days later the sun came out and my Moses basket was put in the snow on the balcony. Sunshine and snow have remained among my chief delights.

My brother John, then seven years old, seemed quite pleased when first told about me. But, on reflection, said that he would rather have had a kitten.

I was christened on 13 June in the Crypt of the House of Commons. Canon Carnegie, who had married Joseph Chamberlain's widow, officiated. Sir Robert Borden, the Prime Minister of Canada, and Sir Henry Wilson, the C.I.G.S., were my godfathers. Mrs. Muriel Ward was my godmother.

My godfathers presented me with traditional silver mugs. But they have remained shadowy figures to me. Henry Wilson was murdered by the Sinn Feiners when I was three years old. Borden went back to Canada, and I did not see him again. Muriel Ward, on the other hand, was a perfect godmother. She gave me a hundred pounds when I was confirmed and a thousand pounds when I became an Under-Secretary. In addition, from my twenty-first birthday until her death, she sent me a Christmas gift of vintage port.

I learnt to walk and talk early. I had golden hair—I still have a lock of it—and grey-green eyes. As a small child I was supposed to look the split image of my father. Later on my build and features changed and I came to look more like my mother.

My earliest memory goes back to when I was about two and a half years old. We were spending the summer at Beaulieu in the New Forest; and after breakfast I observed a pretty insect, striped yellow and black, climbing up a window pane. I thought it would be fun to stroke it. It was a wasp and stung me. This was a great shock. It has left me to this day with a traumatic loathing of wasps. It also showed me that things are frequently not what they seem. Henceforth my innocence was diluted by the grace of suspicion.

Another early memory—I was by then three years old—is of my Aunt Sadie's wedding to Simon Rodney. I was one of the pages. I carried out my part faultlessly until the bridal procession reached the front pew reserved for relations. Here I recognised my mother and asked her out loud, 'Mummy, is this a game?' My voice was clear as a bell and indeed much better heard than the subsequent responses of the young couple. The same question has sometimes occurred to me at other people's weddings since.

Parents tend to treasure the aphorisms of their young, and I have a formidable collection of my early sayings. But only one seems worth recalling. After brooding for some time on the problem of death, I turned to my mother and said, 'When you die, Mummy, will you fade slowly like a flower? or will you pop like a balloon?'

When I was nearly four years old, the Conservatives revolted against Mr. Lloyd George, and Mr. Bonar Law formed a Government. My father became First Lord of the Admiralty and we all moved to Admiralty House. This seemed to me a superior establishment to Embankment Gardens. It had a back door leading onto the Horse Guards Parade as well as the front door onto Whitehall; and there was a one-armed door-keeper who used to salute me when I went out by it. There were suits of armour in the hall and some old cannon outside on which I used to play.

My mother had a large sitting room next to my father's library and when he was out we used to play a game called 'bears'. The principle of the game was simple. I would hide in the library. Whoever was the bear waited a couple of minutes in the sitting room and then had to find and catch me. Mr. Baldwin, Sir Austen Chamberlain, Admiral Beatty and Colonel T. E. Lawrence were among the bears. I cannot remember which of them made the best bear.

Admiralty House has now been broken up into three or four official flats. But, in those days, the First Lord of the Admiralty occupied the whole house. My brother and I had the top floor to ourselves; and, as he was mostly away at boarding school, I was virtually in sole possession. It made a perfect 'box' from which to watch the Trooping of the Colour and other parades.

The First Sea Lord's office was at right angles to my nursery window. Admiral Beatty held the post at the time, and we exchanged salutes and, later, signals most days. He came and played 'bears'. I called on him in his office and was presented with a signed photograph. I thought it would be fun to go into the Navy.

My mother rather liked this idea and encouraged me to come down to the dining room after lunch when there were Naval Officers among the guests. This led to an unfortunate incident. I had been to the Zoo in the morning. Coming down after lunch I found that my mother and the ladies had already left the dining room. 'Are there any admirals?' I asked. My mother said there were; so I marched into the dining room and shook hands with the guests in turn until I came to Admiral Hotham, a famous old 'salt' with a low brow and hairy hands. I stopped, stared and blurted out: 'Why, you're just like the gorilla I saw this morning.' The guests exploded with laughter; but the comparison was rather too apt and seems to have caused the Admiral and my father some embarrassment. At any rate I was ordered out of the room, and further post-prandial visits were, for a time, discouraged.

Presently there was a General Election. Mr. Baldwin's Government was defeated and Mr. Ramsay MacDonald came into office. Grown-ups thought the situation very serious. So did I; for we were driven from the splendours of Admiralty House to dark and dingy apartments in Cadogan Gardens. But the rigours of Opposition did not last very long. Within a few months Mr. Baldwin was back in Downing Street, and my father became Secretary of State for Dominions and Colonies. We now moved to 112 Eaton Square, where I have lived ever since.

In those days an Eaton Square house was considered on the modest side for a Cabinet Minister. But it seemed substantial enough to me. My father had plenty of room to put up his Persian pictures and his books. My French governess and I had three rooms to ourselves. Now, of course, most of these houses have been converted into flats.

My father was very busy and I did not see much of him in these early days. I knew he was very important and held him in some awe. He did not like this and to narrow the gap encouraged my brother and me to call him Coco. This surprised his visitors, but I think it helped him to gain a child's confidence. Later on we would become very close friends.

My mother was for me a creature of pure tenderness and gentle radiance. It was many years, indeed, before I became fully aware of the steel of her will-power and the tribal intensity of her loyalties. But, from the first, there was total confidence between us. I never kept secrets from her, as I grew older, because I knew that her devotion would always be stronger than her disapproval. We often fought about people and ideas, but, when the cards were down, she would always be on my side. So it has continued.

Children in those days saw less of their parents than they do now. The nursery was my world. My nanny, Caroline Meade, had large blue eyes, golden hair and rosy cheeks. My memory of her is a gentle one. She provided, unwittingly, the occasion of my first attempt to remedy social injustice. One winter night an organ grinder and his little son came and played their barrel organ outside our home. The poor man looked hungry and cold in the gathering gloom of a November evening. I wanted to help him. Nanny Meade's wages lay upon the table—a little pile of pound notes kept down by two half-crowns. I put them in an envelope, opened the window and flung them out. Strange, loud, but patently grateful noises came from the street below. The organ grinder ground out a few more bars; and then he and his little son beat a hasty retreat into the night. I was rebuked for dealing so freely with other people's money. But I have since sat in Governments which earned great credit for doing much the same thing.

Most men fall in love with their mother or their nanny. I apparently told Mr. Lloyd George, when he came to tea at Embankment Gardens, that I meant to marry Nanny Meade. But, already, another potent feminine influence was at work in my nursery world.

My brother was in the care of a French governess, Jeanne le Gallen, known as Pipette. Pipette was a Breton girl from Belle Ile, the rugged island off Finistère. Her father, the skipper of a deep sea fishing trawler, had been drowned in a storm off Iceland when she was only five. Her mother had died soon afterwards; and Pipette had been brought up in a convent in Vannes. It was an old-fashioned and strict convent where the girls took their weekly baths, wearing nightshirts for modesty's sake. It was very devout and rather Royalist in tone. But it had given Pipette a sound education and some knowledge of French history and literature.

Pipette was just leaving the convent when the First World War broke out. Her nearest relations had disappeared in the German invasion of the north and she had been sent to England in 1915 as an orphan refugee. She had crossed on a troop ship with an Irish regiment and had lurid memories of the experience. A convent in London soon found her a job as governess to a farmer's son in the South of England. There she and her charge amused themselves in the first week by setting fire to a haystack. She was duly returned to the convent and, a few weeks later, was recommended to my parents by the Mother Superior. She had been with my brother for a couple of years when I was born.

Pipette shared the nursery with Nanny Meade and looked after me on

Nanny's days off. Nanny left us when I was four years old. My brother was now at boarding school; and I remained in Pipette's care. This was to prove a stimulating experience.

Pipette was short, dark and very lively, with long black hair—so long that she could sit on it. She had the true gallic appreciation of good food and criticised our nursery diet freely. She also had the traditional gallic fear of draughts. When we stayed with friends, indeed, she was apt to move the furniture in my bedroom to make sure that I was not exposed to their baneful influence. Pipette never learned to speak English, and I thus grew up speaking English and French with almost equal fluency.

One afternoon—I was aged six at the time—I had been showing off my proficiency in French to my parents. My father, tiring of this entertainment, asked rather sarcastically, 'What is the French for "chatterbox"?' Rather offended, I replied gravely that it would be *bavard* or *loquace* but that if the chatterbox was repetitive it should be *radoteur*. This reply silenced the Secretary of State, and I retired to my nursery satisfied that I had got the better of that particular debate.

Living with Pipette taught me at an early age that there are two points of view about most things. The histories of England and of France are largely concerned with the wars between them. But the version of events taught in my day school was much at variance from the one Pipette had learnt at her convent. Returning home from school I would tell Pipette what I had learnt about the burning of Joan of Arc, the tyranny of Louis the XIV, or the insatiable ambitions of Napoleon. She was indignant that I should be so misled, and gave me her own very different interpretation of these things. Much perplexed I repaired to my father for enlightenment. He explained how the same actions and events could be interpreted and judged in very different ways. Thus I first became aware of the truth of Lord Acton's dictum that history is more often a conflict between right and right than between right and wrong.

It was much the same with religion. My mother was a strong Anglican; Pipette, a devout Roman Catholic who sometimes took me to her church. My father seemed to steer his course by the philosophers of Greece and Rome. I was to go through phases of faith and agnosticism in growing up. But from the age of six or seven I had begun to realise that there are many ways of coming to the truth.

Pipette had a large repertoire of rather tall stories about her life and family in Brittany, and these stimulated my childish imagination. Rome and Athens had been great in their day. Paris might be the capital of Europe, but Vannes was the centre of the world and Belle Ile its enchanted island. I have never dared to visit them lest other and duller accounts of them should prove more accurate than hers.

Pipette had accumulated a mass of historical and general knowledge, largely from reading encyclopaedias, and often invoked the example of the heroes of the past. Faced with a problem, she would ask: 'What do you think Richelieu would have done?' If I was guilty of some childish lapse, she would say 'Can you imagine Napoleon behaving like that?' There are worse ways of giving a child standards.

In politics she called herself a Royalist and read the *Action Française*. For all that, she was rather proud of the French Revolution and sometimes suggested that the British governing classes could do with a little trimming by the guillotine. She also had a thoroughly Jacobin contempt for the rights of property. Her principle on a country walk was to follow the main road until we saw a signpost saying 'Trespassers will be Prosecuted'. This was her invariable cue to turn into the property concerned and then strike across country. This sometimes led to trouble, but we usually extricated ourselves by her inability and my pretence not to speak English.

With my brother away at boarding school, I was virtually an only child. In those days children had much less social life than mine seem to have today. I remember very few parties. There was no television. I had to devise much of my own entertainment. In the absence of other children I invested my toys with living qualities. They mattered very much to me. Indeed, when the Vicar of St. Peter's, preaching at a children's service, said: 'I know you would all be glad to give some of your toys to other children if your mothers asked you to,' I got up and shouted, 'Certainly not.' It seemed a most subversive proposal and I felt bound to stamp on it before it spread.

My toys were two kinds. There were weapons—mostly pistols and daggers. These I regarded as an essential part of my dress. Then there were toy soldiers of which I could mobilise some fifteen hundred. They were of every nationality and period, and of all arms, including artillery and transport. When mustered on the nursery floor for a full dress battle they made a formidable array and seriously impeded the serving of our meals.

I loved to be read to as a small child and, from the age of seven, began to read voraciously myself. My early favourites were the *Swiss Family Robinson*, P. C. Wren's novels about the French Foreign Legion and Dumas' *Count of Monte Cristo*.

At the age of six I went to a small day school in Kensington run by Miss Ironside. She and the school still flourish and, at the time of writing, my youngest daughter has only recently left it. Miss Ironside instructed us in Geography by the simple process of spreading a map on the classroom floor and taking us on journeys to far off places. We had to call out the names of the countries and the principal cities through which her pointer passed and describe the climate, the scenery, the inhabitants and the fauna. It was a simple but amusing way to teach—it also made me long to travel.

It was at Miss Ironside's that I first fell in love. One morning we were joined for our Geography lesson by a very pretty girl with fair hair and blue eyes. She was called Flossie Candler Cobb. During the mid-morning break I found her in tears. She was convinced that Miss Ironside's pointer was a cane and that she would be whipped with it if she made mistakes. I reassured her with all the wide experience of a boy in his second term. From then on she looked on me as her protector and we became close friends. Flossie was American. Her mother had delicious cakes at tea, and there was a tiger skin rug in their flat. I liked her very much and have often wondered what became of her.

Pipette had no sense of time and found it impossible to get from Eaton Square to Miss Ironside's school in Kensington by nine o'clock. I was therefore moved to Mr. Gladstone's school in Cliveden Place which was only five minutes away. The master who taught French there seemed singularly ignorant of the language and made a lot of elementary mistakes. In the interests of the other boys and their fee paying parents I thought it my duty to correct him. Accordingly, after putting my hand up for leave to speak, I put him right both as to syntax and pronunciation. He did not like this at all, all the more as he knew that I was right and that he was in the wrong. But schoolmasters have great powers. In due course he settled accounts with me, giving me two hours extra work for some trifling lapse which would normally have met with a mild rebuke. Thereafter, though often sorely tempted, I never again tried to protect my school-fellows from the vagaries of French as it was then taught—and, I fear, still seems to be—in even the best of our schools.

On the whole I was a serious child, but there was the occasional fall from grace. Sir Luke Fildes had painted my father's portrait while he was Dominions' Secretary. It was to be presented to him, in recognition of his services to the Empire; and a small but select party was invited to the private view. I was about six years old and went with my mother. There were perhaps twenty or thirty people in a smallish studio. On a table I saw a pin cushion. I pulled out a pin and soon discovered that by driving it into the behind of some grown-up I could make him or her jump about and pirouette most amusingly. After each stab I concealed the weapon and assumed an expression of angelic innocence. At first I operated cautiously but then the excitement went to my head. I stabbed too often and, perhaps, too deep. I was caught by Sir Ronald Storrs[1] and led away in disgrace. Storrs later told me that he watched for several minutes before intervening and remembered it as a most entertaining performance.

My life, out of school, was very full. I learnt to ride, at Mr. Smith's

[1] Sir Ronald Storrs: the distinguished orientalist and Governor of Jerusalem and Cyprus.

riding school and in the Row. I learned to swim at the Bath Club. At weekends there were visits to the Zoo, the Natural History Museum and the Imperial War Museum. Presently I graduated to the National Gallery, the Tate and the British Museum. The Italian Renaissance school was my first love and still remains so.

My Aunt May, who was blind and something of a power in St. Dunstan's, often had tickets for the Royal Box in the Albert Hall on Sunday afternoons. Pipette and I used them regularly and I have vivid memories of hearing Toti dal Monte and the Galli-Curci. I have never been able to sing a note myself, and my taste in music remains romantic rather than classical. But these concerts at the Albert Hall were a good preparation for the joys of the Opera.

We had no country house, my father preferring to spend our limited resources on holidays abroad. My Aunt Sadie, however, and her husband Simon Rodney, had a small house in Hertfordshire where we often went for the weekend. When I first stayed there, we were met at the station by a pony trap. Later on they had a motor car, still considered something of a luxury and rather dashing.

Simon was a descendant of the spendthrift Lord Rodney who had lost his fortune on the Turf. He was very handsome and always immaculately dressed. He shot well and rode even better. But, as he had no money, he had been forced to leave the Grenadier Guards after the War and go into the City. At this time he thought business rather beneath his dignity, though in due course he would prosper in it. Years later I remember him telling us of how hard a time he had had as a young man. But when I pressed him for examples of hardship he could only recall his embarrassment, one weekend, at finding that everyone else was wearing a white tie at dinner and he had only brought a dinner jacket. He had been so pushed financially, he explained, that he had only one tail coat and it happened to be away at the cleaners.

Simon taught me to play tennis and the rudiments of fly-fishing. As I grew up he also supervised my wardrobe, a subject in which my father showed no interest at all. Simon's wife, Sadie, was my mother's sister and was to become more a sister than an aunt to me. But that was a little later on.

We usually spent the Easter holidays in Devon. My father's family came from there, and we still had cousins living at Ashburton and around Lustleigh.

At first we used to go to Exmouth by the sea. There I learnt to row and sail and spent hours on the rocks at low tide looking for shellfish and hermit crabs. I also formed a gang of the local fishermen's children. We made wooden daggers and swords for ourselves and careered up and down the beach and along the pier. Other children were given the choice of joining our gang for an entrance fee of a bar of chocolate or of being driven off the beach. One member of my gang, a boy called Francis, took me bird nesting. But the following winter he got pneumonia and died. On his death bed he left me his collection of eggs. I have them still, though I have never gone nesting again.

My teacher in the ways of the sea was an old sailor called Tommy. He was a kindly man much given to singing and joking. He chewed tobacco and taught me to swear. One year we were told that he had died of drink. I was very upset; I had never heard of such things happening.

As I grew older we abandoned Exmouth and spent our Devonshire holidays on Dartmoor. Usually we stayed with a Miss Haynes—a tough Eton-cropped young lady who kept an excellent stable near Manaton. She took me out hunting with the South Devon which used to meet at such romantic spots as Jane's Grave or the Warren Inn on the Princetown Road. Dartmoor may not be the 'Shires, but with its stone walls and bogs, and its long moorland gallops through swirling mists, hunting there is always an adventure.

Occasionally we would go and have lunch or tea with my old cousin John at Ashburton. He had a beard and kept golden pheasants and peacocks. He knew all about the habits of foxes, badgers, otters and other beasts on the moor. He was also a learned man and a die-hard protectionist, typical of what Sir William Lawson called 'the longhorned Tories'.

In the winter holidays we mostly went skiing, usually in the Engadine. I first put on skis in my fifth year and, with the exception of the War years, have used them ever since. I suppose skiing has given me greater exhilaration than anything else.

Since I first skied, the technique has changed continually and come round almost full circle. When I started the great thing was to keep your feet together and lean slightly back. A little later we were told to have our feet apart and to crouch down in the so-called *Arlberg* style. After the War we were made to counter-rotate and lean forward as far as possible. Nowadays we are very much back to where I began.

Crown Prince Ghazi of Iraq, who had just gone to Harrow, spent one winter holiday with us in the Alps. He was an attractive boy and treated me like a younger brother, even helping me to do up my ski boots—a task I still find very irksome. It is not everybody who has had their boots done up by a lineal descendant of the Prophet.

Next summer Ghazi came to stay with my Aunt Sadie, bringing with him the redoubtable Jaaffar Pasha Al Askari, who had played a leading part in the Arab revolt against the Turks and was then a Minister in the Iraqi Government. Jaaffar Pasha was one of the stoutest men I have ever seen. My Aunt Sadie's dining room was furnished with slender Regency armchairs. When we sat down to luncheon, the Pasha lowered himself between the arms of his chair. But though he managed to insert his posterior between them he could not get it through far enough to sit down. The arms were too close together. He accordingly stood up again but the chair rose with him and he had to prise it away. Jaaffar was murdered soon afterwards; and this, alas, is my only memory of Lawrence's gallant comrade in arms.

A little later Ghazi's father, King Feisal,[1] came to London. He dined at home one night and I was allowed down before dinner to meet him. He kissed me on both cheeks and questioned me in French about my school life. Next day he sent me a golden dagger and a golden scimitar. No man has impressed me so much as King Feisal by the perfection of his features and the nobility of his bearing.

Ministers did not work as hard in those days as they do now, and my father usually managed to take two months off in the summer. We would spend a month to five weeks in Switzerland, where he went climbing, and then go on for an 'after cure', as it was called, to the Italian lakes.

This involved staying in hotels. Children are, generally speaking, a nuisance in hotels. But hotels are a great education for children. The business of ordering food, of making yourself understood in different languages and seeing how other people live and behave is all very instructive. I struck up passing friendships with other hotel guests. One I remember was Lilian Harvey, the diminutive star of *Congress Dances* to whom I completely lost my heart. Another was an American who amused himself teaching me to smoke. My father was very cross and promised me a hundred pounds if I kept off tobacco until I was twenty-one. I stuck to the bargain and prize the advantage far above the reward. During the war I smoked Turkish cigarettes for a time, but found the business of cigarette cases, matches and butt ends irksome and dirty and gave it up. I still smoke an occasional cigar; but this is an indulgence not a habit.

One year my father took me to Paris. We went to see Notre Dame, Napoleon's tomb and the Arc de Triomphe. Notre Dame was very dark and I did not really take it in. The eternal flame at the unknown warrior's grave caught my imagination; but it was the Invalides that made the deepest impression. When I got back to England, I read everything I could find about Napoleon. I have pursued this study ever since and at one time began to assemble material for yet another life.

My early study of the Emperor however was presently cut short by more urgent pre-occupations. I was now nine years old and the time had come to wrench me from the bosom of my family and send me to preparatory school.

[1] King Feisal: leader of the Arab Revolt against the Turks in the First World War and first King of Modern Iraq.

My father was a strong believer in a classical education and his choice fell upon Summerfields at Oxford. I was duly taken to see the establishment and was asked whether I would like to go there. I did not really have much choice in the matter, but it was nice to be consulted; and guessing that consultation did not mean the same thing as consent, said that I would do what he thought best.

His diary records that I reported enthusiastically about the school to my French governess. My mother, however, noted that I approached the beginning of term with lively anxiety. The latter view accords more closely with my own recollection.

I was, nevertheless, greatly cheered by the arrival of grey flannel and blue serge suits, complete with long trousers and waistcoats. There is nothing like a new suit for facing an ordeal. When the great day came I was invited to order my farewell lunch. I chose eggs on sweetcorn, a chicken curry and ice-cream. After lunch my mother left us and my father and I stayed to drink my first glass of port. Thus fortified, we all climbed into a large, old fashioned, hired Daimler, driven by a large, old fashioned coachman turned chauffeur, and set off for Oxford.

2

Summerfields

It was a sunny day and, at the start of the drive to Summerfields, the sense of adventure outweighed the fear of the unknown. The nearer we drew to Oxford the lower my spirits sank. We reached the school at about five o'clock. A kindly but distant master showed me my desk in a dingy school-room. My parents and I were then invited to go out into the playing fields. There I found another new boy called Francis Fisher with his parents. We played about together in the ha-ha that separated the playing fields from the Headmaster's private lawn. Then our parents called us over, said goodbye and disappeared. We remained alone. It was all rather strange. But Francis seemed an agreeable companion; and, as yet, nothing actively unpleasant had happened.

Presently a master called us in. We were given tea and taken to our dormitory. This was a pleasant enough room which Francis Fisher and I shared with two older boys, who had been at the school perhaps a year. We questioned them about school life. What they had to say was not altogether reassuring. All the same I soon dropped off to sleep.

With my brother away at boarding school, I had for all practical purposes been an only child. I had had two rooms of my own ever since I could remember and rather enjoyed being alone. Pipette had been my constant companion; my mother had surrounded me with love. I was not 'spoilt' in the sense of having had my whims indulged or my lapses overlooked. But I had spent more time in the company of grown-ups than of other children. I had little experience of sharing; none at all of the rough and tumble of collective life. I held strong opinions on a number of subjects; and some of these, acquired from my French governess, ran rather contrary to the normal schoolboy view. In particular, I had developed a point of honour which would have been excessive in a sixteenth-century Castilian grandee. I took offence at the slightest pro-vocation and was determined to leave no injury unrevenged and never to compromise with principle. These lofty, not to say heroic, sentiments were scarcely calculated to make my life comfortable in a school of a hundred small boys kept in order by a handful of harassed masters.

The first morning started with a cold bath. I had had cold baths for fun in very hot weather. But this was quite different. The day was chilly. To queue up naked with half a dozen boys in a draughty bathroom was uncomfortable and seemed to me undignified. Worse still, when I hesitated to take the plunge, I was roughly submerged by an officious under-matron. We then dressed hurriedly and were lined up in a lobby downstairs with our backs to the wall. From there we were marched to breakfast down a long, stone passage with four prefects picketing the route.

Breakfast started with grey, lumpy porridge—one mouthful of this was enough. Then came a rissole which smelt bad and tasted worse. I pushed it away. I had never eaten *en grand comité* before; and the noise of a hundred small children breakfasting together seemed appalling. Every now and then someone rang a bell. Once the master in charge barked out an order, and two boys at the other end of the room were made to stand in the corner. This seemed ominous. The only decoration in the dining hall seemed to be wooden boards with the names of scholars engraved on them. A lump formed in my throat. I forced it down. Was I really to live like this for three whole months? Tears welled up in my eyes—I drove them back. I was determined to keep up a front.

But, with breakfast over, I felt a passionate longing to be alone and drop the mask, at any rate for a few minutes. But there was no place of refuge. Only crowded schoolrooms with hard benches. Then I had a brain-wave. In the lavatory at least I could be alone. There, surely, I could lock the door and give vent to my feelings for five minutes without arousing pity or ridicule. I found my way to the Vinery, as the conveniences at Summerfields were known. Rather to my surprise they were in a kind of garden. To my consternation they had no doors. To my disgust they were earth closets without plugs. The first seat I tested broke. The stench was appalling. There was no privacy to be found in these privies. My morale sank to my boots. I wandered disconsolately back towards my form room, the tears coursing slowly down my cheeks.

In the passage I passed an older boy. Seeing me in tears, he jeered 'you rotten little cry-baby'. This was too much. He was nearly twice my size, but I flew at him, punching him on the mouth so that his lip split against his teeth. I got much the worst of the subsequent fighting, but, luckily, we were soon separated by a passing prefect who rebuked my opponent sharply for bullying a new boy. This prefect was called Ken Trevaskis. It was his last term, and I did not see much more of him at Summerfields. But I at once formed a very high opinion of him. This was confirmed in later years when we worked together, first in Rhodesia and later in South Arabia where he became an outstandingly successful High Commissioner.

This opening fight was unfortunate. The boy whose lip I had split inflamed opinion against me; and I did not benefit from the indulgence which most schools show to new boys. My first letter home, written four days later, is revealing:

> The world seems very different here. I have already made a few friends and I am sorry to say a few enemies. Please come down. Write and say you can come. Please write a letter to me every day, if you can. I have seen the lavatories. They are most awful with no plugs. Most of the boys are bullies and kick.

Subsequent letters are more cheerful, describing cricket matches, retailing school anecdotes and asking for money. But even these show me counting the days until the end of term.

I disliked the diet, particularly the weekly stewed mutton which was known as 'Cat's meat' and a bread-and-butter pudding which we called 'brother where art thou' because the currants in it were so rare. I hated never being alone and was irked by the lack of quiet and comfort in which to read. I also came in for more than my fair share of bullying during my first year. This, I dare say, was largely my fault. The Head-master certainly seemed to think so.

> *Summer, 1928.* I am pleased with the way he is developing though occasionally the smartness of his tongue brings upon him the wrath of his equals.
> *Christmas, 1928.* His caustic tongue has often brought him into trouble with his peers. I hope he will be more circumspect in the future.

Matters came to a head at the beginning of my third term. I was standing in a classroom, innocently sharpening a pencil with a new scout knife. A boy, my senior by about a year, asked me what I thought I was doing wearing a red silk handkerchief in my breast pocket. In the memor-able words of the Welsh Attorney I 'took the high line and told him to bugger off'. He promptly struck me across the face. I saw red and struck back, but the knife was still in my hand. A long gash appeared just above my victim's right eye; and the blood began to flow. He screamed in fear, I think, rather than pain, and an angry crowd gathered around me. School-boys rightly deprecate the use of *arme blanche*. But I still had the knife and, though 'those behind cried forward', no one dared to come on. At this point a master intervened. My victim was led off to the Sanatorium; I was reported to the Headmaster.

After lunch came the summons to the Study. A large and unfriendly crowd accompanied me to the Study door. They looked forward with evident relish to hearing my chastisement if they could not actually see it. Mr. Williams seemed very angry indeed. He lectured me, at some length, on the iniquity of my action. But though I grasped at once what he thought, I remained uncertain what he would do. By a miraculous coincidence it emerged that he had done the same thing himself when a boy. On reflection, therefore, he had decided not to punish me but to talk to me. I raised no objection to this way of proceeding. He filled his pipe, sat down, and motioned me to take a chair. We then had the first of many man to man talks in which he patiently brought me to understand the importance of turning away wrath with a soft answer and of showing some regard to public opinion as well as to the letter of the law. No community could flourish otherwise. It was all quite simple, but I had not seen it like that before. Children's minds grow up in bits; and grown-ups are often confused by the fact that a child who seems very mature in some ways can still be surprisingly childish in others.

Having satisfied himself that I had taken his words to heart, Mr. Williams went on to talk to me about skiing, mountain climbing and other things which I enjoyed doing in the holidays. Altogether, the interview must have lasted about half an hour.

When I emerged from the study, I was quickly surrounded by a knot of boys. They wanted to know what had happened. I was in an unusually strong position. I could issue my own communique about the meeting, without fear of contradiction. I explained that there had, of course, been no question of punishment or 'any rot like that'. The Headmaster and I had had a cordial exchange of views. I had seen his point; he had seen mine; and we looked forward to close co-operation in future. I was then able to inform them that my victim had had three stitches put into his head, but was making a good recovery. I proposed to shake hands with him when he came back from the Sanatorium. For the rest I regarded the incident as closed.

The effect was electric. Schoolboys are very conventional. If the Head-master saw fit not to punish what they had regarded as attempted murder, they were content to abide by his judgement. Nor did anyone try to bully me again. My victim's scar and the Headmaster's attitude discouraged other would-be bullies. For my part, I learned to keep my temper and my tongue under closer control.

I now settled down in the school, made many friends and began to find life much less unpleasant. I had come to terms with my fellows. I still had to come to terms with the Masters whom I regarded as a species of gaolers.

As a child I had a rather over-developed sense of justice and of what are nowadays called 'Human Rights'. I had not yet learned to accept the basic injustice of the human condition. At lunch one day, Mr. Bolton, a rather formidable senior master, complained that I was making too much noise and told me to stop talking. I had not, as it happened, been talking at all. Springing to my feet, I replied, 'Sir, that is an outrageous statement,

I have not spoken for five minutes.' My neighbours corroborated my story. Mr. Bolton withdrew the charge but declined my request for an apology. I do not know whether the incident rankled with him, but, anyway, a few evenings later he accused me of ragging in the dormitory. I had not, in fact, been ragging on that particular night, but though I protested my innocence, I was given a beating. These two acts of injustice coming from a senior master called, I thought, for some retaliation.

With Francis Fisher's help I proceeded to form a movement which we called 'The Anti-Authority League'. We started by forming cells in the different classes. Then, when no masters were about, I addressed meetings. These were perfectly orderly. There was no violence or incitement to break the rules. I simply aired our grievances, unmasked current examples of injustice and advised my fellows to adopt an attitude of coldness and sullenness towards the masters until authority showed a change of heart. Within a few days something like a third of the school had enrolled in the League.

It so happened—though we were quite unaware of it—that a heated debate was then going on among schoolmasters about how discipline should be enforced. Some favoured the old-fashioned 'Do as you're told and don't argue' formula. Others maintained that rules must be explained and justified as well as enforced. On the whole the Summerfields authorities leaned to the more 'progressive' approach. A leading article in the Summerfields magazine that year (1930) urged masters to co-operate with the boys and to recognise that they might sometimes be wrong themselves. This liberal trend favoured our movement. I was warned, rather like an agitator in the Colonies, that if I broke the rules, there would be serious trouble. But no attempt was made to obstruct constitutional discussion. Better still, the masters actually investigated our complaints and repealed some of the more irksome minor regulations we had denounced.

From then on the masters seemed to take more trouble about me and went out of their way to make themselves pleasant. I responded to this new approach and settled down to become a useful member of the establishment. I had learned the golden lesson that nuisance value can pay handsomely as long as you know when to stop.

The rougher edges had been knocked off me and I now began to get some positive benefit from Summerfields.

The accent at Summerfields was on the Classics and the Bible. The school prided itself on providing the best preparation for scholarships to Eton, and these were, essentially, classical scholarships. It also had a strong Anglican tradition; and the Headmaster, like his predecessors, was a clergyman.

I still believe that a thorough grounding in the Greco-Roman and Semitic cultures are the best academic preparation for an English boy. Quite apart from its religious importance, the study of the Bible is an education in History, Philosophy and the English language. It is essential to an appreciation of European literature, history and art. It also opens the door to an understanding of Islam and the cultures of the Middle East and Central Asia. They taught it well at Summerfields and, for this, I shall always be grateful.

I have more reservations about the way in which they taught the Classics. Learning to read and write Latin and Greek no doubt exercises the mind, stimulates the memory and trains a boy how to work. But we devoted so much time to it and concentrated on such a narrow front that I, for one, grew bored. And boredom is the greatest enemy of learning. I longed that we should study the Classics like the Bible in translation. I still believe that this would be the better course. It would provide a much wider knowledge of the Poets, Historians and Philosophers of Greece and Rome; and they form, after all, the other and more indigenous branch of our European culture.

Concentration on the Classics left little time for History. Our History lessons were dry as dust. Happily they were supplemented by occasional readings from Carlyle, Creasy and other historians. These just kept the flame of interest alive. I am glad they did. My subsequent experience has tended to confirm the truth of Napoleon's admonition, 'Let my son read History. It is the only true philosophy.'

No time at all was given to the Sciences at Summerfields and little enough at Eton. This was a pity. In later years I was to exercise considerable responsibilities in the scientific field. I do not think a better scientific grounding would have altered my decisions. But my ignorance of basic terms and assumptions made the work more burdensome than it need have been. It also inclined me to rely more than I would otherwise have done on scientific advisers who could express themselves in plain English. As it happened, they proved to be the most reliable, but that was just my good luck!

The teaching at Summerfields was by present-day standards intensive and the methods sometimes harsh. Bad work as well as bad conduct was punished by the cane. This produced a rather disagreeable climate of fear, but it certainly achieved its purpose of helping to concentrate the mind.

In accordance with its motto *Mens Sana in Corpore Sano* (a healthy mind in a healthy body) Summerfields gave due prominence to games. In summer we played cricket, and boys were encouraged to follow cricketing form in the newspapers. In winter we played soccer and, in spring, rugger. I enjoyed all three and for a time was very keen on cricket. But I was never really good at any of them and, in the end, grew discouraged.

It is not much fun playing games, especially in bad weather, if you seldom make a run and never kick a goal.

There was also scope for more individual sports like golf and swimming. I enjoyed these much more.

The personal influence of the masters was not the least part of our education. The Headmaster, Cyril Williams, was a clergyman with a vinous countenance and a rather cynical turn of mind. A strong Conservative, he used to say that he hated all change, even change for the better. He affected a rather pedantic turn of humour, largely, I think, because the boys liked it best that way. A favourite exchange was: 'Please, Sir, can I go to the Vinery?' (Summerfields for lavatory). 'I don't know whether you *can*, my boy, but you *may*.'

Williams' principal partner was 'Bobs' Allington, like Williams the son of a former Summerfields Headmaster. Unlike Williams, Allington wore rough tweed suits and held left-wing opinions. He was very approachable and treated boys like grown-ups. This made him popular.

Another partner was Geoffrey Bolton—known as G.B. He was a tall, austere, boney classicist and cricketer, who hated foreigners and loathed Lloyd George. He introduced me to P. G. Wodehouse and to the 'surge and splendour' of Butcher and Lang's translation of the *Odyssey*. But we never really got on.

Kindest of the four partners was John Evans, a gentle creature who affected mock rages and, though infinitely teasable, was withal very wise. When I developed too strong an interest in spiritualism he lent me a book on it from his own library. This was so boring that I soon dropped the subject. Years later he confessed to me that this had always been his purpose.

There were interesting men too among the junior masters. Cecil Day Lewis, later Poet Laureate, taught Mathematics and sometimes Latin, though his heart was clearly not in teaching. L. A. G. Strong, the author of *The Brothers* and other slightly macabre stories, taught French, History and English. His sarcastic and, at times, almost sadistic turn of mind made him unpopular. But if he liked a boy, and he seemed to like me, he took immense trouble, in and out of school, in helping to develop his mind.

Most of my reading at Summerfields was biography. I was obsessed with the great captains of history, Alexander, Julius Caesar, and above all, Napoleon. But a friend, Adrian Batchelor Taylor, convinced me that I was missing a lot, if I only read biography. He introduced me to Bernard Shaw and Henry James. I do not know what became of him, but acknowledge a lasting debt.

For all these academic, athletic and cultural interests, we were still children. Much of our time was spent, and rightly, on flying model aeroplanes or playing with toy cars. I bred white mice in the holidays and though these were not allowed at school I did a brisk business selling them at 1*s*. 6*d*. a pair. Then there were the friendships and feuds of childhood. The feuds are stilled. Some of the friendships were continued at Eton or revived in later life. Most have become memories, jolted occasionally by the realisation that some bald and portly businessman was once Smith minor with his elfin charm and golden hair.

3

The Call to Politics

When I went to Summerfields it was still my ambition to join the Navy. One holiday, indeed, I was taken to Dartmouth to see the place for myself. But powerful influences were shaping a different course for me.

Winston Churchill once remarked that my father seemed to think that the British Empire was his private property. There was a grain of truth in the criticism. The unity and strength of the Commonwealth and Empire were the central themes of my father's life. He had visited all the Dominions and most of the colonies; and news from them figured largely in his conversation. Whether in Office or in Opposition, he felt it his personal responsibility to urge, encourage and advise on every aspect of Imperial policy.

We were a small family, even counting cousins. But all of us had strong Imperial connections.

My paternal grandfather, Charles Amery, though born in Devon, had prospected for gold in Australia, planted tea in Assam, joined the Indian Service and died in the forests of what is now Guyana.

My father had made his name as *Times* Correspondent in the South African War, where he had become Lord Milner's ablest propagandist. Later he had worked with Joseph Chamberlain in the Tariff Reform Campaign.

My father's two brothers had perished in the First World War. But both had moved in the Imperial sphere. Harold Amery had transferred early from the Black Watch to the Egyptian Army. He had served on Kitchener's staff in Cairo and become Director of Intelligence in Khartoum. His younger brother, Geoffrey, had chosen the Far East and become a District Commissioner in the Federated States of Malaya.

I never knew my two uncles; but my father had many stories about them. I used to play with Harold's medals and *tarboosh* and dress up in Geoffrey's Malayan clothes.

The Imperial links were even stronger on my mother's side of the family. Her father had emigrated from Wales to Canada as a boy and there married into a family of American colonists who had stood by us in the American War of Independence and been compensated after Britain's defeat with grants of land in Canada.

The United Empire Loyalist tradition remained very strong in Ontario. It combined a deep suspicion of everything American with an almost exaggerated reverence for the Crown and everything British. I absorbed these sentiments at my mother's knee and they were powerfully reinforced by the rest of her family.

Her brother, Hamar Greenwood,[1] had sat in Liberal Cabinets but his radicalism was 'the radicalism of Empire'. Her eldest sister, Mary, had a fund of stories of Canada in the old days. Being blind, she had a companion, a Mrs. Thatcher, who had been one of the pioneers in New Zealand, and told lurid stories of cannibalism and the Maori Wars.

Family apart, our house was much frequented by visitors from overseas. As a result I soon came to accept differences in race and colour as perfectly natural and to identify places on the map with real people I had met and talked to.

Then, just before I went to Summerfields, my parents embarked on a tour of all the Dominions. This was a new departure for a British statesman in office and attracted widespread interest. The tour lasted six months. I followed it closely in the newspapers and my mother's letters. They came back with a film of the tour and a trunk load of presents for me given by their different hosts.

A year or two later, when in Opposition, my father went to Canada to make the first ascent of Mount Amery, a peak in the Rockies called after him by a previous Canadian Government. He also conquered a new peak, and, at his suggestion, this was called Mount Julian. Then there was my friendship with Prince Ghazi. This opened the horizons of the Middle East to me and these were presently extended by a chance encounter with Dr. Weizmann.[2] We met him on the Orient Express and he offered us a lift from Innsbruck to Bolzano where my mother and I were to join my father. He bought me a box of Austrian tin soldiers at the beginning of the drive and, indefatigable propagandist that he was, talked to me about Zionism during much of the drive.

It is hardly surprising that in this climate of people and ideas I developed a precocious interest in politics and especially in Imperial questions. Politics did not seem at all 'stuffy' to me as they so often do to children; rather the reverse. My godfather, after all, had been murdered for political reasons. Several people had tried to shoot my Uncle Hamar; and, though he had been out of office for eight years, he still had a detective. My father had two detectives who often played with me and

[1] Hamar Greenwood: Liberal Member of Parliament 1906–22. Under-Secretary of State Home Office, Chief Secretary for Ireland, 1st Viscount Greenwood of Holbourne.
[2] Dr. Chaim Weizmann: Zionist leader and first President of Israel.

sometimes let me handle their revolvers. I knew that in America the gangsters had bodyguards. But in England the only people who had bodyguards were the politicians. This made them seen rather important.

In December 1929 I was taken to the House of Commons to hear a full dress debate on unemployment. 'Jimmie' Thomas[1] opened for the newly elected Labour Government, but I found it very difficult to follow him. There were several other speakers. Then Lloyd George rose. I had not recognised the others, but knew him at once. He began very softly so that the whole Chamber was hushed to catch his words. Then gradually the speech gathered strength and took wing. I do not remember in the least what he said. But by the time he sat down, I was spellbound. I wrote to him offering my congratulations and asking for his autograph. I got a very civil reply.

In May 1930 my father again took me to the House of Commons. I do not remember the debate, but as we came away we ran into Lloyd George. He exchanged a few words with my father and then turning to me said: 'What are you going to do, my boy, when you grow up?' 'I'm going into the Navy, Sir,' I replied, giving what was then my stock answer. He frowned, shook his long mane of white hair and said, 'There are much greater storms in politics. If it's piracy you want with broad-sides, boarding parties, walking the plank and blood on the deck, this is the place.' He continued for a couple of minutes comparing modern politics with the naval battles of the seventeenth and eighteenth centuries and then went on his way. But his words had gone home. That evening I confided to my father that what Lloyd George had said had decided my life. I put aside all thoughts of a Naval career. It would be politics for me.

From this time my letters home contain frequent references to the political situation, sometimes quaintly inserted between requests for some toy or enquiries about my white mice. I also began to take an increasingly active part in the School debating society. My admiration for Lloyd George led me to embrace Liberal principles and I spoke in support of temperance and against National Service. Later on I made the main speech in favour of 'Disarmament'; and Mrs. Williams, the Headmaster's charming wife, wrote to my mother, 'Julian won his motion by a large majority. He spoke very well for twenty-five minutes.'

My decision to go into politics brought me closer to my father. I still regarded him with some awe but the gulf between us was narrowed. I was now going into the same business, as it were, and felt I had a new and strong claim on his attention. I began to seek him out and question him about the great issues of the past and present. He responded en-thusiastically, talking to me almost as to a grown-up, and taking my occasional criticism in very good part. That I called myself a Liberal

[1] J. H. Thomas: Labour M.P. and Minister.

did not seem to me in the least inconsistent with our new relationship. He used to say that Liberalism, like measles, was something one had better get over young. In any case my Liberalism was really based on admiration for Lloyd George and never extended to Free Trade or Independence for India.

My father was now in his fifty-eighth year and, though still very strong, was beginning to take his mountaineering and skiing more gently. I was still too young to keep up with him in either sport. But I was already old enough to go with him on his training walks and the shorter climbs. In 1930 we climbed Monte Forno together, which involved a stretch of glacier and a short chimney up which the guide hauled me rather like a fish on the end of a line. Later, in the same summer, we climbed the Corvatsch, more of a walk than a climb, but involving some cutting of steps in the ice and one or two narrow ridges. These expeditions meant nights away in some mountain hut when we spent the evening talking in a way we would seldom have done at home.

My father seemed to enjoy these talks and just before my last term at Summerfields, he took me for a walking tour in the Pyrenees. We spent a couple of days in Carcassonne, inspecting the mediaeval fortifications restored by Viollet-le-Duc. We climbed Mont Canigou and went up to Mont Louis to look at Vauban's fortress. We crossed over into Spain and attempted some spring skiing. These combined activities provided endless scope for discussion of history, travel, religion and politics.

Politics, indeed, were rapidly becoming my main interest in life; but before I could take part in them there were certain preliminary hurdles to jump. The first of these was Public School.

My father had been Head Boy at Harrow and had carried off most of the School's prizes and athletic trophies. He had been very happy there and had wanted his sons to follow in his footsteps. My brother had gone to Harrow but had disliked it so much that he had run away. I was down for Harrow too. But my mother had deep misgivings and persuaded my father that I should go to Eton. I am very glad she did.

Mr. Williams decided to put me in for a scholarship and, along with five other boys, we went up to Eton to sit the Examination. Mr. Bolton came with us and we all stayed at the White Hart Hotel at Windsor. The weather was fine. We worked at our papers morning and afternoon; ate strawberries at most meals, and were allowed to drink cider in the evening. At the end of it all we were allowed home for the weekend. I did not get a scholarship. The reason for this was well summed up by my Headmaster:

> His work has been pretty consistent throughout: but he lacks the patience always to delve into the heart of the matter. He skims the cream and trusts to his native wit to produce the finished article.

This failure was a great disappointment but salutary. It made me begin to realise the need for greater accuracy and thoroughness.

Before the end of the term, those of us who were leaving Summerfields had two meetings with the Headmaster. At the first, he gave us a general lecture on how to conduct ourselves at Public School and in after life. The second lecture was more 'highly classified', and we had to promise not to reveal its contents to the other boys. The subject, needless to say, was sex. It all came to me as a great surprise, and something of a shock. The postures associated with procreation seemed to me inconvenient and rather ridiculous. In due course, however, I revised my views on this important matter and came to see it in a more appreciative light.

I liked what I had seen of Eton and speculated pleasantly about my future at Mr. Howson's House for which I had been entered. These day-dreams, however, were disturbed by a postcard from Francis Fisher who had gone to Eton a term earlier. Mr. Howson's House, he thought I should know, had just suffered a 'general tanning'. Some trivial misdemeanour had been committed, and the culprit had refused to own up. The Captain of the House, Jo Grimond—later Leader of the Liberal Party—and also a strong opponent of corporal punishment—had accordingly beaten every boy in the House. It was nice to learn that Grimond was leaving that summer; and on the law of averages it seemed unlikely that there would be another 'general tanning' in the same House for two or three years. It would, in fact, be three.

I read this news with some concern. But fortunately the horizons of childhood are short, and two months of holidays lay ahead. I spent them with my cousin, John Rodney, at Lord Elibank's estate on the Tweed. I shot grouse and duck for the first time and killed my first salmon. In the evenings we learned to play bridge.

4

Eton

I drove down to Eton on a September evening in 1932 and was welcomed
to Jourdelays House by Mr. Howson and by the Dame, Miss Owen. I
had a room of my own with a bed that folded up against the wall. It was
a small room. It would become a very cold room. But it was my own—
somewhere to read and think undistrubed; a safe harbour where I could
rejoice or even weep alone.

A slightly older boy called Colville came and instructed me in the
customs and traditions of the School. Some of these seemed to me slightly
ridiculous and the clothes we had to wear altogether absurd. I could not
see then—and do not see now—the point of dressing boys up in tail coats
and stiff collars to look like undertakers or footmen. But I thought it best
not to express my views at this early stage. Presently the Captain of Games
looked in and talked to me about the Field Game, the Eton variant of
Soccer. I thought it unlikely that I would shine at this, but showed polite
interest.

My Tutor, Hugh Howson, was a classical scholar and an old Harrovian
with curly reddish hair. Austere in standards and a purist in style, he was
also shy and tongue-tied. It was the custom in most Eton Houses for the
Tutor to go round the rooms after the boys had gone to bed. This gave
him a chance for a few minutes' chat with a quarter or third of the House
every night. Howson forced himself to do this. He would knock on the
door, come in and sit down on the bed. 'Good Evening, Sir,' I would
say. 'How are you, my dear Sir?' he would reply. I would think quickly
of some incident and tell him about it or ask a question which he would
answer briefly. Then there would be a pause. If I could get him on to
mountain climbing, his real love, things went well enough. Otherwise a
rather embarrasing silence developed until with a wan smile he would
wish me goodnight and hurry from the room. I have since learned that a
man can be wise and yet tongue-tied. But Howson's shyness was a barrier
between us, and he had little influence on me.

My dame, Miss Owen, was a rubicund lady in middle life, who bustled
about much faster than seemed likely from her rather comfortable appearance. Like most people in authority who have to process others through

a machine, whether school or hospital or regiment, she had acquired definite views on most issues and developed stereotyped answers to most questions. She wore these like a suit of armour. It became a game for two or three of us to go and see her together in the evening and bring up some subject of conversation previously agreed between us. Each of us would have written down beforehand what we thought she would say, and, if she actually said it, the forecaster scored a point. I once scored twenty-two points, though normally a dozen was a good bag.

The Provost, Dr. James, who wrote perhaps the best ghost stories since Edgar Allan Poe, was already rather ill. I had tea with him once but remember nothing about it. He died soon afterwards, and his successor, Lord Quickswood, though beloved of all the grown-ups I knew, was very remote from us boys.

Dr. Alington, the Headmaster, was of noble appearance and worldly opinions; and both are much appreciated by adolescents. He often asked me to breakfast or tea and made a point of avoiding talk about the School and opening up more general subjects of conversation. I admired but did not altogether trust him. In my second year there were changes in the celestial hierarchy. Dr. Alington went to Durham as Dean and Claude Elliott became Headmaster. Elliott was more a Don than a schoolmaster and lacked the histrionic touch which boys rather need. It was only in later life that we became friends.

Henry Marten was Vice-Provost all through my Eton career. He lived with his sister in rooms above the cloisters. They were large rooms but stacked so high with books that it was not easy to move about them. Marten's breadth of reading, indeed, interfered with his conversation. You only had to mention a subject and he would jump up, burrow in a pile of books and emerge with two or three volumes on it. Once, after breakfast with him, I had to make three journeys back to my room to carry away all the books he had lent me after an hour's talk.

The society of these great men was among the more agreeable features of Eton life. But the real power in the land lay with the senior boys—the Captain of the House, the Captain of Games and the two or three other members of the 'Library'. As a lower boy I was brought into daily contact with them by the institution of 'fagging'.

Fagging was a nuisance, but like most troubles in life could, by giving thought to the matter, be mitigated. There were two kinds of fagging— indoor fagging and outdoor fagging.

Outdoor fagging was the worse. You could be sent on errands to order your fag master's tea, to take his suit to the tailors or to carry messages to his friends in other Houses. It took an unconscionable amount of time and disrupted both work and leisure. But you could only be fagged out of doors in the day time. Here the remedy was to stay away from the

House as much as possible. Attendance at breakfast was not compulsory, and as the gastronomic standard of the House was low, it seemed more pleasant and more prudent to eat out. After sampling various establishments which provided breakfast I settled on a small café beyond Barnes Bridge called Lower Rowlands. After a time Mrs. White, the kindly manager, made a private sitting room available to two or three of us for a very small consideration. We thus had a flat in the town where we could work or spend leisure hours or even entertain without the interruption of fagging.

Indoor fagging was not so easy to escape. Each lower boy had a personal fag master to serve. In addition, any member of the Library might shout 'Boy', at which all the fags would have to run to the call, and the last to arrive would be given the job.

My first fag master, Jim Kenyon, was a kindly man and very tolerant of my inability to light fires. When he left I became fag to Nicholas Elliott whose father was soon to become Headmaster. One Sunday I went to tidy up Elliott's room and found him in a state of great perplexity. He had four essays to write in reply to 'Sunday Questions'. These were upon religious and moral themes, and Elliott could not think what to say about any of them. It so happened that I was familiar with the questions and was able to suggest the line Elliott's answers might take. He was suitably impressed and instructed me to dictate the four essays to him. I obeyed and, walking up and down the room, gained my first experience of dictating English. I do it in much the same way still. To Elliott's delight, and my relief, the Sunday Questions were presently returned with the master's comment in red ink: 'Very good. A great improvement on your previous answers. You have obviously taken trouble.'

From then until I ceased to be a fag, we continued this literary partnership. The hand was the hand of Elliott, but the words were the words of Amery. In return Elliott released me from the ordinary chores of fagging for him. He also told me that if I was ever caught not answering the call of 'Boy' I could plead that I was doing a job for him.

Only once did our partnership run into serious difficulty. One Sunday evening in summer Elliott came back too late for me to dictate his essay to him. I accordingly wrote it out myself during the night and gave it to him before early school. He did not have time to read it or even to make a copy in his own hand, but thought this unimportant as on that particular day he was due to read out his answer instead of submitting it in writing. The subject of the essay was 'Does the end justify the means?' I began by stating the conventional view of the matter. But then took as a more controversial text Armstrong's *Grey Wolf*, a life of the Turkish President Ataturk, which I had just read. Here was a man, I wrote, who was generally hailed as a great and progressive statesman. And yet it was a matter of notoriety that his public conduct and private morals were much at variance with the standards inculcated at British Public Schools. Could it be that murder, cruelty, repeated breach of faith and atheism had all been necessary to his achievement? Was it possible that drunken orgies and lechery had alone afforded him the stimulus or relaxation necessary to his work? Here I described in some detail the extent to which the Pasha had on occasion been besotted by drink and enfeebled by venereal disease. All this and much else in the same vein led up to a satirical conclusion poking fun at accepted principles.

Once embarked upon reading the essay Elliott had no choice but to go on. He could not improvise something else. The other boys showed obvious pleasure and admiration at what they took to be a splendid leg pulling of authority. The master looked rather shocked. But the essay was reasonably well written and showed evidence of research. Nevertheless, the ideas were plainly dangerous, and Elliott was kept back after school to discuss them. In later years Elliott would become something of an authority on the Near East. But, at this time, he had not even heard of Ataturk. Fortunately, he kept his head. The master liked talking better than listening. Elliott parried the questions put to him with questions of his own. 'Well, what do you think, Sir? Don't you think he was a great man?' Presently the master grew hungry for breakfast and Elliott escaped with his copyright unchallenged though his salvation in doubt. But it had been a close shave.

Our room at Lower Rowlands and the sartorial extravagance of youth involved some expense. I had an allowance of £10 a half from my father. This was not enough. But necessity is the mother of invention. When I banked my £10 at the local branch of Barclays Bank, the Manager asked to see me. After expressing his appreciation of my custom, he went on to explain that boys were not allowed to overdraw more than £10. In my innocence, I did not know what an overdraft was, but the Manager explained the idea to me. I thought it a very good one. I reported all this to a colleague who had just opened an account with another bank. He too had been given an overdraft limit of £10, and we decided that this must be the rule among all the banks at Eton. The opportunity was too good to miss. I took £5 out of my account at Barclays and opened a second account across the road. This brought me, as I had expected, another £10 in overdraft facilities. Thus in a couple of days I managed to convert my initial capital of £10 into a line of credit of £30. This, with the help of occasional presents from uncles and aunts, kept me in reasonable comfort until I ceased to be a lower boy and my father raised my allowance from £10 to £40 a half.

I did not shine at games and cordially detested the Field Game. I
played the Wall Game once and thought that quite enough. In summer I
was a 'dry bob', but my early promise at cricket was not sustained. I
sometimes rowed for fun but saw little point in serious rowing. It is a
sport where you exhaust and often strain yourself; and there is something unsatisfactory in proceeding with your back to your goal. But there
was squash and later rackets, both of which I enjoyed. I also took up
fencing and presently got into the school fencing team. Bill McLean was
then Captain of Fencing. Coming away from a match, one day, I asked
him what was his main interest in life. He answered that it was collecting
silver. This struck me as rather an old maidish taste, but I soon discovered
that we had many things in common. Bill was a cousin of Sir Harry
McLean—the Scottish adventurer—who had become Commander in
Chief of the Moroccan Army—and we shared an interest in travel and
adventure. We also enjoyed the good things of life, and Bill was skilled in
organising fencing matches so that we could have a night out in London.
The friendship then begun, was to ripen steadily in the war years and
after.

Much of Eton's charm lies in its friendships. Towards the end of my
first half I made friends with a boy called Hugh FitzRoy. Hugh was fair
haired and blue eyed and perhaps six or eight months older than I. His
father was an impoverished land agent and Hugh's clothes were the
shabbiest in the House. Then various cousins died from accident or illness
and, one morning, Hugh became Lord Euston and heir to the Duchy of
Grafton. All this brought about a welcome improvement in his finances.
Hugh was gentle, imaginative, sentimental, and mocking by turns. We
shared a common love of history, an interest in politics and an impatience
with some of the restrictions of Eton life.

In my second half we decided to 'mess'—eat our tea—together,
along with two other friends of Hugh's, Simon Wardell and Oliver
Thomas.

Simon was a son of Mike Wardell, an Executive on one of Lord
Beaverbrook's newspapers. His mother was a lady of great vivacity and
wit, and dedicated to the pursuit of the fox. Simon had a natural gift of
satire and caricature. He would fasten upon the ridiculous points in a
master or boy with such accuracy that the caricature became the reality.
He had, besides, a great power of puncturing humbug, and exposing
contradictions. I was by nature over serious and too keen on constructing
theories. Simon was, if anything, too flippant and too destructive. But
his influence on me was stimulating. He was far better read in English
poetry than I was. He sharpened my power of expression and gave my
essays shape and balance. His own essays and verses surprised by their
maturity and wit; and Simon seemed likely to become the Noel Coward

or even the Bernard Shaw of our generation. Ill health and finally a fatal accident prevented the fulfilment of his early promise.

The fourth member of our group was Oliver Thomas. Oliver was exceptionally untidy with black hair flopping over thick eyebrows and, usually, with ink stains on his face or shirt. He was short-sighted which may have contributed to his subsequent success as a painter. He was also a brilliant mimic, taking off the masters and the senior boys in turn. Above all, he had a great sense of the practical and brought us down from our wilder flights of fancy to the detailed planning of practical jokes or breaches of the rules. It is nice to think that he became an Eton master.

Tea was the best of the Eton meals. We ordered it ourselves and it was sent up from Rowlands or one of the other food shops. In season, it might include roast pheasant or salmon, or lobster. The hour of day was 6.15 p.m. There were no more classes to attend. This was the time for talk. We read verses to each other, concocted manifestos which, mercifully, were never published, and spent much of our evenings dissecting and lampooning the social, moral, political and religious values of Eton.

Had we been good at games the energies of our little group might have found an innocent outlet. But none of us were. Nor did our work offer us much scope. The early part of an Eton education was geared to the taking of School Certificate, then a basic University examination. I could probably have passed the School Certificate at fourteen but, by the rules then in force, we were not allowed to sit the examination until over sixteen. This meant that for the first three years at Eton we were condemned to an academic treadmill toiling away at the same curriculum.

In these circumstances we found our outlet in flouting school customs and in breaking rules.

Oxford encourages eccentricity. Eton tolerates it, but only just. Our tutor, Hugh Howson, was a patient man. He thought the opinion of our fellows would get us out of our 'difficult phase' soon enough. He was probably right. But, one summer holiday, he was killed along with three other Eton masters in a climbing accident. His place as my tutor was taken by Dick Routh. Routh was a historian who had subdued political ambitions to become a schoolmaster. He was a more energetic man than Howson and determined to make a success of his house. He judged that the boys needed pulling together and that the tone of the House could be improved. These things made the views and activities of our little group irritating to him, and, looking back, I cannot blame him for this. He saw us as a centre of disaffection. We found his leg rather easy to pull.

Teasing authority can be very good fun. But it usually has to be paid for. One day three of us went to a cinema in Windsor. This was, of course, strictly forbidden. On leaving the theatre we ran straight into one of the masters, a Mr. Hartley. We knew him by sight but none of us had ever spoken to him. He did not know us and asked for our names and houses. On the principle that you may as well be hanged for a sheep as for a lamb, we gave false identities. He was completely taken in.

This hoodwinking of a master caused some stir in the stratosphere. If the culprits got away unpunished, authority would be made a monkey. An enquiry was opened. Several groups of boys, our own group included, had been seen coming back from Windsor by other masters at about the time of our escapade. They were all paraded before Mr. Hartley for identification. He thought he recognised one of my two colleagues but was not quite sure. Routh cross-examined us. We stuck to our alibis, but in the night, he broke in on one of my colleagues and rousing him from sleep extracted a confession.

Inexorable retribution followed. Three days later we were summoned before the Headmaster. He sentenced us to lose our Long Leave—half term—and to be 'swiped'—the Etonian slang for birching.

'Swiping' was very much a ceremony. After sentence had been read to us we waited in the cloister outside the door of the Headmaster's office. Presently he emerged accompanied by two senior boys, his private secretary and two servants. We then formed into procession, with the Headmaster leading, and marched up the stairs to the Upper School. At the door of the School a servant motioned to the three of us to stop, while the rest of the procession went in. After a short interval my name was called. At the far end of the Upper School was an ancient wooden block looking like the first two steps of a staircase. Three birches lay on a table beside it. I was told to kneel on the block and to take down my trousers. One of the servants put his hand on my shoulder and gently pushed me forward. The Headmaster did the rest. The birch drew blood but hurt much less than the ordinary beatings administered by senior boys with a cane. My school bills at the end of term included an item 'School Medicine: 7s. 6d.'—the cost of the birch. This, I thought, was adding insult to injury.

Far worse than the 'swiping' was the loss of Long Leave. 1,100 boys went home for a holiday weekend. We three stayed disconsolately at school. So did Dick Routh. This must have been infuriating to him, but, to his credit, he did what he could to make the weekend agreeable. We had to do some work; but he gave us a good dinner and, appropriately enough, took us to a cinema in Windsor.

The next few months were a time of increasing frustration. I was under notice that any further escapades might well lead to expulsion. Mischief was thus barred as an outlet for high spirits. Work and organised games seemed equally distasteful. In a mood of despair I wrote to the Ethiopian Minister volunteering to fight for his country against the Italian invasion. I still have his letter of courteous refusal explaining that 'as you are unacquainted with the language of the Country, we fear that you will not be of any use to us in directing our soldiers'.

I was rescued from these rather wild flights of fancy by my classical tutor, Wyndham Milligan.[1] He understood my boredom with the School Certificate routine and encouraged me to break new ground. He gave me special tuition in Greek philosophy. He also urged me to go in for a prize, offered by the French author, André Maurois. This was for an essay in French on French civilisation. It was intended for boys specialising in French at the end of their school career when they would be about eighteen years old. I was still under sixteen. To the general surprise, I carried off the prize in a paper which Milligan described as 'mature in thought and idiomatic expression to a degree that the examiners could scarcely credit it the work of a boy of his age'.

This paper caught the eye of Eton's senior French teacher, Marcel Ruff. Ruff looked like Mahatma Gandhi and suffered from very bad eyesight. He was also frustrated by the lack of appreciation which the boys and, I dare say, the masters, showed of French culture. My essay, so he told me, gave him hope and he offered to give me unlimited private tuition. I took him up on this and, though it had nothing to do with School Certificate, was presently allowed to work two evenings a week with him after school. Ruff opened to me the treasures of French literature and gave me the rudiments of a French style. He would often keep me back for supper with his highly cultivated wife and encouraged my interest in good food and wine.

At last, in 1935, School Certificate was passed. I now specialised in History, with Ian Macmaster as my History tutor. Macmaster was lame from polio and looked like a benevolent gnome. He treated me like a grown-up and had no inhibitions about discussing other masters in front of me. He was indeed much more a don than a schoolmaster and, like Ruff, would often keep me back for a glass of sherry or for supper after a tutorial.

Under the guidance of these two remarkable men my work shot forward. From being little above average my reports began to speak of me as a likely history scholar. I was at last interested in what I was doing and this quickened a host of dormant faculties.

Dick Routh remained critical of my aggressive support of heterodox opinions and of what were, no doubt, maddening eccentricities in dress. 'Twenty years hence, when he is a great man,' he wrote to my father, 'he may look upon his own follies only as a reincarnation of the

[1] Later Warden of Radley College and Principal of Wolsey Hall.

extravagancies of Disraeli himself.' But he now took a kindlier view of my work.

In one of his reports, in 1936, he wrote:

'This is the best historian in the best division that I have met for ten years or more.'

We now, at last, became friends and he taught me much about the things he loved best, Shakespeare, Italian Renaissance painting and Wagner.

My last two years at Eton brought greater freedom and more varied activity. I joined the Eton Officers' Training Corps. This was supposed to be a voluntary organisation, but when I was told that I would be beaten if I did not volunteer, I joined. We still wore a curious uniform, heather mixture in colour, with green piping. Our legs were encased in puttees, which few of us were any good at keeping up. Boys were supposed to cut their hair for parades. Long hair was rather the fashion, though not as long as nowadays; and on one occasion to avoid the ministrations of the barber I put my hair up. I then tied the excess in a flat knot on the top of my head so that, with my cap on, my appearance was suitably military. An officer came from Windsor to inspect us. He was very critical of the length of hair of some of the boys. They should, he said, pointing at me, try and copy Number 3 in the front rank. He instructed me to step forward three paces so that all could see the proper length which hair should be worn. He then told me to take my cap off. I had no choice but to comply. My topknot was revealed; and the whole parade, including, to his credit, the officer concerned, dissolved into laughter.

I was presently elected to the Political Society. This used to meet in the Provost or Vice Provost's rooms to entertain some distinguished guest. I remember, in particular, a visit from James Maxton, the Clydeside leader of the Independent Labour Party with his long hair, cadaverous features and burning eyes. He began his talk by saying, 'I don't know how many of your parents have been to prison.' This was good shock tactics and gripped our attention at once. 'I suspect many of them deserved to, but few did,' he went on. 'This is a pity because no man's education is complete until he has done a spell inside.'

The Monarchy was very much in our minds in these years. I had watched the Silver Jubilee procession in May of 1935. In 1936 King George V died. As a private in the Corps, I helped to line the route along which the Royal coffin passed on its way from Windsor Station to the Castle. Scarcely a year later came the abdication. My inclination was to support King Edward. But I was curious to know what the man in the street was thinking. Accordingly, Simon Wardell and I went out into the main street of Eton and Windsor and, stopping likely passers by, conducted a kind of public opinion poll. We must have questioned a dozen people. All were against the King.

I had left Summerfields nominally a Liberal. But my political leanings now took a series of different turns. Mr. Baldwin's National Government seemed incapable of solving the unemployment problem at home or exercising effective influence abroad. Its leading members, moreover, seemed remarkably complacent about their failures. In France the situation seemed if anything even worse. Could it be that Parliamentary Government was played out? In this mood I turned to a study of the Russian Revolution and was for a time rather attracted to Communism. But the purges in the Soviet Party and the Red Army suggested that the system did not work out in practice. In any case the break up of the British Commonwealth and Empire was a major Soviet aim, and this alone made Communism unacceptable.

I turned next to a study of the Fascist and Nazi movements. They seemed to have conquered unemployment and to be setting the pace in international affairs. Was something of the kind needed in Britain? Sir Oswald Mosley had just formed his Fascist Party and I went to one of his meetings. But the Anti-Semitism repelled and the black shirt and Roman salute seemed rather ridiculous in London.

The fact remained that the Baldwin–Chamberlain Government seemed to fall well below the level of events. All the ablest people seemed to be outside it. Among them I included, of course, my father and Lloyd George as well as two new figures who now dawned upon my horizon. One of these was Winston Churchill who took the house next door to us in London and came to Eton to judge a Declamation Prize. The other was Lord Beaverbrook. Simon Wardell and I sent him an article which we had written together. He did not use it, but asked us to go and see him in the holidays, when his electric personality made a deep impression.

By degrees, and doubtless under my father's influence, I came to the conclusion there was not much wrong with the British constitution but only with the men who ran it. The problem was not to change the system, but to change the men. By the time I left Eton I regarded myself as a Conservative, though out of sympathy with the leadership of the day.

By the summer of 1936 many of my closest friends had left school. I felt I had had the best of Eton and begged my parents to let me go and study abroad. But my tutors thought I had a good chance of winning the Brackenbury history scholarship to Balliol. I accordingly stayed on until Easter of 1937, but in vain. I did not get the scholarship.

I celebrated my departure with a farewell breakfast to friends. Then on the last evening I gave a champagne party to my fags and another to my colleagues in the Library. Dick Routh looked in, pretended to be very angry and then drank a glass himself.

It is easier to analyse the elements of an Eton education than to define its quality. The prestige of the School and the patronage of influential parents naturally attract the best teachers. Eton still provides the best academic preparation for a British university.

The athletic facilities, though limited by geography, are otherwise as good as money can buy. The strong corporate feeling of the individual houses and of the school as a whole provide the character training popularly, and, on the whole, rightly associated with the British public school system. And yet the Etonian end-product tends to be less stereotyped and more self-reliant than his contemporaries from other schools.

Several things account for this.

Perhaps the most important is that a boy has his own room from the moment he goes to the School. He may have to conform to the rules and customs of the School, but, in the privacy of his own room, he can think what he likes, read what he likes and say what he likes to his intimates. The room is, in fact, a seed bed of individualism.

Scarcely less powerful is the influence of geography. Eton is on the doorstep of Windsor and on the road from London to Oxford. The boys, and even more the masters, are thus continually exposed to the opinions, the fashions and the prejudices of the world outside. The School authorities are conscious, all the time, of operating under the critical scrutiny of sophisticated and influential parents. This ensures that Eton is part of the general life of the British establishment and not an ivory tower. It helps to explain why the School is more tolerant than most. It reflects, after all, the scepticism, not to say cynicism, of society at large. It also explains the reliance on custom and tradition rather than rules.

In this more mature climate, half way between a school and a university, a boy learns not only to obey and to command, but also to persuade. He finds out how to use his personal abilities, his position in the School and even the resources of his parents to achieve his ends. He begins to see that life is not a game played according to definite rules under the supervision of an impartial umpire. He learns instead that it is a kind of cross-country steeplechase where the prizes are not always to the swift or to the strong, but to the bold, the cunning or the well-equipped.

The basic amenities of the School are austere, and much of the accommodation and some of the hours of work would be censured by Government inspectors. One of my school-fellows later wrote from prison that hard labour was nothing to anyone who had got through the Lower School at Eton. Eton indeed teaches a boy how to make life bearable under almost any conditions. I was often struck during the War at how skilful Etonians were, compared to others, at proving the truth of Wellington's dictum 'any damn fool can be uncomfortable'.

I would not want to live my Eton life again, but the fault here lies with me rather than with the School. I was no doubt unreasonably irked by school rules and customs and, though my school life was full and varied, an underlying mood of boredom colours my letters from Eton as well as my recollections of it. By contrast I can scarcely remember a day of boredom since I left Eton in 1937. I say this not in criticism but to the credit of the School. I did not enjoy my schooling, but I have no doubt that it is largely due to it that I have been able to live and enjoy my life so fully ever since. In acknowledgement of the debt, I have sent my son to Eton too.

5

Holidays from Eton

Sir Osbert Sitwell once described himself in *Who's Who* as 'educated in the holidays from Eton'. I would not go so far myself. But it is no disparagement of Eton or of Summerfields to say that I learnt as much about life in the holidays as I did at School.

In April of 1933 my father took me to ski at Gargellen in the Tyrol. This was my introduction to spring skiing, in those days still something of an adventure. We smeared ourselves with a cream used by film actors to keep out the actinic rays of the sun. It was called Butterfly Pancromatic No. 27. There were a lot of avalanches and a fellow guest in our hotel was killed in one just after our arrival. Spring skiing, then, was a strenuous sport. There were no funiculars. This meant starting very early in the morning to reach the top of the run while the snow was still in good condition. We would leave each morning soon after six o'clock and make the top before eleven. By the time we reached the valley the snow was already turning to slush. In the afternoon we walked among the spring flowers or slept and read. The book I remember best was Arnold Zweig's *Case of Sergeant Grischa*. It was a powerful deterrent to any thought of joining the Army.

At Christmas of the same year we went to ski in the Black Forest, basing ourselves on the Feldberg above Lake Titisee. While we were there, the Germans won the plebiscite held to decide the future of the Saar. This was the first of Hitler's triumphs; and the local Nazi leaders made the most of it. All day patrols went off on skis to the remoter villages announcing the news 'Deutsch is die Saar' (the Saar is German). In the evening, there was a torchlight procession on skis. Several hundred people took part. The procession began at the local War memorial where the crowd formed a circle and sang the old German War song 'Ich hatte einen Kameraden'. We then wound our way through the pinewoods to the top of the open slopes above the Feldberg. From there we skied down to the hotel, each skier holding a blazing pinewood torch in his right hand. Quite a few people tumbled, but I somehow managed to keep up. Down at the bottom the procession formed another circle, and there was more singing of the 'Horst Wessel Lied' and other patriotic songs. Presently my father drew us aside, along with General and Mrs. Fuller who had joined us. He issued us with a ration of Vanderhum from a hip flask and we held our own counter-demonstration quietly humming 'Rule Britannia'.

In the following spring (1934) my father took me to see the battlefields of the Western Front. I had read *All Quiet on the Western Front* and other books about the War, but was quite unprepared for what I saw. The long rows of gravestones told their tale all too plainly. More moving still were the monuments to the unidentified and the missing. There seemed to be no trees anywhere. It was fourteen years since the Armistice but on our walks—for we did much of the tour on foot—we often came on barbed-wire entanglements and dugouts. I picked up a German steel helmet, and several clips of ammunition. Ypres was being rebuilt but progress was slow. My father had been there, on General Rawlinson's staff, during the first battle and we managed to find one or two of the civilians who had been kind to him. I remember a Madame Julie, who kept a small restaurant and treated my father very much as one of her boys. I heard the Last Post sounded at the Menin Gate, and, as we stood bare-headed in the evening light, sent up a heartfelt prayer for peace in my time.

From the battlefields of the First World War we went on to Waterloo and spent a day identifying the positions held by the opposing armies. Dominating the battlefields stands a grassy pyramid with a large stone lion on top of it. In my innocence I had assumed that it was a British lion and was rather surprised to read the inscription on the base. This recalled the victory over the Emperor Napoleon of the troops of Orange Nassau with the help—this in rather smaller letters—of their Prussian and British allies.

That summer we went to the Königsee, a dramatic mountain lake under the cliffs of the Watzmann near the Bavarian/Austrian border. Oliver Thomas came with us. Oliver and I walked, fished and drank beer, and visited the famous salt mines whence Stendhal derived his theory that love is a process of crystallisation.

One day my father went off to meet Hitler at Berchtesgaden. Oliver and I went with him. We did not see the Führer ourselves, but drank coffee with some of his aides in a lodge at the bottom of the garden. My father, I remember, thought Hitler rather dull but much less extreme in his views than he had expected.

After a fortnight at Königsee, we moved off to Mittenwald, the home of the German violin industry. From there we set out to conquer the Wetterstein. This was quite an easy climb but long. We started at about seven in the morning and did not get down till after six in the evening. It was the hottest day of the year and we had no water with us. We had hoped to find mountain streams, but all day long never saw even a trickle of water. Our thirst became appalling and was made worse by eating wild garlic. For the last two hours of the descent I could think of nothing but beer. The vision of a foaming mug excluded any appreciation of the view. After an eternity we came to a small pub. But it was closed. It was another half hour before we could at last slake our thirst in litre mugs of ice-cold Bavarian beer. My father in a rare moment of indecision ordered a litre of 'helles'—the light—and a litre of 'dunkeles'—the dark—beer for himself. He looked at both, drank both, decided the 'helles' was the better and went on with that. I followed his example.

In the summer of 1935 we ventured further afield to Lake Bohinj in Slovenia. Slovenia is still Central Europe but there is already a taste of the Balkans in the air. The hotel food was mainly Austrian, but there was Turkish coffee and occasional pungent dishes from Serbia.

My father wanted to climb the famous Triglav. He thought I was still growing too fast for so strenuous an expedition. Instead, I went off to shoot chamois. My host was a young, broad-shouldered Slovene called Rudi Zupan, who had an extensive timber concession and was engaged to the daughter of a certain Rabitch, a hotel proprietor. Rabitch had been a great hunter in his day. But he had grown so heavy that he could hardly move across the garden. He was the fattest man I had ever seen, and accentuated his girth by wearing *lederhosen*. I made my base at his hotel at Moistrana. It was simple but the food excellent and very cheap.

Chamois shooting proved a strenuous sport. We would leave the hotel at one o'clock in the morning, after breakfasting on a cup of Turkish coffee and a glass of plum brandy. We then climbed up steep tracks for some three thousand feet, aiming to reach the chamois feeding grounds above the tree line before dawn. Climbing in the dark with a heavy rucksack and a sporting rifle is tough going. By the time we reached the top, on my first shoot, I was bathed in sweat, worn out and very thirsty. But there was not a moment to lose. About three hundred yards away from us, on the crest of a low ridge, three chamois were feeding. Rudi told me to shoot the middle one. My hands were shaking with exhaustion and excitement. I thought I would never get a steady bead on what, at three hundred yards, is a small target. I squeezed the trigger but nothing happened. The safety catch was still on. One of the chamois had stopped feeding and was looking round. I steadied the rifle, took aim and fired. I saw it fall, kick once or twice on the ground and then lie still. The other two chamois seemed in doubt where the shot had come from. 'Shoot another,' said Rudi. I fired again but the two chamois disappeared over the ridge.

We walked over and picked up our kill which Rudi pronounced a four-year-old buck. He gralloched it, flung it around his shoulders and led the way down towards a small hut on the other side of the ridge where the chamois had been feeding. The hut was only five hundred feet below the ridge, but the ground very broken and as Rudi had the chamois to carry we had to make a detour to reach it. There we breakfasted and spent the day. In the evening, after a long siesta, Rudi swept the hillside with his field glasses and spotted a roe deer looking out at us from behind a bush. I fired. We did not see it run away and thought I might have hit it. We walked across to the bush and followed a dry watercourse for, perhaps, two hundred feet above it. Of the roe there was no sign; but slumped behind the rock we found a freshly killed chamois. It had a bullet through the barrel and must have been the second beast I had fired at in the morning. I had thus scored a left and right at chamois: not a bad beginning.

We slept in the hut for a few hours and set out again an hour before dawn. We climbed along an easy ridge and, as the light came, looked down on the other side of it. I could see nothing from where I was standing. But Rudi crawled down a rock chimney for about ten feet and saw a small herd of chamois feeding on a patch of grass some two hundred feet below us. The chimney was not very steep and getting to him was easy enough. But to shoot I had to lie on my tummy with my head just over the edge of an overhang. Rudi meanwhile held on to my ankles. He pointed out a rather grey looking chamois, slightly apart from the others. It was a female, he said, but at least twelve years old. I took aim as best I could in a near vertical position and fired. The chamois leapt in the air, fell down and never moved again. Rudi was so excited that he let go of my ankles. With a rifle in my hands there was nothing to hold on to and I thought I should fall over the edge to certain death fifty feet or more below. I shouted for help. Rudi roared with laughter but caught hold of my ankles again and helped me back on to my feet. Presently we found our way down to where the old chamois was lying. It had a splendid pair of horns, but was much too heavy to carry back across the ridge. Rudi marked the spot and put his shirt across the carcass. This, he said, would help to keep off eagles or foxes. We now made our way down to the valley and sent up a mule to collect the bag. I went to bed at about four that afternoon and slept till lunchtime the next day.

My father joined us in the evening after climbing the Triglav. We held a dinner to celebrate his ascent and my prowess with the rifle. We were joined, I remember, by the American author, Negley Farson, who was fishing in the same valley. After dinner I received the traditional hunter's baptism according to St. Hubert's rite. This consisted of a bottle of wine poured over my head, a token spanking with a sword by the senior hunter present and the drinking of healths all round.

From Slovenia we made our way through Venice to Sir Edmund Davis' villa, La Fiorentina, at St. Jean Cap Ferrat where I soon learnt both to aquaplane and water ski. I was, I believe, the first person to water ski from Cap Ferrat to Monte Carlo. This was a feat of endurance rather than skill and I would have given up if I had not passed a large fish basking on the surface. It looked like a shark and I thought it better to keep skiing.

Davis was a South African financier with a rather Napoleonic profile. He was opening up the Copper Belt in Northern Rhodesia and was reputed a very rich man. He had no children and, luckily for his friends, enjoyed spending money as much as making it. Among other qualities, he was a great gourmet and would go into Nice most days with the cook to choose the food himself. The cook was very pretty and I often went with them.

It was at La Fiorentina that I first met Lord Lloyd, the former Governor of Bombay and High Commissioner in Egypt, whose pro-consular career had been broken by the Labour Government. He had stepped on a sea urchin the first day of his holiday and had to spend most of the next fortnight lying on a deck-chair. In such circumstances even a schoolboy's company is better than none, and we talked together for hours on end. He was provocative, bitter, intense, cynical and yet romantic, with a vision of Empire which called for sterner stuff than his contemporaries possessed.

Another guest at La Fiorentina was Marshal Caviglia who had re-organised the Italian Army after its defeat at Caporetto. Caviglia was very anti-Fascist but was also violently opposed to British sanctions against Italy during the Abyssinian War. This, he told us, was bound to drive a reluctant Mussolini into Hitler's arms. When I asked him what were the chances of peace, he answered gruffly: 'If England wants war, there will be war.'

Then there was Laura Anning Bell, the widow of the artist, and herself a painter of some merit. She was already over eighty but looked barely sixty; tall, black-haired, untidy, heavily made-up, the ruin of what must have been a great beauty. Laura was part French, part German. She had Napoleon's blood in her veins by one of his German mistresses and showed me an autographed portrait given by the Emperor to his illegitimate son. When she died she left me most of her books, including a much-loved set of Voltaire's works.

One day, Davis gave an afternoon party for the Mayor of Nice and invited several of the affluent English colony staying on the coast. At one point I found myself alone with the mayor. We spoke in French and I soon realised that he took me for a French boy. I asked him about his job. He deplored the boredom of official functions, but then, with an eloquent gesture towards the guests, added, 'but you must admit we're making a damn good thing out of these bloody foreigners'. This remains the best compliment ever paid to my command of the French language.

A.M.—C

Davis showed me great kindness and we stayed at Fiorentina every year until the War. Thinking his own friends rather old for me, he let me bring Eton friends to stay. He also gave me my first shot gun and asked me several times to shoot at Chilham Castle, his home in Kent.

One incident at Chilham afforded an interesting contrast between English and French manners. A distinguished French politician was among the guests. His views were much approved in London at the time, and when he came to dinner on the Friday evening he was warmly welcomed. Over the port he was closely questioned by the company and everyone seemed very pleased with what he said. Next morning, when he came down to breakfast, he found some of his fellow guests deep in the newspapers. They scarcely grunted 'good morning'. He looked pained and, as he obviously had no experience of the British habit of self service at breakfast, I led him across to where the dishes were. On the way he asked me gently, 'Did I make some terrible gaffe last night that they all seem so cross with me?' I did my best to explain our morning habits to him. British taciturnity at breakfast can be a severe shock to foreigners. But on balance I think it preferable to the French *tour de table*. This obliges each guest, however early the breakfast, to shake hands with all those already seated at table; and this without the fortifying effect of an early cup of tea.

As I grew older my father took me with him to see his friends. We touched life at varied points. There was a visit to the Bishop of Lincoln followed by a cruise on board *Westward* with T. B. Davies, another formidable South African millionaire, who had been blackballed from the Royal Yacht Squadron for the obscenity of his language. There were lunches with John Buchan who gave me six autographs to swap at school and with Kipling who balanced a pencil on his eyebrows for my entertainment.

My mother and her sister Sadie continued to be my best allies. Sadie taught me to drive. I bought a third-hand three-wheel car for £30, and my mother risked her life driving across England with me.

Knowing the dangers of the monastic system of our public schools, she took care to invite high-spirited and attractive girls to join us on our holidays. Eton is very close to London and it was easy enough to persuade them to come and console me in school time. I have been reading some of their letters but the thirty years rule should not apply in such matters and I shall make no revelations.

6

German without Tears

My father proposed that I should spend the summer before I went to Oxford learning German. But where? He did not like the idea of Nazi Germany. He thought Switzerland too cosmopolitan. Why not Vienna? He had many friends there, and it was the cultural capital of the German-speaking world.

My father, accordingly, went to see Baron Franckenstein, the Austrian Minister. They talked in German and mostly about politics, but at some point my father asked if the Minister could help him find a suitable place for his nineteen-year-old child to study German. Franckenstein replied that nothing would be easier. He was going on holiday himself next day but would tell his secretary to make the necessary arrangements. My father too was off on holiday, and it was left to the two secretaries to fix up the details. All was soon settled, though with unforeseen results.

I delayed my departure for Vienna a few days to watch the Coronation of King George VI. Some rain fell during the procession, but the prancing horses and the glancing helmets and swords made a brave show. The most brilliant stars to my mind were the Indian princes, and above all the Maharaja of Patiala, with his black Sikh beard worn under his chin like a kind of ruff. After the Coronation came the Naval Review. *Hood*, *Rodney*, *Nelson* led the line which stretched out as far as the eye could see; and, in my imagination, I could picture all the other British warships still on station in the Mediterranean and in Eastern waters. The American Navy was on the point of overtaking ours in size. But we were still reckoned the most formidable naval power in the world.

Two days later I started for Vienna in a light brown open Humber car, a school-leaving present from my parents. Hugh Euston, who was going to study in Karlsruhe, came with me. The car was piled high with all the accoutrement of gilded youth; golf clubs, tennis rackets, gramophones and a banjo. We each had about £30, the equivalent in buying power of more than £100 today. We were on our own for the first time and were resolved to spread our wings to some effect.

We ate our way through Ostend and Bruges to Brussels where we went to a musical comedy and carried off the leading lady to supper. Thence to

Cologne and Bonn where we embarked the car on a Rhine steamer and at last went to bed.

We woke to find the Rhine beginning to narrow as it enters the gorges. It was a brilliant sunny day. Up on deck we secured two deckchairs, and were presently provided by a steward with a jug of *Kalte Ente* which, literally translated, means Cold Duck. I can recommend this mixture. It consists of a bottle of champagne, a bottle of hock, a little orange juice and a glass or two of Kirsch. Thus sustained we glided safely past the rocks where the Lorelei had combed her hair in the sunlight and under the shadow of the tower where the wicked bishop was eaten by the rats. All day we talked and laughed and drank and scarcely left our deck-chairs, till, towards evening, our steamer docked at Mainz. Hugh had planned to leave me there. But it seemed a pity to break up our partnership so soon. We accordingly made our way together to Heidelberg. The guide-book listed several hotels. We decided only the best would do. It was very good. We then drove into the town, made friends with a few students in a bar and carried them off to an expensive dinner.

The bill in the morning showed that we had lodged and dined rather above our station. Funds were low but we drove on undaunted to enjoy the walled city of Rothenburg. Then by sleeping out we managed to save enough money to see the sights of Munich, hear *Salome* at the opera and sup at the Hofbrauhaus. At Salzburg, however, we had to face the harsh fact that Hugh could scarcely pay his railway ticket to Karlsruhe or I the petrol to Vienna. We had come to the parting of the ways.

I continued alone. As I left Linz a man with a rucksack thumbed a lift. We understood each other in a mixture of German and English, though with difficulty. Still there was nothing else to do and we were both too young to keep quiet for long. Presently it transpired that my companion was a Nazi. He had crossed the border illegally and was going to Vienna on Party business. He jumped out of the car in a traffic jam in the suburbs of Vienna and with a cheery wave disappeared up a side street. This was my first encounter with a member of an underground movement.

I was now nearing my destination. This was a Schloss in a village, perhaps twenty minutes' drive to the east of Vienna. I reached it a little after one o'clock. The other members of the academy had already gone into lunch and the servant led me to the dining room. I walked in, and stopped in astonishment. Some sixteen girls were seated around a long table. At the head of it was an imposing Austrian lady in middle life. Another of rather similar appearance sat at the other end. They all looked equally astonished. Somewhere down the line someone had blundered. They expected me all right. But they expected that I would be a young lady.

The scene was pure musical comedy. There was merry laughter all round and I was bidden to stay to lunch. After lunch I was left with the young ladies while the Baroness went off to consult her husband. They faced a problem which I believe economists call 'the marginal factor'. The bulk of the fees received for teaching the girls German was spent on the upkeep of the house, the food and the servants. Only quite a small sum, perhaps the fees of the last two pupils, became net profit in the bank. If I were sent away they must lose half their savings. It was accordingly decided that I should stay.

Accommodation presented something of a problem. Miss Amery was to have shared a room with another girl. By a process of doubling up, however, a spare room was somehow created.

Presently the Baron sent for me. He was a charming and courteous gentleman of the old school, speaking passable English and excellent French. After some light-hearted joking about the imbroglio in which we found ourselves, he assumed a slightly more serious tone. 'I think you will find your stay here useful and indeed enjoyable,' he said, 'but I want to give you a word of advice.' I assumed I was in for a short lecture on how to behave with the young ladies. But then I saw from the twinkle in his eye that it was only mock seriousness. 'When you write home,' he went on, 'I would not explain the position to your parents too precisely.'

I spent the next three months in, or at any rate attached to, a finishing school for young ladies. My teachers taught me to speak and read German reasonably well. My fellow pupils taught me a good deal besides.

I already knew some German both from school and from holidays in German-speaking countries. I now received continuous practice in speaking and began to study German literature and Austrian and German history. My tutor here was an intelligent and sensitive lady called Dr. Brette. Her method of teaching was to take me to some palace, church or museum and then over a cup of coffee or a glass of wine to discuss what we had seen, and explore its significance. It was a very pleasant way to learn.

I used to ride in the Wienerwald most mornings under the critical eye of a retired Austrian general. We would then breakfast together on cheese and beer. After that I would work with Dr. Brette until lunch. In the afternoon I played tennis or took lessons in the guitar from an elderly lady who was said to have consoled the Archduke Rudolf in the days before his romance with Marie Vetsera and the tragedy of Mayerling.

I went often to the theatre. It is one of the best ways of learning a language. Then there was the Opera. The Baron took a box at the Opera for his girls throughout the season. The girls loved the lighter pieces but

sometimes when Wagner was given, I had the box to myself. I love
Wagner. But it is very long; and, on a hard chair, this can be tiring. But
in the back of the box there was a sofa. I moved it forward so that I could
see the stage from a reclining position. I then sent to the bar for a bottle
of champagne. This is the way to hear the Ring.

I began to explore Vienna's night life. My first companion was the
Baron's butler, Hermann. Hermann was an amusing little man with hair
brushed across his head to conceal premature baldness. He had danced
in the chorus in the Corps de Ballet and had been a Franciscan novice.
But he enjoyed the good things of life too much for either vocation.
He loved to please which made him a good boon companion as well as
a good servant. It was Hermann who introduced me to the *Heurige* or
wine gardens of Grinzing, Gumpoldskirche and other Viennese
suburbs.

The *Heuriger* consists of a garden with wooden seats and tables and an
orchestra composed of a guitar, a violin, an accordion and sometimes a
zither. There is only new wine to drink. You chat with your neighbours
if so inclined, or sit silent under the stars and listen to the songs. These
were usually the traditional Viennese drinking songs with an occasional
modern piece thrown in. The *Heuriger* is a very democratic institution.
A litre of wine then cost perhaps 15p and the orchestra was happy with
the same as a tip. The company came from every section of society.

There was also the Prater, a permanent funfair with big dippers and
ghost trains and dominated by a giant wheel. I had never met anything
like this before and spent many happy evenings there.

Once or twice there were private balls, usually given by Embassies,
but attended by the *monde* of Austria and Hungary. There was a particu-
cularly brilliant one at the French Embassy. Most of the men came in
uniform or were covered in decorations. There was one conspicuous
exception. This was Guido Schmidt, the Austrian Foreign Minister, who
looked a stage villain with his jaundiced countenance and burning eyes.
We had a few words together but, like most people present, I had no
idea of the devious nature of his negotiations with Hitler.

The Austrian nobility had been largely ruined by their country's defeat
in the First World War. But they were at this time making something of
a come-back. The Government was well disposed to them and several
members of the Imperial Family had returned to Vienna. One day I saw
an old lady dressed in black enjoying the afternoon sunshine. She was
Frau Schratt, for many years the mistress of old Kaiser Franz Josef.

Among my father's friends in Vienna was Count Richard Coudenhove-
Kalergi, the founder of the Paneuropean Movement, dedicated to the
cause of European unity. Coudenhove was the son of an Austro-Hungarian
diplomat and, on his father's side, had Austrian, Greek and Flemish

blood in his veins. His mother was Japanese. He was exceptionally good looking and, thanks to the high cheek bones inherited from his mother, would keep his looks far longer than most men. He had an original turn of mind and was an indefatigable propagandist. He took great trouble to explain his ideas to me and we talked not just of European unity but of the Balkan problem, of Communism, of Naziism and of the role of the Roman Church in European politics. With him I met several Austrians of his circle. They let me sit and listen to their discussions, and my increasing knowledge of German soon enabled me to follow the argument.

The menace of Naziism hung like a shadow over the land. Again and again conversation turned to the question of how far Austria was German. The aristocrats and peasants said it was something apart. They were mostly anti-Nazi. But there was strong support for Hitler among the middle classes and such working men as I met in the wine gardens. Young men too from every section of society were attracted by the idea of a greater Germany. They saw in it wider opportunities for themselves than the rump state of the Dual Monarchy could ever afford.

Among my friends in Vienna was Djura, son of Count Casimir Esterhazy. He suggested that we should go together to Budapest and stay with his relations. On the first evening we listened for perhaps an hour to Magyari, the famous gypsy violinist who played at one of the big hotels. I had never heard gypsy music before and did not at first give it much thought. But the more I listened, the more it grew on me.

Next evening, after doing the rounds of the city, we explored the smaller gypsy taverns. This was an evening of sheer delight and, by the end of it, the attraction of gypsy music had become a passion. I have never liked jazz. I love the popular songs of Italy and Austria but after a time they pall. Gypsy music is another dimension of popular entertainment. I have sat up all night, more often than I care to think, listening to the gypsies of Russia, the Balkans and Spain. They have made me forget time, place and the obligations of the morning. I do not grudge them a single hour or a single penny. Neither could have been better spent.

We drove back to Vienna along Lake Balaton, stopping in the afternoon, at the house of one of Djura's cousins. Here I was introduced to a very civilised Hungarian custom. The servant who opened the door saw at once that we were hot and dusty from the drive. He first showed us where to wash then as we emerged from the bathroom served us a glass of ice-cold white wine. It was thought wrong that we should meet our host until we were refreshed internally as well as externally.

Another incident of these Vienna days stands out in my memory. I had been to the University in the morning and had agreed to meet seven of the girls from my school at Sachers Hotel to drive them back for lunch.

As we drove out of Vienna, there was a lorry parked on the other side of the road. A man got out of it as I approached and seemed to be examining the wheel. Then, just as I drew level with the lorry, he stepped back into the road and I ran him down. The police came; particulars were taken; and we drove my victim to the nearest hospital. He was concussed and had a badly bruised back. A fortnight later the public prosecutor brought a case against me for careless driving. The insurance company briefed a young lawyer, Dr. Reiss, to defend me. Reiss questioned me and the seven girls about what had happened. He was soon convinced that the accident was none of our doing. He then drilled us carefully as to what we were to say in court.

The appointed day came. The prosecutor made his case and called one or two witnesses, including the victim of the accident. My lawyer called me first and then each of the seven girls in turn. The judge was plainly amused by this cohort of lovely ladies and impressed by their testimony. Reiss then cross-examined the poor lorry driver whose account was, not unnaturally, very confused. The judge found for the defence but went a stage further. He fined our unfortunate victim £5 for dangerous walking on a public highway. I paid his fine and we took my lawyer off to celebrate. This is the only occasion, up to the time of writing, when I have been in the dock.

In August our finishing school moved to Alt Aussee in Styria. This was the most conservative part of Austria, the country of the *White Horse Inn* where Kaiser Franz Josef loved to spend his holidays. Most people then still wore the local dress of leather shorts, embroidered jackets, and hats decorated with chamois brushes or blackcock feathers. Life in Styria was very gay. There was a continuous round of parties in the chalets around Aussee and Ischl. There were also village balls where the gentry and the peasants danced folk dances together. There were expeditions into the hills and drives along the lakes.

Von Papen, the former German Chancellor, came to lunch one day and we went for a walk together. He defended the Hitler régime, though without much enthusiasm, and seemed to think that the peace of Europe rested on a knife edge. This was the first time I took the danger of another war seriously.

My parents joined me in Aussee for a short holiday. I climbed one or two mountains with my father and then took my mother to Salzburg to hear Mozart and watch *Jedermann*.

7

Oxford

I went up to Balliol in October of 1937. For the modest sum of £18 a term I secured a large sitting room and a small bedroom, spacious accommodation by present-day Oxford standards. A 'scout' or man-servant looked after me. He was a cheerful, dark little man and had started life as a partner in a small bicycle shop. But he had lacked confidence in his other partner and had sold out his share in the business for £100 to take service in Balliol instead. The other partner had gone on to become Lord Nuffield.

I had endured Summerfields and Eton rather than enjoyed them. Oxford was love at first sight. School life with its rules and regulations was a thing of the past. We were free to come and go as we pleased; to work or to play; to sleep or to talk; to fast or to indulge as the fancy took us. There was no obligation to attend meals or chapel. There were only two rules that I can remember. We had appointments with our tutors twice a week and were expected to keep them. We had to be in by midnight unless we had secured an extension. To go away for the whole night required some good reason but there was no difficulty about obtaining an extension until six in the morning. This meant that with a hired car it was quite easy to dine and dance in London and get back to Oxford in time.

I read Modern Greats. This school combines philosophy, economics, and politics; the last defined as constitutional and diplomatic history. This is a lot to digest in three years. But it at least makes the student familiar with the general ideas which are the currency of political discussion.

Humphrey Sumner[1] was my history tutor. Sumner was well over six feet tall with long, wavy, black hair, a high brow and angular features out of a painting by El Greco. He looked like a romantic poet. In fact his strength lay in precision and mastery of detail. It was said that in the First World War he had done more than anyone to crack German codes. His own contribution to history consisted mostly of books and monographs on Russian policy in the Balkans in the later part of the nineteenth century.

[1] Sumner: later Warden of All Souls.

Sumner soon put his finger on my weak spot. I tended to adopt a thesis and build up a case to support it. He taught me instead to assemble the evidence, to analyse it objectively and to deduce conclusions tentatively or with confidence according to the quality of the information. On one of my early essays he wrote: 'This is good stuff. One might conceivably get you a first. But you must let the iron enter into your soul. I will explain what I mean when we meet.' When we met, he talked for some time while trying, unsuccessfully, to keep a pipe alight. The weakness of my essay, he argued, was that I had thought it good enough to choose a particular theme and to develop it. How far had I considered alternative possibilities even if only to dismiss them? Had I checked the views of the accepted historians against contemporary memoirs and lesser known works? Had I given sufficient weight to the influence of the forces pulling the strings in the background? Under Sumner's guidance I began to study history as an intelligence officer analyses a military situation. I would have good reason to be grateful for this training.

For a time Sumner was away ill and I took my work to Kenneth Bell. Bell was of undistinguished appearance, with short untidy hair. He looked a practical man but was in fact totally unworldly and, in many ways, eccentric. The first time I went to see him, he sent me away explaining that he had drunk too much at lunch to teach that afternoon. But he had a stimulating knack of fastening on some apparently secondary fact or circumstance and making it the cornerstone of a challenge to generally accepted views.

Sandy Lindsay,[1] the Master of Balliol, was never my tutor but he took a kindly interest in my work and often asked me in for supper or for a talk. Our discussions usually turned to politics and tended to focus on the dilemma which then concerned him most; how to reconcile state direction with individual freedom.

Roy Harrod was the chief exponent of Keynesian ideas and his violent and provocative opinions made him a great favourite at undergraduate lunches. But my own economic thinking was even more strongly influenced by Hubert Henderson. Henderson had worked in the Cabinet Office during the Great Depression and seemed to me much less theoretical in his approach than most of the Oxford economists.

H. A. L. Fisher, then Warden of New College and very much the elder statesman of the University, heard of my interest in Napoleon. He was the leading British authority on the subject and particularly interested in Napoleon's political ideas and methods. Though essentially an academic, Fisher had been Minister of Education and sat in Cabinets. As with Henderson, Fisher's experience of public life seemed to give him a much surer touch as a historian. If I were dictator I should like to decree

[1] Lindsay: later Lord Lindsay of Birker.

that no-one be allowed to teach history who had not helped to make it.

Another academic deeply involved in politics was 'Prof' Lindemann, later Lord Cherwell, one of Churchill's close advisers. 'Prof' gave frequent lunches in his rooms in Christ Church, mixing undergraduates with scientists, politicians and senior officers. 'Prof' loved an argument, was bitterly critical of the Conservative establishment and stoked us up about the German danger.

My father was a fellow of All Souls, and often stayed there at weekends. He would ask me to dine in Hall on Sunday night and I thus came to know most of the fellows. There was the influential 'Cliveden Set' represented by Halifax, Geoffrey Dawson, Lothian and John Simon. They were all personal friends of my father's though in violent disagreement with him over the German danger. I well remember his exasperation when Lothian, fresh from talks with Gandhi, told us he was going shortly to meet Hitler and felt confident he could bring the Führer 'to see sense'. There was Lionel Curtis of majestic appearance but already so obsessed with his Federalist panacea to world problems that it was difficult to discuss other subjects with him. A. L. Rowse, then a right-wing socialist, and G. D. H. Cole, Oxford's leading Marxist, opened my eyes to the strains and stresses within the British Labour Movement. General Swinton, the formidable professor of military history, had invented the tank and easily convinced me that it would prove the decisive weapon in another war. Unfortunately, other people thought him biased. Professor Hudson aroused my interest in Chinese affairs so that I began to understand the background to the Sino-Japanese War and the conflict between Chiang Kai-shek and Mao Tse-tung.

A frequent guest at All Souls was Heinrich Brüning, the former German Chancellor. Brüning was then lecturing at Oxford on the German political scene. His lectures were very restrained but deeply pessimistic; his private conversation even more so. One evening at All Souls, John Simon had expressed hopes of an agreement with Hitler, and asked Brüning for his opinion. Brüning answered rather coldly that Britain could, of course, get agreement with Hitler but only on Hitler's terms.

A German scholar has written a thesis maintaining that pre-war Britain was really governed from All Souls. This is, no doubt, an exaggeration. But by bringing together political leaders and leading academics in the relaxed but objective atmosphere of an Oxford Common Room the All Souls of those days certainly exercised a powerful influence.

My father was also a trustee of Cecil Rhodes' will. This gave me the *entrée* to Rhodes House and the chance to make friends with its scholars drawn from the Commonwealth, the United States and Germany. We had endless discussions about the future of the Commonwealth. Looking back on them I am struck how much we took it for granted that in any major crisis the countries of the Commonwealth would stand together. There were differences of opinion as to how best to strengthen it. No-one seriously contemplated its dissolution.

Oxford then, as now, had a substantial Indian element and a flourishing Majlis Society. Most of its discussions were on a high level. But on one occasion things got out of hand. Sir John Anderson,[1] reputed the most shot at man in Bengal, had been invited to address the Society. Some forty or fifty of its more extreme members had packed the front rows. At a given signal, while Anderson was speaking, they put on false noses, artificial whiskers and funny hats. All then stood up and began blowing whistles and throwing streamers as if at a Christmas party. It was no doubt a disgraceful way to treat a great pro-consul, but I have never seen a more successful attempt to break up a meeting.

The political parties were well represented at the University, and I joined all three in my first term. Fascist and Communist meetings were also open to the general public and I went to some of these as well. Most of the leaders of English political thought came to Oxford. Then there was the Union. Union oratory tended then, as now, to be facetious and to substitute epigrams for experience. But all the great issues of the day were discussed. Some clever things were said; and votes could be swayed by brilliant argument or emotional appeal. I joined the Union at once and heard most of the debates; but it was a few months before I ventured to take part.

Students at universities like London or Birmingham have often told me of their loneliness and depression living in 'digs' in a big city. The undergraduate at Oxford was protected from this by living in College. The College was a community of its own, not in any way exclusive but, like a family, providing a firm base.

The company at Balliol was certainly stimulating. Simon Wardell and I went up together along with another close Eton friend, Sandy Hope, and Maurice Macmillan. I had hardly known Maurice at Eton. But he joined our circle at once and we soon became close friends. Later on he would become my brother-in-law.

Another undergraduate who joined our circle was Hugh Fraser. Hugh was a tall Highland laird, already in his second year. He had true panache, loved paradox and held Disraelian opinions. He was also a Roman Catholic and introduced me to two remarkable Jesuits, Father d'Arcy and Father Ronnie Knox.

D'Arcy combined gentleness with a will of steel and brilliant dialectical skill. We lunched alone one day and spent the whole afternoon until nearly seven o'clock in discussion. Almost he persuaded me, and I shall

[1] Anderson: Governor of Bengal, Chancellor of the Exchequer, 1st Viscount Waverley.

always remember his parting shot: 'With your power of argument you would make a very good missionary.'

A little later, Hugh and I gave a lunch in my rooms for Ronnie Knox and Lutyens, the architect. Lutyens was a militant atheist and poured buckets of sacrilegious fun over the Church. Knox, who was quite unshockable and even more brilliant, kept us in fits of laughter with his description of the torments awaiting Lutyens in hell. It was an object lesson in how two civilised men could clash violently over great issues, on which both felt deeply, without loss of temper or mutual respect.

My interest in politics soon brought me into touch with Ted Heath, then also at Balliol, though two years my senior. Impeccable in dress and precise in speech, Ted was already a leading figure in the Oxford Conservative Association and would soon become President of the Union. He laughed easily, seemed to be everywhere and yet somehow remained a man apart.

On the other side in politics was Denis Healey affecting brightly coloured ties and extreme left-wing views. He became Chairman of the Labour Club but seemed, in those days, more interested in poetry and literature than in politics, and certainly gave no hint of martial tendencies, such as might lead him to his later post as Minister for Defence.

Then there was Niall MacDermot who introduced me to the works of Nietzsche and Sorel, and was perhaps the most original thinker among the Balliol undergraduates. Another close friend was Patrick Duncan, the earnest and baby-faced son of the Governor-General of South Africa. We used to listen together to Beethoven concerts on the gramophone and talk late into the night. He was a man of deep, if simple, Christian convictions and driven by an urge to testify to the truth, whatever the cost. Indeed, the higher the cost, the keener was the urge. This would bring him into serious conflict with the South African authorities in later years.

Another close friend was Ranbir Singh, the son of an old school friend of my father's, Sir Maharaj Singh. Ranbir spoke English with that perfect diction and choice of words of which only Indians seem capable. He had read widely and had all the Indian's gift of subtle and copious exposition. Ranbir loved to talk until the dawn and slept most of the day. I do not think he did much work. But the gravity of his demeanour, although largely contrived, somehow deflected the wrath of the authorities.

Ranbir was of princely descent and not above using his lineage for our entertainment. He had quite a modest allowance from his father but would ring up one of the better known car dealers and express interest in buying a Rolls-Royce. Would they perhaps send one down for him to try? He was planning to go to Newmarket for the races with a few friends. This might be a good opportunity to try out the car. Oxford shops were limited so perhaps the firm would put a picnic lunch including champagne in the boot. At the end of a happy day at the races, Ranbir would write a courteous note thanking the dealer but explaining that the car did not really come up to his standards.

But I suppose I had as many friends outside Balliol as in it. Alan Hare, a close friend at Eton, was at New College. John Orbach, my friend since kindergarten days, had gone to Magdalen, where he had formed a little coterie of friends interested in *avant-garde* literature and art. Among them was Constantine FitzGibbon, who gave luxurious dinner parties, wore strangely coloured shirts and ties and edited a literary magazine called *Yellow Jacket*.

Also at Magdalen was John Biggs Davison. We first met in a debate at the Union. He held extreme left-wing views, but I soon saw that his socialism was of the romantic kind. We dined together and became close friends. We differed violently in our analysis of current affairs, but I was not so sure that our aims were very different. In this events would prove me right.

My interest in France led me to join the French Club and so to meet the group of French undergraduates then at Oxford. Prominent among them was Jean Pierre Giraudoux, a son of the famous French playwright. Jean Pierre carried filial devotion to extreme lengths, and had little time for other authors beside his father. He thought Shaw a bore and wished that Shakespeare had stuck to sonnets. More single-minded perhaps and with a brilliant gift of mimicry was Jerome Sauerwein, a son of the editor of *Paris Soir* and destined to become an outstanding lawyer. These two conspired to make me president of the French Club. With their help we brought over a series of distinguished French speakers. André Maurois came among others, and I was able to thank him personally for his Eton prize.

But we had one great disappointment. Maurice Dekobra, the author of a number of salacious works, agreed to give a lecture on 'Love'. I had read his novels and noted the attention he paid in them to food and drink. I accordingly chose our menu with care and ordered two bottles of a superb Corton Charlemagne. To my horror, Dekobra poured water into the wine and ate scarcely anything at all. Worse still, he had taken his invitation to lecture at the great English seat of learning much too seriously. Five or six hundred students had gathered hoping to be amused and perhaps even shocked. They had instead to endure a very pedestrian comparison of Pagan, Christian and Platonic love, lasting well over an hour.

Oxford was a predominantly masculine institution but there were frequent fair visitors from outside. There was the repertory company where Pamela Brown with her flaming red hair was queen. Then there were the undergraduettes. Some were very pretty. All had two great advantages over their London sisters. They were there. They lived the same lives as we did and so could understand us better. Women are often the mirror in which a young man discovers himself. They stir the desire to please, and the ambition to shine. At parties, on the river and at college balls they were an essential as well as an agreeable part of an Oxford education.

Oxford at this time had two main social clubs, the Grid and the Carlton. Hugh Fraser persuaded me to join the Carlton. Simon Wardell, Maurice Macmillan and Alan Hare did the same. It was next door to Balliol and, as the College food was not very good and the College dinner hour rather early, we came increasingly to make the Carlton our social headquarters. In the end, we took it over; and Hugh, Simon, I and Maurice became its president in turn.

With the exuberance of youth, our little group felt a strong urge for self expression. We were not yet sure of our message. But this seemed a secondary consideration. Form mattered more than content. Accordingly we resolved to start a weekly newspaper. The first step was to find a backer to put up the money. Oswald Berry, Lord Kemsley's son, helped us over this. The next was to find an editor. Here we came upon Woodrow Wyatt, then reading law at Worcester College. Woodrow was short and dark, with untidy hair which often obscured his eyes. He seemed older than we were, and had written articles in the *Daily Mirror*. So began a friendship which has lasted down the years, and across all political divides.

The *Oxford Comment* first appeared early in 1938. I was one of its editorial board and acted as its lobby correspondent. In this capacity I interviewed Harry Pollitt, Oswald Mosley, H. G. Wells and George Lansbury. I remember being profoundly shocked by the stereotyped answers which Harry Pollitt gave to questions. This was my first experience of Communist discipline, of which I had so often heard, but had never expected to extend to Pollitt who, as Secretary, was top man in the British Communist Party. Mosley denied that he sought a dictatorship, which might logically be expected as the ambition of the Leader of the British Union of Fascists. 'No, just a leadership of the people,' he said and rolled his eyes. That spell-binding story-teller of my childhood, H. G. Wells, was also slightly disappointing. Instead of some stunning forecast of future invention, I was fobbed off with the information that religion distorted honest thinking and that whisky was good for diabetes. Lansbury, as Labour M.P. and Pacifist leader, at least did what was expected of him. Hitler was a pacifist at heart, he assured me, and, if only the two of them could get round a table together, there would be no war.

I also interviewed Madame Tabouis the well known French journalist and asked her to give the *Oxford Comment* a 'scoop'. Off the cuff, she forecast the date of Hitler's occupation of Austria. We published it, and were proved right to within four days.

But, it is not enough to be right in the newspaper business. Our revenue from advertising by no means balanced the costs of publication. Oswald Berry had over-spent his allowance. His appeals to Lord Kemsley met with no response. The *Oxford Comment* died after the sixth number. My letters show that I paid up the last £5 owing to the publishers.

I did not do much work in my first year what with discovering Oxford, joining in its politics and helping produce a newspaper. Alan Hare was in the same position. We accordingly decided to spend the summer vacation of 1938 reading our text books in the South of France. We stopped in Lyon on the drive out. It was about six in the evening and I was parking the car when a stranger parked alongside and asked the time. I told him and enquired the whereabouts of our hotel. He volunteered to take us there and then said to me: 'You're Russian, aren't you?' The chance was too good to miss. 'How did you guess?' I answered. 'Oh, I could tell at once by your accent,' he said. 'May I know who you are?' 'Well, very much between ourselves,' I replied, 'I am the Grand Duke Boris. This is my chamberlain, Count Harich, but we are travelling privately so please respect our confidence.' The stranger seemed suitably impressed and escorted us to our hotel. Then he said that it would be a great honour if we would agree to dine with him at his home that night. 'Anything for a free dinner' is a good student rule, and a couple of hours later we entered a comfortably furnished flat. Our host and his wife had laid themselves out for their Imperial guests. They had bought vodka and caviar and there was excellent champagne. The four of us dined very pleasantly, while I told tall stories about my escape from the Revolution as a child, and our hopes of restoring the Imperial family.

Soon after dinner, the bell rang and we were joined by half-a-dozen gentlemen, who turned out to be members of the substantial White Russian community of Lyon.

We sat in a circle over coffee and brandy, myself fortunately ensconced between my host and his wife. One of the Russians made a little speech of welcome in Russian. I nodded appreciatively and when he had finished turned to my host and enquired whether he understood Russian. He did not. Out of courtesy to him, as I explained, I replied in French. I then led the conversation onto the international situation about

The author's mother: a portrait by Olive Snell.

a. I wanted to be a sailor.

b. The young Etonian.

a. The author's father when Secretary of State for India.

b. Participants in the Oxford Union Debate in February 1939. From left to right: the author—with Simon Wardell looking over his shoulder; Randolph Churchill; John Biggs-Davison, with Stephen King Hall to the right in the front row. To the right of King Hall, again in the front row, is Hugh Fraser, then Patrick O'Donovan, bespectacled A. P. Herbert, and Basil Liddell Hart.

a. King Boris of Bulgaria in conversation with General Valkoff, the War Minister, after opening Parliament.

b. King Zog of Albania at work in 1940 during his London exile.

which, fortunately for me, the Russians held strong and conflicting views.

While they argued I led my host aside and explained that he had committed a fearful indiscretion. I had revealed my identity to him in confidence. He had now involved me with the Lyon Russian community who, I said, were deeply penetrated with Soviet agents. He must get us out of the flat quickly or our blood might well be on his head. He took it all to heart, and, as soon as courtesy allowed, Alan and I escaped pleading the fatigue of our journey, and promising to meet the Russians again next day. We went to a night club and were still laughing over our escapade when we saw the six Russians come in and sit down in another corner of the room. Fortunately the club was dark and they were deep in talk. We paid our bill and slipped out unseen.

Clearly Lyon had become too small for us so we pressed on to the coast, stopping to dance, rather self-consciously, on the bridge at Avignon. We found a charming house on the outskirts of Toulon with a garden running down to the beach. We stayed there for the next six weeks reading Philosophy all day and discussing it much of the night. Bacon, Descartes, Spinoza, Butler, Kant, Hegel, Marx and Russell were studied, analysed and discarded in turn. Meanwhile our excellent Corsican cook, Madame Santini, sustained us with a range of Mediterranean dishes extending from *bouillabaisse* to *fricassée* of squirrel. Our house had previously belonged to Bernanos, the left-wing Catholic author. We rented it furnished for £25 a month. I called there some years ago to find that the rent for August had risen to £300. I shudder to think what it is now.

Count Sforza, the former Italian Foreign Minister, lived less than a mile away and kindly asked us to lunch. When I first met him he had just emerged from the sea and was wrapped in a flowing Chinese dressing gown. This led the talk round to China and drew from him an amusing anecdote. As a young man, he told us, he had been very proud of his ancestry, and inclined to boast of it. Presently he was sent out as a secretary to the Italian Embassy in Peking. When he took over his predecessor's house, the servants and gardeners were lined up for his inspection. Each of them carried a piece of parchment in his hand. Sforza enquired what these bits of paper meant. 'Oh,' said his predecessor, 'that's just their family tree.' To Sforza's shame he found that even the humblest garden boy had a far longer lineage than his own 'Since then,' he told us, 'I have never boasted about my family again.'

We went to his house several times and made friends with his son and daughter. After a time we felt we should make some return of hospitality, and sent round a note asking the son to dinner. We then

prepared a suitably undergraduate style of party with dinner laid on
the floor and an old skull, which Alan had found in Toulon, as the centrepiece. To build up our own importance, we instructed the cook to come
in every now and then and summon one of us to the telephone to speak
to Paris, London or New York.

Our preparations were complete, and we were enjoying a glass of
champagne on the terrace, when to our surprise old Count Sforza walked
in. His son, he explained, had had to go to Brussels and he had come
instead. It was much too late to alter our plans, but the old man was in
excellent form and had plenty to say. He seemed delighted to eat off the
floor, and told several stories about skulls which made our centrepiece
seem a happy idea. The dinner and drink were good, and he enjoyed them
freely.

In our embarrassment at Sforza's arrival we had forgotten all about
the telephone calls. But now, every twenty minutes or so, Madame Santini
would come into the room to say that Alan or I was wanted on the 'phone
from Paris or New York. Sforza seemed to regard this as quite natural
and we retailed the news to him from the different capitals until imagination failed and we told the cook to stop.

It was warm, and Sforza stayed talking on the terrace till after midnight. He spoke sarcastically of Mussolini, describing him as 'a great
reader of newspapers'. He believed him to be completely under Hitler's
domination and thought war inevitable. He also predicted that he himself
would be one of the few refugees in history to return to power. He would
be brought back, he said, by the Italian community in the United States.
When he came to London after the War, as Italian Foreign Minister once
more, I recalled our talk that night. He had forgotten the prediction, but
still remembered the skull.

Toulon was not far from Marseilles and we had heard much about
the Vieux Port, as the maze of streets comprising the old and reputedly
criminal quarter of the city was known. We resolved to visit it and, so
as not to look out of place, stopped shaving for three or four days. We
then put on our dirtiest shirts and slacks and drove off to Marseilles.

The sun was sinking as we reached the city and, blinded by it, I ran
into a milk cart. No-one was hurt but a few bottles were broken, and I
was trying to reach an amicable settlement with the milkman when a policeman came up. Alan and I undoubtedly looked disreputable. We had left
our passports behind. The policeman flatly refused to believe that the car
was ours. We must have stolen it. We were taken to the main police
station and pushed into the public lock-up where we spent an hour or so
in interesting, if unsavoury, company.

We were then called into the superintendent's office for interrogation and managed to persuade him to telephone the police at Toulon who established our identity. We were then rebuked and released while a friendly police officer wrote down for us a list of the bars in the Vieux Port which we should be sure to visit. The Vieux Port has since been burnt down and ultra-modern flats designed by Le Corbusier have risen where the narrow alleys once ran. I am glad I saw it as it was.

The reader may think that the Oxford world I have described was frivolous, irresponsible and spoilt. This charge would be unfair. Like youth in every age, we took ourselves if anything too seriously. No doubt our talk and thinking were still very immature, but at least we talked and thought. No doubt we enjoyed more economic security than is common today. But I am not sure that this was necessarily a weakness. Poverty sharpens the mind, but it cramps the style and easily breeds cynicism. In any case, let no-one grudge my generation these few months of gaiety and freedom. If there was a lack of realism about our student life, well, Hitler would give us realism in plenty and soon enough.

II

THE INITIATION

1938–1939

'Viva la muerte!' (Long live death!)
> Motto of the Spanish Foreign Legion

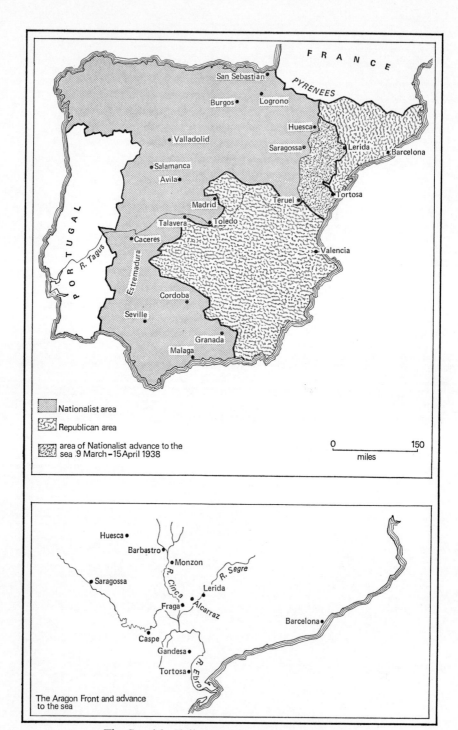

Nationalist area

Republican area

area of Nationalist advance to the
sea .9 March – 15 April 1938

0 ——————— 150
miles

FRANCE

PYRENEES

San Sebastian

Burgos   Logrono

Huesca

Valladolid   Saragossa   Lerida   Barcelona

Salamanca   Tortosa

Avila   Teruel

Madrid

Talavera   Toledo   Valencia

Caceres

PORTUGAL

R. Tagus

Estremadura

Cordoba

Seville

Granada

Malaga

Huesca

Barbastro   Monzon

R. Cinca   R. Segre

Saragossa   Lerida

Fraga   Alcarraz

Caspe

Gandesa

Tortosa   R. Ebro

Barcelona

The Aragon Front and advance
to the sea

The Spanish Civil War: March – September 1938

8

Baptism of Fire

At Summerfields and, indeed, at Eton it had been very much the accepted view that there would never be another major war. War, we were told, settled nothing; and it was unthinkable that the nations of Europe, bled white in the first great struggle, could again put matters to the test of arms. It was, of course, a relief to think that I would never have to fight; and yet it left me with a nagging feeling that this meant missing something essential to a full understanding of life. Much of the world's greatest literature was about war. Many of the heroes of history and romance had been warriors. Could a man be a full man until he had been to war? After listening to pacifist sermons at school, I prayed earnestly that my country might be spared from fighting again. But at the back of my mind I nursed a secret hope that, one day, I would have a chance to see for myself what war meant.

I have already recorded my offer to volunteer for the Abyssinian War, and its courteous refusal. A year later, in 1936, the Civil War broke out in Spain. I followed the campaign closely with an Eton friend, Sandy Hope. We kept a situation map, discussed developments every two or three days, and wondered how we might go out to Spain and in what capacity.

At the time nothing came of our talks. But the Spanish Civil War was still raging when we went up to Oxford at the end of 1937. It had now become the dominant issue in student politics. I decided that I must go to Spain and see something of the War at first hand. This would increase my standing among my fellows. It might also give me a chance to write one or two articles and so begin to make a name for myself in the world outside. The problem was how to get into Spain.

It so happened that Archie James, then a Conservative Member of Parliament and the father of a school friend, David James, came to Oxford. He had just been to Franco Spain and gave a talk about it. After the meeting I opened my mind to him and asked if he could help. He told me that the Duke of Alba, then Franco's representative in London, was coming to lunch a day or two later and suggested that I should come too. The rest would be up to me. At lunch I asked Alba why it was that the Franco authorities would not let observers in to see what was happening on their side. This, I remarked, seemed a pity. My sympathies, I said, were with the Nationalists; but Franco's case was going by default in the universities; and I really did not feel competent to speak out unless I could see for myself what was happening. Alba responded magnificently to this rather obvious challenge. He would be delighted if I and any of my undergraduate friends would care to go to Nationalist Spain in the next vacation. I had only to take our passports to his office and he would issue visas at once.

I reported Alba's invitation to Sandy Hope. We made up our minds to go. Another friend, Michael Lyle, asked if he could come with us and offered to bring his car. Alba was as good as his word, and gave us the necessary visas and recommendations at once.

I was to see a good deal of Alba later, when he was Ambassador in London. He was quite short and slight in stature with an almost Arabian cast of features. Among strangers he seemed to wrap himself in an impenetrable mantle of formality. But among friends he put aside all reserve and indulged in one sparkling indiscretion after another.

My father at first opposed our venture. But mainly, I think, to test our determination. His letters show that he was at heart delighted that we had some spirit of adventure.

We drove across France towards the end of March 1938, and reached the frontier post of Irun at sunset. It was a year since the battle of Irun, but little had been done to repair the war damage. There were very few people about; and the roofless houses and shell torn walls sent a chill down my spine.

By contrast, San Sebastian, where we stayed our first night, seemed very normal. The Hotel Maria Christina was crowded and the menu at dinner showed that there was no food shortage. This was indeed natural. Franco controlled the main centres of food production. The great centres of consumption—Madrid, Valencia and Barcelona—were all in Republican hands. It was indeed a standard item of Franco propaganda to broadcast to the Republican zone menus chosen at random from hotels and restaurants on the Nationalist side. The only sign of wartime austerity was the weekly *Dia del plato unico* or 'day of the one course meal'. No restaurant was allowed to serve more than one course on this day. But they made up for the lack of choice by the size of the helpings and the variety of ingredients in the dish.

Our first morning we presented our credentials to the Governor of San Sebastian, Don Alfonso Velarde. His office was in the former casino guarded by three ragged sentries wrapped in ankle length khaki overcoats. The Governor's ante room, the first of many I was to see in Spain, was crowded with officers and civilians talking in little knots or drinking coffee. The Governor greeted us courteously and asked what he could do for us. We said we wanted to see something of San Sebastian and then proceed to Burgos. He undertook to make the necessary arrangements and told his ADC to take us out to lunch.

Nothing, in fact, happened. We were in the land of *mañana* and it was quite useless telling ADCs and secretaries that we only had three weeks to spare before term started. There was no-one to whom we could turn, and it began to look as if our journey to the war would get no further than a seaside resort at least two hundred miles from the front.

Then fate intervened in the person of the aged Marquis Merry del Val who turned up in our hotel. Merry del Val had been Ambassador in London for many years and I had met him with my father. He at once saw the point of humouring Oxford undergraduates. We might not have any very well defined status, but Alba had thought it worth encouraging our visit and Merry del Val applauded his initiative. By a happy coincidence Merry's eldest son, Pablo, was head of the press department in Burgos. The Marquis looked a very old man but he was still very active. He telephoned to the Governor. He telephoned to his son; and presently things began to hum.

The Franco authorities believed in shock treatment. We had come to see what war was about. Well, they would show us. We were taken off to the Mola hospital for a prolonged tour of the plastic surgery ward. After seeing a row of patients hideously disfigured in battle, we were taken into the theatre to watch an operation by a brilliant Irish surgeon, a Doctor Shean, who was trying to restore the semblance of human features to a man who had lost his nose and as far as we could see his lips. We were then led into the shell shock ward and kept there for several minutes while the patients screamed and made uncontrollable movements with their arms and legs. For boys of nineteen, this was strong meat.

Suitably conditioned by this visit to the hospital, we were then taken to an orphanage run by remarkably pretty girls dressed in blue shirts and black skirts. Everything looked cheerful enough until the Matron began telling us the case histories of the different children. All had lost their parents in the war. About half had been killed in battle. The other half, we were told, had been murdered or executed. I asked which side the parents had been on in the War. The Matron answered laconically 'Both'.

We were now issued with safe conducts to Burgos, Franco's capital, and drove there without incident. Burgos in those days was a small provincial town with an ancient fortress crowning a low hill which ran down to the banks of a largely dried up river bed. Above the river rose

the magnificent mediaeval cathedral and along its banks ran a broad
street known as the Espalon. This was closed to traffic from about six
o'clock in the evening to allow the population to stroll at leisure.

Burgos is 3,000 ft. high and, at the end of March, was still very cold
and windy. Nevertheless, the Espalon was thronged with people walking
up and down or sitting in the cafés alongside. The great majority of the
men were in uniform, dressed in long khaki overcoats or fur-collared
jerkins. A few wore the red berets of the Carlist *Requetés*. Some wore
dark blue, the *Falange* party uniforms. There were several German Air
Force Officers, as well as groups of Italian infantry with black piping and
special regimental flashes. The most striking strollers were the Moorish
cavalry. They were mostly tall men, wearing white turbans and ankle-
length cloaks of light blue cloth lined with scarlet. Every now and then
we saw soldiers dressed in a distinctive grey-green uniform. These were
the famous *Tercio* or Spanish Foreign Legion.

The strollers had not come out for fresh air or exercise. They were out
to look at the girls. These paraded up and down banded together for
safety in groups of half a dozen or so. As the men passed the girls they
would call out bawdy compliments: 'What lovely eyes!' 'Who ever saw
such breasts?' 'How I could pinch your bottom!' 'What a night we could
make of it together!' Nothing was more surprising to a young Englishman,
used to the comradeship of undergraduettes, than this total segregation
of the sexes and the one track train of thought engendered by it.

In the hotel bar, that evening, we got into conversation with an officer
of the Judge Advocate General's Department. He told us that the great
majority of Republican prisoners were either released or conscripted into
the Nationalist forces. He admitted, however, that Republican officers or
known organisers of the Communist or Anarchist parties were executed
on identification. There would, he said, be some executions about two or
three o'clock that morning. If we would like to go and watch them, he
would be glad to take us. We declined the offer and yet could not help
being impressed by its frankness. If this was the form, then no-one was
likely to keep much secret from us.

I think the Colonel thought us rather squeamish. At any rate, before
we parted company he told us a grim jest, then circulating in Burgos.
Sometime that winter a Republican prisoner under sentence of death
had been taken out in an open truck into the Castilian hills to be shot at
dawn. Under the regulations, an officer had to be present at the execution;
but the officer concerned overslept. It was bitterly cold; and the prisoner
and the six men of the firing squad shivered in the icy wind. Presently, the
prisoner complained that this was an infamous way to treat a man on the
last day of his life. 'What are you grumbling about?' said the sergeant in
charge of the firing squad. 'We're the ones who ought to be complaining.

After all, you've only got a one way ticket. We've got to drive all the way back in that bloody open truck.'

The three of us shared a room that night and before going to bed I read the air-raid instructions posted on the door. I slept soundly but towards dawn was woken by a low rhythmic hum. I broke into a muck sweat convinced that hostile aircraft were immediately over the hotel. I was about to rouse my friends when I realised that the hum was only Sandy Hope snoring. I dropped off to sleep again and did not wake until eleven in the morning.

It was past midday by the time we had dressed and breakfasted, and we hurried round to the Ministry of the Interior fearing that we might have missed Pablo Merry del Val. In fact he had only just reached the office. Even at the height of the war, no self respecting Spanish official or officer could be found at his desk much before eleven o'clock. Many stayed on, indeed, not lunching until four and working on after a short siesta till nine or ten at night. But the morning was a dead time.

Merry del Val was tall, dark and strongly built. He had been educated at one of the Catholic Public Schools in England and there was a touch of the school prefect in his tone and bearing, which some of the correspondents rather resented. We found him, however, extremely helpful. He issued us with passes for the battle areas and telephoned to Saragossa instructing the staff there to make sure we saw as much as possible.

We left for Saragossa on 28 March 1938, taking with us a Major Bauer. Bauer was the military correspondent of the *Journal de Genève* and had passed the Swiss Staff College. He was to prove a great help. We had no military experience beyond the Eton Corps and, though Bauer had never seen any fighting, he had made a serious study of war and had attended manoeuvres of both the French and German armies. He knew what to look for.

We reached Saragossa in the evening and went straight to the main hotel, which was rather quaintly called Europa y Inglaterra. The press were already assembled in strength, and the hall seemed to be full of men typing in their shirt sleeves. We knew one or two of them already and were soon made welcome by the others. From what they said, a decisive battle was impending.

The situation on the Aragon front was as follows. The Nationalist forces, under Generals Yague and Moscardo, had launched an offensive to the south-east based on the towns of Huesca and Saragossa. In five days they had advanced nearly a hundred kilometres breaking through the main Republican prepared positions and driving the Republicans back to the strong natural defence line formed by the River Cinca and the River Ebro. The immediate Nationalist objective was to force the passage of these rivers. If this could be done, there would be little to stop them driving through to the Mediterranean. Barcelona would then be cut off from Valencia and Madrid; and the Republican zone broken in two.

There were no rooms to be had in the hotel and we slept as best we could on sofas and armchairs in the hall. In the morning we prepared to join a large group of pressmen who were being taken to Fraga in the hope of witnessing the crossing of the Cinca. But the good Major Bauer had made some logistic calculations of his own and judged that the attack at Fraga would be delayed at least twenty-four hours. He proposed, instead, that we should drive to Huesca, the more easterly base of the offensive and then on to Barbastro, a village on the River Cinca at the extreme left of the line of advance. He reckoned that an attack was likely to develop in that sector. It might be a feint or it might be the real thing, but, in any event, we were more likely to see action there than at Fraga. The Spanish staff respected Bauer as a professional soldier and agreed to his plan. An escorting officer was attached to us and we slipped out of the hotel and set off for Huesca.

Outside Huesca, we came upon a sight of apocalyptic horror. The Nationalists had never lost the town, but until a few days before it had been closely invested by the Republicans. The Republicans indeed had driven in the Nationalist outposts and established an Anarchist company in the walled cemetery immediately outside the town. The cemetery itself made quite a good defensive position; but the country around it was flat and open; and the Republicans often found it impossible to bring up supplies, particularly water, to its garrison. At some point thirst, hunger and continuous shell fire seem to have driven the defenders mad. They tore open the graves, pulled out skeletons and decomposing corpses and set them up in grotesque or indecent postures. In one corner, I remember, a group of skeletons were playing cards. Several were locked in erotic embraces. One was crucified against the wall. Hideous obscenities and lampoons had been scrawled on tombstones. Two Republican soldiers killed in the fighting a week before still lay unburied in a corner of the cemetery. Beside them sat a skeleton with a bottle of wine in one hand and a glass in the other. Even Goya could scarcely have done justice to the scene.

From Huesca, we pushed on towards the River Cinca passing convoys of lorries, mule and donkey trains, and long columns of trudging infantry. The Republicans had blown up most of the culverts and bridges as they fell back; and we had to drive much of the time over roughly made tracks through thick clouds of rich, red Aragon dust.

We stopped for lunch under a tree which served as the command post of a Navarrese battery. To their dismay the artillery men had got their guns into position, only to find that the enemy had retreated out of range. Instead they were indulging in wrestling matches, presumably to work off surplus energy. We shared our rations with the battery Commander and drank some of his wine in return. Then, since all fighting seemed to stop between two and five o'clock, we enjoyed a siesta.

From the battery we drove into Barbastro and just beyond it found an artillery train of pack animals fording the river to try and turn the Republican position at Monzón. We followed them across on foot and stayed while they assembled their guns and began to shell Monzón. We were now on Catalan soil and had managed to get across the river thirty-six hours before any other observers. Bauer's analysis had proved right.

We could make no further progress, however, without the car and so, crossing back, decided to explore along the river towards Monzón. We drove past a column of troops foot-slogging towards the front and then, a little beyond, came on a section established behind some boulders by the road and with their machine guns trained on the road ahead. The officer in charge shouted something at us, but our escorting officer waved our pass at him and told us to drive on. The road ahead was empty and silent. After half-a-mile seeing no troops, we began to feel rather lonely. Presently, we saw some soldiers coming down the side of the hill a mile or more away; but they were coming towards us. Could it be that the Nationalists were retreating? A little further on we saw another section encamped by the road. We heaved a sigh of relief and then Bauer pointed out that their guns were turned our way. It was now clear that we had strayed into no-man's-land. An aeroplane droned overhead; but whose? The road was narrow and it seemed an eternity before Michael Lyle found an opening to get the car turned round. We were well within range of the other side but, for some reason, nobody bothered to shoot at us. When we got back to the Nationalist outpost, we found the Section Commander who had shouted at us, bursting his sides with laughter. It was the natural delight of the fighting officer at seeing a staff officer make a fool of himself. We had made his day for him, and he now produced a goatskin of red wine to celebrate our safe return from the enemy lines.

Back in Saragossa, we found a disconsolate group of journalists in the hall of the hotel. They had hung about all day before Fraga but had neither crossed the river nor seen any action. Bauer thus secured the only 'scoop' of the day. We had no paper to write for, but enjoyed ourselves telling the press men of our experiences with what we hoped was just the right degree of false modesty calculated to provoke them most.

Next day, however, we went with the press to the Fraga sector and towards noon were taken to General Yague's headquarters. The general was in uniform but wore a blue *Falange* shirt. He was a stockily built man with a bull's head and closely cropped grey hair. He led us to the top of a hill a few yards from his tent and briefed us on the battle. Below us ran the valley of the Cinca and we could see plainly the ruins of the bridge across it leading to Fraga. As he spoke we heard sporadic firing and could see groups of Republican troops retreating from the river bank up the hill beyond. The first Nationalist patrols crossed the river in the afternoon and entered Fraga. But Yague judged that a dozen press men would have been a nuisance and we were kept firmly to the Nationalist side of the river. Fortunately, someone discovered a case of champagne abandoned by the Republicans. It was warm and rather sweet, but nonetheless very welcome.

Two days later, on 3 April, we were allowed to cross the river into Fraga and to join the advance towards Lerida. Yague, meanwhile, had moved his headquarters to the village of Alcarraz. We left our cars there and decided to go forward on foot to an artillery post commanding a good view across the River Segre, the next obstacle to the Nationalist advance. Our party, that day, included the three of us, Major Bauer, two English journalists and our escorting officer. Part of the track ran along the crest of the hill and was in full view of the enemy positions on the other side of the river half-a-mile or so away. As we came into this open stretch, I received my baptism of fire from a Republican outpost. My English companions lay down as the bullets whined unpleasantly close overhead. I took cover behind a tree. Our Spanish escorting officer, however, stood quite still in the middle of the road and setting his cap at a rather jaunty angle, turned to us and said, 'Are you afraid to die, gentlemen?' He then explained that we presented almost as good a target lying down as standing up and that, if we cared so much for our lives, it would really be safer to keep walking. We accordingly advanced with more haste than dignity until the track turned back into a wood and we were out of sight of the enemy.

I found this first experience of being shot at rather sickening. It was as if a swarm of angry hornets were after me; and I derived small consolation from the knowledge that when you heard the bullet, that one, at least must have missed.

We reached the artillery post soon afterwards and stayed there through the afternoon. The Republicans were defending Lerida in strength and still had patrols on the right bank of the Segre. We watched them launch a small counter attack but they did not press their advantage very hard. No-one fired at us as we walked back in the dusk to Alcarraz.

We overslept that night and woke to find that the press and escorting officers had already left for the front. We followed them to Yague's headquarters at Alcarraz, but they had gone ahead half-an-hour before. We decided to follow and had just left Alcarraz when a shell burst on the road twenty yards ahead of the car. We stopped; and then two more shells fell not much further away. Bauer judged that the enemy were aiming at the road so we jumped out of the car and took to the fields. By this time shells were bursting all around us. We sheltered for a couple of minutes behind a concrete pill-box and then decided to move towards a deep ditch fifty or sixty yards to our right. We had hardly left the pill-box when it received a direct hit. Sandy Hope, indeed, who had been the last to leave was knocked over by the blast of the explosion. The pill-box itself was shattered.

I was by now very frightened, my heart pounding and my mouth parched. I ran to the ditch, jumped in and found myself beside a Spanish officer of the Moorish *Regulares* and his Moorish orderly. The Republicans kept up the barrage but the ditch was deep and, short of a direct hit, we were tolerably safe. I began to regain my composure and introduced myself to the officer who spoke French. I asked his opinion of the barrage. He said it was the biggest he had experienced and then remarked *'Je trouve notre situation très grave.'* This rather sinister observation coincided with more intensive shelling of our particular area. But the Moorish orderly seemed to be expert at judging where the shells would fall. 'That one,' he would say, 'will be forty metres in front.' 'This one fifty metres behind.' And sure enough the explosion of earth and rock would confirm his judgement. But every now and then he would spread his hands in a fatalistic gesture and say: 'This one? Well, who knows?' When this happened we were generally bespattered by the fall out from the explosion.

I soon found that I could hear each shell coming quite clearly. It made a low whining noise, which turned into a scream as it seemed to slow down immediately overhead. Then came the thud and sickening explosion as it hit the ground. After a bit I began to get used to it though I never achieved the fatalism of our Moorish orderly.

After half-an-hour or so of shelling, the Nationalist batteries opened a counter barrage. Then both sides ceased to fire and there was a lull. I crept out of the ditch to look for my companions and get back to the car. But I had not gone far when the shelling started again. I took shelter in a shallow shell hole and was presently joined there by a tall, fair Spanish officer. I tried talking French to him without much success. I then tried English which he spoke perfectly. This was my first meeting with Peter Kemp, one of the few Englishmen serving on Franco's side and at this time a lieutenant in the Foreign Legion. We were to become close friends and colleagues in the Second World War.

Eventually the barrage ceased altogether. It had probably been put down to cover the Republican withdrawal from Lerida and ended as soon as this was complete. The Nationalist forward patrols now entered the town unopposed. We found the car mercifully intact and followed them.

Lerida looked pretty grim. Apart from a few old people, most of the inhabitants had fled. The inside of the church had been gutted by fire. Part of it had been used as a garage and part as a slaughter house. Most of the buildings around were scarred by shell fire. Several had lost their roofs; and the whole of one street was burning.

The suburbs of the town on the far side were in Republican hands; and the streets running down to the river were still under fire. We had to run to cross them. The centre of the town was full of drunken soldiery; most of them clutching at least one bottle of wine or brandy. Some occasionally fired into the air or used the butts of their rifles to break into the shops and loot the little the Republicans had left behind them.

In a small square, I saw a Nationalist soldier sprawled on his back with blood trickling from under his helmet. I walked over but took him for dead and passed on. Another soldier also took him for dead and bent down to remove his watch. The dead man suddenly sprang to life and hit out fiercely. The thief ran off with the presumed corpse in full pursuit.

Every now and then soldiers would come up and offer us a drink. We feared they might turn nasty if we refused and persuaded the abstemious Major Bauer that he too would be wiser to accept their hospitality. By the time we got back to the car, Bauer was distinctly unsteady. I had somehow acquired a handsome pistol and a rusty old naval sword, inscribed with the date 1890.

The fall of Lerida was the occasion of much celebration in Saragossa; and, after dinner, we repaired to the *Real*, the town's only night club, to watch the fun. The *Real* was a large room filled with plain tables grouped around a small raised platform. On this singers and dancers performed traditional Spanish dances with an occasional attempt at striptease. The audience was made up of officers in every conceivable uniform, of the ladies of the *Real* itself, and of a few other girls who followed the drum. It was smoky, noisy and crowded. Every now and then someone would fire a pistol shot into the ceiling just for the hell of it.

This particular night all the officers we had seen at the front in the last few days seemed to have gathered in the *Real*. We joined up with a group of Andalusian officers. Towards three in the morning, they took us out into a white-washed passage leading into a courtyard and sang *flamenco* songs to us until the dawn.

Spanish officers never seemed to have much difficulty in getting away from the front for a night out, provided they were back in time for the next day's fighting, and this seldom seemed to start before nine o'clock. I have often wondered whether this was one of the reasons why the Civil War lasted so long.

There were often free fights in the *Real* between the very varied elements who fought for Franco. One night, the latent animosity between Italians and Spaniards came to a head. Two Italians and two Spanish officers found themselves at a table together. The talk turned to courage; who was braver, the Italians or the Spaniards? One of the Italian officers drew his revolver, took out five of the six bullets, spun the chamber round and, putting the barrel to his temple, fired. He was lucky; the hammer struck an empty chamber. He passed the revolver to his Spanish neighbour and said: 'Let's see if the Spaniards are as brave as we are.' The Spaniard declined the challenge to Russian roulette. That, he said, was kids' stuff. Instead he took a hand grenade from his belt, placed it in the middle of the table and took out the pin. 'Now,' he called out, 'let's see who leaves the table first.' All four were killed, though it was drink as much as courage that kept them at the table.

The Italians were very much in evidence in Saragossa and, though rather despised by the Spaniards, had in fact fought well in the battle of Aragon. But everyone remembered their rout at Guadelajara the year before. I was once sitting with an Italian officer in the *Real* when one of the dancers came past our table. He called out a compliment. She turned round, hand on hip, and literally spat out the word *Guadalajara* at him.

There were several Germans too in Saragossa but they kept very much to themselves and seldom mixed with the Spaniards or the Italians. They provided much of the logistic support, particularly the maintenance of aircraft and armoured vehicles. They also manned some of the signal units. I came to know one air force officer quite well. He despised Spaniards and Italians as coming from an inferior race and hated Spanish food and girls. He had little imagination and was just doing a job. I have no doubt he did it most efficiently.

General Moscardo now crossed the Ebro and pushed south towards Gandesa and Caspe. We followed through fields strewn with the debris of war and heavy with the sickly smell of dead men and horses. We entered Gandesa with the Army on 5 April; but there was little resistance to the Nationalist advance and none of the looting or drunkeness that we had seen at Lerida. After an excellent lunch, provided by a Belgian pilot in Franco's air force, we drove on to Caspe arriving just in time to see the final assault on the town. The fighting at Caspe had been a good

A.M.—D

deal fiercer than at Gandesa. The town was a ruin. All its inhabitants had
fled.

Moscardo's patrols pushed forward from Gandesa towards Tortosa
and expected, at any moment, to come in sight of the Mediterranean.
We tried to follow them but the road to the south was under heavy shell
fire from Republican batteries and we were ordered back.

Meanwhile, a serious crisis was developing in the Republican camp.
Prieto, the Socialist leader who had been the Carnot of the Republic,
was dismissed. Negrin, the pro-Soviet leader, was now in undisputed
control. Nationalist opinion in Saragossa judged that the collapse of the
Republic was imminent. Such optimism proved altogether premature.
The Nationalists had outrun their supplies. The Republicans were given
time to consolidate their defences. It was several weeks before Moscardo
resumed the offensive and at last reached the sea.

Merry del Val had joined the press for the battles of Lerida and
Gandesa. He warned me that there would now be a prolonged pause on
the front and advised us to see something of the rest of Spain in the few
days remaining to us. Before leaving Saragossa, however, we were taken
to visit a camp where newly captured prisoners of war were under interrogation. With shaven heads and battle-stained uniforms they looked an
unhappy and frightened crowd. The only exception was a group of a
hundred or so British prisoners from the International Brigade. Their
morale seemed high and they were confident of being sent home to
England in a few months. They were delighted to find Englishmen among
the correspondents and to be able to tell us their story. Some had come
out for the money, some for adventure and a few from genuine idealism.
Most had crossed the Channel without passports on day return tickets.
They had travelled comfortably across France and then been smuggled
over the Pyrenees into Spain. They complained that food was very short
on the Republican side and their pay often in arrears. They spoke well
of their officers but had the lowest opinion of the political Commissars
or 'Comic Stars' as they called them. There were a British and an Irish
officer among the prisoners, but we were not allowed to see them. Officers
on both sides were often shot on identification and the Nationalists were
uncertain what to do about these two officers. In the event, both were
kept prisoner until the end of the war.

Back in Burgos, Merry del Val told us that there was a complete lull
on the Madrid front which we had thought of visiting. He urged us
instead to go to Seville. We would be just in time for the Holy Week
elebrations. All the most interesting people in Nationalist Spain would
be there.

We took his advice and drove south, stopping at Valladolid. Valladolid was the headquarters of the *Auxilio Social*. This was the Nationalist

welfare organisation in charge of crèches, hospitals, canteens and welfare centres all over the country. It was run by two remarkable women. One was Pilar Primo de Rivera, the sister of Jose Antonio, a son of the dictator and the founder of the *Falange*. She was a woman of great beauty and distinction, dressed in black, in mourning for her brother, but heavily made up as was the Spanish custom. The other, and perhaps the more practical, was the widow of Onesimo Redondo, another of the early *Falangists*, murdered in Madrid at the beginning of the Civil War.

I have done my fair share of visiting welfare organisations in England and abroad since then. But the *Auxilio Social* stands out in my memory for its gaiety and humanity. The Spaniards may have little sense of discipline, but they have a genius for improvisation. Everything in Valladolid was improvised. Each centre seemed different from the next; and the girls who ran them were as remarkable for their enthusiasm as for their looks. Many came from good families. None seemed bored or harassed. They seemed borne up by a spring tide, such as only develops in time of revolution. Once things return to the normal and the routine, people grow more concerned with what they can get than with what they can give. But in a time of crisis it is different. The breakthrough then achieved is the real justification of revolutions and the main, perhaps the only, compensation for the suffering and destruction which they cause.

From Valladolid we passed through the Baroque glories of Salamanca and into the broad tableland of the Estremadura. In places our road skirted the front; but all was quiet. The Republic's Soviet advisers had foolishly vetoed Colonel Casado's plan to break through the lightly held Nationalist lines in the south. Had they not done so the Republic might well have driven a wedge to the Portuguese border cutting the Nationalist zone in half.

The country, however, was said to be infested with Republican guerilla bands; and, on leaving Caceres, we were told to stop for no-one except the military police and to be sure of reaching Seville by nightfall. Had we been an hour later, the police told us, they would not have let us go on. As we drove we noticed that the bridges and culverts along the road were guarded—something we had seen nowhere else in Nationalist Spain—and several times we saw cavalry patrolling the hills on either side of the road. But towards sunset, the country grew less rugged and as we came into Seville, the air was heavy with the scent of orange blossom.

Seville was the headquarters of General Queipo de Llano. Queipo governed Andalusia in Franco's name but in practice was very much an independent war lord. In Burgos, San Sebastian and other Nationalist cities, the authorities sought to set a puritan tone. Dancing was forbidden

except on the stage. Places of entertainment closed early by Spanish standards. Drinking was discouraged. But General Queipo loved life and would have none of this in Andalusia. Bars and night clubs were open day and night. Dancing was encouraged and the wine flowed freely.

Queipo besides was something of a radical in politics. He had been a Republican in the old days and was said to be a Freemason, which in Franco Spain was a crime. The fact remained that by sheer force of personality he had captured Seville with a stage army of less than two hundred men. He was beloved, moreover, by the people of Andalusia who delighted in his fireside chats over Seville Radio. These were quite unprepared. He would just sit in the studio with a bottle of sherry and say whatever came into his head. And, when so minded, he did not hesitate to castigate the authorities in Burgos.

We were presented to Queipo next day. He was tall, with a deeply lined face and strong cast of features. He welcomed us to Andalusia as if it were his private estate and obviously enjoyed telling us how he had captured Seville. He then gave orders to a staff officer. We were to be taken each morning to see different aspects of his social programme. We were to sleep in the afternoon. The officer was to see to it that we enjoyed ourselves until dawn.

In accordance with General Queipo's instructions, we spent two hours every morning visiting housing schemes, hospitals, military leave centres and the *Falangist* Trade Union organisation. We then refreshed ourselves with platefuls of shellfish and flagons of ice-cold Fino sherry. Fino was very different from the sweeter sherry then in vogue at Oxford and I saw the point of the Iron Duke's comment—'It tastes and looks as if it had been drunk before.' Nevertheless, I soon acquired a taste for it and have remained a devotee.

In the evenings, after a prolonged siesta, we went out to watch the religious processions which are the central feature of Holy Week. The churches in Seville—and there must be a hundred of them—each guard some special image, either of the virgin or of their patron Saint. These belong to *confrerias* or guilds and are dressed in magnificent velvets and brocades and bedecked with real jewellery. In Holy Week the members of the guilds parade, sometimes barefoot and in penitent garb, and carry their statue in procession to the cathedral. The processions began at about six in the evening and went on till after dawn next day. We watched them; we listened to the music in the cathedral. We explored the Barrio de Santa Cruz where the streets are so narrow that you can almost reach across them. In the early hours we went to the gypsies and enjoyed the *flamenco*.

Our group consisted of two officers on leave from the front, the staff officer attached to us by General Queipo and one or two of their civilian friends. Our base was the magnificent studio of an artist called Clemente Camini. It was a double cube room decorated with Camini's pictures and with old swords and pistols hung on the walls. We sat there in the intervals between processions and *flamenco* talking of politics, religion, women, and all the other topics dear to young men. We never saw our beds before dawn; seldom then.

Sandy Hope and Michael Lyle had to leave for Gibraltar to put the car on a boat, but I stayed on in Seville for the Easter weekend. I shall always be glad I did. In the early hours of Good Friday we saw the processions of the Macarena Virgin and the Christus del Gran Poder and followed them on their round of the city. On Sunday there was a High Mass in the cathedral where General Queipo laid up his sword on the altar. After this I was taken to a party on a German U-boat moored in the Guadalquivir. Our hosts were plainly the worse for drink when we arrived. They had been celebrating the Nazi occupation of Austria. One of them said to me: 'Today is Easter Day, isn't it wonderful that God should have sent Christ two thousand years ago and now two thousand years later should have sent us Hitler.' I tried to keep a straight face but the Spaniards with me laughed out loud. One of them said to me: 'Some pretty odd things happen in this country, but no-one is ever likely to talk like that about Franco!'

In the afternoon we went to the Easter bullfight, the first I had ever seen. General Queipo was in the president's box. The greatest *toreros* in Spain were in the ring. The bulls were brave and in my recollection seem larger than those I have seen since.

I knew nothing then of the finer points of bullfighting. But I was thrilled from the first by the enthusiasm of the crowd, the pageantry of the procession, the elemental brute force of the bulls and the courage of the lone *torero* moving into the kill over the horns.

I spent Easter night in a farewell *flamenco* party with my friends. One of them read my character in my hand; but he was killed in action a fortnight later, so the secret remains between us. In the early morning I caught a 'plane and somehow managed to reach Oxford in time for the beginning of term.

9

War Correspondent

I came back to Oxford to find myself something of a lion. Everyone seemed to want to hear about my experiences in Spain. Several societies and dining clubs invited me to talk to them. I also wrote three articles about the Civil War. The first was bought by the *Daily Telegraph* and published as their main feature. The others went to newspapers in Canada and Australia.

The financial return was meagre. The *Telegraph* paid seven guineas and the two Commonwealth papers only five guineas each. Still the whole expedition had only cost me £50, and I reckoned the gain in experience cheap at the price.

During the summer of 1938 I followed events in Spain from the press and was surprised to see that several of our national newspapers no longer had correspondents of their own on the Nationalist side. Some, it seemed, had fallen out with the Franco authorities and been expelled; others had been transferred to more important assignments. Here was my opportunity. I had a valid visa and had made a wide range of contacts in Spain. My article in the *Daily Telegraph* had been well received. Why should I not go back during the long vacation as an accredited war correspondent? I discussed the idea with a very experienced journalist, George Edinger, who put me in touch with Christiansen, the editor of the *Daily Express*. The *Express* were not prepared to put me on their pay role, but they agreed to accredit me as their correspondent and to provide cable facilities and a modest expense account. They would pay in addition for any material they used.

Accordingly, at the beginning of September 1938 I laid aside my vacation reading and crossed once more into Spain, this time as the *Daily Express* correspondent. I drove to Burgos and established myself in the *Condestable* Hotel, popularly known as the *'Detestable'*. There I began to learn the routine of a journalist's life, reading the local press, keeping in touch with the Nationalist press office, and consulting various trust-worthy sources of information. Journalism is sometimes regarded as a cut-throat competition but I have seldom encountered more kindness than I did from the other journalists in Burgos, mostly old hands at the business. They showed me their cables, corrected mine, and often put me on to a story I might otherwise have missed. I also received much kindness from Sir Robert Hodgson, the British Agent, as he was called, attached to the Franco authorities. Hodgson was not very busy and always seemed to have time to help me analyse the Spanish scene. He was a man of very varied experience having served on Admiral Kolchak's staff in Siberia and for some years as British Minister in Albania. He enjoyed talking about Albania and, over dinner, gave me what I can only describe as tutorials about it. I sucked in the information like a sponge. It would soon yield unexpected fruit.

There was a lull on the main battle fronts through September 1938. The Republican attack across the Ebro, their last major offensive, had petered out. The Nationalists were preparing a counter attack but it was to be on a decisive scale and would take time to mount. Meanwhile, the prospect of victory sharpened the struggle inside Nationalist Spain between the *Falangists*, or 'White communists' as their opponents called them, and the monarchists and other more conservative elements. Much of the plotting and intrigue took place in the *Condestable* Hotel; and, though the principals were not very accessible to the press, their aides found time heavy on their hands and were only too glad to drink with us and exchange gossip.

This in-fighting among the Nationalists was of little interest to the readers of the *Daily Express*. But the study of it was a political education in itself and I resolved to make the most of my opportunity. I accordingly worked out a set of questions and asked the press office to arrange interviews for me with the chief men among the Nationalists.

The first to receive me was the Commander-in-Chief of the Navy. I asked his ADC whether the Admiral preferred speaking French or English. 'The Admiral', he answered, 'only speaks Spanish.' The bell rang and, before I could even ask for an interpreter, I was shown in. A short stocky figure in naval uniform motioned me to a sofa and launched into a monologue in voluble Spanish. I could by this time make out the Spanish newspapers and could even follow Spanish if it was spoken very clearly and slowly. But as a midshipman in the Spanish-American War the Admiral had suffered a mishap. He had been standing on deck whistling when an American shell had struck his ship. The shock of the explosion had made him bite off the tip of his tongue. The accident had in no way diminished the natural flow of his eloquence, but it had made his speech very thick and, to me at least, quite incomprehensible. After a quarter of an hour's harangue, the Admiral drew breath and then began firing questions at me. I understood not a word, and thought it best to counter by asking some of the questions I had myself prepared. I am still not sure whether the Admiral thought me a moron or a spy, but mercifully he was summoned to some staff conference, and I was curtly dismissed. Later interviews with other Nationalist leaders proved more cordial as well as more informative. But it is this one I remember best.

In an effort to soften the bitterness of the Civil War, the Powers tried to arrange for an exchange of prisoners between Franco and the Republic and for the mutual withdrawal of foreign 'volunteers'. To further this initiative a special team arrived in Burgos led by Field Marshal Sir Philip Chetwode, a former C.I.G.S.

The Field Marshal's visit was not a happy one. He arrived late at night to find a letter from General Jordana, the Minister for War, offering to receive him at any time next day. The Field Marshal accordingly called at the War Office at about half-past nine in the morning. The night duty officer, the only person there, showed him into the waiting room where he remained till eleven o'clock, the hour at which the General usually began business. It was a bad beginning. But worse was to follow. General Jordana had admitted to the presence of some German and Italian volunteers, but had blandly assured Chetwode that there were no others. By some mistake, however, the Field Marshal was accommodated on a floor of the *Condestable*, which was otherwise entirely occupied by the Portuguese military mission. The Portuguese, indeed, had some 20,000 men fighting on Franco's side. They were nominally in the Foreign Legion but were, in fact, incorporated in units of their own and wore a distinctive uniform. Chetwode asked me who these men were and, when I enlightened him, grew understandably angry.

I thought all this good material for a slightly satirical news story. The censorship refused to pass it. But I was not to be so easily defeated. I persuaded a charming Scandinavian girl, then working for the Red Cross, to smuggle out my notes when she went on leave and to telephone them through to the *Daily Express*. She did so and sent me a postcard from France to say 'Your message safely delivered.' Later on, this would be a cause of trouble.

After some days in Burgos, I resolved to visit the Madrid front. The press office agreed and asked me to give a lift as far as Avila to a Mr. Walter Starkie. In the ignorance of youth I had never heard of Starkie. At the appointed hour a stout middle-aged gentleman of florid complexion arrived at my hotel, sweating profusely. In one hand he carried a gladstone bag, in the other a violin case. He introduced himself and we set off together for Avila. I tried to find out what aspect of the War interested Starkie most—the political, the military or the economic. He answered that the war was a great bore. He was not interested in it at all. His concern was with a particular group of gypsies, some of whom were living near Avila. I now discovered that my companion was Professor Starkie, a world famous authority on Spain and Spanish gypsies. He proved a most delightful companion and the hours flew by as I drove and he talked.

We had planned to sleep at Avila. But soon after dark the car broke down. We sat by the roadside for a time, hoping to stop a passing car. But none came. After a while, we set off on foot to find the nearest village. We had gone about a mile when we came across a sizeable group of gypsies. 'Right, we'll have some fun,' said Starkie, and asked me to go back to the car and fetch his violin. By the time I returned he had gathered a score of gypsies around him. They were drinking red wine from goat skins. I handed over the violin and he began to play. After a time one of the gypsies produced a guitar and the others began to sing and dance. It was about three in the morning before the party ceased and we went to sleep on the ground under borrowed but mercifully clean blankets.

In the morning we got the car repaired and, leaving Starkie in Avila, I continued towards Madrid. The front was quiet. I was given a briefing on the operational situation and taken to an observation post from where I could look through field glasses at the Republican defences and the skyline of the city. There was nothing else to see or do, so I drove back to Avila next day where I dined with Starkie and a Spanish bishop. It was a convivial evening, and, at some point, I got into an argument with the bishop and questioned whether the militant attitude of the Church in the Civil War really conformed to Christ's teaching. The bishop put his hand on my arm and said: 'My dear young man, you must remember that we in Spain were Roman Catholic nearly two hundred years before Christ was born.' He then went on to explain the essential dualism of the Church's mission in Spain. It was no doubt the instrument for the propagation of Christian teaching. But it was more than that. It was the heir to the Roman Imperial Government in Spain, and its first duty was to maintain itself in being. Survival was the first law of life and the pursuit of this end sometimes necessitated the adoption of strange means.

A few days later I paid a visit along with other journalists to a Battalion of the Foreign Legion near Talavera. Our programme started with the Battle Mass of the Legion. The whole battalion was drawn up on the parade ground under a blazing sun. After a few short prayers, the host was lifted up to the accompaniment of a roll of drums and a blare of bugles. Officers and men went down on one knee in the dust. The band then played the National Anthem and the men sang the Legion's song with its chorus: 'Long Live Spain! Long Live the Legion! Long Live Death!'

After inspecting the battalion and its mascots, a monkey and a ram, we were taken across the Tagus to a sector of the front held by another unit of the Legion. The front there had been stabilised for a long time, and was marked by an elaborate network of trenches. The network was confusing in its intricacy, and our escorting officer only spoke French. One of our party was a middle-aged American political author, Mervyn K. Hart. Hart spoke no French and did not appreciate how near we were to the front. He suddenly asked our escorting officer if he might photograph us standing 'over there', pointing to what was, in fact, the parapet of the front line trench. Our escorting officer scrambled up on to the parapet and, roaring with laughter, invited us to follow. I did so reluctantly, but, after a morning of Legionary indoctrination, would have been ashamed to hang back. The enemy trenches were in full view some five hundred yards away. Hart fiddled with his camera for a good three minutes before we were finally released and allowed to climb down. Our escorting officer afterwards told us that we had been in no danger. It was after two o'clock; and between two and four neither side ever fired a shot. Men could even sunbathe on the parapet of the trench without risk.

The Foreign Legion or *Tercio* was very much a *corps d'élite*. At the beginning of the War at least half the Legionaries had been foreigners. But by this time the great majority of the old hands had been killed. In the early days, indeed, regimental tradition had required officers to remain standing under fire. This had led to fearful casualties. By this time more rational orders were in force. The units I saw had very few foreigners left in their ranks and I only met one foreigner that day among their officers.

The discipline of the Legion was extremely strict and breaches of it were punished by severe fatigues or imprisonment. The training was correspondingly tough and the casualty rate the highest in the Nationalist Army. But the Legion was better paid, better clothed and better fed than other regiments; and Legionaries off duty were treated with wholesome respect in places of entertainment.

I still have beside me the 'Legionaries Creed' which I was given at Talavera. Its articles read:

> A Legionary will always try to get to grips with the enemy and if humanly possible go in with the bayonet.
>
> No Legionary will ever complain of being tired until he collapses.
>
> All Legionaries, whether single men or units, will march to the sound of the guns whether they hear them by day or by night, and regardless of whether they have orders to do so.

To die in battle is a man's highest honour. You can only die once. Death is neither as painful or as terrible as it seems. What is intolerable is to live a coward. All Legionaries are brave. Every nation is proud of its courage and of its deeds of fame. The purpose of the Legion is to establish which country is the bravest. Long Live Death!

A few days after my visit to Talavera I went to Logrono to watch General Franco review the Italian Littorio Division and decorate some of its officers and men. After the review there were speeches by Franco and by the Italian Chief of Staff. But the speech of the day was a recruiting speech for the Legion made by its founder, General Milan Astray. General Astray had lost an arm and an eye fighting in Morocco. He was the Spanish equivalent of our General Carton de Wiart. I have not got the text of his speech but this was the gist of it:

'The Legion has the heaviest casualties of any regiment in the Spanish Army. That is why I am calling for new recruits to fill the gap. We are proud of our casualties. We suffer them because we are always in the heat of the battle. Our discipline is of iron. Any cowardice or shirking is punished immediately with death. When called upon to do so, we fight for days, for weeks and for months on end without respite. But, when they are off duty, my men know no restraint. My men are drunk. My men are in debt. My men are with the worst women in the town. And if they're not, by God, they're not my men! I offer you good money to buy some hours of pleasure and a better than even chance to die for your country. Now who will join?'

The response was overwhelming.

I met Milan Astray after the ceremony and, in contrast to the histrionics of his speech, found him a very serious and rather simple man, deeply concerned with the international situation. I was also introduced to Franco and seized the opportunity of asking him for an interview. He declined this, pleading pressure of work, but offered to answer a written questionnaire. He was not impressive to look at, nor in any way magnetic; but I have never met a man who radiated such complete self confidence.

My questionnaire was, in fact, never answered; but I can hardly complain of this. The international situation had by now become critical. Chamberlain had gone to Bad Godesburg but had failed to reach agreement with Hitler. A telegram from my editor read: 'Pipe down Spain, big European situation here dominates everything.'

Opinion in Burgos thought a European War more likely than not. The prospect filled Franco's advisers with gloom. A World War must cut Spain off from Germany and Italy. It might well lead France to give open support to the Republic and so turn the scales against the Nationalists. Besides, after two and a half years of fighting, few Spaniards had much stomach left for a wider conflict.

My Spanish friends were worried about my personal position if war should break out. Merry del Val strongly advised me to leave while the going was good. But Sir Robert Hodgson counselled patience; and, perhaps more decisive, my heart was not wholly my own. So I decided to stay.

News of the Munich Agreement was received in Burgos with immense relief. But, as I read the terms, it became clear that we had suffered a major reverse. This opinion received striking confirmation next day from a senior German officer of my acquaintance. He expressed satisfaction over the Munich Agreement and then, poking me in the ribs, added: 'You must admit that Führer of ours has got the better of you this time.'

The immediate crisis was over: term had begun at Oxford, and *Eros* suddenly turned traitor. I accordingly left for home. At the frontier I was taken into a small office where a counter intelligence officer confronted me with a photograph copy of the postcard I had received from my Scandinavian friend. This, the reader will recall, had stated: 'Your message safely delivered.' What, he enquired, was the message? To have defeated the censorship was, for all I knew, a punishable offence. I answered that it was a purely private message. I had asked the lady in question to telephone my mother and tell her I was well. The officer smiled in disbelief but desisted from further interrogation. I was, however, stripped and searched from head to foot and every article of my luggage was examined for possible documents. The investigation lasted for three hours but revealed nothing worse than my private diaries, all of which were carefully studied but returned to me. The counter intelligence colonel apologised for troubling me and with faultless courtesy accompanied me to the frontier barrier. I was free to proceed but by this time had missed the last train to Paris.

For Spain, the Munich Agreement spelt the end of a serious attempt to bring about a compromise peace between Republicans and Nationalists. Jakob Altmaier, a German Socialist refugee in Paris, was negotiating on behalf of Prieto with an Austrian Monarchist leader who was in turn in touch with Yague. It is not clear how much backing Prieto and Yague could count on, but both men were in very strong positions. According to Altmaier, who told me the story some years afterwards, agreement seemed very near. Franco and Negrin were to be excluded from power. Yague and a group of moderate generals were to form a coalition government with Prieto, Gil Robles and other moderates. The question of a monarchy would be submitted to a plebiscite within two years. This was the Republic's last chance of staving off defeat. But when the Czech crisis broke, Prieto believed that a European War had become inevitable. He concluded that Britain and France would be forced to intervene on the Republican side. He accordingly allowed the negotiations to drag on. Then came the Munich Agreement. The Entente Powers were plainly on the run. It was now Yague's turn to blow cold; and the talks came to nothing. We knew enough in Burgos to realise that relations between Franco and Yague were strained, but of course had no inkling of these negotiations. Now that Yague and Prieto are both dead there can be little harm in telling the story.

After the Munich Agreement, the Republic began to disintegrate. Had the Republican Government followed Casado's advice and maintained a purely defensive strategy, they might conceivably have held out for another year until the outbreak of the Second World War. As it was they exhausted their supplies and lost their best officers in a series of local offensives, counselled by their Soviet advisers, which had no strategic purpose and could only hasten the end. Was Moscow already clearing the decks for the Ribbentrop-Molotov agreement?

At the beginning of March I had a talk with Vernon Bartlett and Gerald Barry, the Editor and Foreign Editor of the *News Chronicle*. It was clear that Madrid would soon fall and they were anxious, so they told me, to send one of their best men to report his impressions of Franco's entry into the capital. I suggested jokingly that they might do worse than send me, but they brushed the suggestion aside. A few days later, however, I heard from them that the Spanish authorities had refused to accept a *News Chronicle* correspondent on the ground that it was an unfriendly paper. Could I go instead? I said I could. I had a valid visa and once inside Spain no-one would care very much which paper I was representing. In any case, the best course might be to stay only a few days and write my articles when I came out.

Against all expectation Madrid continued to hold out and at the end of the Oxford term, I went off to Davos for a short skiing holiday. After three days on the slopes, however, I heard that the Republican command were negotiating a surrender. I hurried to San Sebastian and was lucky enough to get a lift from a Spanish officer who was leaving for the Madrid front. I drove into the Capital a few hours after Franco's advance guards and secured a room at the Ritz. The hotel was freezing. There was no hot water and the only food on the menu was lentil stew. Chicote's Bar was open and had somehow obtained a consignment of oysters. For the rest, the city seemed in a state of collapse. Hundreds of people were still sleeping in the streets without shelter. The soldiers of the defeated army had been ordered to leave the Capital and could be seen literally walking home. *Falangist* posters had been hastily stuck over Communist and Anarchist posters; but there were not enough of them; and on some walls the posters of the opposing sides were ranged incongruously next to one another as in a General Election at home. Meanwhile, the secret police were hunting down the men and women on the 'wanted' list. This was said to number 400,000; and even responsible Nationalists estimated that the number of executions would hardly be less than 150,000.

Statistics mean little in such things, but I recall one poignant example of the bitterness of Civil War. In the Ritz, I ran into a young Spanish officer who had been a friend in Burgos. We had a drink together and then he made to leave saying he had to go and see a girl. I remarked that he didn't seem very cheerful at the prospect. He then sat down again and told me his story. The girl in question had been his fiancée before the war broke out. They had met at the university. He had joined Franco. She had become a Communist youth leader. She was certain to face a long term of imprisonment and possibly a death sentence. The police already had orders to arrest her. But a friend in the police had arranged that the arrest should be delayed until the next day. This was to be their first reunion since the war and probably their last.

In provincial cities like Burgos and Salamanca, Monarchist and clerical influences had predominated. But, now that the Nationalists had gained control of the big cities, the *Falange* were in the ascendant. The *Auxilio Social* was the only organisation capable of feeding the people and caring for the destitute on the defeated as well as the victorious side. The *Falange* besides had a trade union organisation and its rather radical brand of fascism was less repugnant to many Republicans than the clerical monarchism of the old Right.

Within a few days of its capture, Madrid and especially the Ritz was full of Germans and Italians. But they seemed a different type from those I had known in Burgos. These were not military advisers but the first concession hunters and businessmen. Most of my Spanish friends, indeed, spoke as if Spain was already in the Axis camp. They were deeply suspicious of Britain and openly hostile to France. But the more I saw the more convinced I became that Spain was too exhausted to take an active part in a European War.

I concluded the second of two articles published by the *News Chronicle* with these words:

> In all probability Spain is too tired for another War and has not enough supplies of food or munitions.
>
> The general view is that, in the event of War, Spain would maintain a hostile neutralty towards the Entente.
>
> It is felt that General Franco could hardly prevent German or Italian aeroplanes and warships from using Spain as a base for operations but open hostilities on the part of Spain are not expected.
>
> The Spanish army is not to be demobilised till the International situation improves. In the event of war it might man the Pyrenees and so draw off a part of the French army.

These vacation visits to Spain were an important part of my political education. I realise this all the more clearly as I look back on the way they shaped my views.

As a Conservative, my sympathies were on the whole with the Nationalists, and at the beginning I swallowed a lot of pro-Franco propaganda. But even before the end of my first visit, I began to take a more balanced view. I saw much to admire on both sides and much to deplore. Both showed matchless courage and extraordinary skill in improvisation. Both suffered from clumsy and inefficient administration, added to a temperamental inability to follow up success. Both sides were guilty of unspeakable cruelties, individual and collective.

If I had been a Spaniard I would have supported Franco. The Nationalist state was oppressive, no doubt, but at least it was a relatively controlled oppression in contrast with the anarchy and unpredictable witch hunting of the Republic. Moreover, the Franco régime was strongly nationalist and the Communist Party was not. It was tempting, of course, to construct compromise governments, embracing the best elements from both sides. But I soon realised that this was not practical politics. In a Civil War, an individual cannot contract out or pursue his own pet solution. He must either emigrate or take sides and defend the bad against the worse.

I do not see much to alter in this judgement, even with the wisdom of hindsight. Nevertheless a heavy responsibility must always rest on Franco for having started the process which led to a million deaths and retarded the development of Spain by a quarter of a century. There is, of course, a good deal of evidence that Franco's rising merely forestalled a Communist revolution. But it is at least arguable that a Communist rising would have united the rest of Spain against it, whereas Franco's rising drove many Spaniards, who would never have sided with a Communist coup, to defend the Republic. In any case, the only complete justification of a pre-emptive strike is swift success. This Franco failed to achieve.

I tried at first to judge the Spanish conflict on its merits. But, with the Czechoslovak crisis of 1938, I began to relate it to the wider international scene. I now concluded that it was not my business to judge what was best for Spain. As an Englishman, my duty was to try and judge what would be the best outcome of the Civil War for Britain. Where did our national interest lie in all this? During the weeks of the Munich crisis, I became increasingly conscious of the links between Nationalist Spain and the Axis Powers which I already regarded as enemies. My views now began to swing the other way. From the point of view of British and French interests might it not have been wiser to have given open support to the Republic from the beginning? But, by the autumn of 1938 the disintegration of the Republic had gone very

far. Was it still possible then for British and France to save it? In a speech
to the Oxford Union, in November 1938, I reluctantly defended Chamberlain's decision to recognise Franco Spain on the ground that the Republic
was already moribund. Our only remaining chance of counteracting
German and Italian influence in Spain lay in recognising the fact of
Franco's victory and using our economic influence to wean him away
from the Axis.

After my last visit, at the beginning of 1939, my main conclusion, as
I have said, was that Spain was too exhausted to take any active part in
a European War. The event on the whole proved this forecast accurate.
Spain remained neutral throughout the War, though her neutrality was
benevolent to the Axis Powers, and Spanish troops fought alongside the
Germans in Russia.

It can certainly be argued that, ideological considerations apart, a
Republican victory would have been in the best interests of Britain and
France in view of the war with Germany that lay only a few months
ahead. On the other hand, a Communist Spain in the post-war world
would have presented a threat to the whole Western Alliance. So perhaps
it all turned out for the best.

My Spanish experiences were valuable in another sense. They provided
a healthy complement to my university education. Reading Modern
Greats called for much study of economic theory and social and political
trends. Academic historians inevitably tend to impose a pattern on events
and to write as if these developed according to immutable laws. My
practical studies on the ground in Spain were a healthy corrective to any
tendency to generalise. Of course, there are trends in history and currents
in political thought. But the chain of cause and effect is continually broken
at the individual link, and the course of events is all the time deflected
and sometimes turned back by prejudice, ambition or unpredictable
external developments. It was in Spain that I first began to understand
all this.

My experience of the Spanish War was also an education in lifeman-
ship. The business of getting around a country at war, the experience of
front line conditions and the work of collecting and assessing news all
gave me a self confidence and mastery over my own fears which would
stand me in good stead. I had first thought of going to Spain at a time
when I never expected to see a war. In the event, the experience proved a
sound preparation for the five years of war that lay ahead.

10

The Awakening

I was a fortnight late for term when I came back from Spain in the autumn of 1938, but no-one seemed to care very much. Oxford was in the throes of a by-election. Quintin Hogg, the official Conservative candidate, was an ardent defender of Neville Chamberlain and the Munich Agreement. Lindsay, the Master of Balliol, stood against him and called for a Popular Front against 'Appeasement'. Harold Macmillan and Randolph Churchill came and spoke for Lindsay. Oxford Conservatives were deeply divided.

I had looked on Munich, when still in Spain, as a defeat for Britain. What my father told me when I came home only increased my indignation. I felt no great enthusiasm for Lindsay but was determined to fight against the Chamberlain candidate. Along with Ted Heath and several other Oxford Conservatives, I accordingly declared against Quintin Hogg. With the virulent partisanship of youth I even coined a thoroughly unfair phrase which was much used as a slogan in the campaign: '*A vote for Hogg is a vote for Hitler.*' I had forgotten all about this until in 1963 a candid friend wrote to remind me of it. I was then one of Quintin's chief supporters in his ill-starred bid for the Conservative leadership.

Our efforts for Lindsay were of no avail; and Quintin carried the seat with a comfortable majority. But the by-election helped to crystallise opinion.

The following extract from a letter to my father gives an idea of my mood at the time:

> My own impression, while still in Spain, was that a month ago we were the greatest power in Europe, while today we are only equal with Germany and our only real friend, France, has become a second-class power and won't be even that by the time Franco's victory has cut her off from North Africa.
>
> The National Government has been in power two years longer than Hitler with a majority that gave it almost totalitarian authority; but it seems slowly but surely to have led us to a point where we are quite incapable of defending ourselves and where the Dominions must be beginning to wonder whether we are more a protection or a liability. . . .

I don't see how we can trust a man like Chamberlain who has no knowledge or understanding of Europe and who still doesn't seem to realise the
danger we are in.

The Conservatives here are completely split and we gave Lindsay as
much assistance as possible. But for all this it seems to me that the Opposition are almost as stupid as the Government.'

Hugh Fraser had supported Quintin Hogg out of loyalty to the Party
but was scarcely less disillusioned with the Conservative Government
than I was. Maurice Macmillan and Patrick O'Donovan shared our view.
The Oxford University Conservative Association counted for something
in the country; and it seemed just possible that we might exercise some
influence in the crisis that loomed ahead. The four of us accordingly
resolved to secure control of the Association. We would also make a
bid to dominate the Union.

Political organisation is primarily a matter of taking pains. But it is
never easy to find the right men for it. We found just the man in Anthony
Hart-Synnot. Hart-Synnot had been Captain of the Oppidans at Eton.
He had gentle manners; his clothes were usually dishevelled, and he
looked as if he could not hurt a fly. In fact, the loose lip and Charlie
Chaplin walk concealed a man of ruthless and relentless purpose. He was
attracted to our plans and determined to push them through. We got
him elected Agent of the Oxford University Conservative Association.
From then on everything went according to plan. Hugh became President
of the Association at the beginning of 1939, and I became Secretary.
O'Donovan succeeded Hugh and I succeeded O'Donovan. Maurice
succeeded me. Hugh became President of the Union for the last summer
of the peace; O'Donovan was, I think, Librarian; and Hart-Synnot
was confident that he would have the presidency for me the following
year.

Between us we made a point of inviting Chamberlain's Conservative
opponents to come and speak at Oxford. Eden, my father, Duff
Cooper, and Ronald Cartland were among those who answered the
call.

Some years before, the Oxford Union had passed a motion that 'This
house will not fight for King and Country.' This had made a deep impression on public opinion in England and even more in Germany. We
now resolved to reverse the Union's verdict. In the climate of opinion
after Munich, conscription seemed the natural issue on which to join
battle. It has been debated almost every term since I had come to Oxford.
Indeed, I had made my maiden speech in the Union in favour of it. On
23 February 1939, the Union debated conscription with Ted Heath in

the Chair. Hugh Fraser and my father advocated conscription; Christopher Cadogan[1] and Vernon Bartlett[2] opposed it.

The opponents of conscription won the day, but only just. A few weeks later, indeed, Vernon Bartlett changed his mind and announced his conversion to conscription.

On 25 April my father debated conscription in the Cambridge Union, this time against Liddell Hart.[3] Once again he was defeated.

Two days later, on 27 April, the Oxford Union debated the following motion:

In view of this country's commitments and of the gravity of the general situation in Europe, this house welcomes conscription.

Hugh Fraser was President and called on me to propose the motion. Randolph Churchill and Stephen King-Hall[4] came down to speak in support. John Biggs Davison was the leading undergraduate opponent with Liddell Hart, fresh from his victory over my father at Cambridge, as the guest speaker to support him.

The *Oxford Mail* next day described the debate as:

> One of the most outstanding debates in its (the Union's) history. Including the spectators in the gallery there were over a thousand people present, every available bit of space on the floor and on the window sills, and even on the President's dais was occupied. Scores of people were turned away.

I opened the debate in traditional Union style.

> Captain Liddell Hart has come hot foot from his triumph at the Cambridge Union, and his hands still reek of my father's blood. I am not sufficiently presumptuous to imagine that he has come here to cross swords with that father's son, but I welcome him especially warmly since his visit gives me the chance to carry out a filial vengeance.

I continued in a more serious vain:

> After eight years of fatal mistakes in foreign policy, it has become clear that only a policy of power can save the situation. You will never preserve the peace unless you can persuade the dictators that you would beat them in War. You will never save democracy unless you can win the war if it comes. . . .
>
> Our inability to raise large reserves of manpower, before next year, means that the dictators can count on a whole year free from British military interference. In the course of that year, it may well be that Egypt and the Sudan will be engulfed and that Poland and Rumania will pass

[1] Christopher Cadogan: Chairman of the Oxford Liberal Association. Killed in a raid on the Syrian coast—1941.
[2] Vernon Bartlett: Editor of the *News Chronicle* and Independent M.P.
[3] Liddell Hart: military historian and commentator.
[4] King-Hall: Independent M.P. and editor of a widely-read *News-Letter*.

beyond the stage where guarantees are much use. If this does happen, the responsibility will lie with the vested interests in this country who resisted the conscription of industry and with the trade unions who resisted the conscription of man power. Both seem to forget that every day of their resistance has brought nearer the day when a *gauleiter* for England could kick both vested interests and trade unions into the concentration camp. . . .

It has been said that the principle of conscription is undemocratic. Certainly the principle of compulsion is not alien to our constitution. We have compulsory sanitation that our democracy may be healthy. We have compulsory taxation that our democracy may be financed. Yet is it undemocratic that we should have compulsory national service that our democracy may be safe?

A final section introduced personalities and drew some comment from the national press:

There are those who, while admitting the principle of conscription, declare that it can never be entrusted to Mr. Neville Chamberlain. I have never supported Mr. Chamberlain, but the Opposition's petty attacks on a petty man are only rendering a service to the Third Reich. If only the gentlemen who hold this opinion were not marked out for the concentration camp by their other political views, they should be recommended for the Iron Cross in token of gratitude for their services to the Führer. I should be the last to make a defence of Chamberlain's policy, but I would sooner have conscription under Chamberlain than compulsory labour chores under Nazis.'

Randolph was at his most brilliant and provocative. I had found him excellent company at dinner and was deeply impressed by his robust and humorous style of speaking. He brought the house down by quoting the old parody: 'Onward Conscript Soldiers, marching as to war, you would not be conscripts had you gone before.' The debate went on far into the night; but when the vote was taken we had won by 423 to 326. The Union had rescinded the decision not to fight for King and Country.

The Union debate on Conscription attracted considerable attention. Hugh Fraser, Patrick O'Donovan and I accordingly resolved to strike while the iron was hot. On 1 June we issued a *Statement of the Principles of a New Conservatism* and secured its approval by the Oxford University Conservative Association. Much of this manifesto is, of course, out of date. But it is a fair reflection of young Conservative thought and feeling at the time.

The people of England demand a National policy, clear cut and constructive. They are tired of the wrangling of parties and the deadweight of political apathy. This manifesto is an attempt on the part of Youth to satisfy the longing not only of the Youth but of the whole people for a vigorous, planned policy, in which they may believe; a forward drive to Prosperity, Freedom and security.

Liberal Capitalism is as dead as Aristocratic Feudalism, and the conditions of today call for a National policy in the National interest. We will not tolerate the exploitation of the community by a single section of it. We stand instead for the establishment of a state without privilege, where each shall seek to enrich himself through the enrichment of all.

We are well aware that the existing Conservative party has failed to provide the policy we demand, and it is for this reason that we have felt justified in reasserting here what we believe to be the fundamental principles of Conservatism.

We believe that Conservatism is a Nationalist and Imperialist force in that it has but one aim, the maintenance and improvement of the standard of life for the peoples of the Empire.

We believe that Conservatism is a Democratic force in that it has unshakeable faith in the judgement of Englishmen and English women, and in their ability to choose the policy and the men that are best for the nation.

We believe that Conservatism is a Progressive force in that it will always employ, without prejudice, the most efficient methods to attain its ends of a Great and Free and Classless state.

Finally, we believe that Conservatism is Traditional in that it is always mindful of the glories of England's past in the planning of England's future.

These are the cardinal principles on which we have based our programme. They are not the new principles of a new party, but rather an attempt to bring the fundamental ideas of Disraeli and Joseph Chamberlain up to date and into practice, in a National Conservatism that alone is fitted to answer the Nation's call.

But it was the radicalism of the economic section of the manifesto which attracted most comment from the press:

We re-affirm the medieval distinction between the ownership and use of Capital, believing that the State has the right to control any part of the economic life of its citizens. In principle we neither support nor oppose nationalisation of industry; but where it is a means of raising the standard of living, we shall not hesitate to employ it.

We demand an immediate National policy for industry, having as its chief points the subsidising of organised export drives and of shipping and the extension of the rationalising principle through nationally controlled marketing boards.

We believe that British industry is in danger of being driven out of the markets of the world by the competition of cheaper goods produced at a lower standard of living. The only alternative, we contend, to lowering our own standard of living, is to develop closer economic co-operation by preferential treatment with the Nations of the Empire and with those states, such as the U.S.A., France and the Scandinavian nations, whose economic and political aims are similar to our own.

We circulated our statement to all Members of Parliament and to the press. It drew a flood of letters and a good deal of comment. Lord Beaverbrook thought our direction too totalitarian. Lord Iliffe deprecated our flirtation with nationalisation. Left-wing members of Parliament, like Vernon Bartlett and Commander Fletcher (later Lord Winster), were enthusiastic. Harold Nicolson ordered several hundred copies to distribute to his constituents. But the warmest welcome came from Duncan Sandys and Ronald Cartland. Both asked me to go and see them, as soon as term was over.

My meeting with Duncan Sandys was the beginning of a close and lasting friendship. Ronald Cartland would be dead within a year, killed in action in the retreat to Dunkirk. His letter ran:

> I have just seen your statement of Conservative Policy. May I send my congratulations to you. . . . It is, if I may say so, the most refreshing and encouraging thing I have seen for years. Perhaps, when term is over, it might be possible to have a talk on the lines you have laid down—with the possibility of further action.
>
> I have told Ronnie Tree how much I should like to connect up with you and your allies.

Ronnie Tree was then Secretary of the Federation of University Conservative Associations, as well as a popular member of the House of Commons. He arranged that our manifesto should be discussed at the next meeting of his executive committee in October. He also asked Central Office for a financial grant to ensure its wider distribution. But, by October, many things would have happened.

The debate on Conscription and the Manifesto led a number of local associations to invite me to speak to them. I spoke to the Oxford City Association before the end of term and twice in Birmingham after it.

But we did not limit our activities to the Home Front. In the spring Hugh Fraser and I went to Paris and spoke in French to a Congress of French Youth at the Ecole des Sciences Politiques. We called for resistance to German and Italian claims on our Colonies. Paul Flandin, a son of the former French Prime Minister, supported us, as did Jean Daladier, a nephew of the French Prime Minister then in power.

Thanks to our French friends at Oxford, we were agreeably lionized in Paris. Jerome Sauerwein's father, the editor of *Paris Soir*, treated us to a gastronomic orgy at La Pérouse. Jean Pierre Giraudoux's father, the famous playwright, received us in his home. Sir Eric Phipps also entertained us at the British Embassy where I met Hilaire Belloc. Alas, all I remember of our meeting is that he drank beer for tea and that we talked about Napoleon.

It was all very well to advocate conscription and make tough speeches about foreign policy; but after Munich, I had begun to feel that I must do something to practise what I was preaching. It was time to prepare myself for war.

A reading of *All Quiet on the Western Front*, a youthful tour of the battle fields of Flanders and what I had seen of the war in Spain combined to put me off any idea of Army life. If I had to fight, the sky seemed the best place. To begin with, it offered greater individual responsibility. The fighter pilot fought alone like a knight of old and worked, at most, with a handful of colleagues in his squadron. He was one of an élite. The risks might be higher than on the ground, but, by contrast with what I had read of trench warfare, it should be a relatively comfortable existence with hot baths, comfortable beds and reasonable supplies of food and drink for those, at least, who got back to base. I accordingly applied to join the Oxford University Air Squadron and was accepted into it in January of 1939. Membership of the Squadron led in due course to membership of the Royal Air Force Volunteer Reserve.

We did our flying training at Abingdon in yellow biplanes called Avro Tutors. They cruised at about 90 m.p.h. and their stalling speed was not much above 50 m.p.h. The cockpit was open so that, unlike most modern aircraft, these planes gave a continuous sensation of speed.

My first instructor was a Flight-Lieutenant Kirkpatrick. He managed to be fun and thorough at the same time.

My first solo flight was a nerve-wracking experience. I slept little the night before and was rather on edge when I reached Abingdon. The take-off proved easy enough. I put the engine to full throttle, kept the stick forward, until I was level with the tree that was my mark, then gradually eased it back and felt the aeroplane rise from the ground. The circuit itself presented no problem. I was familiar with the controls and only had to watch the air speed indicator to make sure I did not stall. But as I came in to land I began to tremble all over. Would I judge it right? A few feet from the ground my nerve failed. I climbed again and made a second circuit. In the course of it I pulled myself together and came in to make a perfect landing. This was another stage in the conquest of fear. Later on I gained confidence and became quite skilled at looping the loop, doing rolls, going into a spin and getting out of it, all of which were part of the training routine of those days.

I enjoyed learning to fly, but did not, I fear, take the other activities of the Squadron very seriously. On 7 June 1939, my Commanding Officer, Wing Commander Hebbert, wrote to me:

> Ten days ago, I asked P. G. Francis to tell you that I would like to see you as soon as possible. But you have not been round to see me.

On the 1st of June I wrote to ask you to fill in your pilot's flying log book, but you have taken no action in the matter.

Attendance at lectures you treat as something quite unimportant.

In fact you would appear to have joined this Squadron under the misapprehension that you were joining a flying club! I am therefore prepared to accept your resignation from the Squadron as soon as you send it in.

This was a poor start for a future Secretary of State for Air! But I managed to mollify the Wing Commander and, thereafter, we became friends.

I had persuaded Simon Wardell to join the Squadron and, towards the end of June, we went off together to camp at Lympne Airport in Kent. We flew all morning, slept in the afternoon and were meant to attend lectures in the evening. But we had plenty of friends in the neighbourhood and did not always do so.

Flying in those days was not the restricted business it has since become. You could fly at any altitude. There were no traffic lanes to keep to. And it was fun on a summer morning to dive low over a girl friend's house and bring her to the window.

An extract from a letter to my mother gives somes idea of my mood in camp:

I am enjoying this life enormously. Up at 5.30 a.m. and flying all morning above the mists and the clouds, and diving over sleeping villages. There is an independence in the air and freedom from restraint that makes me feel I have realised a lot of my childhood eagle dreams. We live in great comfort with good food which I devour and two hours sleep after lunch. Today it was too rough to fly and I have kept my tent, wrapped in a jackal skin rug and reading *Werther*.

The London Season that year was overshadowed by the march of events. Germany occupied the remainder of Czechoslavakia in flagrant breach of the Munich Agreement. Italy occupied Albania. Britain and France guaranteed the frontiers of Poland and Rumania, though no-one could see how they could be defended in practice. Could war still be avoided? If not what were the chances of victory?

These great issues enlivened the social round. Gossip and trivialities faded into the background. People wanted to see each other to share news and views. The talk at dinner parties was unusually intense, even passionate. Old friendships were sundered and grave statesmen lost their tempers in a way I never saw again until the Suez Crisis of 1956.

At the end of March, the French President paid a State visit to London. In those days all our hopes of stopping Hitler rested on the French Army.

The President's visit was thus the occasion for a great demonstration of Anglo-French solidarity. It also led those who still believed in a deal with Hitler to shakes their heads.

My father took me to the evening reception which the Government gave for the President in the Durbar court of the India Office. Most of the Royal Family were present. The Privy Councillors and other grandees were in full dress. I had to wear knee breeches. It was a brilliant gathering of all the leading men in London come to do honour to our French allies.

In the course of the evening we talked with Sir Neville Henderson, then our Ambassador in Berlin. He was sure there would be no war. But, as we came away, my father told me that he had known Henderson since 1915. He had been a young diplomat in Sofia then and equally sure that Bulgaria would not enter the war against us.

Later in the evening I was introduced to Duff Cooper. He spoke scathingly of Chamberlain and told me that he was having a special walking stick constructed in which to sheathe his umbrella. Chamberlain's umbrella, he explained, had become such a symbol of appeasement, that he would not be seen dead with one.

Later in the summer my father took me to a party given by the Chancellor of the Exchequer, Sir John Simon, at No. 11 Downing Street. This was the only time that I met Mr. Neville Chamberlain. He said jokingly that he was sorry to see that I was following in my father's footsteps and making speeches critical of the Government. He had a striking face but it was not an easy one to describe. Walking home across St. James's Park I remember suggesting to my father that Chamberlain's features were not 'aquiline' but 'corvine'.

There was much social and political activity at Eaton Square that summer. Jan Masaryk came several times to meals. He had a wonderful gift of seeing the ridiculous side of things even in the most serious situations. Count Grandi, the Italian Ambassador, called to say goodbye. He had been recalled to Rome and my father believed would do his best to keep Italy out of the war.

Winston Churchill came to lunch to meet Coudenhove-Kalergi, the President of the Paneuropean Movement. My father had an early appointment that afternoon and I was left to act as host. This presented no problem as both men talked incessantly. Churchill later wrote an article advocating a European Union with which the British Empire should be 'combined but not comprised'. Coudenhove, I remember, forecast that there would be an Agreement between Germany and Russia before the summer was out.

But, of course, it was not all politics at any rate for young people like me. After the Commemorative Balls at Oxford, I joined in the round of social festivities which were more brilliant than usual that year and made slightly hectic by the sense of impending danger. There were two or three dances in London almost every night during June and July. Most have faded from my memory but some still remain. There was a brilliant ball at Holland House soon to be bombed out of existence. Another followed at Blenheim where the palace and the gardens were floodlit. I remember, after the Blenheim Ball, standing on Westminster Bridge with a fair companion and watching Big Ben strike eight. We were both still in full evening dress. People were going to work all around but no-one seemed to think it odd.

Major Astor, of *The Times*, gave a ball at Hever Castle. The night was warm and we sat about on the lawns watching a firework display over the lake. I stayed the night of the ball at Chartwell with Mr. and Mrs. Winston Churchill. He was deeply pessimistic about the situation and talked of nothing else at dinner and afterwards until Mrs. Churchill insisted that we leave the table and go on to the Ball.

Towards the end of July, Hugh Fraser, Simon Wardell, Alan Hare and I spent a weekend with Maurice Macmillan at Birch Grove. I have a dim recollection of meeting a little school girl called Catherine on the stairs. I remember more clearly persuading Maurice's father, Harold Macmillan, to try and make a chicken keep still by drawing a chalk circle round it. The experiment failed. I also remember Hugh Fraser emphasising an argument after dinner with a sword, and drawing Maurice's blood in the process. It would be several years before the five of us dined together again.

11

Go East, Young Man

What with student politics and the Spanish War, my academic studies had rather languished. But, in June 1939, the Master of Balliol wrote to my father:

> I think I ought to tell you that the Modern Greats tutors reported that your boy would get a First if he really made up his mind to go for it hard. He is very able. His temptation is to rely on his ability, but they think he has been doing such good work lately that he could get a First with enough seriousness.

My father showed me the letter, and I resolved to devote August and September to an intensive study of the origins of the First World War and of Economics—two subjects I had neglected. I would go somewhere warm and quiet and thought at first of the French or Italian coast. But then I had another idea. War might well break out before term resumed. If so, where did I want to be?

I reasoned that if I were in France or Italy I would simply be recalled on mobilisation and swept into the training machine with other young men of my age. But if I went East of Italy and Germany, to the Dalmatian Coast for instance, my way home would be barred. This might have dangers but might also offer opportunities. 'The East is a Career' Disraeli had written. There would not be many Englishmen about in Eastern Europe and, if I were one of them, I might well be given more responsible and exciting work than my years and experience would otherwise have justified.

I was revolving these thoughts when M. Subotitch, the Yugoslav Minister, asked me to lunch. One of his guests was Mabel Gruitch, the American widow of a distinguished Yugoslav diplomat. I told her of my interest in the Dalmatian Coast; and she at once asked me to stay there for a fortnight as her guest. She also undertook to find me a flat on the coast for the rest of the long vacation. I jumped at the offer.

My car was still in Spain with a broken crankshaft. But one night in *The Nest*, a Negro night club then in vogue, I was offered a Ford V8 for only £12. I went out into the street to look at it and bought it on the spot. I tried it out the next day and found it reached 80 m.p.h. without difficulty. I packed it to the brim with books and set off on a day of intermittent rain and sunshine. My mother seemed more anxious than usual when we kissed goodbye.

I gave a lift to Paris to a girl friend. When we met again we would both be in uniform.

In Paris, I lunched with my brother John. He had been living abroad for some time; and I was anxious to know his views. He was sure there would be war. He was also sure that France would collapse. 'It's like this,' he said, 'the French eat their potatoes with butter, the Germans without. Both want the butter; but it is much easier to fight to win something than to fight to defend it.' He believed that the French had been badly demoralised by the Munich crisis. They had been mobilised, had suffered a diplomatic defeat and then been stood down. It would be very difficult to rouse them a second time. We would meet again in very different circumstances.

I broke my journey at Strasbourg where a waiter told me in halting French that the situation on the frontier was normal. He was convinced there would be no war. The customs on both sides of the bridge across the Rhine were friendly. Rain storms had flattened out the wheat crop in Germany, and I remember wondering whether it was still true that nations only went to war after a good harvest.

Presently, I left the Rhine Valley and began climbing into the hills towards Ulm. Napoleon's columns had marched the same way in 1805, when they had outwitted the unfortunate Mack. These historical reflections took my mind off the road and at a sharp bend I grazed the mudguard of a supercharged Horch. The owner was furious at seeing his shining new car damaged by my old Ford: but I pacified him by promising to pay his bill if he would send it to me. I reckoned that events might stop him from presenting it.

The pine woods were full of Hitler youth organising their camps or playing games. Once I passed a gang of workers escorted by armed police. This looked more ominous.

I stopped for dinner at a little village outside Ulm and dined off blue trout and *wiener schnitzel*. After dinner, the innkeeper and one of his friends came over for a chat. They argued the German case for annexing Danzig. I agreed that it was a German city but said that we had lost all confidence in the German Government since they had broken the Munich Agreement and occupied Czechoslovakia. We did not believe that Danzig was their last claim. If they got Danzig they would only come back and ask for more. The innkeeper saw the force of the argument and admitted that Germany wanted not only Danzig but the return of her Colonies as well. But after that, he claimed, we should find her the best of friends. I said that friendship could never be built on bad faith: at which the innkeeper's friend remarked: 'I am the leader of the S.A.[1] in this village. I and my friends have always wanted friendship with England. I see your argument and you see mine. If it comes to war, it will be, once again, because of this damned lack of confidence between us. All the same, my friend,' he added, 'if it comes to war we shall win.'

Next day I stopped in Munich and wrote a bread and butter letter to the Churchills. It seemed an appropriate place from which to write to them. I then pressed on along the Autobahn to Salzburg.

It was two years since I had been in Salzburg. It seemed greatly changed. The rich, the beautiful, the witty, the nobly born had disappeared. The town was more crowded than before, but with coach loads of worthy Germans from the industrial north. The streets seemed cleaner and more orderly; and a policeman rebuked me when I crossed one of them at a point where there was no pedestrian crossing.

In a café near the Opera House I ran into some Austrian friends. They asked me to stay the night and I followed them out to their chalet in the Salzkammergut. At dinner we talked about the international situation but they seemed unconvinced when I said that England would fight if Hitler invaded Danzig. Surely England wouldn't plunge the world into war 'just for one small town?' They disliked Hitler's methods but seemed to approve his foreign policy. By contrast they had nothing good to say about the situation in Austria since the Anschluss. No decent Austrian had been given any job of importance. All the key positions were in Prussian hands. No-one who mattered went out in Vienna any more. The theatre had collapsed. Even the opera was going downhill. Taxes were higher. Food was dearer. At school, the children were being taught to despise religion. Even the workmen were grumbling at having to work harder for the same rate of pay. They had never much liked the Jews, but as one noblewoman declared that evening: 'From an aesthetic point of view the Jews are infinitely preferable to the Prussians.'

But before we went to bed my host warned me not to be taken in by all this criticism. Austrian aristocrats might resent the Nazi upstarts; but, since Munich, the Army was solidly behind the régime. So were the middle classes and most German women. Of Hitler himself he spoke kindly, blaming most of the evils of the régime on his lieutenants. I asked if he thought Hitler was determined to attack Poland. He answered: 'If England is going to stand by the Poles, I would advise you not to stay in Germany any longer than you need.'

[1] S.A. *Sturm Abteilung*—the 'assault troops' or 'storm troopers' of the Nazi party organisation.

Next day I crossed the mountains into Carinthia and towards evening came to the Yugoslav frontier. The German frontier guards lifted the barrier and saluted smartly. Twenty yards further on stood a Yugoslav gendarme in a rather theatrical white tunic. He saluted with panache, checked my visa and waved me on.

It was growing dark and I turned away from the main road to spend the night at Moistrana, the village under Mount Triglav, where I had shot chamois three years before. I found Rabitch, the old innkeeper, dozing at the hotel entrance. He opened his eyes and stared at me. Then came a flash of recognition and, smiting his elephantine knees, he summoned his daughters in his husky treble. They all embraced me but then said that all their rooms were booked. Instead they made me dine with them and rigged up a bed for me under some trees in the garden. Nor would they let me pay a penny when I asked for my bill next day.

From Moistrana I drove in broiling heat over what even by Spanish standards were very bad roads. I kept losing my way and had begun to run out of petrol when suddenly through a gap in the hills I caught my first glimpse of the Dalmatian Coast: a blue sky soft with mist, a sea of brighter blue and the jagged grey cliffs and islands of the *karst*.[1]

I followed the coast to Crikvenitsa and, at the biggest hotel in the town, asked for beer and information on the whereabouts of Mabel Gruitch's house. Beer there was in plenty but no-one seemed to have heard of Mabel Gruitch. I consulted the telephone book but this afforded no clue. The porter made several enquiries but in vain.

I drove on a couple of miles in search of somewhere to swim and made more enquiries in a little snack bar on the beach. The man behind the bar pointed across the bay to a square building standing right on the water's edge. That, he explained in broken German, was my goal.

Villa Alta, as the house was called, was in two parts. The main building stood on the water's edge with an unbroken view across the bay to the Isle of Krk. Above the villa, at the top of the garden, was a small Greek temple, where I was given two rooms. One contained a large double bed with three pillows which I nicknamed Serbia, Croatia and Slovenia. The other was a small study. I went for a swim before dinner, but was urged not to go out too far. There were sharks in the bay, they said. I did not believe it at the time. But, two days later, a Czech girl was taken, less than half a mile away; and a week later the tunny fishermen killed a shark at least nine foot long and found her remains inside. I have since been told that sharks seldom attack in the Adriatic. But, in those days, several of the big hotels along the coast kept their beaches netted to give bathers confidence.

We dined by the water's edge. There was lemon instead of vinegar

[1] The Dinaric Alps.

in the salad. The wine was stronger and had a slightly musty taste. Two middle-aged men joined us for dinner and we sat very late talking about Tolstoy. I had never spent an evening with a Slav family before and was struck by the length at which everyone seemed to talk, and the wealth of anecdote with which points were illustrated.

Mabel Gruitch was no longer young, and walked slowly and with dignity. But she proved a most entertaining companion. She had gone to Athens as a girl before the First World War to study archaeology. There she fell in love with Slavko Gruitch, a handsome young secretary at the Serbian Legation. They married and returned to Belgrade where he became secretary to the Serbian Cabinet. Mabel must have been a beautiful girl and the gossips said she had enjoyed herself freely. But she had also worked hard for her husband's success, and their house had become a centre of social life in Belgrade before 1914.

In the First World War she had served with the Serbian Army and followed it in the retreat through Albania. She had often been under fire and had received a high decoration from King Peter. After that she had toured the United States raising funds for 'Gallant Little Serbia'. In the 'thirties she had persuaded King Alexander to make her husband Minister to Britain and, thanks to her skill as a hostess, had put the Yugoslav Legation on the social map of London.

Her husband had died three years before and she had returned to the United States. There she had dyed her hair blonde and, so some speculated, had her face lifted. Certainly everyone said she looked much younger than when they had seen her last.

Mabel was thrilled to hear that I was studying Balkan history in the period leading up to the First World War. She had known many of the leading personalities involved and presently invited one or two older people staying on the coast to come and contribute their recollections. These informal seminars were both pleasant and useful.

After a fortnight at the Villa Alta, I moved to a small flat in Crikvenitsa with a balcony overlooking the sea. My landlady was a kindly Viennese, the widow of an Austrian Naval Captain. Meals came from a restaurant across the way. They were brought by Mathias, a Slovene waiter, who had worked in Paris and Monte Carlo and had served in the Austrian Army during the First World War. Mathias was a keen student of politics and kept me in touch with the world outside.

For the best part of a month I read for ten hours a day about the forty years leading up to 1914. I devoured Dickinson's *International Anarchy*, Grant Robertson's *Eastern Question*, Percy Sykes on Persia, the German and Russian archives, and many other textbooks, whose titles, authors and, alas, whose contents I have largely forgotten. Partly, perhaps, because I was living in Yugoslavia I became especially interested in the struggle between Austria and Russia for control of the Balkans.

I saw very few people during this time. Apart, indeed, from a weekly visit to Mabel Gruitch and an occasional word with English or German acquaintances in the café opposite my flat, I kept my own company. I swam for an hour or so at midday and slept for an hour after lunch. Otherwise, it was study all the time.

At the end of a month or so I had finished my books on the origins of the war. I now turned to economics and began with Professor Pigou's work on Banking. The sky that day was overcast and a strong wind was blowing. I found it hard to concentrate and was relieved when the worthy Mathias arrived with dinner. He looked cheerful and sweaty as usual, but was also obviously excited. Even before he had put down my tray, he blurted out his news. The Germans had signed a pact with the Russians. Steeped as I was in nineteenth century diplomatic history, my first reaction was that Bismarck would have thoroughly approved. Hitler was re-opening 'the line to Petersburg'. But if the news was true, it could only mean that Hitler had decided on war and was taking steps to avoid fighting on two fronts.

After dinner I went out in search of information. In the town I ran into a Yugoslav friend. She confirmed Mathias' story and added that Ribbentrop was expected to leave for Moscow next day. I said 'This means war.' She answered bitterly 'Yes, or capitulation by the Western powers.' 'God save us from that' was my reply. Her suspicions, as I found in the next day or two, were widely shared by Yugoslav opinion. Most people expected Britain and France to run out again.

I did not see myself how the British or French Governments could now pull back. And yet a doubt lingered. With no confidence in our leaders on either side of the Channel, it was all too easy to conjure up the spectre of another futile compromise. My main fear that night was not of war but that we might once again shirk the issue.

I now put aside Pigou and scoured the town for foreign newspapers. I also listened closely to the German radio to which the café opposite kept tuned in for the benefit of its mainly German clients. I talked to some of them. They seemed convinced that Hitler would somehow pull a rabbit out of the hat once more and get Danzig for Germany without fighting.

Next evening, 30 August, I received a telegram from my father:

> Air Ministry orders you report Middle East Command Egypt. Think you should begin moving eastwards not later than the end of the week. Will telegraph further instructions if peace should break out. Meanwhile keep telegraphing prospective movements.

Mathias woke me at half past seven next morning to say that Hitler was due to broadcast in half-an-hour. I dressed hurriedly and walked over to the café opposite. It was already crowded with Germans. Hitler's speech was quite calm. But there was no mistaking his meaning. The invasion of Poland had begun; and the Poles had invoked the British and French guarantees. When it was over a German acquaintance walked up, shook hands with me and said: 'Goodbye. We are leaving for home. What a pity human beings should be so stupid.' He did not specify which human beings, and, anyway, we were not yet officially at war. In the circumstances I saw no point in starting an argument. Back in my flat I found my landlady in tears. Her son was a German citizen and had just received his call up papers. She wanted my advice as to what the boy should do. I could see no alternative for him but to obey.

When she had gone I wrote two letters—to my mother and to a friend. I then packed. The first stage of my journey to the East would be through Bosnia to Belgrade. I accordingly went to see Mabel Gruitch to get advice about the journey and to ask for introductions in Belgrade. Her eyes lit up when I told her of my plans, and I asked if she would like to come with me. She accepted at once, delighted at the chance to do 'her bit' in the Second World War. She would need a few hours to pack and asked me to delay our departure until next morning.

That evening, the first of September, I went for a long walk by the sea. The water lapped against the rough limestone rocks. Every branch and leaf on the trees stood out clearly against the sunset. When it got quite dark I sat down under a tree by the water's edge. Across the bay I could see the lights of Seltse.

In all honesty I have to admit that my strongest feeling at the time was one of relief—relief that the issue with Germany had at last come to a head and that this time we could not shirk our duty.

I measured, of course, the suffering and loss that war must bring, and with some bitterness; for I believed the disaster could have been averted had our Government stood up to Hitler in time. As it was, my generation would have to pay for the blindness and hesitations of the men in power. But, perhaps, it was only war that could rid us of those men and bring in new men who would help England find her soul again.

For myself I felt no regrets. Thanks to Hitler, my 'first' would remain a might-have-been. But I would at least be spared the gloomy prospect of having to climb the ladder of the bar or journalism from the bottom rung. All previous bets were off. War would provide adventure and—who could tell?—the chance to do big things. I felt that night that I had come of age.

A.M.—E

III

WITH CLOAK AND DAGGER

September 1939–November 1940

'And I then decided that, if there were to be further assassinations, I would be on the side of the assassins.'

King Ferdinand of Bulgaria

12

Attaché: Belgrade

I came downstairs on the morning of 2 September to find a small group of my Crikvenitsa friends gathered to see me off to Belgrade. They helped me load my luggage into the car and tied a Union Jack on to the mudguard. As far as they were concerned, I was the first soldier leaving for the front.

The gathering at Villa Alta was more sedate. The luggage was already at the door. Mabel Gruitch came slowly down the steps, like some Roman Empress. The servants kissed her hand. I started the engine and we drove off in a cloud of dust.

We followed the coast road towards Senj where two barren islands of grey rock rise out of the sea. The water between these islands is continually churned up by the interplay of wind and current. Encrusted in the cliffs opposite the islands is the town of Senj with its ancient fortress dwarfing the little harbour and the houses around. The princes of Senj were pirate chiefs, descendants, it is said, of Crusaders wrecked on their way back from the Holy Land. The country around was poor and barren; and in recent years more than half the population had emigrated to the United States. The women were all dressed in black and looked prematurely aged with work and child bearing. They turned away from us as we passed.

The young men of Senj, by contrast, were reputed very handsome. It was said that they used to club together to send one of their number to the United States. His task was to marry an American heiress, bring her back and carve up the proceeds with his partners.

From Senj we followed a steep road zig-zagging up the face of the *karst*. At the top we stopped to look back at the bright hard beauty of the Gulf of Senj. A few yards further on and the sea vanished from sight. We were now in rich and wooded country, the Lika, where Kaizer Franz Josef had recruited his bodyguard. The peasants there wore flat round *fezes* decorated with a long tassel. The men sat and smoked leaving any manual work to their women. They had good horses and lived well from timber and maize. On the coast the religion was Roman Catholic. The Lika was Serbian Orthodox. A few miles further on we reached the linked lakes of Plitvitse, bright as green jade in a forest of dark pines. We crossed into Bosnia. The houses had long sloping roofs. The women were heavily veiled. The farms seemed prosperous.

We drove along a steep river valley and, rounding a bend, came upon the town of Bihatch with half a dozen minarets rising above a cluster of red roofs. There was an untidy Moslem cemetery, shaded by green trees; and ahead of us along the white and dusty road marched a grey column of soldiers. We drove past some hovels and across an old Turkish bridge into the market place. Some of the men there carried rifles and walked with their veiled women following a yard or two behind. Others sat on long low stools, their *fezes* pushed back from their foreheads. Most of them wore black baggy Moslem breeches. Everyone seemed to be smoking cigarettes or long pipes. Little boys were moving about serving coffee from brass trays.

The Hotel Bosna produced two reasonably clean rooms. It was an old world *caravanserai* built around a courtyard where the merchants used to unload their carts and hobble their horses. We gave orders for dinner and walked out to see the town. The main mosque was still open and a peasant girl pulled back the rush matting on the floor to show us the fine carpets beneath. It was the first time I had been inside a mosque.

We wandered through the streets, bought water melons and at my request had our dinner carried down to the river bank. 'You're like a Turk,' said Mabel, 'They always like to sit by water.'

Next day, we struck out across north Bosnia meaning to spend the night at Banja Luka. But the road was winding and very rough; and we were lucky to reach Pryedor by nightfall.

It was *Ramadan.*[1] The minarets were all lit up and the taverns and cafés full of revellers. After dinner I wandered through the narrow streets and went into a bar where *slivovitz*—plum brandy—was solid in diminutive bottles. Here I was joined by a couple of Bosnians in *fezes* and baggy trousers. We had no common language but were soon drinking to the health of England and France and to the death of Hitler, Mussolini and dictators in general. Quite a crowd gathered, including military and police. We all got on famously. About one in the morning, the party escorted me back from the tavern to the hotel. When they saw the Union Jack on my car their enthusiasm was redoubled. Somebody went into the hotel and came out with several bottles of wine and we had to drink further toasts all round.

Next day we continued to Banja Luka where a crowd gathered around the car attracted by the Union Jack. One of them was a student who spoke a little English. Radio Belgrade, he told us, had just reported the

[1] *Ramadan* is the Moslem equivalent of the Christian Lent, with the difference that total abstinence from food, drink and smoking is required between sunrise and sunset, but after sunset any indulgence is allowed.

British and French declaration of war against Germany. Banja Luka is only an hour or so by car from Sarajevo. It seemed appropriate to learn the outbreak of the Second World War so near to where Printsip had fired the fatal shots leading to the First World War.

We stopped by the River Bosna to drink coffee, and were joined by a Serbian officer and his family. He had fought in the First World War and said it was Serbia's duty to fight again alongside her old allies. There seemed no doubt where Yugoslav sympathies lay.

We crossed the River Drina next morning and came into Serbia. The country here was flatter. The peasants, all Orthodox Christians without any Moslem element, wore tall sheepskin caps. The road was, if possible, worse than in Bosnia. It had been shelled during the First World War and never repaired. We made slow progress until we reached the banks of the River Sava. Here the road broadened and led us straight into Belgrade.

I had a letter of introduction from my father to our Minister in Belgrade, Sir Ronald Campbell. I, accordingly, telephoned to ask when I might present it. His secretary told me that the next day would be a public holiday and asked me to come on the day after that. With the self-centred eagerness of youth, I thought this rather dilatory. So did Mabel Gruitch. She declared that our diplomats were 'a lot of Munichois' and that she would launch me on Belgrade herself.

For a start, she took me to the palace where I signed the Prince Regent's book. The Marshal of the Court, Bojidar Cholak-Antitch, then carried us off for lunch to his villa at Dedinye in the hills outside Belgrade. It was a large house by Serbian standards with a small racing stable.

Among the guests was a General Antitch, who had been one of the conspirators in the murder of King Alexander Obrenovitch and Queen Draga in 1904. I had read several accounts of the murder in my studies and had little difficulty in getting Antitch to give me his version. The worst moment, he told me, was when the lights failed and the conspirators, some of them rather drunk, stumbled through the palace in the dark looking for their victims and occasionally shooting at each other by mistake.

After lunch, Mabel took me to the Foreign Office and introduced me to the Foreign Minister, M. Tsintsar Markovitch. He was very friendly and then and there asked his permanent Under-Secretary, Dr. Stoyan Gavrilovitch, to begin my education in Yugoslav foreign policy. Gavrilovitch duly led me off to his office and gave me a lucid *tour d'horizon*.

All this seemed a good beginning and I spent the rest of the day exploring Belgrade. The city was a curious mixture. There were some imposing if rather heavy Government buildings. The main streets were broad; and private enterprise had put up a number of cheap-looking

modern apartment blocks. In striking contrast to these were the traditional houses of old Belgrade, little single storey buildings with Regency
porticos and windows. There were still a few such houses in the main
streets; and, in the side streets, they predominated. There was a fine
Orthodox cathedral, but unfinished for lack of money. Beside it stood a
small Russian church and the chapel where the Obrenovitch dynasty
were buried. There was also a substantial Turkish house with big bow
windows. It had been the *Konak*[1] of the last Ottoman Governor.

But the building I liked best of all was the Kalemegdan, the old Turkish
fortress built on Roman foundations. This jutted out into the water, like
the prow of a ship, dominating the confluence of the Danube and the
Sava. The Kalemegdan had become a public garden and I spent many
hours on its ramparts looking out across the rivers and over the great
plain stretching north-west to Hungary.

The public holiday next day was in honour of the King's birthday;
and the Marshal of the Court had given us tickets for the 'Te Deum' in
the old cathedral. Mabel and I arrived early. It was a hot day and we
stood for a time in the sun watching the Royal bodyguard in their shakos,
blue tunics with gold facings, and red trousers. The cathedral inside was
white and rather bare. As in most Orthodox churches there were no pews
or chairs, and this made it seem larger than it really was. Slowly the nave
filled up with officers in grey, white, or blue uniforms. The members of
the Government were there in morning dress and the foreign diplomats
with their military attachés. The latter included the German Attaché in
the uniform of the Wehrmacht. Mabel was the only woman present, and
this by virtue of the military decoration she had won in the First War.

The Yugoslav officers formed into little groups talking quietly but
intensely. While we stood waiting, Mabel pointed out to me some of the
different racial types among Yugoslavs: the dark, lean Montenegrins with
aquiline features; the bull-necked, thick-skulled and heavy-jowled Serbs
and Bosnians; and occasionally a Slovene with blond hair and blue eyes.
Suddenly an officer barked out a word of command to the guard of
honour outside the cathedral door. The talking ceased. A lean, sallow
faced man in a general's uniform moved quickly up the aisle. He had
an aquiline nose and high receding brow. This was the Prince Regent
Paul. The Prince's features and bearing showed distinction rather than
strength. He looked ill at ease. I wondered what he thought of the tough,
battle-scarred officers in the congregation, and what they thought of him.

Presently we heard chanting from behind the altar screen and clouds
of incense slowly filled the church. The bishops now appeared wearing

[1] Official residence.

crowns of gold and embroidered robes. Their hair reached to their shoulders and their beards to their waists. In front of them stood the Prince Regent. Behind him were the officers and the politicians; to one side the foreign diplomats. Here, as if on a stage, were the principal characters in the Yugoslav drama.

In the afternoon, Stoyan Velkovitch, a dark young Serb who had studied at Oxford and owned my hotel, drove me out to Avala. Avala—the black mountain—is a tree-covered cone that rises sheer and solitary above the low rolling hills south of the Danube. On the summit stands the tomb of the Unknown Warrior, designed by the great sculptor Mestrovitch in the classical style and made of polished black and green stone. The caryatids supporting the canopy are statues twelve feet high of South Slav peasant women. They represent the different provinces of the Yugoslavia which the Unknown Warrior and his comrades had died to create.

From Avala the view stretched northwards over the roofs of Belgrade to the great plains beyond the Danube. To the east, the river flowed through marsh lands past the ancient walled city of Smederovo and towards the Iron Gates. To south and west ran the green valleys and leafy slopes of rich Shumadia, the heart of Serbia.

Standing at Avala I reflected that little Serbia with a population of only five million had lost over a million dead in the First World War. But out of the bloodshed and the sacrifice had risen the new state of Yugoslavia, already some fifteen million strong. Had the survivors built soundly? Or had the dead died in vain? How would Yugoslavia stand up to the testing times ahead?

That evening I went out with two young Yugoslav officers and their wives. They introduced me to young sturgeon, sucking pig, and the skewered grilled meats eaten with strong salads of garlic, egg plant and red peppers, which are such a feature of Serbia cooking. They made me try their wines—the dry white wine of Smederovo and the strong 'black' wine of Nish. It was all very much to my taste.

After dinner we visited several *kafanas* or coffee houses. Most of them were big functional rooms, but brought to life by gypsy orchestras and singers. In one of them, The Dardanelles, a dingy, crowded place, I first saw Turkish belly dancing performed by gypsies from Macedonia. We ended up in the Kasbek, a small White Russian night club where Tania, one of Bruce Lockhart's heroines, still sang and her husband danced Cossack sword dances and threw daggers held between his teeth.

I walked to the Legation next morning and saw Peter Garran, the Third Secretary. I had never seen the business side of a diplomatic mission before and was surprised by his small and dingy office. I told him of my journey through Bosnia. He was polite but uninterested. He promised, however, to give my father's letter of introduction to the Minister. I then went down to a basement to report to the Air Attaché. He asked me what I wanted to do. I suggested going to Warsaw to join our Mission with the Polish forces. He seemed doubtful about this but agreed to telegraph to Warsaw. While I was with him, a telephone message came from the Minister asking me to lunch next day.

Sir Ronald Campbell was a classical type of British diplomat. He was slight, dark and agile; impeccably dressed, and with the informal good manners which quickly put young people at their ease. We lunched alone. He questioned me closely about my drive through Bosnia. He seemed genuinely interested in what I told him and especially in the strength of pro-Allied sentiment I had met everywhere on the journey and indeed since I had come to Belgrade. Then, to my surprise, he said that pro-Allied sentiment among the Serbs was the thing that worried him most. There was no question of the British and French opening a new Salonika front. It was, therefore, important to check any signs of war fever in Yugoslavia. We must try to prevent the Yugoslavs provoking the Germans and keep them on ice until we could use them to best advantage. Starting from this premise, Campbell deprecated the attitude of the Opposition leaders in Belgrade and said they were simply trying to ride back to power on a wave of pro-Allied sentiment. The only wise course was to work closely with Prince Paul and his ministers. They were our friends and would help us as much as they safely could.

I felt doubts about his line of reasoning but, though I put some questions, thought it wiser not to argue. I was flattered, besides, by the interest which Campbell seemed to show in what I had told him. I cannot believe that what I had to say was very new to him. But by showing interest he encouraged me to give of my best. This made me enjoy the lunch and perhaps made it less boring for him. I have often thought of his example in later years and tried to follow it.

After lunch Campbell raised the question of whether I could be of any help to him. He said he needed someone in the cipher department but thought this would bore me stiff. Now that he had seen me he would like to talk the problem over with his First Secretary, Terence Shone. Would I, perhaps, come and see Shone the next afternoon?

Shone looked rather like Anthony Eden, and, indeed, was sometimes mistaken for him. He was a great gourmet and later began my education in wine and cigars. I had expected him to talk about my future. Instead he gave me a short briefing on the Yugoslav situation, as if I had been a visiting Member of Parliament. I asked a few questions and he then led me off to have tea with Campbell. Campbell said he had no immediate work for me, and yet was reluctant to let me go. He thought that with my experience of journalism in the Spanish War I might be able to help him on the public relations side. He accordingly asked me to call on the Press Attaché, Stephen Childs.

In appearance Childs might have been a provincial bank manager. He was going bald. He had a round red face and wore horned rimmed glasses over a slightly hooked nose. But he had a very wide range of experience. He had fought in the First War and with Wrangel's army in South Russia. He had organised the resettlement of Russian refugees in Eastern Europe and had worked in South America for the League of Nations after the Gran Chaco War between Bolivia and Paraguay. He had also written two entertaining books about his adventures.

Childs now invited me to become his deputy. I would rank as an Attaché at the Legation and would receive a modest salary. The job would be very much what I chose to make of it and we would decide my duties as we went along. I decided to accept. Warsaw had already fallen to the Germans and there was little chance now of active service in Poland. The Balkans seemed likely to be drawn into the War before long; and a job in our Legation should provide a firm base from which to operate.

I now adorned my ancient Ford with C.D. plates and hauled down my Union Jack after the Minister had politely intimated that he was the only member of the Legation to fly one. My name was added to the Diplomatic List; and, in accordance with protocol, Oakley the Legation messenger, left my visiting cards on all members of the diplomatic corps not actually at war with us. They sent me back their own cards in return. To my surprise, one of these came from the *Chargé d'Affaires of His Imperial Majesty the Tsar of all the Russias.* Yugoslavia had never recognised the Soviets and still gave diplomatic privileges to a White Russian representative who lived in the old Tsarist Legation.

My work for the first few weeks consisted of listening to the B.B.C. at seven in the morning and at five in the afternoon. I then dictated a short news bulletin based on the broadcast and, with the help of guidance telegraphed from London, composed a commentary on it. These were distributed to perhaps a score of the leading people in Belgrade. Since local censorship was strict and foreign newspapers often delayed, my bulletins soon became quite influential. It was surprising how quickly the contents of a score of bulletins spread round Belgrade.

I also delivered copies of the bulletins personally to the editors of the three Belgrade newspapers. This gave me a pretext to discuss the day's news and try to influence their presentation of it.

There were three main papers. *Politika* claimed a circulation of 200,000 copies. It was the oldest paper in Belgrade and published articles of inordinate length. Its proprietor and editor, Vlada Ribnikar, was friendly but reserved. He was thought to have pro-Soviet sympathies and indeed later proved to have been a secret Communist. This led him, after the Ribbentrop-Molotov agreement, to adopt a strictly neutral line.

Vreme was a more modern newspaper owned by the Government. Its editor, Gregoritch, had orders to follow a neutral course, but he had been persuaded—to put it kindly—that the Germans would win the war and favoured them accordingly. All the same, Gregoritch was personally very friendly, and we sometimes played chess in his office while waiting for the paper to come off the press.

But my favourite paper was *Pravda*, owned by the seven brothers Sokitch. One brother I never met, as he lived in the country. The other six were all over six feet tall, very broad and most of them well furnished with gold teeth. Each brother was responsible for a section of the newspaper, except for one brother, who sat in the outer office wearing a hat, dressed in a crumpled suit and often unshaven. He was called 'the responsible editor', and it was his name which appeared at the top of the paper each day. His job was to appear in court and sometimes spend a few days in prison whenever his brothers had printed some article particularly offensive to the Government.

The Sokitch brothers were voracious trenchermen and no less greedy for money. They were genuinely pro-Allied but had no scruple in seeking to capitalise their sentiments. One day, lunching alone with the six of them, I was asked for a subsidy of a million dinars, about £20,000, from the British Government. I must have looked slightly surprised, for one of them said in his very special brand of Balkan French: *Pourquoi pas? c'est honnête, c'est loyale, c'est morale; car nous n'avons jamais cessé de manger* (he had, of course, meant to say, *de marcher*) *avec L'Entente.* They were by turns absurd, alarming and yet good friends. They remained loyal throughout to the Allied cause and wept like children over the fall of France.

Another office which I visited most days was the press section of the Yugoslav Foreign Ministry. I took great pains to show understanding of their difficulties, and steadfastly refused to press little points against them. My plan was to build up a credit balance against a day of need. This came soon enough. One day, *Vreme* devoted most of its front page to an obviously exaggerated German account of the sinking of British ships in the Atlantic. The British version of the sinkings was not published at all. Childs was ill, and I drew up a strongly worded *démenti* and demanded that it be published in the next day's issue. The Head of the press office refused my request and we had a very heated argument. I came away convinced that I had failed to persuade him. Next day, how-ever, the *Vreme* carried my *démenti* on its front page and splashed the British version of the sinkings under banner headlines. The Minister and Childs sent little notes of congratulation. More important, they now began to listen to what I had to say.

My contacts with the Belgrade newspapers had convinced me that the great majority of Yugoslav journalists had pro-Allied sympathies. What they wanted was to be able to show their editors, and, if necessary, their Government, that any news or views they published had reached them from a responsible source. I discussed this with Childs one evening on Belgrade railway station and suggested to him that we might start a news agency. This would be on the lines of Reuters but more propagandist. It would issue its bulletins through a commercial office in Belgrade selling them to the newspapers at a nominal rate. The bulletins themselves could be prepared in the Legation with the help of friendly Yugoslav journalists. The Ministry of Information might also supply material. Childs liked the idea; we worked on it and presently 'sold' it to the Ministry of Information. They sent out an energetic journalist called Donald Mallet who helped us set up the *Britanova* News Agency. *Britanova* consisted of a couple of rooms where Kozomaritch, a former editor of *Vreme*, concocted bulletins based on the B.B.C., the British Press and material supplied from the Legation. As well as being a good journalist Kozomaritch was reputed to be pro-German. This gave the whole operation an appearance of im-partiality and made it easier for the Yugoslav Government to turn a blind eye to *Britanova's* activities.

Another successful venture was the publication of a Yugoslav magazine called *Britannia*. This was planned as a fortnightly and contained articles by such eminent contributors as Churchill and Lloyd George. They did not, of course, write the articles themselves but allowed us to pirate articles they had already written and even, with the help of scissors and paste, to concoct new articles from their speeches and writings. The first number led off with a strongly pro-Allied editorial and was quickly sold out. We doubled the circulation for the second number and again for the third. The German Legation, of course, protested. The editor was fined, and the magazine closed down. We paid the fine, appointed a new editor, and produced further numbers under another name.

Another of my duties was to brief Yugoslav journalists on their way to London and to give such help as I could to British correspondents in Belgrade.

The Balkan correspondent of *The Times* was Patrick Maitland.[1] He was married to a daughter of the Marshal of the Court and was of more help to me than I could ever be to him. With Patrick was Ralph Parker who had been *The Times* correspondent in Prague up to the outbreak of War. I saw much of Ralph and of his attractive Czech wife, Milena, and we became close friends; but more of that later.

Another journalist who did much for my education in things Yugoslav was Lovat Edwards. Edwards was more of a don than a newspaper man and had some difficulty in adapting his style to the requirements of Beaverbrook Press. But he had explored every corner of Yugoslavia, spoke the language fluently and had friends everywhere. One day at lunch he introduced me to a Mr. Printsip, who turned out to be a brother of the Gavrilo Printsip who had killed the Archduke Franz Ferdinand at Sarajevo. This Printsip was a timber merchant and in every way a solid citizen. I asked him about his brother, but he only said: 'He was a good boy, Mr. Amery, a very good boy. I often think of him and wish he were alive to help me with my business.'

Reuter's correspondent was Peter Brown. Peter's hair hung black and lank over his ears and collar. His face had somehow collapsed around his bright, dark eyes and he had never learnt to shave properly. He seemed to possess only two suits. An orthodox but stained grey suit for the summer and a golden brown corduroy suit which appeared with the first snowfall. But he knew the country and its language well and had very useful contacts with the Yugoslav left wing. The Communist Party was banned in Yugoslavia but it remained influential in the universities and capitalised on the traditionally pro-Russian and Slav sympathies of the average Serb and Montenegrin.

In addition to resident correspondents, we had a constant stream of distinguished journalists and other visitors sponsored by the Ministry of Information. I used to arrange interviews for them, brief them as best I could and take them round Belgrade. The strangest visit, perhaps, was a goodwill mission of three Anglican bishops sponsored by the Religions' Division of the Ministry. In advance of the visit I went to the Patriarchate to discuss a programme. An Orthodox bishop there, a jolly fellow who spoke a little English, remarked: 'It is good that they come. I once knew your Bishop of Gibraltar. He was a good man. I took him to— how you say?—a nunnery. When he came out he looked very satisfied.'

The Anglican bishops were clean shaven and, no doubt, clean living men with a business-like manner. They made a strange contrast with their bearded patriarchal hosts who looked on washing and exercise as luxuries unbecoming to holy men, but who also tended, in the intervals of fasting, to eat and drink copiously. The link man between them was Canon

[1] Now the Earl of Lauderdale.

Douglas, 'the Anglican Foreign Secretary'. Douglas was well versed in Orthodox traditions and used to stroke the Serbian bishops' beards. Unfortunately, he suffered at this time from an uncontrollable cough and sometimes left big lumps of phlegm behind. They seemed not to notice or else were glad of the chance to practise the Christian virtue of forgiveness.

I piloted the party to the Patriarchate and round the monasteries of Frushka Gora. The Serbs are not a devout or fanatical people; but the Serbian Church is a strong political organisation; and these early meetings with its leaders would prove useful later on. But the visit had an unfortunate ending. The secretary to the Mission was a young clergyman who acted as liaison officer between the Ministry of Information and the Church of England. He was very anxious, as clergymen sometimes are, to show that he was neither a prig nor a puritan. I happened to be taking a small party of English journalists to see the night spots of Belgrade and, as he was in my office at the time, I asked if he would like to join us. He accepted, and we had a very convivial evening. I thought no more about it. But a few days later the *Völkischer Beobachter*[1] published a large photograph of our young friend in his dog collar seated between two scantily dressed Macedonian belly dancers. The Ministry of Information were not amused.

Another of my duties was to draft despatches for Childs and the Minister on the attitude of the Belgrade Press and the state of Yugoslav public opinion. This work of drafting marked an important stage in my literary education. My essays at Oxford and my articles on Spain had attracted favourable comment. I thought I knew how to write English. I was, accordingly, a little surprised and hurt when Childs, after reading my first draft, said: 'This is full of good stuff. What a pity you can't write English.' It was about eleven o'clock in the morning. He now pushed all other work aside and took me back to his flat. With a brief interval for lunch with his attractive Russian wife, we spent the next five hours going through the draft despatch line by line, and discussing how it could be improved. Childs' main concern was that the meaning of each sentence should be absolutely clear to the reader and so phrased that it could mean nothing else. He held that the first purpose of all writing was to convey information. For this reason he deprecated the use of subjective adjectives which could mean different things to different people. He would not accept, for instance, that I should write of 'a large and disorderly demonstration'. I must either give an estimate of numbers and say in what way it was disorderly or else use no adjectives at all.

[1] The main newspaper of the Nazi Party.

I acknowledge a lasting debt of gratitude for that day's lesson in the art or at least the craft of writing.

At the end of a tour of South East Europe Lord Lloyd, then chairman of the British Council, described our press office as 'the only good one for propaganda in the Balkans'. My work there certainly kept me busy, but I still found time for discovering and enjoying Belgrade. Until the snow came I used to ride, most mornings, with a group of young Yugoslav officers. I also took lessons in Serbo-Croat from a Croat official in the Foreign Office and met a number of his friends. There was a good deal of entertaining within the diplomatic corps, and I explored the restaurants and night life of Belgrade with Yugoslav and British pressmen. Sometimes our high spirits got the better of us and led me to depart from the traditional decorum of diplomacy.

One evening half a dozen members of a German purchasing commission came into the Kazbek night club. Germany was very short of fats and we knew that they had come to try and buy butter from Yugoslavia. We accordingly ordered a large piece of butter and stuck on it a little flag—'*With the compliments of the British Legation.*' The orchestra, who were friends, struck up with a martial air, and one of the waiters carried the butter across the room and presented it with elaborate ceremony to the Germans. The other guests in the Kazbek thought it all very funny. But the Germans took the joke badly. They paid their bill and left. We had thought this might happen, and, while laying on the presentation of the butter, one of us had already nipped out and let down the tyres of two German C.D. cars parked outside. It was snowing at the time and rather late to get a taxi. When we left an hour later, the cars were still there with their flat tyres and we presumed that our German friends must have had a long and cold trek back to their hotel.

Another night, one of the German Service Attachés came in to the Kazbek with a very attractive Montenegrin dancer. I admired her with perhaps more freedom than discretion, and he either took offence or thought it a chance to impress the lady. In any case, he came over and in good English asked me to leave the Kazbek or to come outside and fight it out. He was a big fellow, but I thought it best to take the high line. I told him to go away, adding that if he wanted to fight, I was armed. As if to emphasise the point I put my right hand to my left armpit pretending to feel for my gun. The bluff worked and my German turned on his heel and went back to his table without a word. I decided to follow up success and continued staring at the lady. She was obviously enjoying the whole situation and suddenly flashed back a smile of encouragement. I got up at once and asked her to dance. She accepted and, when we had finished dancing, came back with me to my table. I reckoned it was game, set and match to me.

I carried off a more practical coup a few days later. I was lunching alone in my hotel when a German official came into the dining room carrying a heavy brief-case. He too was alone and put down the brief-case on a chair beside him. While he ordered his meal, I slipped out and encouraged the hall porter to come in, a few minutes later, and call him to the telephone. When the summons came, the German, as I had hoped, went out, leaving the brief-case on the chair. No-one seemed to be looking, so I picked it up and drove off with it to our Legation. Some of my colleagues thought this was pushing total war rather too far, but the contents of the brief-case proved interesting; and the Naval Attaché, a tough old pirate called Despard, commended my initiative.

13

A Balkan Education

In our four days' drive from the Dalmatian coast, Mabel Gruitch had taught me much about the principal factions and cliques in Belgrade and Zagreb and of their links with the European Powers. She had also told me something of the private lives of the leading men from the Prince Regent downwards. I was at an age when memory is very retentive and, by the end of our journey, could have written a passable thesis on political trends in Yugoslavia.

Once established as a member of the Legation I began to meet members of the Government and of the Court. But official relations with them were the business of the Minister and the First Secretary, and I had to be careful not to say anything which could cross wires with my seniors.

I felt much less inhibition about contacts with the leaders of the Opposition. Most of them had been out of office for several years. Some were friends of my father, and there was no reason why I should not sit at their feet, provided I was careful what I said myself. Nor, at this stage, were they at all shy of seeing foreigners. Prince Paul's régime was a dictatorship in the sense that there was no parliamentary control of the executive and no protection against arbitrary arrest. For all that, the climate was not oppressive. People criticised the Government freely. Political leaders had their telephones tapped spasmodically but were seldom watched themselves. The secret police was a ramshackle and rather venal organisation; and even dangerously subversive elements like the Communists or the Croat *Ustashi*[1] had little difficulty in evading its vigilance.

The first Opposition leader whom I came to know at all well was Dr. Momchilo Ninchitch. Ninchitch had been Foreign Minister from 1918 to 1925 and had since become a distinguished historian. He asked me to lunch soon after my arrival. Then in his middle sixties, Ninchitch was a small man with a big nose and beady eyes. He was rather deaf and, perhaps because of this, talked all the time. At our first meeting, indeed, he talked with scarcely a pause from one o'clock until nearly five, and I could hardly suppress a smile when, towards the end of his monologue, he

[1] A terrorist organisation led by Ante Pavelitch and advocating Croat separatism.

said to me: 'The trouble about King Alexander was that he never would listen to me.' For a busy man Ninchitch's flow of talk must have been a bore. But, as a young man of twenty, I was fascinated by the way in which he marshalled his facts and, despite copious detail and lengthy parentheses, somehow managed to draw all the threads together to a logical conclusion. Like Oliver Twist I went back for more; and this first meeting was only the beginning of a series of tutorials in contemporary Balkan politics.

Ninchitch's views were not, of course, unbiased. He had played a leading part in Office and in Opposition and still hoped to return to power. But our talks together convinced me that, if a young man wants to learn about politics, he should seek the company of elder statesmen who have passed the years of discretion and no longer hesitate to say what they really think.

But my chief mentor in Yugoslav politics was Jakob Altmaier. Altmaier was a German Jew from Frankfurt. He had been a non-commissioned officer in the First War and had seized power for the Socialists in Frankfurt after the 1918 armistice. For ten days he had been 'boss' of Frankfurt but lacked sustained ambition. One day after hearing a pretty girl practising *Lieder* in his hotel, something broke inside him and he took the train to Berlin leaving the revolution and a political career behind him. Altmaier later turned to journalism and was for many years correspondent of the *Frankfurter Zeitung* and of the *Manchester Guardian* in Belgrade and in Sofia. He left the Balkans in 1936 to play an active part in the Spanish Civil War. But, after the fall of the Spanish Republic, came back to Belgrade and was staying with Milan Gavrilovitch,[1] the leader of the Serbian Peasant Party.

With a narrow clipped moustache and grey wavy hair, Altmaier looked rather like Adolphe Menjou, the film star of the 'thirties. I first met him when Childs sent him over to my office to discuss some proposals he had made about British propaganda to Yugoslavia. I asked him to lunch, and we talked until late in the afternoon. I was impressed by the depth as well as the originality of his ideas, and was not surprised when Harold Nicolson later told me that he thought Altmaier the most intelligent man he had ever met. From the time of this first meeting I saw him almost daily for the next six months.

Altmaier knew everyone in Belgrade and opened every door to me. But he did much more than that. Until then the main formative influences on my political thinking had come from the right wing in politics: from my father and his friends, from mainly Conservative school teachers and dons, and from friends in Nationalist Spain. I was now, for the first time, brought into daily touch with a brilliant and experienced colleague whose political roots were Marxist. Altmaier taught me to distinguish between

[1] No relation to the Dr. Stoyan Gavrilovitch mentioned in Chapter 12.

the truth in Marxism and the errors. More important, he accustomed me
to apply the Marxist social and economic method of analysis to current
political problems. This would add another dimension to my thinking.

At an early stage in our acquaintance, Altmaier took me to see Milan
Gavrilovitch. The Gavrilovitch family lived in a large and rambling house
on the outskirts of Belgrade. The furniture was nineteenth-century Central
European. There were Turkish carpets on the walls and one or two icons
framed in silver. It was a house out of a Tolstoy novel. So was the family.
Milan Gavrilovitch's mother-in-law was the unchallenged matriarch. She
was a tall, slender old lady in her seventies with white hair and eyes so
dark that she must have had gypsy or *Tsintsar*[1] blood. She held herself
like an Empress, spoke beautiful French, and was passionately interested
in politics. Her husband, Alexander Genchitch, had been the brains
behind the coup d'état against the Obrenovitch dynasty in 1904. But he
had directed the coup from abroad and she alone had known the full list
of the conspirators against the King. These had worked in cells of three
or four, unknown one to the other, and each, in her husband's absence,
had reported to her. She had kept the list in her bosom adding names to
it and subtracting them as the plot developed.

Madame Gavrilovitch, her daughter, remained rather subdued in her
mother's presence. She had the same dark eyes and dark complexion, but
her nature was more passionate and she was easily moved to indignation.
There were three Gavrilovitch daughters, still in their teens, who had all
written novels and poems, and a handsome dark-eyed son. Milan
Gavrilovitch himself had a massive head with grey curly hair, small
rather slanting eyes and a skin that looked as if it was made of parchment. He smoked incessantly. His clothes looked as if he slept in them,
and he only had one necktie. This was an annual present from his wife,
worn daily and thrown away at the end of each year.

Nothing happened on time in the Gavrilovitch family. Dinner could
be two or three hours late and Madame Gavrilovitch never really knew
how many people were coming. Half a dozen unexpected guests often
turned up and the maid was then sent down to get extra food from the
nearest tavern. The talk passed from Serbo-Croat to French without
difficulty and ranged over every topic under the sun.

After dinner, on my first visit to the family, I was standing talking to
Milan Gavrilovitch, when I was suddenly seized by both arms and legs
and bumped against the floor three times by his children. This proceeding,

---

[1] The Slav name for the Vlachs living in Macedonia and believed to be a mixture of
Slav, Greek and Roman blood. For a full account of this people see *Encyclopaedia
Britannica* 1960, vol. 23, pp. 229–230.

in the middle of a serious conversation seemed so absurd that I lay on the floor convulsed with laughter. I asked the children why they had done it—they said it was to see how I would react. Would I be cross? Would I be embarrassed? Or would I think it funny? Different people, they said, took it in different ways. I had apparently passed the test rather well.

I was invited once more to dine with the Gavrilovitchs and then told that there would be no more invitations. I was to come whenever I wanted to, but they expected me to come at least once a week.

My friendship with this delightful family was cemented in a curious way. Sir Ronald Campbell had been followed as Minister—rather confusingly for Belgrade society—by a Mr. Ronald Campbell. 'Little Ronnie', as the new Minister was nicknamed, kept Dalmatians. These produced a litter of puppies and one day Campbell asked me if I knew anyone who would like to have two of them. It so happened that only a few days before I had heard Madame Gavrilovitch say that she would never keep a dog again unless it was a Dalmatian. I accordingly took two of Campbell's Dalmatian puppies and went off uninvited to dine with the Gavrilovitchs. I released the dogs in the hall wondering, this time, how they would react. Nothing I have ever done before or since has met with such enthusiasm. There were whoops of joy and I was embraced several times by every member of the family, including the grandmother.

Milan Gavrilovitch, as the leader of the Serbian Peasant Party, aimed to set up a federation of the four South Slav peoples—Serbs, Croats, Slovenes and Bulgars—based on peasant co-operatives. He was a strong Serb patriot but soon persuaded me that I must visit Croatia and Bulgaria if I was really to understand the South Slav problem. He was in close touch with the powerful Peasant Parties in both countries and promised to recommend me to their leaders.

Accordingly, at the beginning of December, I went for three days to Zagreb to exchange views with Stephen Clissold, the press officer at the British Consulate there, and to give a lecture explaining why Britain and France were bound to win the war. The lecture was well attended and the press next day reported that 'Sir Amery, former First Lord of the Admiralty, spoke in Zagreb last night'. The German Legation was said to be very disturbed by this news.

The political scene in Croatia was dominated by the Croat Peasant Party, led by Dr. Matchek. The Party exercised immense influence through its network of co-operatives. It owned most of the press and controlled local government. Matchek was away at the time of my visit but I had long and interesting talks with his chief lieutenant Dr. Kosutitch and with his main ally, Dr. Vilder, the leader of a smaller party representing the Serbs living in Croatia. The Croat Peasant Party had joined the Government shortly before the war and their leaders naturally showed more reserve in talking to me than did the Opposition leaders in Belgrade. Nevertheless they were frankly critical of their Serbian colleagues in the Government, and spoke of them as 'unrepresentative'. They thought it would strengthen Yugoslavia's position if the Opposition parties could be brought into the Government and the Parliamentary constitution restored.

Opinion in Zagreb was less outspokenly pro-Allied than in Belgrade. But, though there were no memories of the Salonika Front to stir the blood, there seemed to be a deeper loyalty to the cause of Parliamentary Democracy. The Roman Catholic religion, moreover, served as an antidote to pro-Russian and pan-Slav sentiment. I was encouraged by my first impressions of Croat opinion. But Stephen Clissold warned me not to underestimate the influence of Ante Pavelitch and his terrorist *Ustashi* movement. They were stronger in the middle classes and the Church than was generally believed and could be a dangerous fifth column in a crisis.

It was too cold to see much of Zagreb or anything of its surroundings; but I liked what I saw of the old city with its narrow streets and quaint medieval houses. Zagreb is a much finer place than Belgrade; and yet I knew at once, that I liked Belgrade more. Zagreb is still part of Catholic Central Europe, though an outpost. Belgrade belongs to the Balkans, with their Byzantine and Ottoman traditions.

A few days later, I took my lecture to Sofia. Our Minister there, Sir George Rendel, showed me great kindness and talked to me about the Balkan situation as he saw it. He was convinced that King Boris had no wish to follow his father's example and become involved in a war against the Allies. He would do his best to keep neutral. No less important, he would serve as a built-in obstacle to any Soviet penetration of Bulgaria. Rendel saw the King as a friendly influence in the Balkan scene and thought we should try to persuade Prince Paul to make territorial concessions to him.

Gavrilovitch had given me letters to the Bulgarian Peasant Party leaders, Obov and George Dimitrov.[1] Obov was very reserved at our first meeting and I soon sensed that King Boris' dictatorship was a fiercer thing than Prince Paul's.

[1] George M. Dimitrov, popularly known as 'Gemeto' and not to be confused with George Dimitrov, the Secretary General of the Comintern and first Communist leader of Bulgaria in 1946.

Gemeto Dimitrov was of peasant origin but had earned the money for his school fees as a railway porter on Varna station. He had later qualified as a doctor and at this time still practised spasmodically. He had been active in the Bulgarian Peasant Movement since boyhood and twice sentenced to death and reprieved.

I telephoned to Dimitrov only to learn that he was ill and could not see me. Yet, within half an hour, one of his men came round to my hotel. Dimitrov's telephone, he explained, was tapped and he did not like making appointments over it. He would, in fact, be delighted to see me any time after dark. It was winter and soon after five o'clock I followed his emissary to a dingy two-roomed flat, perhaps ten minutes walk away. Dimitrov seemed very glad to meet an Englishman, especially one from Belgrade. Unlike Obov he was very outspoken. His main theme was that King Boris was the enemy of democracy, of Bulgaria and of peace in the Balkans. The only hope for the Balkans was a union of all the South Slav countries including Slovenia, Croatia, Serbia and Bulgaria. This could never happen so long as King Boris remained in power. British policy, he understood, was to support King Boris. 'Well, he will stab you in the back just as his father did.'

Dimitrov's personality made a strong impression on me. Though of humble origin, Dimitrov was of very distinguished appearance. The gaze was frank and open, the mouth rather scornful, the hair wavy and brushed back from a high forehead, the hands long and tapering. He spoke French, though with more eloquence than regard for grammar; and I could well believe that he was a great orator in his own language. I did not try to argue with him. I did not know enough about Bulgaria. But I thought he had made a better case than Rendel.

There was too much snow to go out into the country, but Rendel's daughter, Ann, and Michael Padev, *The Times* correspondent, showed me Sofia by day and night. The city was cleaner and more orderly than Belgrade; its atmosphere less exuberant. By comparison with the Serbs, the Bulgars seemed dark and dour people, though with smouldering depths.

Back in my office in Belgrade I found Peter Brown, of Reuters. 'What are you doing for Christmas?' he asked. 'Nothing,' I said. 'I suppose we'll have to go to the Minister's party for the British colony.' 'I am going down to the Sanjak,' said Peter, 'to hear a left winger speak. Why don't you come too? We can leave tonight by the eleven o'clock train.' The Sanjak had been Turkish until 1912. Its capital was Novi Pazar, once the cockpit of the Balkans.

Our train, of course, was late, and we spent a chilly hour walking up and down the platform, discussing the questions of the hour. Prince Paul; was he really pro-Allied? The Opposition leaders; did they represent anyone but themselves? Serbian love of Russia; was it inspired by Communism or pan-Slavism? The left wing; how significant was it? The Legation; was it in touch with what was really going on? At last the train came in and we settled down in a crowded carriage and slept as best we could.

I was woken at six by a police official making a routine check of identity papers. He saluted smartly when I showed my diplomatic pass. We were running through rocky, desolate country deep in snow. There were high barren hills on both sides of the railway line, and the sky was clear. About half past nine in the morning we reached Rashka, a Serbian town on the border of the Sanjak. A five minute walk took us to the café where the first meeting was to be held. A crowd was already collecting. Most were peasants in homespun Serbian dress with sheepskin caps and bast sandals curling up at the toe; but a few wore Albanian skull caps with turbans wound round them and narrow jodhpur-like trousers cut below the hips. Only a handful were in town clothes. Two or three armed gendarmes stood around.

The orator we had come to hear and whom I now met for the first time was Dragolyub Jovanovitch, the leader of the left-wing Serbian Agrarian Party, a break-away from Milan Gavrilovitch's Peasant Party. He was a history professor at Belgrade University and spoke perfect French. Then in his early forties, he was short with rosy cheeks, a soft moustache, well fitting clothes and a broad-brimmed black hat. He was reputed never to drink or smoke or eat meat; and this gave him considerable prestige among a hard-drinking and, when money allowed, essentially carnivorous peasantry. In Belgrade he was widely regarded as a secret Communist. Green was the Peasant Party colour, and he was often compared to a water melon, green on the outside but red inside.

Jovanovitch had been exiled from Belgrade to the Sanjak during the dictatorship of Stoyadinovitch,[1] and was now returning in triumph. He spoke for some two hours and held his audience spellbound. Even with my limited knowledge of Serbian, I managed to follow most of his argument. He began with home affairs, dwelling at length on the mistakes of the different post-war Governments. The main economic problem, he went on, was how to modernise agriculture and ensure that the fruits of the peasants' labour were not stolen by the middlemen. His remedy was to develop agricultural co-operatives both for production and for distribution. He was against the collectivisation of agriculture. The Serbian peasant must never give up his land. It was different in Russia where there had been collective ownership in the *mir* even before the Revolution. Turning to the foreign scene he called for the union of all the South Slav peoples in a federation, stretching from the Adriatic to the Black Sea. He praised Britain and France for at last standing up to Germany, but argued that there need have been no war but for our earlier policy of

---

[1] Dr. Milan Stoyadinovitch, Prime Minister and virtual dictator of Yugoslavia 1936–39 —generally regarded as pro-Axis in his sympathies.

appeasement. He blamed us too for having driven the Russians into the arms of the Germans. But this, he forecast, could not last.

After the meeting the local peasant leaders invited Peter Brown and me to join them at lunch. We climbed to an upstairs room and were revived from the cold with much needed glasses of plum brandy, followed by a banquet of cheese pancakes and sucking pigs. One or two of the guests were Moslems, but seemed to enjoy the sucking pig and the plum brandy just as much as the Christians.

Dragolyub now asked us if we would like to join him for the rest of his tour. He was going on to Novi Pazar and then Syenitsa, where we would spend the night. We accepted at once and presently set out in a ramshackle car with Dragolyub and a henchman.

Just out of Rashka we entered the Sanjak and passed the grey stone barracks where, under the terms of the Treaty of Berlin, the Dual Monarchy had kept a garrison on what then was still Ottoman soil. The country was wild and barren and covered in snow. The villages—mostly Christian—seemed desperately poor. The little towns were in the main Moslem. We broke our journey at Novi Pazar, wandered round the town and into the big mosque built of red brick. The streets were filthy with slush, and there seemed to be no electric light.

Dragolyub's business in Novi Pazar was with his party committee and took some time. When we drove on it was pitch dark. But, presently, the moon came out and we could see the road ahead of us, winding into the flank of a cliff which rose some 2,000 ft. above the plain. At the top we found ourselves on a plateau, covered with snow and stretching away to the horizon. We drove on for about an hour and then came to a small town with two or three minarets. We went into the only restaurant, a bare barrack room with a single long wooden table. I drank hot plum brandy. Dragolyub drank tea. It was about nine o'clock in the evening.

We fell to talking about the peasant problem and I asked about their circumstances and their psychology. What did they eat? How did they think? What did they want? Dragolyub soon realised that no amount of explanation could really convey much about Serbian peasant life to a young Englishman. 'Do you really want to know our peasants?' he asked. I said I did. 'Very well,' he said, 'we shall go now and see them.' A few minutes later we were driving back along the plateau. We drove for perhaps twenty minutes. Then he got out of the car and leaving the road led the way across country. We had nothing to light us but the moon.

An observer would have found us a curious party, the peasant leader stumbling about in the snow in his town shoes and broad-brimmed black hat and talking all the time like a character in a Russian novel. 'The Peasants . . . All that is good comes from the land . . . They are real aristocrats yet there is no privilege or corruption among them . . . Such great souls, such great poverty. . . .' Behind him followed the henchman, the chauffeur, Peter Brown and myself. Above us the moon.

After an hour or so, we came upon a straggling cluster of long low buildings. I was rather surprised that no dogs barked, though later in the night we heard the howl of wolves. There were no lights shining. Dragolyub knocked on a door. There was an exchange of shouts; a door opened and we were led into a long bare room with two big square box beds and some benches arranged around a rough table in an angle of the wall. At the other end of the room a fire glowed on an open hearth.

Our host was a grizzled open-faced Serbian peasant. With him was his brother, their male children, and an army officer who had resigned his commission two years before 'to go peasant'. The womenfolk, big-boned, ruddy-cheeked, and dressed in thick padded garments, came in to greet us and then stayed in the background awaiting orders.

These peasants were too poor to offer us meat. They could only serve us cheese, sour milk, bread and gherkins, and offered a strong white spirit, but made of grapes not plums, to drink. In summer they had to walk two miles to the nearest well. In winter they simply melted snow. For wood they went fifteen miles to the nearest mountains where there were still bears. But their wants were few. All their clothes were homespun. All their food home grown. Their only luxuries were paraffin, coffee, salt and sugar.

We were welcomed with grave ceremony and the family plainly felt honoured at having two foreigners as guests. After the initial courtesies, I got them with Dragolyub's help to talk about themselves. One of the older men remembered life under the Turks. No, it had not been so bad. There was great freedom. The terrible thing was the insecurity. If you had a good horse, it would be stolen sooner or later by a Turkish officer. Justice was arbitrary and so weak that you had to be your own policeman. In those days, everyone had been armed.

When we had finished eating, one of the brothers brought out a *gusla*, a one-stringed musical instrument, played with a primitive bow. For the next hour he sang us some of the Serbian epics. The first one was about the battle of Kossovo when King Lazar had chosen certain death and defeat rather than submit to the Sultan. But by the end of the evening my host was singing about the Balkan Wars, and the Salonica Front.

I shared a bed with Peter Brown and one of the brothers. The bed was of straw and sacking, but I was tired and slept heavily. It was rather a shock on waking to find what bed fellows I had collected.

I got up and washed my face in the snow. The sun was just rising and the day fine. Breakfast consisted of the same raw spirit we had drunk the night before, and again cheese, sour milk, bread and gherkins. It was

Christmas Day and we told them of our holiday customs at home. They listened gravely and then removing a floor board produced an ancient rifle. We went outside with it and they let off a few rounds in our honour.

Presently, a crowd began to collect; Peter took photographs; and the word went round that Dragolyub Jovanovitch was there. People came over from neighbouring villages, the richer peasants riding on stocky ponies and many carrying rifles and knives. There was much milling around, and then we set out together, an army some three hundred strong marching on Syenitsa. On our way we made frequent halts to drink coffee and talk with influential villagers. As we progressed our army grew and we must have numbered five or six hundred when we debouched onto the main square of Syenitsa. A crowd of townsmen was already gathering. It included Orthodox priests and Moslem *hodjas*, Serbs, Albanians, soldiers from the garrison and a few gendarmes. Altogether there must have been an audience of two thousand.

Dragolyub spoke for nearly three hours. There was snow on the ground, but it was quite warm standing in the sun. He made a few sly digs at the priests and *hodjas* and at the gendarmes. There was much applause at this and once or twice some angry but approving growls when he attacked the Government. The rest of the speech was on the same lines as the day before.

After the meeting, Peter Brown and I went to look at the town. Syenitsa was, I believe, largely destroyed in the Second World War. In those days it was mainly built of wood with a solid Turkish fort and a domed mosque both of red brick. About four o'clock there was a lunch. It consisted mostly of sucking pig, but this time, out of deference to the Moslem guests, there was also sheep. When it was over, we drove back through Novi Pazar and just caught the night train to Belgrade.

Most of the Serbian Opposition leaders wanted Yugoslavia to align herself more closely with Britain and France. Unfortunately, neither of the Entente Governments was in a position to give them any serious backing. Very different was the situation of Dr. Milan Stoyadinovitch, the former dictator. Stoyadinovitch was generally regarded as the friend of Germany; and Germany was the dominant economic influence in Yugoslavia as well as the strongest military power on her borders. These things made Stoyadinovitch the most powerful man in Belgrade outside the Government and potentially the most dangerous.

I thought it would be interesting to meet Stoyadinovitch. A mutual friend spoke to him and I was told to ring him up direct. I did so and was put through to the great man himself. He invited me to come and see him next day. 'Yes, Your Excellency,' I answered, 'that would suit

me very well. When would you like me to come?' 'Oh,' he replied, 'Come
in the afternoon.' 'Yes, Your Excellency,' I said, rather shyly. 'But when
would you like me to come in the afternoon, at what time?' 'Oh,' he said,
'you British are impossible. Come punctually between three and six.'

On reaching his house I was shown into a small study crowded with
photographs. Stoyadinovitch was heavily built with a rather florid face,
sparse black hair and a black moustache. He gave an impression of energy
and for a man of his weight moved surprisingly quickly. He motioned me
to an armchair and offered me tea and whisky in turn. I explained that I
was trying to learn about Yugoslav politics and was anxious to hear his
views at first hand. It was so easy for a man's views to be misrepresented
by his enemies. He laughed at this and said that I had, no doubt, been
told that he was pro-German and Hitler's man. Well there was no truth
in this at all. He was neither pro-German nor pro-Italian and never had
been.

As he spoke my eye wandered round the signed photographs in the
room. Hitler glared sternly out of a silver frame. Mussolini's chin stuck
out from behind tortoiseshell. Ciano was there. So were Goering and
Goebbels. He must have caught a look of incredulity in my face; for he
went on to say that, though I might find it hard to believe, he hoped that
Britain and France would win the War. This would be much the best
thing for Yugoslavia. 'But then, my young friend,' he went on, 'I am not
so sure whether you will.' He then explained at some length that he had
pursued a policy of friendship towards the Axis Powers, partly because of
our weakness over Abyssinia and the Rhineland, and partly because this
was the policy that London and even Paris had advised. It was not he but
the Western Allies who had undermined the Little Entente and allowed
the annexation of Austria and the rape of Czechoslovakia. As a result of
our mistakes his country now had a common frontier with Germany
and, to the best of his knowledge neither Britain nor France was in a
position to send a single soldier or aircraft to help Yugoslavia if she were
attacked. In these circumstances, he thought it his duty to be a realist
and to keep his relations with the Axis leaders in good repair. There was
a real danger that the Germans might think it in their interest to break
up Yugoslavia and throw the bits as so many bones to their Italian,
Hungarian and Bulgarian satellites. The Allies were in no position to
stop them from doing so. But, by skilful diplomacy, the Yugoslavs
themselves might deflect the thunderbolt. They could never join the Axis
camp; but they must play for time and hope for a compromise peace
between the Axis and the Entente before the War spread to the Balkans.

I suggested that Stoyadinovitch's line was not very different from
Prince Paul's. He agreed but went on to say: 'The Prince is neither a
Serb nor a soldier. He is a White Russian and an intellectual. He knows

what has to be done. But he has not got the personality to carry the Army or the people with him. I am perhaps the only man who could.'

He asked me to come for another talk two days later, which I did. There was an attractive buccaneering quality about the man best illustrated perhaps by an anecdote then circulating in Belgrade. According to this, Goering had taken Stoyadinovitch over the Mercedes-Benz works, in the course of an official visit, and had presented him with the latest model of the car. Stoyadinovitch had declined the offer. His people, he had explained, would not understand if he accepted such a present from the Germans. But he would like to buy one of the cars. How much did they cost? Goering had replied with a bow, 'For you, Prime Minister, it would be £100.' 'In that case,' said Stoyadinovitch, 'I'll have six.'

I do not believe that Stoyadinovitch was a German agent. But he saw himself as a rival to Prince Paul and might well have tried to outbid him for German support. Prince Paul evidently thought the same; and, on my second visit, I noticed there were two policemen outside his door who took the number of my car. Not long afterwards Stoyadinovitch asked me to lunch. But before the appointed day came round, the Government had exiled him to a remote village in Serbia.

I had learnt a lot during these six months in Belgrade; and the Minister seemed pleased with my work. Yet during the first month or two of 1940, I began to wonder whether that work was serving any good purpose. My duty as a Press Attaché was to try and influence Yugoslav opinion in favour of the Allies. But Legation policy was to keep the temperature low, to support Prince Paul, and at all costs avoid provoking the Germans. To reconcile these two aims was a difficult and frustrating business.

Meanwhile my twenty-first birthday came upon me. I only had a small flat, but as a diplomat could buy drink duty free. I accordingly invited as many of my friends as the flat could hold. There were speeches, some gypsy players were imported from a neighbouring café, the wine flowed freely, and several glasses were shattered against the wall. The sun was already well up when the last guests departed; and I barely had time for a bath and shave before my first appointment in the office.

14

Revolt in Albania

Early in 1940, the staff of the Legation was strengthened by the arrival of an Assistant Naval Attaché, Lieutenant Sandy Glen.[1] Glen was short, prematurely bald, with small eyes glinting behind powerful spectacles. He had been to Balliol, had explored the Arctic and had worked as a banker. He pretended to know all the answers, though very much with his tongue in his cheek, and did, in fact, know quite a lot of them. We soon became friends and, presently, decided to pool our resources and take a spacious flat with a view to enlarging our circle of Yugoslav acquaintances.

Glen spoke little of his professional activities. But it was soon clear to me that they had little to do with the Navy, and were by no means as blamelessly 'diplomatic' as my own. I was, therefore, not too surprised when one evening soon after my twenty-first birthday, he told me that 'The Chief' of his 'Show' was on his way to Belgrade and would be using our flat as his office. Their work, he implied, was very secret. So would I please keep out of the way and not mention the visit to anyone, even to the Minister?

The Master Spy duly arrived, self-enveloped in an aura of mystery and urgency. He had grey wavy hair, thick horn-rimmed spectacles, a green complexion and long tapering fingers. He ensconced himself in the flat and proceeded to hold several meetings with Sandy and other members of the British community whom, in my innocence, I had hitherto regarded as ordinary businessmen.

I kept out of the way, apart from bed and breakfast. But on the second day of the visit, Sandy came into my office looking distinctly worried.

'The Chief,' he said, 'has asked me for a note on the situation in Albania. Of course it's got to be different from what the F.O. give him. I know nothing about the beastly place, and wondered if you could help me?'

The reader will remember that during the Spanish Civil War, I had had one or two talks about Albania with Sir Robert Hodgson. This was

[1] Now Sir Alexander Glen.

the limit of my knowledge of the country. It had seldom figured in my talks in Belgrade except as a possible base for an Italian attack on Yugoslavia. Most Serbs, indeed, were as ignorant of the Albanian mountains as most Englishmen, in the seventeenth century, had been of the Scottish Highlands. Nevertheless, Albania seemed an intriguing subject and I sensed rather than saw an opportunity of more interesting work than the press office could offer.

'Yes, of course,' I answered. 'I'll try and let you have a short memo. on the latest trends by dinner tonight.'

For a moment after the door had closed behind Sandy, I was at a loss to know how to begin. Then I rang up Ralph Parker, of *The Times*, and asked if he knew any Albanians.

'Yes,' came his imperturbable reply. 'I know two. If it's really urgent I'll try to get them round for a drink this evening.' I said it was urgent.

Accordingly, at six o'clock, I went round to Parker's flat and there was introduced, as a fellow journalist, to Gani Bey and Said Bey Kryeziu. They were the first Albanians I had ever met and I had no real idea at the time who they were. We talked for perhaps an hour; and they told me what they knew of the situation inside Albania. I then went back to the Legation and concocted a short memorandum based upon our talk. I handed it to 'The Chief' after dinner, modestly expressing the hope that 'it might throw some light on the general picture'.

The great man glanced thoughtfully at the paper. 'This,' he said, 'is very significant.' He asked me one or two questions about it; and, as he knew even less about Albania than I did, I had little difficulty in answering. He then asked if he might take the paper with him to Athens where he was going next day. I made no objection. There, as far as I was concerned, the matter rested.

'The Chief' was, in fact, Chief of the Balkan Unit of the 'D' Section. This was the creation of a resourceful Major of the Sappers, Lawrence Grand, a man gifted with unusual powers of persuading his superiors and enthusing his subordinates. 'D' Section was quite distinct from 'C' Section, the Secret Intelligence Service. Its object was to subvert the enemy's war effort in his own and in neutral territories. By subversion was meant those operations against the enemy which lay outside the province of the Armed Forces and the Departments of State. It included such things as the sabotage of enemy factories or ships, the blowing up of his communications, and the organisation and support of 'Resistance' in occupied territories.

Later in the War, as the Resistance Movements grew in importance, 'D' Section became first 'SO2' and then 'SOE', with a Minister in the Cabinet and a galaxy of generals and high officials on its establishment. But, at this time, it was still a very small and intimate club, so secret that even our heads of mission were kept in ignorance of its exact activities and personnel. Its official funds were very limited; but Lawrence Grand had persuaded his friend Chester Beatty, the mining magnate, to second a number of his staff to 'D' Section while keeping them on his payroll.

Now it so happened that Lawrence Grand and the 'Chief' had set their hearts on organising a revolt against the Italians in Albania. They believed that it would tie down large numbers of Italian troops and weaken Italy's ability to wage war. The Foreign Office, however, took a different view. We had great interests in the Mediterranean but very limited military power. Our first object was to try and keep the Italians out of the war and not to provoke them by fomenting a revolt which in their view would probably go off at half cock.

The strength of the Foreign Office position was that they were supposed to be the experts on Albania. Several of their officials had served in Tirana. No-one in the 'D' Section had ever been there. My meeting with 'The Chief' changed all this. He quickly convinced himself that he had discovered a real expert on Albania and, being an active man, set out to convince others. From Athens he penned a dispatch to Lawrence Grand which, among other doubtless more profound observations, contained the following statement: 'Our staff in Belgrade would be greatly strengthened by the co-option of Julian Amery, whose expert knowledge of Albanian affairs would be an invaluable asset to the organisation.' With it he enclosed my report which at least had the merit of containing fresh and as it happened accurate news from Albania. This was duly circulated in Whitehall, though without quoting its source, and rather inaccurately described as 'an example' of the kind of information on Albania available to the 'D' Section.

With the help of this new ammunition, Lawrence Grand managed to win this particular battle in the Whitehall war. 'D' Section was authorised to prepare plans for a revolt in Albania and to open communications with potential Albanian centres of resistance.

In the process of arguing their case, the high-ups in the 'D' Section had ended by convincing themselves that I really was an expert on Albania. Their Chief man in the Balkans, Julius Hanau, was accordingly instructed to ask me to take the work in hand.

Hanau was a very experienced arms dealer, steeped in the cultures of France and Germany and learned in history. He was no less familiar with those subterfuges which, then as now, play an essential part in the sale of arms; the exploitation of personal rivalries between Ministers, the bribing of officials and the making of suitable presents to the right people. The Balkans held few secrets from him; and it was in his hands that the threads of our network throughout the Peninsula came together.

Hanau asked me to lunch and told me of his instructions. He knew much more about Albania than I did, but he was not seriously concerned by this. I was not, of course, the ideal choice for the job, but, if he were once to query my appointment, the whole decision to prepare a revolt in Albania might be put in question. Nobody knew much about Albania anyway, and the few Englishmen who did were probably quite unsuitable for the job. There was no reason why I should not quickly become an expert. Albania was, after all, a very small place and I was young enough to learn. Anyway, he added, the best revolutionaries had usually been young, and, taking down a book from his shelves, he checked that Danton and Robespierre were both only thirty-four when the guillotine fell. At twenty-one, thirty-four sounded to me like maturity, but I kept my own counsel on this and said I would do my best.

Hanau asked me to tell no-one of this new assignment but to continue my work as assistant Press Attaché. Presently, he would have a talk with my immediate chief. Meanwhile, I should just have to do two jobs and make do with less sleep. If I needed money for the Albanian project, I had only to ask. Then as I left him he said: 'Remember we want live heroes, not dead heroes, and if there are going to be any dead heroes, let them be Italians or Germans.'

Childs by this time had gone to Paris and his place as Press Attaché had been taken by Ronald Syme, the historian of the Roman Revolution. Syme was as frustrated as I was by trying to make pro-Allied propaganda for a Legation which only wanted to keep down the temperature. He was all for cloak and dagger work and gladly agreed to turn a blind eye to my new activities.

So there I was entrusted with the preparation of a revolt in Albania. It was only a few days since my twenty-first birthday, but the dreams of boyhood were coming true with a vengeance. I thought myself very lucky.

The first thing was to build up an organisation. It so happened that 'D' Section had just sent out to Belgrade a young lawyer called John Bennett.[1] He was a wild man, gaunt, loose limbed and prematurely bald. The operation which he had come to work on had been cancelled and he was at a loose end. I accordingly asked him to help me over Albania. We had wireless and bag communications with 'D' Section in London and now began to ask them for reports, statistics and guide-books. These slowly trickled in; and Sandy Glen was able to get the latest Italian order of battle in Albania from the Yugoslav General Staff.

Skoplye was the most important Yugoslav centre near to the Albanian

[1] Later H.M. High Commissioner in Barbados (1970).

A.M.—F

border. We had a Consulate there and I thought it would be useful to have a man of our own attached to it. One morning out riding with Ralph Parker, I asked him if he would take on the job. He was a trained observer and had had some experience of underground work in Prague, where he had helped to rescue Czechs from the Gestapo. He at once agreed and resigned from *The Times* to take on the job.

Greece also had a land frontier with Albania. And we, accordingly, asked 'D' Section to open Albanian sections in Athens and Salonika. In the longer run, a revolt in Albania would also need support from the Middle Eastern Command. We accordingly secured the appointment of Major Cripps, a former instructor of the Albanian gendarmerie, to Wavell's staff.

I also remembered that Hodgson had spoken very warmly of a Colonel Frank Stirling. Stirling had been military adviser to Lawrence in the Arab Revolt. Then, after the First World War, had raised a team of British instructors to train the Albanian gendarmerie. Later he had reorganised the Albanian administration and had remained an adviser to King Zog until the Italians had made his position untenable.

Stirling was at length tracked down in some recess of the censorship department. He became a King's Messenger and, in this guise, maintained liaison between the different Albanian groups in Belgrade, Athens and Istanbul, and with Wavell's headquarters in Cairo.

Such was the British framework of our Albanian organisation. But while it was still in the making, we also were busy looking for potential allies in Albania and among the Albanian exiles.

On Altmaier's advice, I went to consult Yovan Djonovitch. Djonovitch had at one time been leader of the Republican Party in Yugoslavia. Later on, however, he accepted an invitation from King Alexander to become Minister in Tirana for the specific purpose of counteracting the growth of Italian influence in Albania.

Djonovitch was a Montenegrin with pale blue eyes and a little imperial beard. He was the most forceful of the Yugoslav politicians I met and, like Odysseus, a man of many devices.

Djonovitch had kept in touch with Albanian affairs, and I spent many hours learning from him about the country's tribal structure and its factions and leading men. Like most Montenegrins, he loved talking, and thanks to his instruction I soon became quite knowledgeable about Albania.

The most important Albanian exiles in Belgrade were in fact Gani and Said Kryeziu, the two I had met in Parker's flat. The Kryezius were a family from Kossovo with a powerful following on both sides of the Yugoslav-Albanian border. They were said—for such was the political currency in Albania—to be worth two thousand rifles at short call. The family had been in exile for several years and there was a blood feud between them and King Zog whom they accused of having murdered their elder brother, Tzena. But in the interests of national unity, they were ready, so they told us, to accept Zog's leadership until Albania was free again.

Gani was short and fair with an open countenance and a distinctly military bearing. He was a man of few words, but when he chose to speak, very clear and concise. He impressed me by his accuracy and by his refusal to bargain in negotiations. This was so unusual in a Balkan politician that I, at first, thought it must conceal some doubly tortuous design. It did not.

Gani's younger brother, Said, was studying in Paris but on Gani's instructions returned to Belgrade, pawning his gold watch to pay for the railway ticket.[1] Said was tall and dark, and, although from a noble family, had left-wing sympathies. A third brother, Hassan, lived on the family estates near the Albanian border and maintained a close connection with the family's following inside Albania.

With a little help from us this connection was developed into an effective courier system and we were soon receiving regular reports from the whole of north and central Albania down to the capital, Tirana. Parallel lines of communication were opened from Skoplye, Salonika, and Athens with the help of other groups of exiles. Thus within six weeks of the start of the operation, we were beginning to get a clear picture of what was happening in Albania. This suggested that the people were impatient of Italian rule and well disposed towards the Allies, though still uncertain of our victory. In the mountains the tribal chiefs encouraged our approaches promising but also asking much.

The collation of intelligence was an essential preliminary to our work and also a good test of our organisation. But it was only a means to an end. Our end was to organise a rising against the Italians. The first step, here, was to form an Albanian Revolutionary Movement which would include as many enemies of Italy as we could persuade to work together. It was still too soon to launch such a movement inside Albania. So we decided instead to build up our organisation in Yugoslavia. There were more than half a million Albanians in Yugoslavia and, so long as the Yugoslav authorities turned a blind eye, we could recruit agents and even guerrillas from among them and begin feeding in propaganda and rifles across the border. The Revolt might thus be securely mounted on neutral soil and carried into Albania if war should come to the Balkans.

[1] In 1949 after years of imprisonment, fighting and exile Said stopped in Paris and found the watch still at the pawnshop. He redeemed it and gave it to me as the author of most of his troubles.

On the advice of the Kryeziu brothers we invited Abas Kupi, who was then living in Istanbul, to join us. Abas Kupi could neither read nor write. Indeed, it was only with difficulty that he could sign his own name. But he had been a famous guerrilla leader in his own country against King Zog and then, poacher turned gamekeeper, had become the most successful of Zog's gendarmerie commanders. He had put up the only effective resistance to the Italian invasion in 1939, and, by holding up the Italians for thirty-six hours, had covered the King's escape. This had made him a national hero.

I was struck, at my first meeting with Abas Kupi, by his pronounced likeness, especially in profile, to certain portraits of Napoleon, a likeness accentuated by a lock of hair brushed forward on his forehead to hide a scar. He spoke little but with a charm of expression and gesture and a warmth of tone which overcame the impersonality of interpreted conversation. Although illiterate, the man was no peasant, but delicately made and with all a highlander's grace of movement.

Abas Kupi was a staunch Monarchist. But with his and Gani's encouragement we now approached Mustafa Djinishi, a member of the Albanian Communist Party. The influence of the Albanian communists was said to be small. But we wanted to have Djinishi for his personal qualities and were curious to see whether his party would let him work with us. Rather to our surprise he accepted.

By bringing the Kryezius, Abas Kupi and Djinishi together, we had in effect created a united front of Albanian Resistance. Until that moment these three men had been at daggers drawn. Now, thanks to our intervention and encouragement, they had come together. They became great personal friends, but would sometimes tell us that, as soon as they had driven the Italians from Albania, they would have to fight it out among themselves. We smiled indulgently at such prophecies. In the summer of 1940, the headaches of victory still seemed remote.

The United Front was the fruit of long hours of patient planning in the extra territorial security of the Legation, and of conspiratorial meetings in dark corners of Belgrade. We changed our meeting places frequently, though our favourite was a deserted flat on the top storey of a modern building. It was unfurnished except for a rickety table and two benches left by the owner.

We took infinite pains to keep these meetings secret and would approach the *rendezvous* by devious routes, changing taxis on the way or parking our cars some distance off. The Italians, indeed, were soon on our trail. But we tended to overrate their efficiency. Some months later, when I had left Yugoslavia and was living in Istanbul, we intercepted an Italian intelligence report. This said that I was still living in Belgrade but had grown a beard and was living under a spurious name! It turned out that the Italians were busy shadowing the innocent and unsuspecting representative of the British Council.

The Albanian leaders were of exemplary discretion. But the same could not always be said of their followers. One afternoon I returned with Sandy Glen from lunch to find two or three hundred Albanian wood cutters, variously armed with axes and knives, squatting on the pavement outside the Legation. A few of them were in earnest conversation with John Bennett. He presently explained what was afoot. Someone, it seemed, had told them that the British would pay them a hundred dinars each to go and wreck the Italian Legation. They were keen on the job, but being prudent men, had come to collect their money in advance.

Nevertheless, the work made progress. Our couriers passed through the Kossovo into Albania, preaching the aims of the United Front and gathering political and military information. Next, by way of propaganda, we began to send wagon-loads of maize across the border and distributed them to our supporters. Later, rifles and ammunition were concealed beneath the maize.

15

An Austrian Mission

By the end of April Hanau's activities in the Balkans had been largely 'blown'. The Germans demanded his expulsion from Yugoslavia and he judged it wiser to return to London. His place was taken by Bill Bailey.

Bailey was a powerfully-built metallurgist from Chester Beatty's organisation. He had a round head with straight black hair parted in the middle and hooded eyes which seemed to jump open when he was surprised or amused. He reminded me of photographs I had seen of Al Capone. Bailey had a remarkable gift for languages and spoke French, German, Russian and Serbo-Croat fluently. He loved the good things of life; but in the isolation of mining camps had also read widely.

I had first met Bailey some months earlier when he had rung the door bell of my flat at seven o'clock in the morning. He carried a letter of introduction from Sandy Glen in one hand and a heavy suitcase in the other. Would I be good enough to keep the suitcase till the evening. He did not like to leave it in his hotel or in his car. I asked what was in it. 'Dynamite,' he replied in his velvet voice and pushed it under my bed. It was, indeed, some explosive which he had brought from the Treptcha mine in South Serbia the day before and would take away that night for use in a sabotage operation.

I had found him from this first experience excellent company and wholly reliable. If we had to lose Hanau, I could have asked for no better Chief to work for than Bailey.

Bailey, like Hanau, had to run considerable risks to get our operations moving fast enough to keep up with the war. The Gestapo, we thought, were already after him and, since we only wanted 'live heroes', he spent a strange conspiratorial existence, sleeping each night in a different flat or hotel. For the same reason, he seldom made exact appointments, on the sound principle that it is much easier for 'them' to 'get' you, if they know where you are going to be and when.

I had asked him for an urgent meeting and expected him in my office at the Legation in the course of the morning. The Battle of France was going very badly. The French Government had left Paris; and, I was anxious to get Bailey's approval of our plans for emergency action against the Italians in Albania.

He came into my office at about midday on 14 June and handed me a telegram. 'Here, read this while I put a call through,' he said. I read:

Telegram from London to Belgrade . . . following personal for Bailey.

A. Chiefs of Staff consider every attempt must be made to divert Axis efforts from France.

B. R.A.F. have agreed drop ammunition and small arms in Austria in event of revolt breaking out there.

C. Situation critical. Advise earliest what prospects of revolt in Austria.

It seemed a forlorn hope but then it was a desperate situation.[1]

'Is there anything I can do to help?' I asked.

'Yes, there is,' said Bailey. 'You will leave tonight by car for the Austrian frontier and take with you Dr. Becker. He is our Austrian expert and will tell you all about our Austrian friends in the car. But the doctor is erratic and has only just come out of jail. He will travel with false papers. If the Yugoslavs stop you, your story is that you are going to the British Consulate in Ljubljana and that Becker is an agricultural expert interested in buying food for the Army in the Middle East. But your main job is to get him there and back safely—your diplomatic immunity should help here—and to see that he doesn't get knocked off by the Gestapo. You may also have to keep him on the rails in any talks with the Austrians. It will, in any case, encourage them to see a real Englishman. Tell the Legation you are down with 'flu. I'll come round to your flat at about eight tonight and you should be ready to start an hour later.' He paused for a moment and then added: 'This is a dangerous game. As you know, we have already had one man killed in Zagreb. The Doctor is a marked man, and you may well have both the local secret police and the Gestapo after you. You had better be armed. Take this one. It is light but quite powerful enough at close quarters.' And he handed me a small automatic pistol.

I spent the afternoon discussing our Albanian plans with Bailey and John Bennett and then went back to my flat for a short rest. When I got up again I had a look at the pistol. It was loaded with a bullet 'up the spout'. But the safety catch was on. I thought it as well to test the catch and, aiming at the pillow, squeezed the trigger. There was a loud report, and a neat hole appeared in the pillow case. A few minutes later Bailey came in. I told him what had happened and asked if he could mend the catch. He fumbled with it for a moment and then pointing it at me said:

[1] The text of the telegram quoted above is taken from a note made from memory a few days later. It is unlikely, therefore, to be an exact reproduction of the original, though the sense is clearly the same.

'Now it's as safe as houses.' I must have looked scared for he turned the gun instead towards the bed. There was a second loud report. He put it in his pocket and gave me his own—a rather heavier one—instead.

Bailey led me in his own car as far as the bridge across the Sava, where he had arranged to meet Becker. It was pouring with rain and the mud from the roads had already obliterated our number plates. Just before we came to the bridge Bailey drew into the kerb. A man in a raincoat stepped out of the shadows and, after a quick word with Bailey, walked over to my car and got in beside me. We crossed the river and drove northwards.

Dr. Alfred Becker was a stout, jovial fellow of about forty-five with a prominent chin, but rather weak eyes. He loved good living, as I presently discovered, but cared even more for his ideals and had accepted poverty and hardship for them. The son of an eccentric Prussian Junker, he had fought in the First World War and then had made a considerable success of managing his estates. But his 'parlour pink' opinions and his marriage to a Jewess had put him in the bad books of the Nazis. He had found life under Hitler intolerable and had emigrated rather than put up with it. He had worked with different German *émigré* groups in France and Austria and eventually when his funds ran out had retired to Belgrade where he earned a small retainer from the Ministry of Agriculture.

From Belgrade Becker had tried to make contact with Socialist friends in Austria and, in the process, had been brought into touch with the Slovene Irridentist Movement. There was a sizeable Slovene population in both Austria and Italy and it was a long-term aim of the Belgrade Government to bring the districts where Slovenes were in a majority—notably Istria—into Yugoslavia. The Yugoslav authorities thus gave discreet encouragement to the Irridentist Movement. One of its leaders, indeed, was a high official in the Ministry of Interior and controlled the organisation from his office.

In the course of their struggle against Hitler and Mussolini the Slovenes had made working arrangements with Austrian and Italian Socialists. Here plainly was a golden opportunity to penetrate into Germany and Italy, and Becker had put the Slovenes in touch with Hanau, acting himself as the go-between. In the hope of Allied backing for their cause after the war, the Slovenes distributed subversive propaganda for us in Austria and north Italy and collected intelligence. They also opened a line for us to the Austrian Socialists and began with them to attack German railway communications. Becker's part in all this was suspected by the Gestapo; and the German Legation had asked for his expulsion. This the Yugoslav Government refused. Instead they had put him in prison for a couple of weeks to cool his ardour, and to show the Germans they were doing something. He had only been let out the day before.

Our immediate plan was to see the Slovene Irridentist leaders in Ljubljana. It seemed just conceivable that they could start some sort of diversionary movement in Austria and persuade their Catholic and Socialist allies to join in. The Doctor was not too sanguine. Intelligence, propaganda and sabotage was one thing. To start an insurrection was another. On the other hand, there were hardly any German troops left in Austria. So there was just a chance that something could be done.

We drove through the night without incident, reaching Osiyek, with its big Bata shoe factory, about dawn. Here we turned south to the Zagreb road and pulled up, at about nine o'clock in the morning, to breakfast at a small inn off wood strawberries, coffee and brandy. Petrol was our chief worry. It was strictly rationed in the provinces and even diplomats needed a written order from the local chief of gendarmerie to buy any. Our tank was running low and I kicked myself for not having brought a couple of spare cans. We should look pretty silly if the Battle of France was lost because our car was immobilised on the road to Zagreb.

The village where we breakfasted boasted a single petrol pump. I blew my horn and was answered by a small boy. He had never seen a diplomatic identity card before and clearly could not read. But he was longing to pump some petrol and was easily persuaded that I was entitled to it. He filled up the tank and provided us with two extra tins. We drove on through Zagreb and reached Ljubljana about seven o'clock in the evening. I had driven for nearly twenty-two hours with very few stops and over appalling roads.

I asked the receptionist at the hotel if there was any news from France. He said there were rumours of a Cabinet crisis but nothing certain except that the Germans were still advancing. We dined in the Doctor's room and, at about midnight, managed to reach our contact with the Slovenes on the telephone. I found him in an all night café and asked him to arrange an urgent meeting with the Slovene leaders next morning.

We met them about ten o'clock on the morning of 16 June and explained our purpose. The telephone lines across the border were still open and our Slovene friends presently reported that they had got through to their colleagues in Austria. Two of them would come over towards evening and meet us at an inn near the border.

We changed to look like holiday makers out for a day in the mountains and then drove off with one of the Slovenes. We reached the inn in the late afternoon and found the parlour deserted. A radio was blaring in the corner. An hour or so later two other 'tourists' walked in. They were Slovenes from the Austrian side and had crossed the border on foot.

Becker explained our plan to them in German, stressing the urgent need to help the Battle of France. They discussed it in Slovene with our Slovene companion. Presently, they reverted to German and said they were willing to try if supplies arrived. But they would need the best part of a week to consult their colleagues and arrange for the reception of parachute drops. We had begun discussing a possible timetable when the music stopped and the radio went over to the news. The announcer reported that M. Paul Reynaud had resigned and that the aged Marshal Pétain had become Prime Minister. It was expected that he would ask for an armistice. There was no point now in continuing the discussion. The Battle of France was lost. We were too late. Our friends from the Austrian side shook hands with us sadly and went out into the night. It would be a long night for all Europe.

We thought it wiser not to delay in Slovenia after this meeting, and we accordingly drove south eastwards, spending the night in a bug-ridden café near the Hungarian border. There was no hurry now to get back and we continued next day at a leisurely pace, taking turns at the wheel. We reached Novi Sad at sunset and went to the best restaurant promising ourselves a good dinner.

In the washroom of the restaurant we were stopped by an agent of the Yugoslav Secret Police who wanted to see our papers and asked where we had come from. I told him that I was a British diplomat and that he could wait for answers to his questions until I had answered the calls of nature. Just then a Serbian officer, whom I had not noticed, came up and said to him: 'The gentlemen say they are from the British Legation. Stop worrying them. They've got enough trouble on their hands without you.' The policeman slunk away, and, after a good dinner, we continued to Belgrade with the Doctor at the wheel. Back in my flat I telephoned to Bailey: 'Too late I am afraid.' 'Lots of things will be too late now,' he replied, 'it may well be the Balkans next.'

16

A Coup d'État?

The fall of France transformed the situation in the Balkans. The balance
of power in Europe was shattered.   On the Continent the only counter-
weight to the Wehrmacht was now the Red Army; and any hope of
Soviet intervention seemed forlorn. The only land forces engaged anywhere against the Axis Powers were the British Armies fighting far away
in Libya and Abyssinia.

Yugoslavia, meanwhile, was encircled by a ring of hostile powers.
The Germans and Hungarians threatened her from the north; the
Italians from Istria and from Albania. Bulgaria looked greedily at the
Macedonian provinces. The only friendly frontier lay across the narrow
corridor of the Vardar valley running south to Greece.

For Yugoslavs the moral consequences of the fall of France were
almost graver than the material. Until then no Serb and very few Croats
had been prepared to take an openly pro-German stand. Everyone knew
that Yugoslavia was a creation of the Allied victory in 1918 and that all
her neighbours, save Rumania and Greece, had territorial claims against
her. A German victory was almost bound to mean the dismemberment
of the State, and though his Government might be formally neutral, no
patriotic Yugoslav could be neutral at heart. But with the collapse of the
French Army there was a new situation. Germany's victory seemed the
most likely outcome to the War; and now the Croat Separatists, the paid
Fifth Columnists and the defeatists crept out from the holes where they
had been hiding. Worse still, even respectable citizens, whose sympathies
were all with the Allies, began to face the fact that they might have to
come to terms with a victorious Germany.

The German Legation now became the dominant power in Belgrade.
Their influence was soon felt. Our news agency and magazine were sup-
pressed. Henceforth, only the German viewpoint was presented in the
press. Pro-British editors or journalists were dismissed or transferred.
Radio Belgrade passed under the control of a known German agent.
Officials in the Police or Ministry of Interior who had worked with us
lost their jobs. The General Staff withdrew their support from the Slovene
Irridentist Movement. The Masonic Lodges, long a stronghold of Serbian

patriotism, were banned. There was a new drive to suppress Communism in the universities; and the first anti-semitic slogans appeared. Meanwhile 'Instruction Battalions' of German troops had entered Rumania where King Carol had been forced to repudiate the now useless British guarantee.

I caught something of the growing mood of despair in the course of a drive with two members of the Peasant Party. We stopped in a village and they took me to a very poor farm, the home of one of their supporters. The old man showed me round his small plot grumbling all the time. He wondered how he would feed himself through the winter and, pointing at his only pig, a lean grey beast, said to me with a high-pitched laugh: 'I call him Churchill; Yes, Churchill.' I was inclined to take offence but he put his hand on my arm and explained: 'I call him Churchill because he is my last hope.'

In fact, many Serbs also nursed another hope. Under the Tzars it had always been Russian policy to prevent the Germans and Austrians from dominating the Balkans. The Russians were, after all, the big brother of the Slav family. Surely national self interest and Communist ideology would force Stalin to stand up to Hitler? Could the Soviets really allow the Germans to put their hands on Belgrade, Sofia and Constantinople?

On the surface the Soviets remained loyal to their pact with Germany. But there were some small shifts of policy. Before the fall of France, the Yugoslav Communist Party had been more anti-Allied than anti-German. Now there came a change, and Communist leaflets and slogans began to call for resistance against 'Fascist' infiltration of key positions. These were only straws in the wind, but Serbian opinion fastened on them gladly.

Brooding in the solitude of the White Palace, Prince Paul watched the rise of Nazi influence in Yugoslavia with distaste and fear. But he had a weak hand and perhaps judged it weaker than it was. The British could offer no support. He had no faith in the Soviets, and, though quite prepared on occasion to 'play the Soviet card', would, in the last analysis, have preferred a German to a Russian occupation.

His policy, in fact, was to play for time and to make use of every device in his Byzantine repertoire to delay the spread of German influence. He no doubt hoped something might turn up to save him. Perhaps the British would make peace with Germany. But he probably accepted that, unless they did, he would in the end have to accept Hitler's terms.

Prince Paul's conception was not very heroic, but it was, at this time, largely accepted by the British Legation. Our diplomats felt that he had to bow to German pressures and made the most of his skill in playing for time. One initiative in particular seemed to confirm their faith in his realism and diplomatic shrewdness. This was the decision to establish diplomatic relations with the Soviet Union.

One evening shortly after this had been announced, I received an urgent summons from Milan Gavrilovitch. He led me out into the garden and told me that Prince Paul had asked him to go to Moscow as the first Yugoslav Ambassador. Only the Soviets could still prevent Germany from taking over Yugoslavia. His whole inclination was to accept. The chances of active Soviet intervention, whether military or diplomatic, were no doubt remote, but no patriot could afford to leave this stone unturned. His mind, he repeated, was pretty well made up. But he wanted to know what the British Government thought before giving the Prince his final reply.

I was back two days later with a positive message from London, and we fell to discussing the prospects of his mission. He was frankly pessimistic. I asked him, at one point, what would happen to Yugoslavia if no help came from Russia. The choice, he answered, lay between war and occupation or capitulation without war. Of the two, he favoured war but knew that defeat was inevitable. The real struggle would begin after the occupation had taken place, and it would be waged by the peasants. The Germans would find it easy enough to keep down the townsmen whether workers or middle class. But the peasants would be a much tougher proposition. They were scattered. They could feed themselves. The woods and mountains would protect them from pursuit. Above all, they had a long tradition of guerrilla resistance against the Turks and the Austrians. Serbia, he went on, would be the natural centre of Resistance for all the Balkans, and his Peasant Party, with its links with Bulgaria and Croatia, would be the natural spearhead.

Gavrilovitch now asked whether we could help him build up the necessary organisation. He would need wireless sets to communicate with the British after occupation and clandestine presses to print propaganda. He might also need our help to build up caches of arms and explosives. If I was interested, and I assured him I was, he would arrange for me to meet his deputy, Milosh Tupanyanin, who would be in charge of the Party after he had gone to Moscow. Tupanyanin and I, he suggested, might draw up a plan and then we could all meet together to settle details before he left for Moscow.

A day or two later I went with Altmaier to meet Tupanyanin. He was a great bull of a man, dark enough to be an Arab and with a deep loud voice and violent gestures. Between us we drew up a plan. This was in two phases. Phase One aimed at expanding the Peasant Party's activities while Yugoslavia was still neutral. It was directed to stiffening the Government's resistance to German demands and to creating a climate of opinion hostile to capitulation. Phase Two was concerned with the organisation of propaganda, sabotage and guerrilla warfare in the event of a German occupation.

Bailey and I agreed a final version of this plan with Gavrilovitch and
Tupanyanin two days before Gavrilovitch left for Moscow. But we had
still to negotiate it with London. The 'D' Section organisation had not
previously contemplated covert support for a political party in a neutral
country. Nor did the Foreign Office like the idea of British involvement
in the building up of a para-military organisation behind the back of
Prince Paul. After some weeks of telegraphic discussion, phase one of
the plan was finally authorised. This was something to start with.

The growth of German and Italian influence in Belgrade had serious
consequences for our work in Albania. The police officers who had
connived at the smuggling of propaganda and arms across the border
were now transferred to other work. Ralph Parker was expelled from the
Consulate in Skoplye. Abas Kupi was restricted to a remote village. The
Kryeziu brothers were forbidden to visit their estates in the Kossovo.
Even the intelligence reports about Albania which we had been getting
from the Yugoslav General Staff now ceased.

Djonovitch knew of our difficulties; and I sought his advice on how
to overcome them. We met in the small dark study in his house. He sat
behind his desk, chain smoking from a long black cigarette holder. I sat
in an armchair opposite. On the walls were bookshelves and a Turkish
carpet hanging down and draped over a divan. It was a very hot morning,
and old Djonovitch was in his shirt sleeves. With his blue eyes, heavy nose
and imperial beard he looked rather like the Third Napoleon. His daughter
served us each a spoonful of jam with a glass of water according to
Serbian orthodox custom and then Turkish coffee. After that she left us,
and for some time we could hear her practising the piano in another
room.

I told Djonovitch about our Albanian problems but he brushed them
aside. Albania, he said, was no longer the issue. The issue was Yugoslavia
itself. Then, speaking very slowly and quietly, he began to analyse his
country's political situation. The Serbian people in their great majority
were bitterly anti-German. The German was their traditional foe. They
were pro-British because Britain had been Serbia's ally in the First World
War and one of the founders of Yugoslavia. They were pro-Russian and,
in their hearts, still looked on the Russians as the protectors of the Slavs.
These were the true feelings of the people and of their representatives in
the Political Parties, the Army, the Patriotic Societies and the Church.

Even if they wanted to, the Yugoslavs could not do a deal with
Germany. Whether they fought or surrendered, the Germans were bound
to carve Yugoslavia up to meet the claims of Italy, Bulgaria and Hungary.
But, if they surrendered without fighting, the soul of the nation would

die; and even if the war ended in an Allied victory they would never be able to put the country together again. Honour was the soul of a nation. Serbia had survived five hundred years of Turkish domination because she had never given in. But Prince Paul's policy could only lead to capitulation. We were wrong to put our faith in this White Russian Prince. Paul was no hero and no leader. He had no following among the people. Of course, he was clever enough and was playing for time. But every concession he made to the Germans carried the moral disintegration of the country a stage further. 'The Prince,' said Djonovitch, 'is already an unconscious agent of the Germans. You will soon find him a conscious one.'

The right course for the Serbs, he went on, was to stand up to the Germans even if this meant war. In a war they could give a good account of themselves and, though military defeat might follow, they would have a place of honour at the Conference Table and would share in the fruits of victory. Little Serbia had suffered heavier casualties in the First World War than the British Empire. The whole country had been occupied. But at the end of the day, Serbia's sacrifices had proved to be the title deeds of the new Yugoslavia. No-one could read the future, but if Yugoslavia stood up to the Germans now, she might be able at the next Peace Conference to extend her frontiers to include Bulgaria in a federation of all the South Slavs.

Britain, he repeated, was wrong to put her faith in Prince Paul. In such a critical hour we should rest ourselves upon our true friends and the true representatives of the Serb people. These, he repeated, were the Army, the Church, the Patriotic Societies and the Political Parties. There was no time to lose. Already German troops were in Rumania, and Rumania's dismemberment could only be a matter of months away. It would not be long before the Germans crossed into Bulgaria with the full consent of Bulgaria's German King. Every day that went by narrowed still further Yugoslavia's freedom of action.

Djonovitch paused at this point and then asked me whether I knew his friend, Voivoda[1] Ilya Trifunovitch Birchanin. I had never met the *Voivoda* but knew him by reputation as the greatest of the Serb guerrilla leaders in the Balkan and First World Wars. He was then President of the *Narodna Odbrana* or National Defence League, a powerful patriotic society, some two hundred thousand strong with branches in every town and big village where there were Serbs. The *Narodna Odbrana* had been formed at the beginning of the century to organise guerrilla war against Turks, Bulgars and Austrians. One of its off-shoots had been the *Black Hand*, a secret society of Serbian officers which, among other things, had

[1] *Voivoda* is the Serbian equivalent of the military rank of Marshal but has also been used traditionally as the title of a guerrilla chief.

organised the killing of the Archduke Franz Ferdinand at Sarajevo. These were 'serious' people. Djonovitch now told me that he had been in consultation with Birchanin for several days. They had examined every possible course of action and had come to a solemn but radical conclusion. The only way to save their country from capitulating to Hitler was to overthrow Prince Paul's régime by a military coup d'état. Birchanin had taken soundings among his friends in the Army and was satisfied that the job could be done. Several senior officers, indeed, were already pressing him to give a lead.

Djonovitch, for his own part, had also discussed his analysis of the situation, though not his conclusions, with the chief men in the Opposition parties. They shared his views and would all be prepared to serve in a Government of National Unity. Bishop Nikolai Velimirovitch, the most dynamic of the Serbian Orthodox priests, would probably be the most acceptable figure to head this Government either as Prime Minister or as Regent for King Peter.

If the coup succeeded they must expect a strong reaction from the Germans. But they had some good cards to play. The Yugoslav Army could hardly expect to resist a German attack for very long. But they were more than a match for the Italians. If the Germans began to mass troops against them, they could at once attack the Italians in Albania and throw them into the Adriatic.

But there was another string to their bow which he must now describe. In the First World War, the Serbs had finally collapsed when they had been stabbed in the back by Bulgaria in the autumn of 1915. This time, if we knew how to play the hand, the Bulgars could be on our side. King Boris, of course, had already sold out to the Germans; and he had more support among the Bulgarian middle classes than Prince Paul had in Yugoslavia. Nevertheless, the strongest forces in Bulgaria—the Peasant Party, the *Zveno* group of officers and the *Protogerovist* section of the Macedonian Revolutionary Organisation—IMRO were sworn enemies of the King and of the Germans.[1] Most of them, too, wanted to federate Bulgaria with Yugoslavia. If the ground was well prepared a successful coup d'état in Belgrade might well be followed by a similar coup in Sofia.

If Yugoslavs and Bulgars could make common cause, the Germans would be faced with a tough proposition and one which they would hardly dare to tackle in a winter campaign. The pressure on Britain would be relieved. Even the Russians might be drawn into the struggle.

I was about to ask one or two questions, but Djonovitch put up his hand and said that he would rather say no more that day. He had talked

---

[1] The *Zveno* was a secret military society led by Colonel Damian Valtchev then in prison in Sofia. The *Protogerovists* were the anti-régime section of the IMRO in contrast to the followers of Vancho Mihailov who supported King Boris.

a. King Peter II of Yugoslavia, Prince Regent Paul on his left, reviews the Royal Guard in Belgrade

b. An evacuation party waiting for one of H.M.'s ships from Bari in 1944. From left to right: standing, Captain Jovo Babovitch; Major Voja Luka-shevitch, eventually executed by the *Partisans*; Colonel S. W. Bailey; and Lt.-Colonel Bashovitch, Mihailovitch's notorious commander in Hercegovina and lower Dalmatia; and, kneeling, Captain Walter R. Mansfield, U.S. Marine Corps, who was the first American liaison officer with Mihailo-vitch's *Chetniks* in the field; and Captain Todorovitch, a Yugoslav air-force officer attached as interpreter to Mansfield by Mihailovitch, but with the actual task of detaching Mansfield from the British Mission and enabling Mihailovitch to play the Americans against us.

a. Prince Mohammed Ali.

b. King Farouk and Queen Farida.

a. Sir Miles Lampson, later Lord Killearn, with Nahas Pasha in 1943.

b. General Sir Claude Auchinleck and General Sir Archibald Wavell.

a. General Mihailovitch, the Serbian Chetnik leader, who was later executed by Tito's orders, drinks a toast with a peasant woman.

b. Marshal Tito (*extreme right*), with some of his cabinet ministers and supreme staff, at his headquarters in the mountains.

to me without reserve because he had watched my work in Albania and believed that I would understand. '*Je vois que vous êtes bon pour ces choses,*' he said. He wanted no material support from Britain for what was to be done in Yugoslavia. But he needed our moral support and wanted to know that we should treat the Revolutionary Government as friends. He would also need our help in Bulgaria. He and his friends could do little to organise the Opposition in Sofia while they were still in Opposition themselves. This, like the preparation of the revolt in Albania, would be a task for Britain. Djonovitch rose from his chair to signify our talk was over. He asked me to come again next day at the same time when Birchanin would be with him.

I went back to my flat and cancelled all my engagements for the rest of the day. I wanted time to think. My first reaction was one of admiration for Djonovitch's moral fibre. Here was a man who deliberately rejected the easy course of a gradual surrender to the Germans and chose instead one that must lead to war and almost certainly to defeat and occupation. And he had made the choice from a conviction that his people's honour was more precious than their material possessions and more crucial to their future greatness. It was in the tradition of Tsar Lazar, who on the even of the Battle of Kossovo had chosen the 'heavenly crown' of the Martyr rather than keep his earthly crown as a vassal of the Ottoman Sultan.

Scarcely less strong was my sense of wonder at the ruthless resolve of this old man who, for the sake of his ideals, was prepared to organise a conspiracy which, if detected, would almost certainly cost him his life. As to the merits of his proposal, the more I looked at it, the more attractive it seemed. I could, indeed, see objections from a Yugoslav point of view. These were the materialist considerations which informed Prince Paul's and Stoyadinovitch's policies but which Djonovitch had faced and rejected.

But from a British point of view, I could see only advantage. If Yugoslavia stood up to Germany, some, at least, of the pressure on Britain must be relieved and there was just a chance that Russia might be drawn into the war. At the very worst, it meant that the Germans would have to fight for the Balkans, instead of picking them up for nothing; and war has a way of leading to unexpected consequences.

I went back to Djonovitch's house next day and met the *Voivoda*. He was sturdily built with a square low-browed head, jutting out from slightly bent shoulders. An empty sleeve stuck in his pocket showed that he had lost an arm. He addressed me for about twenty minutes in a deep, rather melodious, voice. His people, he said, were for freedom and against the hereditary German enemy. They were for the old Allies of Salonika days and for the Russians. They had a long tradition of war.

They would soon see off the Italians. As for the Bulgars, he had fought with them and against them, but basically they were brothers. They too wanted a great South Slav State, stretching from the Black Sea to the Adriatic. That has been the dream of his friend *Apis*[1] and of the old *Black Hand*. Now was the time for action. He and his friends were ready to do the job and put a true Serb at the head of the Government. All they wanted was to know that, in our hearts, whatever we might say officially, we were with them.

Bailey had gone to Cairo for discussions with Wavell's headquarters. In his absence, I discussed Djonovitch's proposals with Glen and Bennett. We judged them sound; but, plainly, they raised large political issues reaching beyond the purview of the 'D' Section. We accordingly told the Minister of what was afoot. He reported to the Foreign Office, but recommended that we should discourage Djonovitch and his friends from any action against Prince Paul. The Foreign Office reaction was less negative. They suggested that we should keep in touch with the conspirators and, while discouraging immediate action, try to form our own assessment of how much support Djonovitch and his friends could rely on. I found even this answer frustrating. But it gave me a cue. I would conduct my own survey of opinion among the Political Parties, the Church and the Army.

I began with the leaders of the Opposition; Nintchitch, the former Foreign Minister and spokesman of the Radical Party, Milan Grol, the professorial leader of the Democratic Party, and Yeftitch, who had been King Alexander's Prime Minister and Foreign Minister. I took the line with them that the situation was growing increasingly dangerous and that we needed their advice. We had, of course, complete confidence in Prince Paul's wisdom and pro-British sympathies. He knew what he was doing. But was there anything more any of us could do to prevent disaster? The identity of their views left me in little doubt that they had been discussing the whole issue among themselves and with Djonovitch. We were wrong, they said, to trust Prince Paul. The Prince was playing the German game. If things went on at the present rate Yugoslavia would be a German satellite in a matter of months. When I asked what could be done, they mostly spread their hands leaving me to draw my own conclusion. But old Yeftitch was more outspoken. In 1904, he said, there had been a King who had been an enemy of the Constitution and a friend to the Germans. In those days men had known how to handle the situation. They had

[1] *Apis* (Colonel Dimitrievitch) the founder of the Black Hand and executed at Salonika in June 1917 for alleged conspiracy against the Prince Regent Alexander. *Apis* was still regarded as a National hero by many Serbs in 1940.

killed the King and thrown his corpse out of the window for all to see. Desperate situations called for desperate remedies.

I turned next to the Church, which had been the inspiration and often mainspring of Serbian and Montenegrin resistance during five centuries of Turkish occupation. For a start I drove out with Altmaier to the monastery at Zenitsa to see Bishop Nikolai Velimirovitch, the man who figured in Djonovitch's plan as the head of the Revolutionary Government. The Bishop was a fine bearded patriarch and spoke good English, the result of a stay at Oxford during the First World War. We drank coffee with some of his monks. Then he led us out into the sunshine to where a carpet had been spread by the bank of a silvery river. I asked him about the situation in much the same terms as I had used in my talks with the political leaders. He spoke of Prince Paul with sorrow mounting to indignation. Paul was a man who neither understood his people nor the needs of the hour. We should place no confidence in him. His approach was crassly materialist. His only concern was to avoid war. He would rather capitulate than fight. But the life of a nation was made of more than material things. Gaps in the population could be filled. Wealth could be rebuilt. What mattered was the spirit of a people. He would far rather see his monastery destroyed, and his diocese under the Nazi jackboot than see the Serbian people dishonoured by a shameful capitulation. He had led the fight against the *concordat* which Prince Paul had tried to conclude with the Vatican. He had overthrown Stoyadinovitch. He was beginning to wonder where his duty lay now.

My other friend in the Church was Bishop Valerian Pribitchevitch, whom I went to see in his monastery at Jazak. His views were much the same as Bishop Nikolai's and if anything more outspoken. We lunched together and afterwards he suddenly said: 'Before you leave I would like to show you my cellars.' I thought at first that his purpose was convivial. But it soon became clear that his real concern was that I should see how extensive was the network of rooms running under the monastery. 'Soon,' he said, 'there will be war, or if there is no war, there will be occupation. In either case you may want to hide people or store weapons. I simply wanted to show you the facilities we have to offer. They are yours whenever you need them.'

Sounding opinion in the Army was a more delicate business. But it so happened that Sandy Glen and I had asked a certain Colonel Draja Mihailovitch to dinner. Mihailovitch was then Chief of the Operations Bureau of the General Staff, and known as an expert on guerrilla warfare. We had consulted him more than once on Albania; and he was now coming to dinner, for the specific purpose of telling us something of his plans for fighting a guerrilla war, if the Germans should overrun Yugoslavia. Mihailovitch was usually very self controlled and rather professorial in his bearing, but his mood that night was violent and bitter. When we asked him how his plans for guerrilla warfare were going, he replied acidly that they all depended on fighting a regular campaign first. As things were going, the country seemed to be heading not for resistance, but for capitulation. Sandy and I judged that Mihailovitch was probably too disciplined an officer to lead a military coup, but we had no doubt which side he would be on, if one was made, though we were far from guessing the role he was destined to play.

What did the ordinary people think? This was not so easy to discover in a country where most men are liberally endowed with the grace of suspicion. The 'D' Section, however, had a chauffeur who looked after all our transport. He was an ex-policeman and spoke French. I got him one day to take me to his village. There, and at one or two villages on the way, we stopped to drink coffee and talk with the village elders. They were much better informed than I had expected and genuinely worried as to where Prince Paul was leading them. The British and the Russians were their traditional friends; the Germans their worst enemies. When I asked what they thought should be done, they mostly answered that they put their trust in the Church and the Army.

These talks seemed to confirm that Djonovitch had judged the mood of Serbia aright. The political leaders, the bishops and the senior officers had no illusions about where Prince Paul was heading. They would welcome action, even revolutionary action, to bring about a change of policy. Feeling as they did, it seemed on the cards that some sort of revolt would break out spontaneously at some stage. But then it might be too late. If a reversal of Yugoslav policy was to be really fruitful, it should come at a time of our own choosing and not simply when Hitler decided to bring matters to a head.

I reported these impressions and conclusions to my colleagues in the 'D' Section and to the Minister. The Minister listened very patiently, but, though we had two long talks, it was clear to me that I had failed to convince him. He knew and trusted Prince Paul. They had, I believe, been at Oxford together. He looked on the authors of the coup d'état proposal as Balkan adventurers of the worst type; and his whole nature revolted at the idea of getting involved in their plots and intrigues against a man who was his friend.

In normal times the natural thing for someone of my youth and inexperience would have been to accept the Minister's judgement however reluctantly. But these were not normal times. Britain was in desperate straits. We had no ally in the world outside the Commonwealth. We still had to pay cash for every purchase from the United States. The U-boat threat to our supplies was growing. Our armies had been shattered in the retreat to Dunkirk and so desperate was the shortage of rifles that our old men were being issued with pikes to resist the invasion Hitler was preparing. Now suddenly the movement stirring in Yugoslavia cast a ray of light in the gathering gloom. A reversal of Yugoslav policy would not of itself decide the outcome of the war. But if it relieved the pressure on Britain, or embroiled the Germans with the Soviets, or drove the Italians out of Albania, it might prove a turning point. Here, perhaps, was the key to our survival. And yet here was a senior diplomat recommending that we should throw the key away not for any good reason connected with the war, or with Britain's interests, but because, if he had been a Yugoslav, so I suspected, he would have felt like Prince Paul.

With the ardour and certainty of youth, I decided that the matter could not be left where it was. If I could not convince the Minister, then I must mobilise the 'D' Section to raise the Djonovitch proposals at the highest level in London. Foreign Office officials, formed in the long years of appeasement, might cling pathetically to Prince Paul or King Boris; but surely Churchill and his friends would have the realism and the toughness to break with the past and set new forces in motion.

I talked these plans over with my colleagues in the 'D' Section and, with their agreement, decided to take a few days' leave in Istanbul. I would stop in Sofia on the way and try to assess the chances of a coup against King Boris. In Istanbul I would brief Hanau who was then on a visit from London and would be leaving soon for Cairo and home. He could raise the issue as soon as he returned.

On arrival in Sofia, I got in touch with Obov again. I carried with me a letter from Djonovitch. Obov received me in his house sitting at a small desk topped with a map of Europe under a sheet of glass. I set the ball rolling by saying that as far as we knew the situation, the Bulgarian Government intended to stay neutral. The King was no doubt under heavy pressure from the Germans, but we counted on his friendship to keep Bulgaria out of the war. I got no further. Obov banged the table so hard that I thought the glass must break. Boris, he said, was a German and the son of a German. He had come to power over the corpses of Stambuliski and thirty thousand Bulgarian peasants. He was kept in power by the police and by a chauvinist group in the middle class who were moved solely by jealousy of Belgrade and Athens. There was nothing we could do to win over either Boris or his supporters. Had we been winning the war, they might have stayed neutral. As it was, they were bound to play the German game. Far from counting on the King's friendship we should reckon with his deep-seated hostility. If Britain wanted friends in Bulgaria, she should look for them among the democratic forces and in the first place in his own party, the Peasant Party.

Was it not the case, I asked, that the Peasant Party was split into three factions? Obov replied that, since the fall of France, he and George Dimitrov had joined forces. They were, besides, very near to agreement with the third group led by Gichev. For all practical purposes, they were once more reunited. They also had powerful allies. The most important of these was the *Zveno* group of officers who followed Damian Velchev and Kimon Giorgiev. They could also count upon the Protogerovist section among the Macedonians.

I asked about their relations with the Communists. He said that it was difficult to work with people who depended so much on Moscow for instructions. But, since the fall of France, the Communists had dropped their propaganda against British Imperialism and were working in parallel, though not in partnership, with other Opposition Parties to resist the spread of German influence. Obov had no doubt, from what the local Communist leaders had told him, that Moscow was dismayed and alarmed at the prospect of a German occupation of the Balkans.

I asked Obov whether he and his friends could bring enough pressure to bear to make the King stand up to the Germans. He shook his head. The only hope lay in direct action. The King must be overthrown and replaced by a National Government pledged to form a common front with Yugoslavia against the Germans.

While we talked, Dimitrov had called Obov on the telephone and presently came round and joined us. I put much the same questions to him as I had to Obov and drew much the same replies. Dimitrov weighed his words more carefully than Obov and did not conceal the difficulties ahead. But he was plainly determined to do all in his power to overthrow King Boris with British support or without it.

Obov arranged further meetings for me with Gichev, the most pro-Government of the Agrarian leaders, and with two other Opposition leaders, Mushanov and Bobochevski. Gichev and Bobochevski confirmed Obov's analysis of the political situation in Bulgaria but without going so far as to advocate direct action.

Mushanov was rather more reserved. He was very tall with long silver hair, falling over a high winged collar onto an old-fashioned black coat. It was like talking to Mr. Gladstone. He spoke with admiration of Britain's steadfastness in defeat. He recalled his own country's grievances over twenty years. The Germans could satisfy many of Bulgaria's claims; and, yet, he prayed that the King would resist the temptation and hold fast to a policy of neutrality. I asked if this was hope or faith. He smiled and answered: 'I wonder whether the present dictator intends to stay neutral for long.' He would oppose the drift to war and make a fine speech against it. But, I felt, it would only be for the record.

Obov also arranged for me to meet a representative of the *Zveno* group of officers. This was a rather more clandestine operation. I drove to the address I had been given. There, two men were waiting and after an interval drove me to another flat. I stayed there perhaps a quarter of an hour and then another man escorted me on foot to a third flat where Colonel Karakulakov was waiting. He was a tall dark man about forty-five years old and spoke good French. We sat on very low wooden chairs, drank Turkish coffee and smoked long Bulgarian cigarettes. The Colonel was courteous but laconic.

When I asked him about the King's real intentions, he answered: 'You know his nationality. He is a German. He behaves like one.' He then said to me: 'There is nothing to hope for while this Government continues. The problem is how to change it. The difficulties are great; and my friends and I have measured them closely. We have decided to act; but on one condition. We could not make a successful coup d'état here, unless the Yugoslavs first take a much stronger line towards Berlin.'

I told Sir George Rendel in very general terms of what the Opposition leaders had told me, but without disclosing Obov and Dimitrov's advocacy of a coup d'état. Nor did I mention my meeting with Colonel Karakulakov. This reticence sprang from a growing mistrust of Foreign Office thinking but was unwise.

Rendel, for his part, thought the influence of the Opposition leaders very limited and still believed that our best policy was to support King Boris. Yet, on this score, even he was much less sanguine than he had been in the winter. If Yugoslavia and Greece had only made some concessions to Bulgaria, before the fall of France, Boris might have taken a stronger line against the Germans. As it was, he admitted, the temptation for Boris to join Hitler was very strong. Other members of his staff, and particularly Geoffrey McDermott, believed that the King had already gone over to the Germans. But they had no confidence in the Opposition and were still very reluctant to do anything which could increase Russian influence in Bulgaria.

British policy in the Balkans, between the wars and especially in the years of appeasement, had been at least as anti-Soviet in its orientation as anti-German. This tendency had been strengthened by the Ribbentrop-Molotov agreement. All this was quite natural and, doubtless, conformed to British interests. But after the fall of France, the whole situation was changed and called for a drastic reappraisal. Old habits of thinking, however, die hard. Our officials were very slow to see that any counter-weight to German influence in the Balkans would be to our advantage, even if it had a Communist label. Later on, after the German attack on Russia, the pendulum would swing to the other extreme until any warning about Soviet ambitions was regarded as heresy.

I left Sofia by train for Istanbul and as the Bulgarian countryside glided past, tried to draw up a balance sheet of the Balkan situation. My talks in Sofia certainly seemed to confirm Djonovitch's estimate of the situation in Bulgaria. They also showed that the *Zveno* officers were prepared to strike at the King. But it was equally clear that nothing would, in fact, be done in Bulgaria unless Yugoslavia first gave the lead. And here time was working against us. The Germans were quietly taking over Rumania. Every day saw an increase of repressive measures against the Opposition in Sofia. Unless the Yugoslavs moved quickly, it might be too late for the Bulgars to move at all.

I saw Hanau in Istanbul next day and told him in detail of the Djonovitch proposals and of my reasons for thinking that we should support them. We spent some hours discussing them in the seclusion of the old Embassy in Pera and on a launch on the Bosphorus. Hanau endorsed my analysis and agreed with my conclusions. Bailey arrived from Cairo a day or two later and was of the same mind. We telegraphed a summary of our views to the 'D' headquarters. Hanau then left for London determined to raise the issue at the highest level.

I had become a strong advocate, within the 'D' Section, of the Djonovitch proposals. I had, however, been very careful, in Belgrade and even more in Sofia, not to give any encouragement to the conspirators until a decision was taken in London. The 'D' representative in Sofia, Colonel Alec Ross, however, became confused in his own mind between the account I gave him of my talks with the Peasant leaders and Colonel Karakulakov and my own views of what should be done. Whether by design or inadvertently, he led Rendel to believe that I had been actively encouraging the Bulgarian Opposition to overthrow the King. Rendel was, very naturally, annoyed and reported the matter to Campbell in Belgrade. Campbell telegraphed to me in Turkey calling for an immediate explanation.

With the help of our Ambassador in Ankara, Sir Hughe Knatchbull-Hugessen, I was able to satisfy Campbell that I had committed no indiscretion. I had said nothing to any Yugoslav or Bulgarian which ran counter to his or Rendel's policy. The fact remained that I had continued to collect information for the specific purpose of changing that policy; and this when I knew full well that he and Rendel were strongly opposed to the change I was advocating. Worse still I had tried to use the 'D' Section to get the existing policy changed from London.

It was true that I had been working for some months for 'D', but I was still a member of Campbell's staff and on the payroll of his Legation. In the circumstances he was not prepared to give me Legation cover to work against his policy and asked that I should not return to Belgrade.

I cannot blame him. My personal loyalty had for some time been to Hanau and Bailey; but my action had undoubtedly been insubordinate in so far as Campbell was still my nominal chief. But there was a war on; and I was satisfied in my own mind that events would soon justify what I had done.

I spent a week in Ankara setting down on paper the full extent of the connections I had developed with different political and other groups in Yugoslavia and Bulgaria. John Bennett joined me in Istanbul and we made arrangements for him to take up the threads.

I was sorry to leave Belgrade and my Serbian friends. But Bailey now made me his chief assistant in Istanbul, and this put me at the hub of all 'D' operations in the Balkans. It was a good base from which to contribute to the radical change I wanted to see in Britain's Balkan policy.

17

Special Service: Istanbul

I shall never forget my first morning in Istanbul. It was the beginning of August; and I had arrived early on the night train from Sofia. The station, like stations everywhere, seemed dirty and drab.

I took a taxi to the Park Hotel in Pera. The streets on the way to it were narrow and gave me no idea of the city.

The night porter was still on duty at the hotel. He knew nothing about my reservation and invited me to await the arrival of the receptionist. Few things are more depressing than hotel halls in the early morning. This one was no exception. The air was stale. Half empty glasses and coffee cups lay on the tables. The ashtrays were still full of last night's cigarette ends. Two pale and unshaven men in grey denims were washing down the marble floor and sweeping up the dust. Apart from them my only companion was a life-size bronze statue of Kemal Ataturk in evening dress.

I waited about an hour. One or two people left the hotel; and then a smart young gentleman, speaking French, announced that he had found me a room. It was, he said, as if to console me for waiting, a room with a fine view.

I followed him rather crossly into the lift and up to the top floor. The room was still shuttered. The bed had not been made. The previous occupant had left without pulling the plug or emptying the bath. I asked for a maid to clean out the room. Then, remembering the receptionist's patter about the view, opened the shutters and stepped out onto the balcony.

I was quite unprepared for what I saw. Before me lay the whole skyline of old Stamboul rising steeply from the crowded waters of the Golden Horn. To the right were the great mosques of Bayazid and Suleiman surrounded by a maze of houses, each of which seemed to have a courtyard with trees growing in it. Straight in front of me rose the six minarets of the mosque of Sultan Ahmet and beside it the vast dome of Santa Sofia. From there the ground ran down to the exquisite Seraglio Palace jutting out into the sea. Beyond were the jagged Isle of Dogs and the low rock where Bulwer Lytton had built his palace. Then to the left, across the gleaming blue of the Marmara, lay the coast of Asia with Scutari guarding the entrance to the Bosphorus and the mountain of Chamblidja above it. The only blot on the landscape was a large mound of rubble, immediately below the hotel, which had plainly been there for a long time. When, later, I asked the manager why it was tolerated, he gave me a curious explanation.

Some time before his death, Kemal Ataturk had arrived unannounced at the hotel around midnight, to watch the sun rise from the balcony of the dining room. The other guests dining or dancing there were summarily expelled—though the orchestra was detained—so that the President could take his ease and get into the right mood. Unfortunately, on that particular morning, the sun rose precisely behind the dome of a mosque that then stood where the rubble now was, producing, so far as Ataturk was concerned, the effect of a total eclipse. Ataturk was not amused. He left abruptly saying that he would be back the next day to *see* the sun rise. The point was quickly taken and, by evening, Turkish Army engineers had blown up the offending edifice. Ataturk's cryptic order, however, had not been interpreted as covering the removal of the debris. His wish had been fulfilled but no one saw the need, or would risk incurring expenditure for any other purpose than its prompt gratification.

It had been about half past nine when I went out onto the balcony. I never left it until lunchtime when I was due to meet Hanau. In these hours I lost my heart to Istanbul and have never got it back.

Clandestine operations know no hours and involve endless waiting. I thus had plenty of time to explore the city and its surroundings. Nermin Okyar, whom I had known at Oxford, and her brother, Osman, introduced me to the delights of wandering through Stamboul on foot. This became a favourite pastime, and I would often spend a morning losing my way in the narrow unmarked lanes or resting from the heat beneath the dome of one of the great mosques. Sometimes, Osman's mother would ask me out to her country house on the Isle of Princes. She was the widow of Fethi Okyar, one of modern Turkey's founders, and helped me to enlarge my circle of Turkish friends. Among them was Raif Meto who took me sailing on the Bosphorus and showed me something of its marble palaces and sculptured wooden *yalis*.[1] Raif knew all the talk of the town and taught me much about modern Turkey as well as about its past.

I had little money to buy carpets or jewellery, but, in the course of exploring the great covered bazaar with its vast cisterns, came upon the

[1] These are delightful wooden villas built on the shores of the Bosphorus and, for the most part, rising straight out of the water.

booth of Abdullah Güdrek. Abdullah and his brother, David—who
somewhat improbably had been a member of the Arsenal reserve team—
soon saw that I was an unpromising client. But they took a liking to me
and often showed me their treasures, explaining the finer points of
Turkish and Russian jewellery or Turkish and Persian carpets. If ever my
ship comes home, I should be more qualified than most to buy these
things.

The Güdrek brothers often took me out in the evening and so I came
to know many of their friends; Turks, Armenians, Greeks, and Jews.
They also taught me the delights of Turkish cooking. With the noble
exception of the *kebab*, this is not, of course, Turkish but Byzantine,
and closely resembles the food of the Ptolemies and the Caesars. With
them, too, I acquired a taste for *raki*, the delicate but powerful spirit
flavoured with aniseed which the Turks and Lebanese love to drink with
sundry little dishes of *meze* or hors d'œuvres.

Many Turks do not drink for religious reasons. But even among
drinkers there is a much more developed appreciation of water than we
have in the West. I have known Turks savour water as a Frenchman
savours wine; and good water is a very good drink. I was, all the same,
rather surprised when a Turkish friend commended a restaurant to me
as having 'the best water in the town'.

The British Embassy proper was in Ankara. But the 'D' Section had
its offices in what had been Stratford de Redcliffe's Constantinople
Embassy. This was a fine, eighteenth-century house, built in a spacious
garden on a hill in Pera. We had been allocated two noble but sparsely
furnished rooms. Each contained a desk, an armchair and a hard chair.
It was not much but it was enough. We also had a big safe. In this we
kept our cyphers and telegrams and the gold *sovereigns* and *napoleons*
in which we did much of our business. One of our agents called this safe
'the stables'; when I asked him why, he replied: 'That must be where
you keep the Cavalry of St. George.'

My work was a mixed bag. Some of it consisted in drafting telegrams
and reports for Bailey. But by temperament and for reasons of security,
he was allergic to paper work. Most of my time was thus spent in briefing
agents according to his directives, and in de-briefing them and reporting
to him orally.

There was also a good deal of liaison work with colleagues outside
our organisation. There was the Secret Intelligence Service or 'C' which
supplied us with much of our information. There was Arthur Forbes,[1]
our talented Air Attaché in Bucharest, who had an aircraft of his own
and flew out several of our agents from different Balkan countries when
the secret police were too close on their heels.

[1] Now the Earl of Granard.

There was Eliahu Epstein[1] of the Jewish Agency. Epstein was organising the escape of Jews from the Balkans; and we were sometimes able to help him with documents and travel facilities. He, for his part, helped several of our agents to penetrate as far into Europe as Germany itself. Epstein was a man of broad culture and deep understanding of the Middle East. We became and have remained close friends.

We also worked closely with the Czech and Polish intelligence organisations. Among the Poles was Christine Granville, who had been smuggling members of her organisation out of Poland. Many had travelled across the High Tatra and the Carpathians in the boots of cars driven by Andrew Kennedy. Kennedy had an artificial leg and many valuable rolls of microfilm were brought out in it. Christine was one of the gentlest looking girls I have ever met and it was hard to credit her with some of the bravest clandestine achievements of the war.

Perhaps the strangest of my contacts was a certain Lefoglu, a quick-witted Armenian from Bulgaria. He was in Istanbul ostensibly as a journalist but, in fact, on our payroll. His job was to pick up snatches of information and to watch suspicious characters for us. He was very good at this, for he was one of Nature's Peeping Toms and kept me in fits of laughter with his reports of what he had overhead in the hotel lavatory or seen through some bedroom keyhole. He was quick besides to sense the feuds between the different British agencies and often supplied us with unsolicited and embarrassing reports about our fellow countrymen. Lefoglu enjoyed a varied war in different branches of intelligence and, when peace broke out leaving him unemployed, joined a private detective agency. The last time I saw him he was acting for them in a nudist colony. 'Cold work,' he said, 'but very low overheads.'

A tragic case, by contrast, was Ralph Parker who, with his wife, spent some days in Turkey on his way home to England. The Germans had secured Parker's expulsion from the Consulate in Skoplye where he had been working for 'D' Section on the Albanian side. One of his colleagues, however, had accused him of working for the Germans. There was no serious evidence to support the charge, but there was a good deal of spy mania at the time, and the authorities were taking no chances. Parker was, accordingly, ordered home though without explanation. He knew he was under a cloud but had no idea what charges might be brought against him. I was sure of his innocence and sorry to lose him as a colleague.

His life now descended into tragedy. From Istanbul, he went to Egypt, where he was virtually placed under arrest and embarked in a troop ship for England. His wife, who was expecting a child, went with him. The bombing of London had begun, so he left his wife in Cape

[1] Now Eliahu Elath and later Israeli Ambassador to Britain.

Town to await the child's birth. Back in England he was confronted with a series of accusations. He cleared himself completely and went back to *The Times* a bitter and disillusioned man. But this was not the end of his troubles. His wife died in childbirth in South Africa. The baby was presently brought back to England and entrusted to the care of Parker's parents. It turned over in its cot and was smothered.

In the first winter of the Russian War Parker left England to become *The Times* correspondent in Moscow. I have been told that, at this time, his mind was virtually unhinged and that he twice tried to commit suicide on the boat. In Moscow he fell under the influence of an attractive but dominating Soviet agent who manoeuvred him by degrees into the Communist camp. He was dropped by *The Times*, wrote spasmodically for the *Daily Worker* and later published a foolish book about the activities of the 'D' Section in Yugoslavia. Eventually he settled down to live in Moscow, mistrusted by the British Community but never accepted by the Russians. There he died.

Parker's personal tragedies may not excuse his subsequent actions, but it does much to explain them. As he was my friend and, since I brought him into paths which led to his undoing, it seems only right to record these things.

The great enigma for all of us was Soviet policy. What would Stalin do to check the advance of German influence into the Balkans? Our Yugoslav and Bulgarian friends could not believe that the Soviets would surrender what the Tzars had looked on as a vital Russian interest. Nor could such well informed observers of the Moscow scene as Walter Duranty, the distinguished American foreign correspondent, whom I saw several times that summer. And yet the Soviets made no move. Then, one day, in September, a strange thing happened.

One of my colleagues in Istanbul was a Czech intelligence officer who had helped us sabotage consignments of minerals and other strategic goods as they passed through the Balkans on their way to Germany. This officer now told us that he had been approached by an official of the Soviet Consulate General. The official has asked him for advice about how to organise similar Soviet sabotage operations against the Germans and for information as to what the British were doing in this field. The Soviets, this official had explained, did not want, at this stage, to work directly with the British. They feared we might think it our interest to betray them to the Germans. They wanted, however, to co-ordinate their plans with ours through the help of an intermediary. They hoped my Czech colleague might play this part.

Our headquarters in London feared the Russian initiative was only a plot to penetrate our organisation. But Bailey persuaded them at least to allow us to explore the possibilities of the Soviet proposal. We, accordingly, indicated sectors of the Balkan railway and shipping network which the Soviets might be better placed to attack than we were.

It was not very easy to hold meetings in Istanbul without attracting the attention of the Turkish police and the different German and Italian Services working in Turkey. In the poorer parts of the town strangers were soon recognised. In the few hotels, there was pretty effective surveillance. The most secure as well as the most agreeable meeting places were, in my experience, the mosques of Stamboul. Tourists were part of the Stamboul scenery; and two European sightseers sitting in the courtyard of a mosque were unlikely to arouse much suspicion.

The Soviets, on their side, would only hold meetings in their Consular offices or in motor cars. This seemed to me rather less secure, but that was their business.

I had several meetings with my Czech colleague in different mosques, and he in his turn would be picked up by Soviet agents at some convenient street corner.

Once, one of the Russian agents came into the Mosque of Suleiman with my Czech colleague. I was already there by arrangement. They did not talk to me, but on leaving the mosque the Russian made a little bow towards me. The Czech explained that his Russian contact had volunteered to take this risk as a sign that the Soviets were acting in good faith. He thought they were considering establishing direct links with us.

Another meeting had more comical consequences. It was late on a Friday afternoon. I was sitting in a mosque waiting for my Czech colleague. He was late, but this was not unusual. Presently, one or two people came in and sat down nearby. I looked at my watch and decided to give him another half hour. Long before that quite a crowd joined me and I found myself in the middle of the third row of what was evidently a congregation assembling for the evening prayer. Had I known as much of the kindliness and tolerance of Islam as I do today, I would have got up and left without embarrassment. But I had heard so many tales of fanaticism that I hesitated; and, while I hesitated, the prayer began. There was nothing to do but watch the man in front and do what he did. It was not very difficult but more strenuous than I had expected.

These contacts with the Soviets were delicate and bedevilled by suspicion on both sides. But they bore some results. We began to get reports of acts of sabotage against the Germans for which we certainly were not responsible. The Soviets never admitted to them, even to my Czech friend, but it was hard to see who else could have been at work.

After a time, the Czech officer was called by his superiors to the Middle East and though alternative arrangements were suggested the Soviets let the contact lapse. But it had been a straw in the wind and gave us some encouragement.

But the most interesting part of my work was the discussion of plans and policies with Bailey. Like most men of action, he was a great believer in talking out a problem. On the top balcony of his flat at night, in a launch on the Marmara, or on some hillside overlooking the Bosphorus, he would spend hours analysing a situation and deciding what action to take. Sometimes we would be joined by Altmaier or other colleagues. Almost always we came away with fresh ideas and definite things to do. Bailey was a man of vision and courage, though like many self-made men not always quite sure of himself. But his greatest quality was his receptiveness to new ideas. He saw the advantages in any proposal more quickly than the drawbacks. Some of his initiatives failed in consequence, but, in the final score, he achieved far more than a more cautious man would have done. In a desperate situation—and 1940 was as desperate a year as any in British history—the only unforgiveable sins are the sins of omission. Bailey was never guilty of these.

18

The Fall of Rumania

I went to see Bailey early on the morning of 5 September 1940. He was holding a meeting with some Poles on the balcony. So I sat down in his room and began to read Istanbul's French language paper, *La République*. Clearly something—perhaps everything—was rotten in the State of Rumania.

The Rumanian leaders had been summoned to Vienna by Ribbentrop and Ciano and, there, had agreed to the virtual dismemberment of their country. Transylvania was ceded to Hungary and the Dobrudja to Bulgaria. The Soviets had already grabbed Bessarabia some weeks before.

According to *La République* the Rumanian Army was withdrawing from Transylvania in a state of near mutiny. Telephone and telegraph communications had been cut. There was said to be rioting in Bucharest and other towns. The principal figures in the drama were King Carol, General Antonescu,[1] the Iron Guard[2] and the Peasant Party. It was not at all clear who stood for what or with whom. It looked, however, as if what remained of Rumania might soon pass altogether under German control.

Rumania was within Bailey's operational area and there was a representative of 'D' Section in Bucharest called de Chastellain.[3] Was there anything we could do either to influence the immediate course of events or to prepare for resistance against Germany in the longer term? The only way to answer these questions was to send someone at once to talk things over with our man in Bucharest and to make sure that he was given any necessary financial backing that might be needed. But whom should we send? It was out of the question for Bailey himself to leave Istanbul. In the circumstances, I thought it might as well be me.

Presently the Poles left, and I put my ideas to Bailey. He smiled and then, walking to the edge of the balcony, stood for some time looking

---

[1] Antonescu: then Prime Minister.
[2] A greenshirted fascist type organisation.
[3] Now Lt. Cd. A. G. G. de Chastellain, D.S.O. The D.S.O. was awarded for subsequent operations in Rumania leading to his capture and lengthy imprisonment.

A.M.—G

out to sea. 'All right,' he said at last 'Get on to the office and let them fix your passage. If you're to go you must leave at once.'

He then sat down and wrote a letter to de Chastellain authorising him to take any action, in agreement with me, which the situation might call for. As I left him, he said: 'You will have to make your own decisions and there may well be no time to refer back to me.'

I sailed in the afternoon from Galata aboard the Rumanian liner *Bessarabia*. We glided up the Bosphorus past the *yalis*, the palaces and the castles of Europe and Asia. At sunset we turned into the Black Sea steering a north westerly course towards Constanza.

I dined on board with Gordon Young of Reuters, but he seemed to be as much in the dark about what was happening in Rumania as I was. Nor did a stroll on deck in the moonlight produce any further inspiration. I would have to play it by ear.

We docked just before dawn; and, presently, I could make out the Tartar mosques with beehive domes and squat minarets on the cliffs behind Constanza. Two gunboats rode at anchor in the harbour but they seemed to have no-one on board. As I stepped off the gangway a policeman separated me from the other passengers and led me to an office. There I was brought before a fat swarthy individual dressed in the green shirt of the Iron Guard and flanked by two officials in plain clothes. He asked for my passport and then said in indifferent French, 'Diplomat? That is not a profession. What kind of diplomat are you?' In the circumstances I thought it wiser to avoid answering questions of this kind. I accordingly took the high line. 'You are quite right. Diplomacy is not a profession. It is a career.' He seemed taken aback and after a few more routine questions let me go.

I joined Gordon Young on the train to learn that there had been shooting in Constanza during the night and several casualties, but there was no news of what was happening in Bucharest. Caviar was cheap so I had some for breakfast and settled down to watch the Rumanian countryside. We crossed the Danube at Chernavoda and, at about eleven o'clock, pulled into Bucharest.

At the station newspaper boys were selling special editions. These consisted of a single sheet with a headline 'The King abdicates'. Below was the text of the deed of abdication in favour of Prince Michael. General Antonescu remained Prime Minister.

I managed to find a taxi and drove through crowded streets—plainly no-one was at work—to the Athene Palace Hotel. The hotel looked on to a square opposite the Royal palace. Outside the palace a large crowd was milling around composed partly of curious onlookers and partly of organised youths shouting slogans. Once or twice one of the organisers fired a pistol in the air; but no-one seemed seriously excited; and the crowd thinned out visibly with the approach of lunchtime.

Between the hotel and the palace was a restaurant with a garden. It seemed as good a vantage point as any from which to watch developments. So, after making one or two appointments, I walked over to it and enjoyed a lunch of Parisian excellence.

Presently, a car drove up to the palace. Inside it was Queen Helen, King Michael's mother, just arrived from Greece. The crowd stopped the car; but when they recognised the Queen fell back again and gave her a spontaneous cheer.

After lunch, I was joined by Hugh Seton-Watson. Hugh was a son of the famous professor who had done much to shape the post-war map of Eastern Europe after the First World War, and would himself become a historian of equal distinction. Hugh looked like a friendly bear, with crumpled clothes, untidy hair and rather awkward movements. With strangers he was at first rather self-conscious but forgot himself as soon as he warmed to a theme. He would then speak much faster and louder and gesture without reserve. At our first meeting in Belgrade I had judged him an austere Wykehamist Scholar. Scholar he certainly was. His knowledge of the Balkans was already encyclopaedic; and, unlike most academics, he had a sure grasp of the mainsprings of political action. But, by the end of our first lunch, I had to revise the label 'austere'. I have seldom known anyone derive more pleasure from good food or show more discernment in choosing it. Moreover, being an intellectual, Hugh enjoyed the idea of a dish, whether in anticipation or in recollection, almost as much as the eating of it.

I had been instrumental in bringing Hugh into the 'D' Section and he was at this time combining work for us with a rather nominal job in the Legation. His account of what was happening in Rumania was depressing but clear.

The Army was retreating from Transylvania in accordance with the terms of the Vienna Agreement and was reported very demoralised. One officer, it was said, had recently turned up on parade in plain clothes. When asked to explain his conduct he had replied: 'My uniform is at the cleaners. I pissed on it when I heard of our Government's surrender at Vienna.'

Which way would the Army incline? To the Iron Guard or to the Peasant Party? The Iron Guard was wholly committed to the Germans, but King Carol had smashed its organisation and killed its ablest leaders.

The Peasant Party was numerically the strongest movement in the country and its leaders, Maniu and Michalache, were staunchly pro-Allied. But they were old men and did not want to accept the responsibilities of Government in the hour of their country's humiliation. Maniu had talked to Hugh that morning about summoning a congress at Alba Julia to protest against the Vienna *Diktat*. If he did so, the Army might rally to him. But this would mean war with the Hungarians, and perhaps the Germans. At the end of the day, so Hugh forecast, Maniu would not risk it.

The most likely outcome, in his judgement, was that Antonescu would stay in power to become a kind of Rumanian Pétain collaborating with the Germans but trying to retain such independence as he could.

In the evening I went to see de Chastellain, our man in Bucharest. De Chastellain was an oil engineer. He had lived in Rumania for some years and spoke the language fluently. He was a short, fit-looking man, with fair hair and a slightly nasal intonation.

I explained that Bailey had sent me to discuss what could be done to organise resistance to German penetration of Rumania. Substantial funds were available for any political party group which would resist the Germans and carry out sabotage operations against them. Bailey and I could not judge who would be the best people to work with. I had come to learn this from him and to see if we could make a plan together.

De Chastellain explained that his mission until then had been confined to sabotaging transport carrying Rumanian oil to Germany and to co-operating with the Berthoud[1] mission which was intended to destroy the Ploesti oil fields. He had, accordingly, regarded the organising of political resistance as outside his brief. He had, however, a number of political friends, especially among the Peasant Party leaders, and believed that something might be done with them on the lines I had suggested. He would try to see Maniu and Michalache that night or the next day and we would meet again after that. Like Seton-Watson, he doubted if anyone else could be of much use.

I met Maniu briefly that evening. But it was in a crowded restaurant and he was surrounded by henchmen. There was thus no chance of a serious talk. He did, however, tell Seton-Watson that he had given up the idea of a congress at Alba Julia. The Army, he had been advised, was in no condition to fight.

De Chastellain, who saw him and Michalache next morning, confirmed

[1] This was a special mission led by Mr. (now Sir Eric) Berthoud and designed to implement a 'scorched earth' policy in the Rumanian oilfield. It had little chance to demonstrate its capacity in Rumania but was subsequently more successful in dealing with Burmese oilfields in 1942.

that they had decided not to take office in what they regarded as a hopeless situation. They could not fight against the Germans. They would not work with them. In the circumstances, they saw no choice but to remain in Opposition and try to resist German and Iron Guard penetration as best they could.

De Chastellain has asked whether there was any way in which we could help them in their resistance. They believed that there was. We could help in the production and distribution of propaganda in the immediate future. We could also help them to develop an underground organisation to carry out guerrilla and sabotage operations if the Germans should take over what remained of Rumania. They would draw up detailed plans over the next few days and de Chastellain would bring these to Istanbul for Bailey to confirm.

It was clear from all this that there was nothing we could do to organise resistance to the Vienna Agreement. Rumania was already in the German grip; and German penetration was likely to grow into something like occupation. Had we given support to Maniu and the Peasant Party at an earlier stage, it is at least possible that they would have seized power before the Vienna meeting and stood up to the Germans instead of surrendering. The Germans would then have had to fight for Rumania, and the vital oil fields could have been put out of action. As it was, the enemy had won a bloodless victory; and there was nothing left for us to do but try to build up an underground organisation for propaganda, intelligence and sabotage. For this, the Peasant Party seemed the best allies available. Their leaders were scarcely men of revolutionary timber; but there was no-one else to turn to.

Before leaving Bucharest I dined with Hugh Seton-Watson. He was suffering from a form of dysentery and could only eat boiled rice. He selected my menu, however, with his usual enthusiasm. Years later, he told me that he had enjoyed ordering the meal, but that watching me eat it while he kept to his rice had probably been his worst moment in the whole war. I walked back with him to his rooms and then continued on foot towards my hotel. On the way a smartly dressed police officer came up, saluted and asked me for £10. He wanted the money, he said, for the Transylvanian refugees. I explained that I was a British diplomat and asked to be excused. He answered that I could please myself but that, if I chose not to pay up, I should spend the night in a cell at the police station. I should, no doubt, receive an apology in the morning but it would be a very uncomfortable night. So, I paid up; and he courteously escorted me to the hotel to ensure that none of his colleagues should ask me for a further contribution.

I returned to Istanbul next day and de Chastellain followed soon afterwards with detailed proposals agreed with the Peasant Party leaders. These seemed sound to us, and Bailey commended them to the 'D' Section in London.

All through September and October the tide of German influence rose steadily through the Balkans. Unless something was done, it could only be a matter of months before Bulgaria and Yugoslavia followed Rumania into the Axis camp. The only course of action open to us, as we saw it, was to return to the Djonovitch proposals for overthrowing Prince Paul and King Boris and replacing them with men committed against the Germans. We had put these proposals to the Government at home but they had been turned down. The question was how to bring them forward again.

Our opportunity came out of the blue. As so often in politics, the unexpected happened. Mussolini attacked Greece. To the general surprise, moreover, his legions failed to break through the Greek defences and, instead, were hurled back into Albania. The war had come to the Balkans though in an unexpected quarter. There was now a new situation. It would call for new policies. Eden, the Secretary of State for War, was in Cairo to confer with the Commanders-in-Chief. Bailey was determined that they and the Government at home should have his views on what could still be done in Yugoslavia, Bulgaria and Albania. He, therefore, decided to send me at once to Cairo to report to Wavell. After that, if Wavell agreed, I was to go back to London and fight the battle for a change of policy there.

IV

HOME TO A MIXED RECEPTION

November 1940–March 1941

'The road to resolution lies by doubt: The next way home's the farthest way about.'

Francis Quarles

19

At Wavell's Headquarters

Before leaving for Cairo, I drove up to Chamblidja, the highest point on the Asian Shore, for a last look at Istanbul. The sun was already low and a mist was rising from the Golden Horn. The domes and minarets of the great mosques stood out above it, but the ramshackle buildings in between were already lost to sight. Directly below us was the broad blue Bosphorus. In the distance rose the dark hills of Thrace.

I have seen Istanbul from many points of vantage: from Haidar Pasha, in the morning haze, when it is a city out of an Eastern fairy tale; from the minaret of the Blue Mosque at midday, when it is hard and clear like a Canaletto; and from the Seraglio point at sunset, when the towers and minarets cast strange shadows. It remains for me the most beautiful city in the world; blessed in its God-given setting of water and steep hills; majestic in its man-made mosques and palaces; fascinating in its variety; mysterious in its contrasts of quiet gardens and milling crowds. From Chamblidja you can see that it is 'the key of the world': the point where Asia and Europe come together.

The next day I again crossed the Bosphorus to Haidar Pasha where I caught the Taurus Express. The country along the Gulf of Izmit was green and smiling, with its orchards and gardens. Then, after an hour or so, the train began to climb up to the great plateau of Anatolia with its broad expanses broken only by flat-topped hills of red earth and rock. I remember thinking that the plateau would be ideal country for tank warfare, if the Germans ever got that far.

My reading for the journey was Kemal Ataturk's speech when he reported to the National Assembly upon his Revolution. It is not a very objective account of what happened, but it remains impressive as a soldier's account of what he did—a modern version of *de bello Gallico*. It took six days to deliver and must have been a physical *tour de force* for the orator as well as a severe test of endurance for the members of the Grand National Assembly.

We reached Ankara in the evening, and when I woke next morning were just entering the Taurus. By afternoon we had dropped down again to Adana and crossed the frontier into Syria just before nightfall. Syria and the Lebanon were still administered by the Vichy Government of Marshal Pétain and the customs officials confiscated all our newspapers.

Towards midnight we reached Aleppo, where I left the train. A horse-drawn *fiacre* carried me through cobbled streets to Barons Hotel where Kemal Ataturk had made his last headquarters before the Armistice of 1918. Next morning I saw something of the town with its huge square citadel and untidy graveyards, its veiled women, Kurdish tribesmen from the hills, and camel caravans.

From Aleppo I took the train through Homs and Hama to Tripoli. The population was now entirely Arab. Many had noble faces. But I was shocked by their poverty which exceeded anything I had seen in the Balkans or even in Turkey. Several members of the Italian Armistice Commission were on the train. One of them took me for a Frenchman and tried to console me for my country's defeat. I played up to this and, with heavy irony, paid tribute to the glorious part Italy had played in defeating the French Army with so little help from the Germans. He did not like it at all and presently went and sat elsewhere.

In Beirut I spent a delightful evening with a Lebanese lawyer, the father of an Oxford friend. He hoped the British would take a firm line with Vichy and place both Lebanon and Syria under British protection.

Next morning I left Beirut for Palestine. At the frontier post of Ras Nakourah a French inspector of police came up and saluted: 'You are Mr. Amery?'

'Yes I am.'

'We have orders to detain you.'

I argued that there must be some mistake and begged him to telephone Beirut for confirmation. My papers were in order and included a Diplomatic Visa and *laissez-passer* issued by the French Embassy in Ankara. After half an hour he got through but only to receive confirmation of the order to send me back.

While waiting for transport, I passed the time in the frontier post canteen drinking *arak* with some Foreign Legionaries. They had never heard the story of *Beau Geste*,[1] so I told it to them.

I now spent three very comfortable days in the Hotel St. George as the guest of the Vichy Government. As I had diplomatic status, I was not formally under arrest but was told to consider myself as interned. My telephone was cut off and I was asked to take my meals in my room. I was, however, allowed to go for a walk twice a day, though in the company of a police officer. The weather was fine. The hotel first-class.

[1] *Beau Geste* (1924), a novel by P. C. Wren about the Foreign Legion; much in vogue between the wars.

I had nothing to complain about. Nevertheless, I was worried. The influence of the Axis Armistice Commission was very powerful. The Italians and the Germans presumably knew of my activities in the Balkans. Would I be handed over to them or interned for the duration?

After three days I was summoned to the Grand Serail by M. Conti, the political secretary. He asked me a few questions, indulged in a little general conversation and then apologised that I should have been detained. It was all a mistake, he said, and I was free to leave. Next day, therefore, I drove again to the frontier, where I was greeted by the same inspector. 'It was all a mistake,' I said. 'No doubt that's what they told you,' he answered.

Twenty years later at a dinner in Tunis I happened to tell the story of my internment in Beirut. Someone asked me why I thought the French had stopped me. I said that I had never been able to find out. At this point another of the guests intervened. He could solve the mystery. This was the Emir Farid Shehab. He was then Lebanese Ambassador to Tunisia but, at the time of my arrest, had been deputy chief of police in Beirut. He remembered the case clearly. The Axis Armistice Commission, as I had feared, had asked that I should be handed over to them. This the French had declined. They had then asked that I be interned in France for the duration of the War. The French had agreed to consider this request. They never intended to comply with it, but, as if to show that they were in earnest, had stopped me from leaving the country and confined me to my hotel. Once I was safely in Palestine, they had told the Axis Commission politely but firmly that, after due consideration, they had felt bound to release me. Such decisions turn largely on personalities. Had my case been in the hands of a zealous 'collaborationist' instead of M. Conti, this book might have told a very different story.

The British side of the Palestine-Lebanon frontier was guarded by a single sentry in shorts and a pith helmet. He was the first 'Tommy' I had seen since the outbreak of war and his presence, after my detention in Beirut, was reassuring.

I spent the night in Haifa where I dined with an officer of the Palestine police. He brought two girl friends with him. One was Arab, the other Jewish. This seemed encouraging.

I had hoped originally to visit Jerusalem on my way to Egypt. But there was no time for this if I was to reach Cairo before Eden left for home. I accordingly spent a tiring day in a stuffy train passing through Jaffa and Gaza and crossing the Suez Canal at Kantara. After the Bosphorus the Canal was disappointing. It did not emphasise enough the division between Asia and Africa.

I had an Egyptian *laissez-passer* but this did not stop the Egyptians searching my luggage. They pounced on Ataturk's Six-Day Speech and seized it on the grounds that it had been printed in Leipzig. It was sent back to me two years later.

After the rather provincial atmosphere of the Balkan capitals, Cairo seemed astonishingly vital. I was staggered and at first shocked by its contrast of wealth and poverty: shiny limousines and caravans of camels and donkeys; stout pashas and starving beggars; well-to-do young *effendis* in smart lounge suits and *tarbooshes*; *fellahin* in turbans and what seemed to be night shirts. The military were everywhere, dressed in the simple tropical uniform of the desert, with every now and then the red tabs of a brass hat or the distinctive cap of a French or Polish officer. All was noise, bustle and hurry.

I had carefully memorised the address of the 'D' Section office and gave it, as clearly as I could, to the driver of a horse-drawn *garri* or fiacre. He seemed puzzled at first and I wondered if I had forgotten the full formula. Then a smile lit up his face. 'Ah,' he said, 'you mean the British Secret Office.' This was only the first of my surprises that morning.

A few minutes later I rang the bell of a pleasant looking flat in the Garden City of Zamalek. The door was opened by a familiar figure dressed as a Corporal. This was Whittaker, who had been, for many years, butler to Simon Wardell's grandmother and had abetted many of our youthful escapades. He led me to the receipt of customs where I found Simon's sister-in-law, Hermione Ranfurly. She was then secretary to George Pollock, the head of the 'D' Section in Cairo. Between them Hermione and Whittaker brought me up to date with what had happened to several of my friends over the past year. They then piloted me into Pollock's office.

Pollock was a barrister sprung from a distinguished legal family. He was prematurely grey but with a fine presence and exuded vitality. I gave him an outline of Bailey's views. He asked me to condense them into a memorandum. I did so the same afternoon, and he sent copies of it at once to Eden, Wavell and Wavell's two directors of intelligence, Clayton[1] and Shearer.[2]

I was still asleep next morning when the telephone rang. It was the hotel porter to say that Wavell's ADC was on his way up to my room. It was nearly eleven o'clock and I feared that to be still in bed so late

---

[1] Sir Iltyd Clayton: then deputy director of Intelligence, responsible for political analysis.
[2] Sir John Shearer: then deputy director of Intelligence, responsible for the analysis of the enemy's order of battle and intentions.

must make a bad impression on the Commander-in-Chief's entourage. To my relief and delight the door opened to admit my old school friend Francis Fisher.

Francis was known as the General's 'Playing ADC'. He played golf with him, flew aeroplanes with him, rode with him and generally looked after his relaxations and his visits to the front.

Wavell, Francis told me, had read my report and wanted me to come and dine that night. I was also to see Eden earlier in the evening.

We spent what was left of the morning talking together in my bedroom and were presently joined by another friend of Eton days, Jimmy Boyle. Jimmy had a sparkling gift of mimicry. He had also developed a parlour trick which I first saw demonstrated that morning. We had ordered drinks; and, when Jimmy had finished his, he proceeded to eat the glass down to the stem. He claimed that if you ground it finely enough it could cause no harm. Sir Richard Grenville had done it before the sinking of the *Revenge*; but then, he had gone down with his ship the same day. Jimmy went on doing it for another five years but, to the lasting sorrow of his friends, died just after the war, from cancer of the stomach. I have often wondered how much the trick was responsible.

Eden had not read my report when I met him in the evening. He was just back from Greece and showed some interest in what I had to say about Albania. But, when I tried to tell him about the possibilities in Yugoslavia and Bulgaria, he cut me short. He was only Secretary of State for War, he explained, and these were matters for Lord Halifax, the Foreign Secretary. This seemed a strangely bureaucratic approach and I wondered whether it concealed some jealousy over spheres of influence within the Cabinet.

My first meeting with Wavell was a rather intimidating affair. He greeted me with kindliness, sat me down in a chair and then remained silent for two or three minutes. After this he seemed to wake up and said that he had read my report and was asking Clayton and Shearer to discuss it with me the next day. It all seemed very sensible to him, though what he really wanted was more tanks. He then lapsed into silence, smiling benignly. I tried to develop one or two ideas in my report to which he said: 'Yes, yes, you're probably right. But what I really need is more tanks.' I could not at first see how I was expected to produce tanks out of the 'D' Section. But this, as I later discovered, was Wavell's way. He would concentrate on a single point and bend all his energies to securing it. Anything else was then delegated to his staff. By stressing his need for tanks to any visitor, however junior, he doubtless hoped to pressurise Whitehall to send him what he wanted.

Presently we went into dinner, where we were joined by Lady Wavell and her three daughters. Dinner was austere—not much to eat and only whisky or water to drink. Wavell was no conversationalist but told some amusing anecdotes about my Uncle Harold who had been a close friend of his in the Black Watch. In an effort to draw him out, I asked him how he had reacted to the fall of France. He had learned the news, he said, on one of the greens of the Gezira Golf Course. 'I thought for a moment if there was anything I could do about it. There wasn't. So I went on with the game and was rather pleased that I did the next two holes in three and four.'

Next day I had long talks with Brigadiers Shearer and Clayton, the two Directors of Intelligence. It would be difficult to imagine two more opposite personalities. Shearer was smart, good looking and exuded confidence. He had left the Army several years before and made a name in business by reorganising the Sales Department of Fortnum and Mason. He seemed to have taken account of every factor in the military situation and gave me a brilliant account of the War in the Western Desert and its prospects. He praised my report but stressed that there was little the Middle East Command could do about it. Their commitments already exceeded their forces; and they could not contemplate a Balkan entanglement. But I would go to London with their blessing and if, later on, I would like to join his staff he would be glad to have me.

Clayton was a brother of Gilbert Clayton who had worked with Lawrence. He was a large, rugged and untidy man. He asked me a lot of questions about the Balkans in rather haphazard order. He did not see how we could prevent a German occupation of the Balkans. The real problem was how to keep them out of the Middle East. This would call for political warfare as well as fighting; and he thought I might find this interesting work. In any case, I was to come and see him as soon as I was back in Cairo.

In the intervals of talks and writing reports, Francis and Jimmy showed me the highlights of Cairo. They took me riding at Gezira, and showed me the Sphinx and the Pyramids in the sun and by moonlight. We drove up to the Citadel and went shopping in the *Musky*. There was also the usual round of restaurants and night clubs. I hoped the war would bring me back to Cairo.

20

Across Africa

Shearer and Clayton had advised Wavell that I should go to London and report to the 'D' Section. But this was not, in those days, an easy journey. The only aircraft capable of flying to Malta and Gibraltar was the Sunderland flying boat. There were very few of these and the R.A.F. kept them for operational purposes. The only other way, apart from joining a convoy round the Cape, was to go by air to the south of the Sudan and then hook westwards across Free French territory to Lagos in Nigeria.

The plane for Lagos went about once a fortnight and it only held seven passengers. But Wavell's word was law and I was soon on the next plane to leave. My fellow travellers turned out to be four generals and two senior naval officers.

We stopped the first night at Wadi Halfa and flew on next day to Khartoum and El Obeid, which already seemed to me well beyond the pale of civilisation. El Fasher, our next stop, was little more than a sprawling native village.

Another hour's flight brought us to an airfield at El Geneina which was not even that. No village was in sight, though there were a few beehive huts dotted around. The heat was infernal. I felt it all the more as I was dressed in a London suit. I was also, as it chanced, wearing my old school tie. A smart District Officer met us. He suggested, I thought a trifle curtly, that I should stand in the shade under the wing while he 'fixed up the Senior Officers'. He would come back for me presently. I watched rather disconsolately as he led them away each to a beehive hut. Presently, he came back and with grave courtesy said: 'I observe that you and I were at the same school. I have the only civilised house within three hundred miles. I also still have some champagne. I hope you will be my guest tonight.' This is the only occasion on which I have derived positive advantage from wearing my old school tie. I have sometimes worn it since when travelling in the hope of another windfall. But the score so far has only been a touch for a fiver—from another Old Etonian on the Golden Arrow—which I never got back.

Next day we flew over the great marshy swamp of Chad to Fort

Lamy, the French Equatorial Colony which had rallied to de Gaulle and from there we continued to the walled city of Kano, in Nigeria. Beyond Kano we at last left behind us the dreary featureless scrub country or savannah which had been our constant companion. Below us now was the lush steaming rain forest of the Western African Coastal Belt. In the early afternoon we reached Lagos. It had taken us four days to fly a distance which a modern jet would cover in as many hours.

With its promenade along the lagoon, its surburban villas and its neo-Gothic cathedral, Lagos seemed oddly English, except that the people were black and the colours bright. We put up at the one and only hotel which was called, I think, the Grand. It was small and dirty. The rare bathrooms were smelly and infested with large though apparently in-offensive spiders. There was no question of air conditioning or even of fans in the bedrooms. I shared a minute room with a Naval Commander. He was tall, anaemic and conventional and talked about his wife as 'my Madam'. I was not sure at first whether we would get on. In fact, we soon became good friends.

The hotel was crowded with people waiting for a passage on to London or back to Cairo. Some had been there for several weeks, never quite achieving the necessary priority to get on to the next plane.

The climate was hot and very damp. Coins mildewed in my pockets; little fungi sprouted on my shoes overnight. I love heat but found the dampness trying and, for the only time in my life, developed an almost insatiable craving for alcohol towards evening. Fortunately whisky was in plentiful supply. One night I also tried the native palm wine which tasted like a sort of fermented barley water. I was assured that it was very potent but did not find it so.

We stayed in Lagos for a week. I read the *Odyssey* in translation, and played golf at the Akerri Club. One night my golf bag, which I had dragged through the Balkans and the Middle East, was stolen. I have scarcely played since. On the Sunday I went to church and found a very respectable middle class African congregation. It was exactly like a service in a country town at home except that everyone sang a good deal better.

The equatorial sun was still thought dangerous and I was sharply rebuked on my way back from church for going out without a hat. A few months later, the doctors pronounced that dark glasses were a sufficient protection against sunstroke—a pronouncement now equally exploded—and topees were at last laid aside to become 'props' for charades or status symbols for semi-literate Africans and Asians.

This was my first visit to a British Colony; to judge from the hotel, we were not spending a great deal on ourselves. To judge from the public buildings, hospitals and new housing, we had done quite a lot for the local inhabitants. They certainly enjoyed more freedom and security than the Serbs, Bulgars and Turks among whom I had been living.

Then one morning we were suddenly roused at four o'clock with the news that our flying boat, the *Clare*, had come in. We were given an hour to pack and dress. A launch took us out across the lagoon to the flying boat. Half an hour later we taxied out beyond the reef and soon after daybreak took off across the Atlantic.

The *Clare* was the most comfortable aircraft I had seen. The seats were big armchairs, and there was a promenade deck where you could stretch your legs. Food was austere but there was plenty to drink. We landed in the harbour of Freetown. Freetown looked most attractive, nestling in the centre of a broad bay with green hills rising up behind it; but there was an epidemic in Freetown itself and we were not allowed ashore. Instead we spent the night on a liner in mid harbour.

Around us lay several British warships. Two were still listing heavily from wounds suffered in the ill-fated attempt on Dakar a few weeks before. I met the captain of one of them. He did not think the Free French to blame for the failure of the operation. He argued, indeed, that the attempt could have succeeded if only the Royal Navy had been allowed to take a more active part and to press home the attack.

We continued along the Guinea and Senegal coast, and landed just before lunch at Bathurst in the Gambia. We scrambled out into a creaking, leaking launch and clambered up a crumbling jetty where a small crowd of Africans had collected. The few buildings in sight looked damp and dilapidated. The Colonial Secretary took me off to his house where I had a very welcome bath in a spacious hand-filled tub and attended to other duties on an old-fashioned thunder-box. After that there was an excellent, if for the climate rather heavy lunch, washed down with claret and followed by vintage port.

Bathurst seemed very remote but was, in fact, almost in the front line. Vichy reconnaissance aircraft often flew over from Dakar and an invasion was thought quite likely. Occasionally Free French supporters escaped to Bathurst through the jungle.

Despite the heat, the Colonial Secretary returned to his office as soon as lunch was over. His wife showed me something of the town and explained the virtues and vices of its leading citizens. We then drove inland along the river hoping to see a crocodile. I was disappointed in this and so, by way of alternative entertainment, was taken to a leper colony. The wretched victims of the disease cowered round the car with a terrifying humility. Some had lost whole limbs or features; others were covered with what seemed to be scales. In those days, there was no known treatment for leprosy. The memory of the visit haunted me for some twenty years until I visited a modern leper colony in the Pacific and came away with much happier impressions.

We left the Gambia after sunset and flew through the night landing at about ten o'clock in the morning in the mouth of the Tagus. This was the longest leg of the journey and about as much as the *Clare* could manage with a full load. Lisbon seemed cold and windy after Africa and we devoured a vast lunch at Estoril. Our gastronomic standards had been low since leaving Cairo; and the austerity of wartime Britain lay ahead.

We took off in a drizzle on the last lap of our journey. To avoid enemy action we had to keep as low as two hundred feet crossing the Bay of Biscay, and this made the flight very bumpy. I was not air sick; but very nearly. We landed at Poole; but by the time we had finished with Customs and other controls, the last train to London had gone. This was just as well as Waterloo Station was badly bombed that night. Instead an elderly lady drove us in a large taxi to a hotel in Bournemouth. The rooms were unheated and the menu Spartan; but everyone seemed cheerful and anxious to help.

In the morning I took a train to London but it only ran as far as Ealing. Beyond that the line had been blocked by bombing. From Ealing I found my way back by underground and taxi to Eaton Square. My mother and father were just back from the country and had no idea I was coming home. We fell into each others' arms and spent the rest of the day in a detailed unfolding of all that had happened to us.

21

A Bone of Contention

I reported next day to an office block in Baker Street. A modest name plate at the entrance proclaimed that this was the office of I.S.R.B. or the Inter Services Research Bureau. It was, in fact, the Headquarters of the 'D' Section. I asked for Hanau, who was now Chief Adviser to the Balkan section, and eventually found him in a dingy room in a rabbit warren of offices. After a long talk he took me to see George Taylor who was in charge of both the Balkan and the Middle Eastern sections.

Taylor was a short, dark man with sharp features and had been in the oil business. He was an Australian, a Roman Catholic, and a keen student of politics. He was plainly deluged with routine work and could only spare me a few minutes; but I said enough to engage his interest, and he asked me to dine that night. We met in a small restaurant, also in Baker Street, where he had most of his meals. We dined there on the two following nights as well; and I was surprised to see that he ordered exactly the same dinner for himself each time. I asked him why, and he told me that it was his way. He would take a fancy to certain dishes and eat them till he got bored. Then he would give them up completely and try something else.

For three nights running I told Taylor in detail what Bailey and I thought could be done in Albania, Yugoslavia, Bulgaria and Rumania. I have seldom met a more stimulating man to talk to. Very quick to grasp new ideas, he nevertheless probed them until he had extracted the last ounce of relevant information. He would then marshal all the departmental and military arguments for and against the course of action involved. When these brought him up against a difficulty he never tried to evade it, but worried away at it until he had found a solution.

After these private talks, Taylor held meetings in the office to try and define the 'D' Section's policy towards Yugoslavia, Bulgaria, Rumania and Albania. As a result 'D' Section requested authority to support the Peasant Party and the Djonovitch group in Yugoslavia, the Peasant Party and the *Zveno* officers' group in Bulgaria and the Peasant Party in Rumania. They also recommended that King Zog should be made the leader of the Albanian exile movement and if possible infiltrated into

Albania to raise guerrilla forces to support the Greek Army. The Foreign
Office tended to resist these policies. They refused to make any commitment to King Zog and were helped in this by the Greek Government.
The Greeks hoped to annex much of Southern Albania—or as they called
it Northern Epirus—after the war and did not want to be under any
obligation to the Albanians.

Our proposals to support the Rumanian Peasant Party, however,
were accepted. There was no-one else in Rumania to whom we could
turn. Even so, the decision was taken only just in time. Under German
pressure, Antonescu presently broke off diplomatic relations with Britain
and our mission had to be withdrawn; but not before de Chastellain had
made the necessary arrangements for co-operation with the Peasant
Party and for maintaining communications with them.

On the vital issue of the Djonovitch proposals, the Foreign Office
rejected the idea of supporting direct action against Prince Paul and King
Boris. But opinion in the rest of Whitehall was growing increasingly
sceptical of the merits of these two gentlemen. In the end, therefore, it
was agreed that we should keep in touch with Djonovitch and our other
friends in the Yugoslav and Bulgarian Opposition and give them discreet
support as a reinsurance against the possible defection of Prince Paul or
King Boris. It was an uneasy compromise and did not take account of
the momentum of the German advance in the Balkans. Nevertheless it
was a step in what I thought to be the right direction.

Taylor now proposed that I should go back to Belgrade or possibly
to Sofia to take charge of our contacts with the Opposition groups. But
the Foreign Office would not agree to this. They might be forced to
accept some change of policy; but it was too much to ask their representatives to accept the return of the very junior official who had helped to
inspire the change.

Taylor, accordingly, proposed that I should return to Bailey's staff in
Istanbul. But this too was opposed. I had become a bone of contention
between two powerful departments; and, since co-operation between them
was important to the war effort, the 'D' Section concluded that the easiest
solution would be to post me back to the R.A.F. from which I had hitherto
been seconded. But, at this point, word of the 'Amery case' reached Dr.
Dalton, the Minister of Economic Warfare, who, unknown to the general
public, was also the Minister responsible for the 'D' Section.

Dalton had been Under-Secretary at the Foreign Office in the second
Labour Government. He knew Europe well and regarded our policy in
the Balkans as a hangover of the years of 'Appeasement'. He sent for me.

At our first meeting he seemed rather larger than life. He was tall
and broad. His head rose to a mightly bald dome. His voice boomed,
and he accompanied his expansive gestures with an ominous rolling of

the eyes. It was, indeed, the joke of the office that he would not have lasted long in the days of 'shoot when you see the whites of their eyes'. It was also rumoured that he had a special chair so designed as to fall to bits at very slight pressure. According to the story, he would take a running kick at this when he wanted to impress a visitor with the strength of his opinions.

Yet I have never known a kinder man or one prepared to take so much trouble to help his subordinates and young men generally. He cross-examined me for most of a morning beginning with my school days and making me relate the whole story of my life.

He asked about my political views and whether I had read certain books on economics. When I confessed to ignorance of the particular titles he mentioned, he boomed out: 'Aha! I see you are not very familiar with my works. I will send them to you tomorrow and then examine you upon them!'

Then, at last, he turned to the matter in hand and questioned me in detail about the Balkans. He seemed at first to be arguing the Foreign Office case but this was only to take my measure. Suddenly he brought his fist down on the desk and declared: 'Of course you are right and they are wrong. It is useless to expect any help from King Boris or Prince "Palsy".' And he repeated the word 'Palsy' several times obviously relishing his own lampoon which Churchill would one day make famous. At the end of our talk he said: 'I want you to work for me in the Balkans; and, when I want something, I usually get it. You will be hearing from me.'

Dalton duly raised the 'Amery case' personally with the Foreign Secretary but was rebuffed. He did not change his mind about me but decided to bide his time. He instructed me meanwhile to go the R.A.F.

Dalton asked Hanau, as my first Chief in the Balkans, to put his view of me on record. Hanau wrote:

16 October 1940. In the spring of this year . . . it was found necessary to appoint a Liaison Officer with our section. The choice fell on Mr. Julian Amery, Assistant Press Attaché.

Very soon we found that his special qualifications could be put to good use by our section in other directions also, especially on the political side. . . .

Amery was employed by us principally in connection with our Albanian and Bulgarian schemes, where he displayed a political flair very exceptional in most Englishmen.

His political judgement we found to be mature and to a degree quite astonishing in one quite so young. He is only twenty-one years old. Added to his political sense, young Amery has a good historical background with an unquenchable thirst for more knowledge.

Moreover he has that quality, so rare in Englishmen, of being able to ingratiate himself with foreigners of all races and convictions. . . .

Far be it from me to question in the remotest degree the wisdom of the Foreign Office. I can only judge Amery from the point of view of 'D' section and as a man under whom he served. In that capacity I have nothing but good to record of him. . . .

Employed on the kind of work for which his intellectual qualifications and moral qualities fit him so admirably, he would be worth a battalion of infantry. As an N.C.O. in the R.A.F. he would really be one of many thousands and his rare talents would run to waste.

In my opinion we should make the strongest possible efforts to induce the authorities to allow us to retain Julian Amery in our section.

May I add in conclusion that he would be one of the first men selected by me as a collaborator on any new mission with which I might be entrusted.

22

Sergeant R.A.F.

Towards the end of November 1940 I received orders to report to the R.A.F. training organisation at Torquay.

In the same railway carriage going down were two privates from a Yeomanry Regiment and a vigorous old lady, bursting with patriotic sentiment and praise for 'the boys doing their bit'. These two soldiers were clearly out for some fun. They told the old lady that they were conscientious objectors and had decided to desert. They were sure Hitler would win the War and wondered if she would hide them in her house until the Germans came. The poor soul took it all literally and threatened to denounce them to the police. They pleaded piteously with her to spare them and eventually promised to be good boys and return to their regiment. At this she tipped them each ten shillings and bustled off at the next station, obviously feeling that she too had 'done her bit'.

I had already become a Sergeant in the R.A.F. Volunteer Reserve when at Oxford. This seemed to present a problem to the authorities. In 1939 the training wings had been filled with officers and N.C.O.s from the Volunteer Reserve, and it had been easy to form them into separate groups. But by November 1940 I was the only one. Nobody quite knew what to do with me. Questions of rank are of absorbing interest to the fighting services; and the discussion of my status was prolonged. But eventually authority gave its ruling. I was to be paid as a Sergeant, dressed as a Sergeant, and accorded a Sergeant's privileges. At the same time I was to be accommodated with the rest of the wing intake who were all Aircraft-men Second Class and to take my meals with the instructors who were corporals.

I was then marched off to a dilapidated hotel on the sea front, where my squadron—'A' Squadron—was billeted. The rooms were as bare as a prison and each contained several narrow beds. There was no heating at all, save for a coke fire in the guard room, and there was no hot water at night.

The squadron was some forty strong, drawn from every part of the country and every possible walk of life. In charge of us was a young

Welsh corporal. He had been a P.T. instructor in private life and was a strong Christian Socialist.

My fellow recruits were a pleasant enough crowd. One had the courage to say his prayers at night; and the others mocked him for it until I defended him. I was two years older than most of them, and, as a Sergeant, had a shadowy authority. The most congenial were an amusing boy called Geoffrey Lloyd who borrowed my books and what is more returned them, and an Anglo-Mexican, Harry Hambledon, who had flown in the latest Mexican Civil War. He and I were the only two recruits in the wing who held pilot licences. This gave us prestige among our fellows but none at all with the authorities.

Flying training was still some way off. For three weeks life consisted of making beds, learning how to lay out our kit in approved fashion, to polish boots and buttons, to clean floors, windows and fire grates. We did some drill and P.T. and went for occasional runs across country. Every now and again we had a lecture on the history of the Air Force, in those days still mercifully short, and on venereal disease, a subject with which authority seemed obsessed.

One day we were all marched off to the Medical Officer's quarters. There we were told to strip and then proceed through three separate rooms. At each door was a medical orderly with a blunt syringe. He stood behind the door so that you could not see him until you went through it. Almost as soon as you saw him he jabbed you in the arm. When we came out ten minutes later we had been injected against typhoid and tetanus, vaccinated against smallpox, graded for blood group and weighed and measured. At least half a dozen people fainted. I noticed that they were all fair-haired. We were given the rest of the day off but this was little consolation. A typhoid injection makes most people feel as if they had 'flu, and the second day is with me worse than the first. We sat in our barrack room, cheerful at first but growing progressively despondent as the injections took effect and, by doctor's orders, denied the comforts of alcohol.

It all reminded me very much of school. The food was slightly worse than at Eton in peace-time, though not I imagine much worse than at Eton in the war. I accordingly ate out as much as possible. I got round the different chores in much the same way as I had done at school. Some of my colleagues found it difficult to write letters, and I was much in demand to help with begging letters to parents and love letters to girls. In return, they made my bed or polished my boots. There was 'lock up' which meant that we had to be in our billets by ten o'clock. But as the N.C.O. in charge was a corporal and I was a sergeant, we soon came to an understanding about this. Generally speaking, I found discomfort and discipline much less irksome than I had done as a child. I found too that

I minded them a good deal less than many recruits from less comfortable homes. I have often heard it said that the importance of comfort increases with age. This has not been my experience, at any rate so far. The only thing I really minded was unrelieved cold. This I found just as trying in the R.A.F. as I had at school. In one of my letters home I wrote:

> The weather is Arctic. . . . It's funny that people have never pictured hell as an icy cavern with howling draughts where the wicked freeze to all eternity tantalised by imitation furnaces.

By way of reply my father sent me a copy of the *Inferno* flagging the passage where Dante provides frozen sections of hell for the punishment of the very worst offenders.

My life in the Balkans had called for constant vigilance and put considerable responsibilities on me. In the R.A.F. it was quite different. I wrote in another letter:

> Life is so simple and there is so little to worry about that it is rather a relief. Nobody expects me to be intelligent. Nobody asks questions. Nobody has any questions to ask. Better still, nobody has to be questioned.

As I already held a pilot's licence I thought it reasonable that I should be excused the Initial Training Wing and allowed to go straight to the Elementary Flying Training School. There at least I would see an aeroplane, though, even then, it would be at least a year before I could hope to join a squadron. With my Commanding Officer's support I accordingly applied to authority for the necessary permission. The high-ups were still considering this petition when the rest of 'A' Squadron moved on to the Initial Training Wing. My Commanding Officer ruled that I should stay behind. The prospect of flying raised my morale:

> . . . it seems that I shall part with my fellows and proceed to an Elementary Flying School while they do a further course of drilling, etc. This is a relief both because it means that I shall be treated as a slightly higher type of worm and because I can get a real interest out of flying. I hope that Hugh (Dalton) will have acted by then, but if not I shall be at least more intelligently occupied than at present.
>
> You can imagine what it feels like to spend hours a day polishing, making beds, and listening to elementary talks on the Official Secrets Act when I know what my friends are doing out East.
>
> Nonetheless, I am full of admiration for the R.A.F. training organisation which does make a pretty successful attempt to explain the service to would-be pilots and spare them unnecessary trouble or discomfort. The officers I don't see, but most of the N.C.Os. are a nice lot. . . .

My duties while waiting consisted in supervising the furnishing of two hotels which the R.A.F. had taken over to accommodate recruits. I also seem to have acted as a temporary medical orderly.

Yesterday I rubbed ether on the chests and forearms of some three hundred candidates for inoculations. Big chests, hairy chests, bony chests, flat chests, heaving bosoms, in short every possible variety, colour, texture and smell of chest. This I suppose is flying training.

But most of the time there was nothing to do at all. I went for walks on the cliffs and read *War and Peace*. I thought it then, and still think it, the greatest novel ever written. There is hardly a facet of life—birth, death, love, poverty, business, family life, hunting, battles or politics— which is not portrayed with truth and often with genius. Tolstoy may underrate the influence of individuals upon events, but there are limits to what human beings can do, and when things are going wrong I have often found his philosophy comforting.

Kind friends also provided some relief. Lady Allenby, the widow of the Field Marshal, had a house near Torquay and loved to talk of Egypt and about Wavell. Professor Max Mallowan, the archaeologist, also gave me the run of his house and garden. He knew the Middle East well and I spent many hours discussing its problems with him and with his wife, better known to the public as Agatha Christie. She has the heart of a woman but the mind of a man.

Presently, the authorities wanted the hotel where I had been staying for another batch of recruits. I was accordingly allotted a billet in the town. I set off humping a bursting kit bag and after a long trudge found the right address. A comfortable looking old woman showed me up to a bedroom, furnished with a small double bed and a wash stand. She was just leaving when I noticed another kit bag behind the door. I pointed to this and suggested that she must have shown me the wrong room. 'That's all right,' she replied, 'I think you'll find the bed plenty big enough for two and quite comfortable.'

My bed mate when bed time came was a spotty young man with a fair moustache and a Lancashire accent. He had been a clerk. The bed was narrow and I must have taken more than my fair share of the covers, for my partner woke from the intense cold and grabbed them back. We repeated the process several times. The next night was even worse, and so on the following morning I applied for leave. It was granted at once. Later on, when I was parliamentary candidate for Preston, I was asked whether I had any close experience of the Lancashire working man. I almost replied: 'Well I've been to bed with one,' but then thought better of it.

On the first night of my leave, 4 January 1941, the Germans bombed the City and burned much of it down. I went with my father to watch the fires put out and to gaze on the smouldering ruins of what had been the financial centre of the world. Somewhere amid the devastation we ran into Brailsford, the left-wing journalist. He judged the devastation symbolic of what the war meant for Britain's future. It was hard to gainsay him; but my father found some consolation in the thought that the Great Fire would provide an undreamt of opportunity to clear the area around St. Paul's—he wanted to build a square in front of the cathedral and let public gardens run down from its south side to the river. He also spoke of building a mosque in the Stambouli style on the opposite bank of the Thames in recognition of Britain's connections with the Moslem world. Money was raised to build a mosque, but for some reason the fund-raising committee settled on a less imaginative site in Regent's Park. After the War, Duncan Sandys fought hard to prevent new building from again choking the view of St. Paul's. He is the most determined man I know in English public life, but vested interests proved too strong even for him.

I had scarcely been twenty-four hours in London when a telegram came cancelling my leave. Training Command had turned down my request to go straight to the Flying School. Instead I was to rejoin my old Squadron at their Training Wing at Paignton.

We were billeted once again in a hotel on the sea front. As a sergeant I shared a room with the corporal of the Guard, a sly fellow who had worked in a shipping firm in the Cape Verde Islands. Unlike the other barrack rooms, our room was never inspected, and I was thus spared the tedium of kit inspections. Life, however, was more strenuous. There was more P.T. and drill; there were also more marches and lectures. I was living the life of an ordinary pilot under training and had no cause for complaint. But after a year at the heart of things in the Balkans, it was frustrating to be a prisoner of the machine unable to make any contribution to what for Britain was the supreme crisis of the war.

A few random extracts from my letters show my mood:

> This is just like being back at school with no prospect of any action for over *a year*!
>
> The novelty of discomfort and second-rate company is wearing thin, but I guess I can take it. . . . I am already enormously rested. Soon I will be restive.

I remember walking out along the cliffs on a stormy winter afternoon trying to assess Britain's situation. The danger of invasion was thought to have receded. But it was difficult to see how or where we could take the offensive in Europe again. The Russians seemed prepared to swallow anything from Hitler. My letters from America were full of pro-Allied sentiments, but held out no hope of action. We might well be excluded from the Continent for a decade, existing precariously as a dependency of the United States. The only rays of light came from Libya, where Wavell had routed superior Italian forces, and from Epirus, where the Greek Army was still holding its own. But if inferior forces could achieve such victories, could they not do the same in Yugoslavia and Bulgaria? And yet the situation in the Balkans was crumbling rapidly and every day the papers reported further signs of German penetration. I felt convinced that I had a contribution to make in Belgrade or Sofia and that no-one else perhaps could make it.

> I am living a sort of half life shut in on myself. Only you will under-
> stand how bitter it is to be right out of everything at this of all hours.

All this time my friends in 'D' Section had been active on my behalf. Hanau and Bailey pressed repeatedly for my return. Dalton told my father at Cabinet that events were proving me right and that he was more than ever determined to get me back.

His first attempt, made in the middle of December 1940 failed. Hanau wrote to me:

> Yesterday I was told that all efforts had failed to get you released from
> the R.A.F. and back into our section. I am truly sorry as I feel convinced
> that you would have contributed so much more effectively to the War
> effort with us than in your present job. . . .
>   The Amery case has become quite a *cause célèbre* and petty intrigues
> aided by that accursed demon of block-headed officialdom have brought
> us up against a blank wall.
>   Any way you have the profound satisfaction of having helped very
> efficiently in a mighty interesting job of work and of seeing the adoption
> of your policy.

Indeed the signs that King Boris was preparing to go over to the Germans could no longer be ignored. In January, Dalton came on a particularly pessimistic report from Bulgaria. He spoke to Eden, who had recently become Foreign Secretary. The Foreign Office, he boomed, were virtually working for the enemy. They were still backing King Boris although it was now quite clear that Boris was a German agent. They wouldn't even let the 'D' Section use young Amery. And why? What was his crime? He had been against Boris and that other German agent, Paul. Well, they would have done a great deal better if they had listened to Amery instead of to their own hide-bound officials.

There was a good deal more, I have been told, in the same vein; and, Eden gracefully conceded what was, after all, a very small point. Looking back I have always thought it immensely to Dalton's credit that, in all the press of business and at a time when he was running two major departments, he should have spent so much energy in putting right an injustice to a very junior member of his staff.

At the end of the afternoon parade on 22 January, I was called before the Commanding Officer. He told me that the Ministry of Economic Warfare had applied for me and that the R.A.F. had authority to release me. Did I really want to leave? He was a fine type of man, passionately devoted to his Service. He supposed that I was going back to an office job in London; and when I said 'Yes', I could see in his eyes that he was shocked and hurt.

I longed to tell him that I would be in action at least a year sooner than if I stayed with the R.A.F. But the secrecy of our work in the Balkans had been so drilled into me that I said nothing.

So ended my R.A.F. career. It was hardly a glorious one, and I have sometimes blushed when chairmen at political meetings have spoken with pride of how 'Mr. Amery served in the Royal Air Force during the Battle of Britain.'

I knew it was right for me to go back to the Balkans. And yet I should like to have fought an air battle alone above the clouds. Life, however, has its consolations. I left the R.A.F. as a Sergeant. When I returned to it twenty years later, it would be as Secretary of State for Air.

23

Baker Street

I came back to London to find that the 'D' Section had been drastically reformed. Among other things it had changed its name and was now known as the Special Operations Executive or S.O.E.[1]

Lawrence Grand was dismissed and posted to India. There he earned high praise from both Auchinleck and Wavell for his work on the re-organisation of the Indian Army's rail and road communications. Grand's disregard of Whitehall conventions, his love of the Nelson touch, and his ruthless ways of cutting through red tape had made him a thorn in the side of the Government machine. But such men are necessary in time of crisis; and, without his vision and driving force, the work would never have begun. Those who followed him enjoyed much greater backing from the Government; and their achievements were on a correspondingly greater scale. Yet a large part of the credit for Britain's acknowledged pre-eminence in the waging of Resistance and subversive warfare belongs to Grand.

Grand's place was taken by Sir Frank Nelson, a former Member of Parliament with extensive business experience. Charles Hambro, a distinguished banker, became his second in command; and a number of able men from the City and industry were brought into the organisation. A proper command structure was introduced and, with it, a semblance of bureaucratic procedures. All this was necessary as the work grew in scale. But something of the original impetus and comradeship was lost.[2]

I sensed something of the change on the first day of my return to Baker Street. Although I had worked for nine months for the 'D' Section, I had never been on the organisation's books nor paid a salary by them. I was now formally enrolled on the establishment of S.O.E. and commissioned in the Army with the rank of Captain. This was rapid promotion seeing that I had only been a Sergeant a few days before, and it at last

[1] To be strictly accurate it was first called S.O.2; S.O.1 being the organisation responsible for 'Black Propaganda'. These names were later changed to S.O.E. for S.O.2 and P.W.E. (Political Warfare Executive) for S.O.1. For the reader's convenience, however, the organisation will henceforward be described as S.O.E.

[2] For a full account of the work of the 'D' Section and S.O.E. see *Baker Street Irregular* by Col. Bickham Sweet-Escott.

enabled me to do without any further allowance from my father. I was also made to fill in a mass of forms, including the Official Secrets Act, and issued with various passes admitting me to the more sensitive sectors of National Defence.

Despite these tendencies to bureaucratisation, S.O.E. was still very conspiratorial. We were under instructions when travelling from the office to some clandestine appointment always to change taxis on the way, in case we were being followed; though as taxis grew scarcer this rule was allowed to lapse. Each of us, too, had a code name. Mine was AHA. I was always referred to by it in correspondence, at formal meetings or over the telephone.

Dr. Dalton soon sent for me. He had decided, he said, to keep me in the London Office for a couple of months and then send me back to the Balkans. I was accordingly attached to the Balkan section in Baker Street. To my regret Taylor had left London to take personal control of our work in Belgrade. Hanau, who knew more about the Balkans than any living Englishman, had unaccountably been put in charge of the East and West African sections of S.O.E. My immediate chiefs were first a solicitor and then a steel executive. Both were able men but knew as much about the Balkans as I did about their business.

I had no specific responsibilities in the section but was given a small office and shown the telegrams and reports as they came in. I commented on these and did my best to follow up requests from Bailey or Taylor.

My dentist, however, presently reported that I was suffering from seriously impacted wisdom teeth. He advised an immediate operation.

The Germans chose to raid London on the day of the operation and the blast from one of their bombs knocked down my anaesthetist on his way to the hospital. He gave me an overdose of anaesthetic. The dentist somehow managed to crack my jaw.

I came round in a gloomy cellar surrounded by groaning bodies lying on truckle beds or stretchers. The raid had been heavy and prolonged; and all the hospital patients had been moved down into an improvised shelter. The body in the bed next to mine began screaming. A nurse came and gave each of us a strong shot of morphia. This put me to sleep again, and when I woke up I was back in my room.

The operation left me weaker and more shaken than I had expected, and the doctor prescribed a fortnight in the country. This was not so easy to arrange in wartime, but fortunately Pam Churchill, Randolph's wife and a life long friend, carried me off to a house which she and Diana Sandys were sharing in Hertfordshire. Pam's son, Winston, was newly-born and slept most of the time. Julian Sandys was an alert three-yearold with a mass of red hair. He seemed surprised that anyone else should be called Julian and rather disapproving.

At the end of my convalescence Pam drove me back to London. We called at 10 Downing Street and found a message inviting her to dinner. She asked if I could go too. It was a small party but included Winston Churchill and Averell Harriman. Towards the end of dinner, the talk turned to the War. There was agreement that we had probably escaped invasion. But no-one could quite see how we could get back into Europe and win the War. Someone asked Churchill what he thought. He picked up an orange from the table and said that, if he were a worm and wanted to get into the orange, he would go on walking round it until he found a hole. He might have to go on walking round it until the orange went rotten and a hole appeared. But he would get in in the end, if he did not starve first. And, here, he turned to Harriman and began talking to him about the importance of supplies from North America. I know of no better description of Britain's grand strategy in the year when we stood alone.

Back in London, I stayed at our home in Eaton Square which my mother somehow kept going despite conscription, raids and rationing. She was helped in this by our cook and two old servants, and by a steady stream of food parcels from the Commonwealth. There is little gratitude in politics, but my father's work for the Empire received tangible recognition all through the War in the shape of food parcels. These enabled us not just to feed ourselves but to keep something like open house.

My relations with my father now entered upon a new phase. I had always loved and admired him but inevitably there had been a gulf between man and boy. In some ways Oxford and Spain had narrowed it, but the arrogance and impatience of an undergraduate had deepened it for a time as well. Now, as far as I was concerned, the gulf disappeared. My experience of the Balkans had taught me some humility and I, at last, began to appreciate fully the breadth of his vision and the vigour and audacity of his thinking. I now know from his diaries that he felt the same:

> Julian has certainly matured enormously in the last year and his judgement on political matters is remarkable.

As an officer of S.O.E. I saw a wide selection of Foreign Office telegrams, Intelligence Reports and other Government papers. I was on the inside of Government; and so my father felt free to talk to me about many of the great issues with which Ministers were grappling. All this taught me much about the inner workings of the Government machine, as well as about the broader problems of War—supply, strategy and diplomacy.

These lessons were complemented by meals at home with some of my father's Cabinet colleagues, our military Commanders or Allied leaders like Dr. Beneš or General de Gaulle. By the time my twenty-second birthday came round in March of 1941, I knew a good deal more about the conduct of the war and the problems ahead than did most of my superiors in the office.

There are obvious dangers for a young man in being on the 'inside track'. But my work in the Balkans had taught me to keep my own counsel. I occasionally took advantage of my information and contacts for some serious purpose but otherwise made it a rule never to parade my knowledge of what was going on.

I had found it very helpful in Belgrade to sit at the feet of older men, especially those who had the leisure of retirement. I thought I would do the same at home. I had been deeply depressed by my experience of Foreign Office policy in the Balkans and, accordingly sought out Lord Tyrell, one of its greatest Permanent Under-Secretaries, to learn his views on what should be the aims of British Foreign Policy. We had several talks together. I made no notes of them and much of what he said was, no doubt, ephemeral. But he had one constant theme. This was the paramount importance of associating France—and this meant in his view de Gaulle—with as many of our decisions as possible. Britain, he kept saying, had never been a very great Power on her own account. We had achieved a dominant position in recent years only by combining our leadership of the Empire with our alliance with France. After the War we should have to fight for our very survival, and, in this, would need France almost as much as France would need us. As for the Balkans, he was inclined to agree with my criticisms of our policy. It was, he explained, the inevitable consequence of our withdrawal of support for the Little Entente and for a forward French policy in Eastern Europe. Like Dalton, in fact, Tyrell seemed to see our support for King Boris and Prince Paul as a 'hangover' from the attempted 'appeasement' of the Axis Powers.

All this time the situation in the Balkans was steadily deteriorating.

In Rumania there was little or no resistance to the advance of German influence. Our co-operation with Maniu's Peasant Party had come too late. It yielded a dividend, indeed, in terms of intelligence. More important perhaps, it enabled Maniu to keep his organisation in being and this of itself was a source of anxiety to General Antonescu and to the Germans. But by the beginning of 1941 the German take-over of Rumania was virtually complete.

In Bulgaria our friends in the Peasant Party and the *Zveno* officers' group showed more spirit. There was widespread sabotage of the road and

A.M.—H

rail communications along which the Germans planned to bring their forces from Rumania to the Yugoslav and Greek borders. At the beginning of February, indeed, it seemed possible that, given energetic Yugoslav and Turkish support, Dimitrov and his friends might bring down King Boris.

I talked over this possibility with my father, and he sent a minute to Churchill and Eden suggesting:

> We should urge Turkey and Yugoslavia to force Bulgaria into line at once, giving them a definite promise of the whole of Wavell's Army and further reinforcements if they did so. I have no doubt it is the right policy . . . but I doubt if we shall rise to it.[1]

We did not rise to it; and, in any case, Prince Paul was in no mood to provide the essential Yugoslav co-operation. As a result, King Boris managed to recover his grip on the situation. German troops now entered Bulgaria, and most of the Opposition leaders were put under arrest. Dimitrov, however, escaped and was brought by us to Istanbul in a diplomatic bag.

To be more precise Dimitrov travelled in a large packing case under diplomatic seal which purported to contain part of the British Legation archives. Expecting the journey to last some twenty-four hours, Dimitrov had taken with him a couple of pounds of butter to provide energy and some oranges to quench thirst. He also carried a long-nosed Luger automatic, and enough ammunition to fight his way out or sell his life dearly in the attempt.

The packing case was loaded with others on to a van. The van in its turn was escorted by Norman Davies, the S.O.E. representative in Sofia, who drove his own car. Both vehicles had diplomatic plates, but in the rush someone had forgotten to provide the van, as distinct from the car, with a separate diplomatic *carnet* and *laissez-passer*. The van was accordingly stopped by security police at the Bulgarian frontier post of Svilengrad.

Norman Davies fortunately had diplomatic status and managed to prevent the security police from searching the van. But it took him several telephone calls to Sofia, lasting over seven hours, before the frontier authorities were instructed to let the van proceed.

Finally, after some thirty hours' travel, the van drew up in the garden of the old British Embassy in Istanbul. It was 4.30 a.m.; but Bailey had waited up for this precious consignment. He recalls that Dimitrov's first words after scrambling out of his diplomatic dog kennel were: 'I have a great deal to tell you, and many matters to discuss before we leave for Belgrade. When can we start?' They started then and there and it was

[1] L. S. Amery: *Diaries*, 10 February 1941.

after nine o'clock before Dimitrov could be persuaded to go and take some rest.

With the collapse of Bulgarian resistance the centre of the Balkan drama shifted to Yugoslavia. There, despite the pathetically earnest entreaties of the British Legation, Prince Paul prepared to come to terms with the Germans. When this became clear, Gavrilovitch's Serbian Peasant Party withdrew their support from the Government. They and the other Opposition leaders decided to organise mass demonstrations in Belgrade. There was no need. The people were already crowding into the streets spontaneously shouting the slogan 'Better War than the Pact.'

Djonovitch and Voivoda Birchanin now resolved to move against Prince Paul. Birchanin was soon in touch with his friends in the Army and the Air Force only to find that Major Knezevitch of the Royal Guards and Colonel Mirkovitch of the Air Force were already making their own plans for a coup d'état.

There was little enough we could do in London; but I suggested that, as the only member of the Government who spoke Serbian, my father might usefully broadcast to Yugoslavia. The B.B.C. agreed and on the evening of 25 March he made a stirring appeal to the Yugoslavs to be worthy of the traditions of Kossovo and to choose the path of honour rather than capitulation.

The speech was widely heard in Belgrade and may have contributed to the general spirit of resistance. More important, perhaps, it was heard by some of the officers who were preparing the coup d'état. They afterwards told me that they took it as a public sign of British support for themselves and were strengthened by it in their determination to act.

Despite the demonstrations, Prince Paul's Government signed their pact with Hitler. *Nemesis* followed swiftly. On the night of 26/27 March Colonel Mirkovitch of the Air Force, Major Knezevitch of the Royal Guards and Voivoda Birchanin with four hundred men of the *Narodna Odbrana* seized the key positions of Belgrade. They roused General Simovitch and invited him to become Prime Minister.

Prince Paul was arrested and handed over to Britain. King Peter was declared of age. A national Government was formed. It included a number of my old friends, among them Nintchitch, Yeftitch and Grol. Yugoslavia had declared against Hitler.

It would be idle to claim that S.O.E. organised the coup d'état of 27 March. There has never been a more spontaneous revolt in history. But S.O.E.'s co-operation with the Djonovitch/Birchanin group and with Gavrilovitch's Peasant Party undoubtedly strengthened both these and helped them to create the climate of opinion in which a coup became inevitable. The coup itself was the work of three men: Colonel Mirkovitch, Major Knezevitch and Voivoda Birchanin. Of these only Birchanin was in direct contact with S.O.E.

The new Yugoslav Government faced a desperate situation. The Army was ill-equipped; the Air Force wretchedly weak. The country was surrounded by hostile forces on every frontier, save the Greek. Croatia was riddled with Fifth Columnists. Their only hope was to withdraw the Army from the northern provinces and concentrate it to defend the mountains of Bosnia and Serbia. At the same time, all available forces should have been thrown into Albania in an attempt to destroy the Italian Army in the Balkans before the Germans could attack. Such a strategy would not have averted ultimate defeat. But it would have forced the Germans to fight the Yugoslavs in the tangled mountains of Serbia and Albania instead of in the northern plains. It would also have given the Greeks a chance to switch some of their forces from Epirus to the defence of Macedonia.

The Yugoslav leaders were fine men but they had been out of office a long time and seemed incapable of decisive action. Instead of taking the initiative against the Italians in Albania, they played for time hoping that the inevitable Nazi offensive might somehow be delayed. The German attack on 6 April—the Orthodox Good Friday—found them equally unprepared to defend their mountainous heartland or to strike at their more vulnerable foe. The result was catastrophe. In less than a week Belgrade fell to the Germans, and the greatest of the Balkan Armies was utterly defeated.

The Yugoslav Government escaped to the Middle East; the High Command capitulated; and whole divisions were made prisoner. The Battle of Yugoslavia, however, lasted just long enough for S.O.E. to send Colonel Oakley Hill[1] and the leaders of the Albanian United Front back into Albania. They advanced with a small force as far as the outskirts of Scutari; and were warmly welcomed by the tribes. Had the Yugoslav armies been able to stand their ground, the whole of Northern Albania might well have risen in revolt against the Italians. But with the capitulation of Yugoslavia, the leaders of the Albanian Front were changed from the vanguard of a powerful army into a small band of fugitives. The Kryeziu brothers escaped back into Yugoslavia where they fell into Italian hands and were imprisoned. But Abas Kupi and Mustafa Gjinishi stayed as outlaws in the Albanian mountains. They would be the seed from which the Albanian Resistance Movements would grow.

With the collapse of Yugoslavia, the German armies swept on to

---

[1] Colonel Dagvall Oakley Hill had served in the Albanian gendarmerie before the war and had been sent to Belgrade by S.O.E. as a liaison officer with the Albanian United Front.

overwhelm the gallant Greek Army and its handful of British allies. All the Balkans were thus lost to Hitler.

The coup d'état of 27 March may well have been a turning point in the war. It forced Hitler to clean up Germany's Balkan flank before attacking Russia, and so delayed the Russian campaign by more than six weeks. These six weeks probably saved Moscow and may thus have turned the tide of the war. And yet I believe that Britain missed an even greater opportunity by not supporting the Djonovitch proposal to overthrow Prince Paul when this was first made to us in the summer of 1940.

Had we given our blessing then to a coup d'état in Yugoslavia it would probably have been attempted in the autumn. Now at the end of October 1940, as it happened, the Italians invaded Greece only to be driven back in disorder into Albania.

Had there been a pro-Allied Government in Belgrade at the time, the Yugoslav Army could have attacked the Italians in North Albania and might have thrown them into the Adriatic. In the autumn, moreover, there were still no German troops in Bulgaria. The Bulgarian Opposition would have been greatly encouraged by a coup in Belgrade; King Boris might have been overthrown; and Yugoslavs and Bulgars might have made common cause with Greece. The Germans would scarcely have relished the prospect of a Balkan campaign in winter; and by the spring of 1941, there could have been an effective Balkan Front in being. Instead Greece was left to fight alone. The Italians recovered their balance in Albania. Bulgaria admitted German troops; and, when at last Yugoslavia 'found her soul', it was, for all practical purposes, past midnight.

To say all this is not to decry the value of the coup d'état of 27 March. It remains one of the noblest gestures in Serbian, indeed in European, history. It gave Yugoslavia a place among the Allies and ensured that it was not broken up into its component parts. It may even have saved Moscow. But for the defence of the Balkans it came too late.

V

OF RESISTANCE

1941–1943

'I believed I was on the right road . . . But fate was merciless to me when it threw me into this maelstrom. I wanted much. I started much, but the gale of the world carried away me and my work.'

General Draja Mihailovitch: final speech at his
trial in Belgrade 11 July 1946

Explanatory Note

My life for the next three years was lived in two watertight compartments. My working hours and main energies were devoted to the organisation of Resistance in the Balkans. But this was secret service and its concerns could be shared with none but a few close colleagues.

At the same time, as a young staff officer with political connections, I was an interested observer and occasional participant in the broader struggle of which the Balkans were only one sector and a minor one at that.

In London, I saw much of my father's colleagues and friends. In the Middle East, Wavell and Auchinleck showed me kindness and hospitality, while Lampson, our Ambassador in Cairo, Smart, his Oriental Secretary, and Clayton, the Director of Intelligence, encouraged and helped me to meet the political leaders of Egypt and other Middle Eastern countries. War, besides, is not all grim and earnest. London and Cairo offered entertainment in plenty; and I had my fair share of this.

To tell the story of this Jekyll and Hyde existence in chronological sequence would be confusing. It seems better, therefore, to separate the two themes—the secret and the overt.

I will, accordingly, begin with my recollections of Balkan Resistance and revert in later chapters to other experiences in the Middle East and at home.

24

Picking Up the Bits

Immediately after the coup d'état in Belgrade, Bailey asked for me to join him in Istanbul. His request was at once approved.

My immediate problem was to get to Cairo. The best way was by Sunderland flying boat. But there were very few of these to spare for communication flights. Twice I was booked to fly and then pushed off by someone with a higher priority. This was just as well since the second Sunderland never reached its destination.

On the night of 10 May 1941, there was a heavy air raid on London. I had gone to bed late and was still fast asleep when my office telephoned to say that I must leave for Plymouth in half-an-hour. I reached Plymouth towards six in the evening to find it even more bomb-scarred than London. A staff car took me to a combined Naval and Air Headquarters on a cliff above the harbour. From it I could see our Sunderland riding at anchor a hundred yards or so from the mole. The sea was choppy and the wind rising; but the Sunderland was a vulnerable target and there could be no question of leaving before dark. It was double summer time and so we waited till nearly ten o'clock uncertain to the last moment whether the sea would be calm enough for take off. As it grew dark we drove down to the harbour and then out by launch to the Sunderland. Looking back, I could see a row of houses on the crest of the hill. But they were only bombed-out shells of buildings with what was left of the daylight shining through them.

I slept soundly through the night flight, though the pilot told me next day that the Germans had chased us over the Bay of Biscay. He had confused them by flying 'on the deck', and after a time they had turned back, probably from lack of fuel.

We spent the day at Gibraltar and, thanks to Hugh Quennell, the S.O.E. representative there, I was able to see something of the defences of the Rock and to climb to the top of it for the view across the Straits.

Ever since, Gibraltar has seemed to me a symbol of Britain's military genius and an extension of her naval tradition. It is not a colony but an unsinkable aircraft carrier, a coiled spring of sea, air and land power, commanding the cross roads between two seas and two continents.

During the Spanish War, I had often heard Gibraltar dismissed as a military anachronism. It did not look like that to me in 1941. Indeed, without it, we could never have made the landings in North Africa in the following year. Its military significance may well grow again with the current increase in Soviet naval power in the Mediterranean.

We resumed our journey after sunset and landed at first light at Malta. I was eating an early and austere breakfast in the R.A.F. mess at Kala Frana when a formidable figure bore down on me. 'You must be Julian,' she said. 'I shall look after you.' This was my first meeting with Mabel Strickland, the daughter of my father's old friend, Lord Strickland, the Catholic Prime Minister of Malta, who had suffered excommunication rather than support Italian claims to the island.

Mabel was then editor of *The Times of Malta* and, in a period when the Maltese constitution was suspended, had constituted herself the main channel between Maltese opinion and the Governor's Palace. She inspired and directed everything; relief, welfare, civil defence and above all, the civic pride and patriotism of the islanders. She carried me off to her mother's house, the Villa Bologna, when we sat in the garden and drank champagne, while she briefed me on the state of the island and the virtues and shortcomings of the Governor and the military commanders.

Malta had been in the front line since the summer of 1940; and the evidence of bomb damage was everywhere. That the island had survived at all was a miracle. At the beginning there were only three serviceable British fighter aircraft. They were known as Faith, Hope and Charity. Faith and Hope had long since been shot down. Charity I saw; but it was by then more a mascot than a weapon. The Fleet had left the Grand Harbour; and if the Italians had pressed home their attack, the island must have been theirs. But they lacked the courage or vainly imagined they could starve the defenders out.

The Governor, General Dobbie, took our party—they were all very senior officers except for me—on a tour of the island's defences. Dobbie was a Cromwellian soldier and believed as much in the power of prayer as in that of arms. From what I saw of the defences, I could only hope his prayers would be heard.

The tour brought us out on to one of the bastions overlooking the Grand Harbour. Suddenly three waves of Italian bombers flew out of the sunset to drop their bombs on the ships and harbour defences. They made a second pass, but, by that time, our AA batteries were in action and they disappeared flying low across the sea. They did little damage; but two Sunderlands had been destroyed in similar raids; and we were relieved to learn from the Kala Frana base that ours had not been hit.

I had now sat up two nights running and, on the next lap of our journey, slept on the floor. It was hard, but it was a luxury to stretch out at full length. When I woke we were already taxiing along the Nile just below Cairo.

Bailey was in Istanbul but returned a few days later bringing with him several of my friends from the Balkans, including Djonovitch and Tupanyanin from Belgrade and Dimitrov, the Bulgarian peasant leader. Most of the S.O.E. mission in Yugoslavia had been captured; but Bennett and Altmaier had managed to reach Cairo; and we were now joined by Ian Pirie, the head of the Greek section, who had just escaped from Crete.

Pirie was an old Harrovian, an Oxford history scholar and a boxing Blue. He was short, square, red faced, with twinkling blue eyes. His practice was to get to the office every morning at least half-an-hour before anyone else. It was not that he was hard working. Quite the contrary. But he had discovered that by arriving early, he could slip away towards the middle of the morning for a snooze in his bedroom or an early drink in the bar. It never occurred to anyone to question the absence of someone so obviously punctual and thus presumably so industrious. If he was out of the office, it was assumed that he was out on business and, since his work was secret, no-one was in a position to check.

Pirie was what the Americans call 'an ideas man'. One of his best coups had been the discovery of an invisible paint which turned black when exposed to sunlight. Greece is full of white-washed walls; and Pirie had his agents paint suitable slogans on such walls at night. Next day after an hour or two's exposure to the sun, slogans like 'Death to Hitler' would appear, as if by magic, on a wall opposite some crowded café. The customers would laugh their heads off. The Germans were made to look ridiculous; and it would be several hours before a bucket of whitewash could be found to blot out the offending *graffiti*.

Our mission, as Bailey now explained to us, was to re-establish contact with the organisation we had built up in the Balkans before the German invasion and with any new Resistance Groups that might emerge. We had left wireless sets behind. But wireless sets were unwieldy things in those days, far too heavy and gluttons for almost equally heavy batteries. We could not rely on making wireless contact and would therefore have to introduce couriers through Turkey or Switzerland or even by parachute or submarine.

But first there were some political hurdles to clear. The Greek and Yugoslav Governments in exile were our Allies and we should need their general approval for our work and might sometimes want their help. It was also important to bring them to work with each other and with our friends in Bulgaria and Albania. Our agents might then pass through one country to the other and be cared for on their way.

The King and Government of Yugoslavia were in Jerusalem. Bailey and I, accordingly, went there, at the beginning of June 1941, to lay the foundations of our future co-operation with them.

King Peter and his staff were lodged in a small villa outside the city. The King was eighteen years old, slightly built and rather shy. But he seemed alert and was certainly outspoken. He was convinced that Prince Paul had decided to 'kick him out' and probably to 'finish him off'. Twice before the coup d'état, he told me, efforts had been made to persuade him to abdicate.

We hoped then that he would play a major part in the reconstruction of the Balkans after the War. It seemed important, therefore, to get him to London as soon as possible to complete his studies and show him something of English life. This was easily arranged.

His Ministers presented more of a problem. They and their staffs had been billeted together in the monastery of Tantura. This was a noble building; but the bedrooms were cells and the washing facilities primitive. There was only one telephone. The NAAFI food was of a low standard and it was very difficult to get transport into Jerusalem, some five miles away. More galling still to the Ministers was the knowledge that Opposition politicians who had also escaped from Yugoslavia had secured rooms in the King David Hotel and were enjoying good food, a good telephone service and taxis galore.

Sir Reginald Hoare, previously our Minister in Bucharest, had been appointed Ambassador to the Yugoslav Government in exile.

Hoare was a wise and kindly man, but he had passed the stage in life when men can get things done without the help of efficient secretaries. Yet, in Jerusalem, he was virtually without a staff. His telegrams went through the already over-burdened cypher department of the Palestine High Commission. His only assistant, Sturrock,[1] was a heavy fellow with an artificial leg who found the heat of the Palestine summer quite unbearable. Worst of all, Hoare suffered from acute asthma and could scarcely speak above a whisper. The Yugoslav Foreign Minister, Dr. Nintchitch, was stone deaf. This complicated the transaction of business.

When I reached Jerusalem, I found Hoare and his assistant in hospital and the Yugoslav Ministers seething with impotent frustration in their monastery and quarrelling fiercely among themselves.

Winston Churchill had asked me to take a signed photograph of himself to General Simovitch, the Yugoslav Prime Minister. This was no more than a friendly gesture. But to the exiled Yugoslavs it was a sign that I was Churchill's personal representative. Hoare and his assistant

---

[1] Sturrock had been commercial secretary to the Legation in Belgrade. He collapsed and died a few months later in a valiant attempt to rescue aged and sick refugees from a fire on board the ship in which they were leaving Egypt for South Africa.

were forgotten; and I was literally besieged in the King David Hotel by groups of Ministers seeking anything from British approval of some plan for the reconstruction of the Balkans to bag facilities for questionable commercial deals.

General Simovitch, a man of great dignity as well as great courage, found the situation extremely distasteful. He begged me to get his Ministers away from Jerusalem and, if possible, to London. This was clearly the best course and very welcome not only to the Ministers but also to the Mandate authorities. The latter already had nightmares that the British Government was planning to establish another National Home in Palestine, this time for the South Slavs.

It was not, however, so easy to arrange. For political and practical reasons the Egyptian Government and our military authorities had agreed that the Yugoslav Ministers should not stay in Cairo on their way to London, but merely change planes. It was, therefore, arranged that they should only leave Jerusalem when Hoare received a coded message from Cairo, to say that their 'plane to London was ready.

Bailey, Bennett and I were sitting together on a Saturday evening when we received an angry 'phone call from our Cairo office. What had happened to the Yugoslav Ministers? Their aircraft had been standing by for hours. The coded message had been dispatched at midday. Could the Jerusalem plane have crashed?

The first thing was to locate Sturrock. He had been out to dinner but his host said he had gone to bed. There was no answer from his room at the King David Hotel but the porter said he had taken his key. After knocking on his door in vain we finally persuaded a maid to open it with a pass-key. All the lights were burning; Sturrock lay on his bed in a stupor. His artificial leg dressed in a tartan sock and shod with a white-and-tan correspondent shoe was propped against the wall.

The poor man had plainly dined all too well, and it was some time before we could get any sense out of him. In the end, it emerged that he had received the message, had decoded it, and had delivered it in person to Hoare in the early afternoon.

We dashed off to the Carmelite nunnery where Hoare was being nursed by the Sisters of Mercy. The guardian not unnaturally refused to let us in. Finally, the Night Sister was persuaded to parley with us.

The Ambassador was in bed and though not yet asleep had taken a sleeping pill and was distinctly drowsy. Still it was easier getting our point across to him than it had been to Sturrock. 'Ah, yes,' he muttered finally, 'I do remember Sturrock bringing me up something. Kindly pass me my trousers.' He pointed to his clothes which lay in a heap on a chair under the window. Hoare fumbled in the hip pocket, extracted a crumpled sheet of paper, and handed it to Bailey. 'I'm afraid I didn't bother to read it,' he muttered. 'I thought it was just another piece of "bumph" from the Foreign Office.'

The piece of 'bumph' was indeed the magic authorisation and a few hours later the Yugoslav Ministers were on their way to London.

General Simovitch was delighted to be rid of his colleagues and gave Bailey his blessing for our general plans to resume contact with Yugoslavia. He appointed our old friend, Djonovitch, as his delegate in the Middle East and asked us to work closely with him and with the Yugoslav General Staff who would remain in Cairo.

Pirie meanwhile had been working along parallel lines in Cairo with M. Tsouderos and the other leaders of the Greek Government. In some ways his task was easier than ours. There was a large and prosperous Greek community in Egypt; and he was not much troubled with practical problems of accommodation or diet. On the other hand, the feuds within the Greek Government were even fiercer than among the Yugoslavs. King George of Greece and Tsouderos were in frequent disagreement. The Greek officers who had escaped to Egypt were sharply divided between Royalists and Republicans. Pirie, however, also secured the appointment of an old friend, Spiromilio, as the Greek Government delegate authorised to co-operate with S.O.E.

We now brought Tsouderos and Simovitch together in Cairo. They soon agreed to work with us and with each other in the task of resuming underground contact with their own countries. They also discussed for the first time how their two countries might work together after the war.

A more difficult business was to bring the Yugoslav and Greek Governments to accept co-operation with our Bulgarian friends. Dimitrov was no chauvinist but he was a man of strong principles and determined, besides, not to be branded as a Yugoslav, Greek or even British agent. He wanted to be recognised as the leader of a Free Bulgarian movement on the lines of Free France. This neither Simovitch nor Tsouderos were prepared to concede.

The skein was becoming unusually tangled when a new and formidable Bulgarian character appeared on the scene. This was Kosta Todorov.

Todorov had been a sergeant in the French Foreign Legion and had been dropped by the French behind the Bulgarian lines during the First World War. Later he had become a Minister in Stambulisky's post-war Agrarian Government and then Bulgarian Minister to Belgrade. He had lived in exile since the counter-revolution of 1923 and the killing of Stambulisky.

Dimitrov had asked for Todorov and, so as not to excite Greek or

Yugoslav suspicions, arrangements had been made for him to travel from Canada, where he was then living, on false papers and under the alias of Albert Thomas. As Todorov knew no English he had to masquerade as a French-Canadian; but I have no idea why whoever chose his *nom-de-guerre* should have hit on the name of the founder of the International Labour Office.

I was in my room in the King David Hotel, one evening, when the porter rang and announced the arrival of Mr. Thomas. In the hall stood a short thick-set man with a heavy jowl, looking rather like a caricature of Mussolini. 'I am Kosta Todorov,' he said in a loud voice, extending his hand. Then, as everyone began looking round, he added, 'You look very young. But never mind, at your age I had already been condemned to death twice.'

Todorov proved to be a man of immense vitality. He ate and drank copiously and needed little encouragement to break into the songs of his own country or of the Foreign Legion. On the surface he seemed much rougher than Dimitrov. In fact he was very flexible.

Despite our requests, the Yugoslav and Greek Prime Ministers had avoided meeting the Bulgarian exiles. Todorov soon broke down the barriers. He and Djonovitch were old friends. He accordingly waited until Djonovitch was in conference with Simovitch at the King David Hotel and then broke into the room brushing the secretary aside. He and Djonovitch embraced. After that Simovitch could hardly refuse to recognise his existence.

Todorov then wrote to Tsouderos explaining that his mother was from Crete and claiming that they were cousins. Greeks have a strong family sense, and Tsouderos thought the claim might possibly be true. At any rate he received Todorov and the two men got on very well.

This rather unorthodox diplomacy served its purpose; and, within a few days, Bailey, Pirie and I attended a meeting with Simovitch, Tsouderos, Dimitrov and Todorov. No formal agreements were concluded, but we reached a broad understanding to help each other in all forms of underground work. There was also general agreement that the three countries must co-operate closely together after the war and at least consider setting up a Balkan Federation.

Exiled leaders seldom return to power, and agreements between them are thus of limited value. But we had got what we wanted. We had authority for S.O.E. to work underground in Greece, Yugoslavia and Bulgaria. We had also established a sufficient understanding between the leaders of these three countries to claim that the purpose of our work was not only to liberate the Balkan countries from the Nazis but also to promote a new deal for their peoples based on co-operation and demo-cracy. Here was a banner under which the Balkan peoples might unite against the Germans instead of being played off by the Germans one against the other.

But now the march of events took a dramatic and unexpected turn. On 21 June 1941 Hitler attacked the Russians. For the first time since the fall of France, a gleam of hope lit up the dark horizon. If the Red Army could hold out against the Germans, then the Allies had every chance of ultimate victory. But, for those of us concerned with the Balkans, fear followed close on the heels of hope. If the Germans were held and then driven back, who would liberate the Balkans? The British? Or the Soviets? And what local forces would come to the top? Nationalists and Democrats? or Communists?

I was sitting on the terrace of Shepheard's Hotel in Cairo, with Altmaier, Djonovitch and Dimitrov, when the news of the German attack came through. Within an hour or two all these questions were clearly formulated in our minds. The problem was how to answer them. Over lunch that day and in meetings afterwards with Bailey, the outlines of a solution began to appear. The first essential was to build up centres of Resistance in the different Balkan countries and seek to influence their character by giving them money, arms and political guidance. Britain should take the lead in this in association with the legitimate Governments of Greece and Yugoslavia. But we should also seek, as soon as possible, to associate the Soviets with us in our work. It should prove easier to commit Moscow to support our friends while the Soviets were still fighting for their lives, than it might become later, if the tide should turn in their favour.

Our headquarters in London accepted these views. It was, accordingly, decided that Bailey should go to Istanbul with Djonovitch, Tupanyanin and Dimitrov. They would try from there to reopen communications with Yugoslavia and Bulgaria. They would also seek contact with the Soviets. I was meanwhile to stay in the Middle East to keep in touch with G.H.Q. and with the Middle-Eastern Section of S.O.E.

My work over the next few weeks was spasmodic and irregular. Among other things I was involved in a rather farcical attempt to assassinate Hitler. As part of their contribution to the war effort, our Bulgarian friends had produced a Macedonian terrorist who travelled under the assumed name of Vilmar. Vilmar was a stout middle-aged man with an ugly leg wound gained in some Balkan skirmish. He would sometimes pull up his trouser leg and show his scars to emphasise a point. He suffered from cancer, so he told us, and had only a year to live. To die in bed in wartime seemed an ignoble end. He, accordingly, volunteered to try and kill Hitler. He wanted no money other than living expenses and the promise of a commission and posthumous decoration if he died in the attempt.

Vilmar was very emotional and, in his cups, sometimes wept like a child. I had the gravest doubts as to whether he would make an effective killer but he was certainly a crack shot with a revolver; and our Bulgarian friends vouched for his sincerity and past experience in terrorism. Political assassins, I reflected, were likely to be rather unbalanced. Many, indeed, had been lunatics. As there was nothing to lose but the few hundred pounds of expenses involved I recommended that we take the chance. The results were pure comic opera.

Our organisation had a section, largely staffed, it was said, from forgers 'doing time', which specialised in fabricating passports and other documents. It was thus easy enough to fit Vilmar out with papers, establishing him as a bona fide Bulgarian businessman. There was no problem either in infiltrating him through Portugal as far as Switzerland. There he was to remain studying the German press and radio until he got news of some occasion when Hitler was likely to appear in public. He was then to go into Germany, as if on business, and make his attempt.

Some months later we received the following account of what happened next. Vilmar somehow learned that Hitler would be visiting Vienna. He arrived there two days before the Führer was due. He reported to the Bulgarian Consulate, spoke in glowing terms of his admiration for Hitler and said that he wanted to meet him, or at least to see him. The Consul told him that a meeting was out of the question, but that he would be glad to take Vilmar to some ceremony to which the Consular Corps had been invited and where he would at least see the Führer.

Vilmar was a crack shot and might conceivably have achieved his aim. But wine and women proved his undoing. On what he thought to be the last night of his life, he went to a night club, ordered champagne and invited the prettiest girls. As the drink rose to his head he displayed his gun-shot wound. A little later he also showed his revolver. One of the girls grew suspicious; the police were sent for and Vilmar was arrested. His documents stood up to examination and after a few days he was released and deported to Bulgaria. There he was again arrested and, as far as I know, never heard of again.

For the rest most of my time was spent in piecing together intelligence reports and talking to refugees or travellers from the Balkans. Until the beginning of July most of the news reaching me concerned conditions under German and Italian occupation, fighting between Serbs and Croats and the arrest of our friends in Belgrade. Now, all of a sudden, we began to get news of another kind. Yugoslavia had risen in revolt.

25

Operation Bullseye

In a long-drawn war an army can be destroyed and a nation's will to resist overpowered by hard pounding and sheer exhaustion. This did not happen to Yugoslavia. The Germans had administered a 'knock out' blow to the Yugoslav Army. They had not ground it to pieces. With the capitulation of the High Command whole divisions were taken prisoner and led off to Germany. But many units, especially in Serbia and Macedonia, fell back into the hills instead of surrendering. In accordance with plans laid down by Colonel Mihailovitch, the former Chief of the Operations Bureau, they now went underground. This simply meant that they put on peasant costume, hid their weapons and ammunition and lived in the villages or in the woods.

Where possible they went back to their own homes, subject to recall at short notice; but a small cadre remained permanently under arms and were kept supplied by the peasants. Gradually Mihailovitch linked up his headquarters with these different groups, exercising as much command over them as couriers and the primitive W/T field communications he had managed to salvage could ensure. Mihailovitch's first objective was to build up the *Chetniks*[1], as his underground army were called relying primarily on regular soldiers and on the *Narodna Odbrana*—or National Defence League—of our friend Birchanin. His plan was to keep his powder dry until the right time came to raise a general revolt against the Germans.

In parallel with Mihailovitch's essentially regular and planned Resistance Movement, a quite different movement also took shape, almost spontaneously. The German occupation threatened the lives and freedom of thousands of individuals. Communists and Jews were in immediate danger. So were other known enemies of the Germans or of their Allies, and in particular Serbs living in Croatia.

All through the early summer such people slipped out of the cities and closely garrisoned districts and fled into the wilder parts of the country, particularly Bosnia, Herzegovina, the Sanjak, and Montenegro. In these rugged and mountainous regions, they were safe enough from

[1] From the Serbian word *cheta* meaning a band, usually of guerrilla fighters.

pursuit. But how were they to live? The country was as poor as it was wild; and the first snows would fall by the end of October. Here Tito and the Yugoslav Communists showed something approaching genius. They organised this rabble of fugitives into a fighting force and taught them that it was only by fighting that they could get food and shelter. In principle, they were to fight against the occupying forces; but this definition was soon stretched to include any Yugoslavs left in positions of local authority and who could thus be accused of 'collaboration' with the enemy, or, indeed, any who had been associated with the pre-war dictatorship of Stoyadinovitch and Prince Paul, and could be called 'enemies of the people'.

The *Partisans*—as these Communist-led fugitives called themselves after the Russian guerrillas who had harassed Napoleon's retreat from Moscow—were not very popular with the villages; since their operations drew down fierce Italian and German retribution on the local population. But sometimes these reprisals worked in favour of the *Partisans*. Where, for instance, a village was burnt down many young men went and joined the *Partisans* partly because they were homeless and partly to revenge themselves upon the Germans.

There was thus, from the beginning, a fundamental difference between Mihailovitch's *Chetniks* and Tito's *Partisans*. The *Chetniks* were a regular organisation, loyal to King Peter and the Serbian Establishment. Like Territorials, their rank and file lived as civilians in their villages waiting to be called up by the different commands under which they were organised. The *Partisans*, by contrast, were Communist-led and cut off by geography and circumstances from civil life. They had to fight to survive. This made them, inevitably, the more dynamic of the two movements; and with action came increasing popular support.

Most of the German troops had been withdrawn from Yugoslavia for the war with Russia; and the local population soon took the measure of the Italian garrisons. On 13 July 1941, a general rising broke out in Montenegro and freed the Montenegrin countryside, except for the main towns, of Italian troops. In the climate of Pan-Slav fervour created by the Russian War, the movement spread rapidly to the Sanjak, to Bosnia and to Serbia.

Mihailovitch thought the rising premature, but he was powerless to restrain the upsurge of popular feeling and so tried to put himself at its head. By the end of July most of Yugoslavia between Belgrade and the coast had been cleared of enemy troops; and even big towns like Ujitze and Kraljevo were in insurgent hands. On the whole Mihailovitch was the predominant influence in Serbia; Tito in Montenegro and the Sanjak. Both had substantial support in Bosnia. There was contact between their forces but not much co-operation. Mihailovitch claimed the overall

leadership of the insurrection as the senior officer in the field. Tito refused
to accept this. He argued that the old Yugoslav Establishment had failed
the people and that the rising must be led by the peoples' own representatives.

It was some time before we fully grasped the dual nature of the
Yugoslav Resistance Movement. But reports of a large-scale rising soon
began to reach Jerusalem. A Moslem businessman arrived in Turkey
from Bosnia and reported that it was no longer possible to travel from
Sarajevo to Belgrade. The railway was cut. Our Intelligence reported
unexpected Italian and German troop movements towards Yugoslavia.
The German press carried obituary notices of officers killed in action in
Yugoslavia.

Then, towards the end of July, I received a message from Djonovitch
in Istanbul. He had just had a courier from Mihailovitch, a certain
Rakitch, who reported that Mihailovitch and a Major Misitch were in
the mountains and had nearly a hundred thousand men under arms.
Their headquarters was at Suvabor, a high plateau in Serbia. They
requested that we send an aircraft with liaison officers and wireless sets
to establish regular contact with them.

I had known Mihailovitch as Director of Operations on the general
staff in Belgrade, and along with Sandy Glen had often discussed guerrilla
warfare with him. I did not know Misitch personally but he was a son of
Voivoda Misitch, one of Serbia's heroes in the First World War. We now
had something definite to act on. We knew already from other sources
that a major revolt had broken out. We now knew the location of one at
least of its headquarters and the identity of some of its leaders. Our clear
duty was to send a mission to Mihailovitch to establish regular communications between us and assess what could be done.

I left at once for Cairo to seek approval and facilities for the necessary
operation.

But in the Cairo office of S.O.E. all was chaos. There had long been
a bitter feud between G.H.Q. and the Middle East Section of S.O.E. Sir
Frank Nelson, then head of S.O.E., had been summoned to Cairo and
had just carried out a drastic purge of the Middle East Section. Much
worse, from my point of view, he had also decided to recall Bill Bailey
and replace him by Tom Masterson, a much older man who had taken
part in the destruction of the Rumanian oilfields in the First World War,
but whose knowledge of other Balkan countries was sketchy. Terence
Maxwell, a distinguished banker married to Austen Chamberlain's
daughter, Diane, had been placed in overall command of both the Balkan
and the Middle East Sections.

I went to see Maxwell and asked for his help to get an aircraft from the R.A.F. to take in a liaison mission to Mihailovitch. But he knew little about the Balkans or, indeed, subversive work of any kind and plainly regarded my proposal as a tiresome distraction from his main task. This was to build up an efficient organisation, with a proper civilian and military establishment and a carefully prepared budget. He listened politely enough to what I had to say but then went back to the task of interviewing candidates for jobs and of framing estimates. The Serbia proposal, so his secretary told me, was put into the 'pending' tray. And yet there was no-one else to whom I could turn. Bailey, my old chief, was still in Istanbul. Masterson, the new one, had not yet left London. I returned to the charge several times but in the end was firmly told that no decision could be taken until Masterson had arrived. This, I learned, might not be for two or three weeks. Such a delay seemed to me unacceptable. Tens of thousands of Serbs had taken up arms against Germany and Italy. For the moment, they had the initiative; but an enemy counter-attack might develop at any moment. It was our plain duty to get in touch with them at once and see how we could help them. If we acted quickly the revolt might spread to Albania, Greece and Bulgaria, thus creating a major diversion from the Battle of Russia. If we failed to act, the Yugoslav Resistance Movement might well be crushed for good and, even if it survived, we should lose our best chance of influencing its development. It was intolerable that so grave an issue should be neglected because of bureaucratic arguments about organisation, establishments and jobs.

I was, of course, in close communication with my father and had kept him informed of my general impressions of what was going on in the Middle East and the Balkans. But, until then, I had been careful not to involve him in departmental controversy. But this, the fate of the Serbian revolt, seemed a different matter and one which justified cutting through the red tape and going to the top.

I wrote to him as follows:

15 August 1941
Our own work has reached rather a crisis. The reorganisation of our Middle East activities is now being carried out too late to be of any use but just in time to hold up important—and I think essential—action in the Balkans. I have always regarded your stories of inter-departmental intrigue in the last war as rather exaggerated. Now I know better . . . issues of world importance are being neglected while personalities and internal organisation are discussed by the hour.

Briefly I believe the time has come to launch a general revolt in the Balkans. First, because something like a general insurrection has already started in Serbia and Bosnia. Second, because the peasants there and in

Greece have not yet been effectively disarmed nor their organisations destroyed by the Germans. Third because the fortunate coincidence of Democrat and Communist, Anglophil and Pan-Slav interests creates a solid anti-German block representing not far from 90% of the Balkan peoples south of the Danube. Finally, because the Germans are so deeply committed in Russia that either they won't divert troops to suppress the Revolt, or they will and this may provoke a diversion which will help the Russians to hold out and thus help preserve the first glimmer of a chance of victory since the War started.

If you think these views sensible you might pass them on. They are at present under consideration from our office and I will write more fully if the present apathy continues. All I am asking, at the moment, is for the Air Force to lend us one or at most two 'planes to drop people into the Balkans to organise and encourage. If they don't make up their minds soon, the winter will come and the wretched guerrilla leaders will be forced down into the valleys to go into permanent hiding or surrender to the tender mercies of the Gestapo.

My father at once passed on the gist of my letter to the Prime Minister and suggested that he should call for a report. Churchill prodded Dalton. Dalton prodded Maxwell in Cairo; within a very few days, I had the pleasure of finding that my proposal to send a mission to Mihailovitch had been lifted out of the 'pending' tray and had become business of the first priority.

Armed, now, with Maxwell's warm support, I went to discuss possibilities with R.A.F. Headquarters. But the difficulties of an air operation were judged insuperable. There was no airstrip in insurgent hands that could take a long-range aircraft. We had too few bombers to afford a crash landing. A parachute jump at night—without a reception committee—was judged unacceptably dangerous.

Maxwell, however, was not prepared to take 'no' for an answer. He was by now determined that Operation Bullseye—to call it by the code name he had given it—should succeed. If we could not get an aircraft, why not a submarine? This seemed to me a very good alternative. Montenegro was thought to be in insurgent hands and the great thing was to get a mission into the country and establish communications.

Maxwell went himself to see the Commander-in-Chief Mediterranean. He sent for me next morning to say that a submarine would be ready at Malta in ten days' time. It was then 3 September 1941.

I knew that Djonovitch had a small team of volunteers ready to go back to Yugoslavia. I accordingly telegraphed to John Bennett in Istanbul explaining that Operation Bullseye was now approved, and asking him to send the team urgently to Cairo. For security reasons, I was forbidden to let him know that the mission would be infiltrated by submarine. John Bennett thus remained under the impression that they would be flown in to Suvabor as Mihailovitch had asked. So did Djonovitch's team.

I had next to find a British officer to accompany the Yugoslav mission. He had to speak Serbo-Croat well and yet not know too much about our organisation in case he fell into enemy hands. Bill Hudson, a mining engineer who had worked with the 'D' section in Yugoslavia, volunteered for the job. Meanwhile, Maxwell's newly recruited staff officers set about collecting the mission's basic equipment: a portable wireless set with batteries, iron rations, personal weapons and gold.

On 5 September, John Bennett arrived from Istanbul with news that Voivoda Turbitch and another Yugoslav officer would reach Aleppo next evening. Time was short, if we were to keep our rendezvous with the Navy, and I accordingly flew up next day in an old Anson, dragged Turbitch and his aide out of their sleeping car and brought them to Cairo.

Voivoda Vasili Turbitch was a Serb from Prilep in Macedonia. He was already over sixty years old and, indeed, had made his name as a *Chetnik* leader in the Balkan Wars of 1912–13 and the Salonika Campaign of 1918. He was short, stout, with a shaven head and virtually no neck. His assistant was a callow youth whose chief function was that of interpreter and ADC.

Turbitch was older than I had expected but his morale seemed high and he ate a hearty lunch in my flat. After lunch, John Bennett and I began to brief him on our plans. Almost at once we struck a reef. Turbitch was expecting to go to Macedonia or Serbia where he was a local hero. But Montenegro was quite another matter. Nothing would induce him to go there. He knew little of the country or its people and disliked the little he knew. I tried to persuade him that he need only spend a few days in Montenegro on his way to Serbia; but he was impervious to argument. He would not go to Montenegro.

We faced a crisis. It was by this time six o'clock on the evening of 7 September.

The R.A.F. had agreed to fly our mission to Malta on the following night in a Sunderland. And now the essential part of the mission had melted into thin air.

John Bennett and I conferred briefly. It was clear to both of us that unless we could produce an alternative mission by the following afternoon, we would never again be taken seriously either by the new leaders of S.O.E. or by G.H.Q.

Leaving Turbitch and his aide in my flat, John and I drove round to see Colonel Jarko Popovitch, the Yugoslav Director of Intelligence. Popovitch was a highly professional officer, trained at the French Staff College and with experience of both Tzarist and Soviet Russia. He was also the owner of the largest collection of pornographic photographs I have ever seen. His flat was on the sixth floor; and on the way up to it the lift jammed. For nearly twenty minutes John Bennett and I were prisoners, wondering if this was to be the end of Operation Bullseye.

Eventually someone got the lift to work and we reached Popovitch's flat to find the Colonel in bed and, it seemed, not alone. His first reaction at our intrusion was one of resentment, but when we told him that we wanted one or two really good officers to leave for Yugoslavia next day, his whole mood changed. He seemed not the least surprised at the very short notice we were giving him, and perhaps took it as evidence of a highly developed sense of security. He asked one or two questions and then said that he would have two reliable officers and a wireless operator ready by ten o'clock next morning. After that he showed us out and, so we presumed, went back to his bedroom 'to finish the game'.

For our part, John and I went back to the office and worked with the Staff Officers till midnight checking on the last details of the operation. After that I walked back to my flat to snatch some sleep. It was rather a shock to find Voivoda Turbitch snoring peacefully in my bed. Under the pressure of work I had forgotten all about him and his colleague; and, having nowhere else to go, they had made themselves at home. I accordingly spent the night on the sofa.

In the morning I went to Popovitch's flat and there was introduced to two Montenegrin air force officers, both over six foot tall. Major Ostojitch was very dark with a huge hooked nose and looked as strong as a horse. Major Lalatovitch was fairer and of slighter build. With them was a tough young sergeant, also a Montenegrin, who claimed to be a trained wireless operator.

I took them to our headquarters and introduced them to Bill Hudson. They were then kitted out with pistols, knives, and bags of gold. Maxwell shook hands with them, but, as they had no common language, never realised that they were not the original team. Nor for that matter did anyone else in S.O.E.

In the aircraft to Alexandria I began to take stock of the 'scratch' team we had collected at less than twenty-four hours' notice. Physically they were well above the average. From that point of view, indeed, they were far superior to the aged Voivoda Turbitch and his rather lacka-daisical aide. All three moreover were Montenegrins and knew the country where they would land. On the other hand, none of them had any personal prestige in Montenegro nor did they know much about politics or guerrilla war. They should be ideal for the job of establishing contact with the insurgents. Afterwards there would have to be a follow up. This, I reflected, would be a very suitable job for me.

I was under orders to go no further than Malta, since I was thought to know too much about S.O.E. to risk falling into enemy hands. But in these first few minutes of our flight I resolved to accompany the party at least as far as the Montenegrin coast. It would be useful to have first-hand experience of the problems of landing from a submarine, and, if I came back safely, my indiscipline would no doubt be overlooked.

We flew without adventure to Aboukir, and drove through sand dunes to the flying boat base outside Alexandria. The R.A.F. knew nothing about our mission and had not been told how much equipment we were carrying. The captain of the aircraft refused point blank to accept it. I ask him to telephone to Cairo for instructions, but the lines were blocked. In the end, I took a sympathetic intelligence officer into my confidence and he persuaded the captain to turn a blind eye.

As we stood on the beach in the fading light, waiting for a launch to take us out to the Sunderland, I reflected that Yugoslavia was nearly a thousand miles away. To try and support a Revolt at this range with virtually no aircraft and only one submarine at our disposal seemed quite an undertaking.

The sun was sinking behind the palm trees as we clambered into the launch. A few minutes later we were scrambling through the narrow door in the flank of the Sunderland. Our fellow passengers were mostly R.A.F. air crew and ground staff bound for Malta. We took off just before dark, and towards midnight, I dropped off to sleep. We were due at Kala Frana, the Malta flying boat base, at about five in the morning.

When I woke my wrist watch showed six-thirty. Other passengers were already commenting on the delay. Presently the captain came into the cabin and told me that his wireless was out of order. So was his compass. It was cloudy and, like the Turkish Admiral in an earlier war, he simply could not find Malta. He had only enough petrol left for thirty minutes more flying and had therefore decided to land on the open sea. Malta expected us and there was at least a chance that a rescue patrol would find us before the enemy did.

A few minutes later we struck the sea with a fearful thud. It seemed as if the bottom of the flying boat had been torn out. Great wings of foam shot up on either side, and I thought at first that we were going right under the water. Then, in a moment, all became quiet and we were left swaying and bumping on the switch back of the waves.

As we tossed up and down I wondered whether we would be rescued or drowned or machine-gunned on the water, or possibly taken prisoner. The captain left me in no doubt as to our plight. 'Another hour of this bumping about,' he said 'and the boat may break up. You had better tell your team.' Enquiry revealed that there was only one rubber dinghy on board and no-one except the crew had a Mae West. In the circumstances I saw no point in telling my Yugoslav friends how serious our situation was. They might well have started a fight to get control of the dinghy.

Then, with the motion of the flying boat we began to grow sea-sick, and I don't think I cared any more about my fate until I had finished spewing up what there was to spew. After that someone offered me a *Camel* cigarette and I remember thinking what an excellent advertisement it would have made.

My Montenegrin colleagues seemed very fatalistic and moved with greater deliberation than usual as if to show off their courage. I watched them carefully. It was a good test of nerve and they stood up to it well. I told them so afterwards. They replied that they had watched Hudson and me with the same thought in mind.

There was nothing we could do except wait. But it was a bitter thought that, after all the preparation and planning and all the will-power and mental effort that had gone into the operation, we should end here in a stupid accident at a point equi-distant from our target and our base.

We had been tossing on the waves for about an hour when the Sunderland's observer reported "plane in sight'. Was it friend or foe? I looked through the window and could see a small black aircraft bearing down on us like a hawk out of the sky. Our guns were manned and then someone recognised the aircraft as one of ours. It circled over us a couple of times and signalled us to follow. The Sunderland's engines were started up again. We pitched through the waves and with an immense effort wrenched ourselves out of the sea and into the air. Twenty minutes later we glided down to Kala Frana. By nine o'clock we were sitting down to breakfast with the R.A.F. as if nothing had happened.

S.O.E. lodged us in a house in Valletta, situated appropriately enough at the corner of Amery Street, so called after a short-lived constitution my father had given to Malta in the early 'twenties. It was an attractive early nineteenth-century building with ample accommodation and a big garden.

This was just as well; for there were thought to be Italian spies in Valletta and we were advised not to show ourselves at all. We kept to the house and garden all day and every day, going for quiet walks after dark and avoiding all contact with Maltese or English friends. Nevertheless, there was plenty for us to do. The mission's wireless set proved defective and had to be replaced. Hudson had to be taught the code in which to send his messages. This was simple enough but still took some hours to learn. Above all, I had to brief Hudson and his colleagues collectively and separately on the situation in Yugoslavia, as we knew it, and on the kind of information we wanted.

I also tried to discover what private instructions Popovitch might have given his two officers. They did not give much away; but it was clear that the Communist danger was very much in their minds.

On the night of 12 September, three days after our arrival in Malta, I dined with Lieutenant-Commander Woods, the captain of His Majesty's Submarine *Triumph*, and his First Lieutenant Janfryn. Woods was a tall burly sea dog with a zest for adventure. Janfryn was lightly built, with delicate features, a rather sensual mouth and bright green eyes. I sketched out what we knew of the Revolt in Yugoslavia and explained the object of our mission. They saw the point at once and were obviously pleased at the chance of taking part in what might be the beginning of a big thing. This was a great relief as I had feared they might think our cloak and dagger operation a tiresome distraction from the serious business of sinking ships. As it was, I was soon convinced that they would take considerable risks to ensure the success of our mission.

Our cruise, Woods explained, should in any case be interesting. We were to be the first British submarine to try and enter the Adriatic since the fall of Yugoslavia in the previous April. There has been reports that the Straits of Otranto were netted, but Woods discounted these. He reckoned besides that even if they were we could get under the net by diving deep enough.

After dinner I took Woods and Janfryn back to our house and introduced them to Hudson and the Yugoslavs. They studied the proposed landing point on the map together and asked a few questions. The Yugoslavs were impressed by Woods' frankness and buccaneering disregard for danger and for irrelevant detail. They called him 'a real sea wolf'.

Next afternoon we drove to the submarine base and were led to one of the submarine pens. We approached the *Triumph* along a narrow gang plank, scrambled up the conning tower and were taken down the hatch and through the control room to the Wardroom. It all looked very cramped.

About five o'clock we glided out of the submarine pen and I went up to the conning tower with Woods to watch the land recede and hear him explain our daily routine. This was quite simple. The submarine, he told me, surfaced at nightfall and travelled on the surface all night. This was when we covered distance, charged our batteries and filled up with fresh air. We would dive before dawn and spend the day under water. Our underwater speed would be much slower.

In those days, a submarine cruise in the Mediterranean in summer was uncomfortably hot. There was virtually no ventilation and we spent the day sitting stripped to the waist and sweating as if we were at the bottom of a mine. Towards evening the air became rather stale and people tended to grow listless and irritable. It was only when we surfaced at night that we got cool at all.

Accommodation was very cramped and, as long as the Bullseye party were on board, the officers had to work a 'hot bunk', sleeping in the bunk of whoever relieved them on the watch. Food was plentiful, though mostly tinned, and there was no shortage of beer and other drink. We would spend the day in the wardroom talking, reading or playing cards. At night I would spend an hour or so in the conning tower getting some fresh air. Every now and then we visited the control room where the officer of the watch would explain our position and allow us to look through the periscope. We also visited the crew's quarters, which were even more cramped than our own, and admired the incredibly complicated engine room. Almost as complicated were the 'Heads', as the lavatory was called. To work the 'Heads' you had to operate three knobs and two levers in a prescribed order. If you got the order wrong, the contents of the pan was quite likely to jump out at you. Partial flushing could be done at any time of the day. But total flushing was only allowed at night. This was to ensure that our spoor should not betray us to enemy sea or air patrols.

Our first day's cruise was uneventful, but early on the second morning (15 September) we sighted a 6,000 ton Italian tanker steaming towards Crotone. We were almost on a collision course and had no difficulty in coming within range. Woods took charge of the operation and invited us all into the control room to watch. He gave us plenty of opportunity to look at the target through the periscope as we moved into position. Then he took over himself. It was a tense moment; and he showed his excitement by a violent scratching of his balls. Presently he gave the order to fire. The first 'fish', as the submariners call their torpedoes, struck the tanker amidships. A second went wide. The third struck her aft just below the waterline sending up a column of spray.

Within minutes an Italian destroyer appeared as if from nowhere and we dived as deep as we could. We then stayed motionless while the destroyer dropped depth charges around us. I was told that these came rather close. They made a rattling sound like sudden gusts of hail on a tin roof and shook the submarine a little. But the sound was muffled and nothing like as frightening to me as the whining of shells or even the 'ping' of rifle bullets. We spent the time playing cards.

After a couple of hours the depth-charging ceased; and, half-an-hour or so later, we rose from the depths and put out our periscope to see what was going on. There was no sign of the destroyer; but we watched our tanker sinking just outside the harbour wall of Crotone where the relief tugs had dragged it.

We were all heartened by this successful engagement; and our spirits rose still further when we surfaced in the evening and heard the news on the B.B.C. This gave a detailed account of the rising in Yugoslavia based on reports in the Swiss press. It made us feel that we had a decisive part to play in a decisive theatre of the war.

On the morning of 16 September we dived deep and passed through the Straits of Otranto without incident. There was no net. We spent the day checking over the mission's equipment and seeing how best it could be carried. Our staff officers, in Cairo, had unaccountably forgotten several essential items. The wireless set, for instance, weighed as much as a heavy suitcase but no thought had been given to constructing some kind of harness so that it could be carried on a man's back. But the Royal Navy has a genius for improvisation, and Sub-lieutenant Douglas Donne somehow rigged up harnesses both for the set and for its batteries. We had forgotten, too, to bring field glasses. Woods thought these a 'must' and generously gave Hudson his own.

The night was fine, and towards dawn, the wind dropped. Through the periscope we could make out the Albanian coast and the mouth of the River Boyana. About midday we were opposite Bar just north of the frontier between Montenegro and Albania. We had now to determine our exact landing spot.

Our wireless operator knew the coast well but had considerable difficulty in identifying the little town of Petrovatz. He had often been there but had never before seen it from the sea. At last we got an exact fix and moved in under water until we could see the houses of Petrovatz clearly and watch an occasional lorry driving along the road. A little to the north of Petrovatz, we came on a sandy cove, Perisicadol Bay. This was a crescent of rocks with a small beach in the middle. On the beach stood a ruined house. It was roofless and so presumably uninhabited but would help to conceal our party and its gear from anyone passing on the road above. From the house, a steep path led some two hundred feet up the cliff and on to the road.

We explored the coast a little further but soon decided that Perisicadol Bay should be our landing point. It was easy to approach from the sea. The ruined house afforded some cover and the cliff path provided the first stage, at least, of a route inland.

Our minds made up, we put out to sea again and spent the rest of the afternoon under water at a healthy distance from the coast. Once an Italian 'plane flew overhead. Otherwise we were undisturbed.

At about nine-thirty in the evening we moved towards the shore. There was no moon. At ten-thirty we surfaced and nudged our way to within six hundred yards of the beach. We now assembled all our gear on the forecasing of the submarine, and began to ferry it ashore in two small rubber dinghies. It was then stacked inside the ruined house.

Towards one o'clock in the morning, the work was done, and I wen ashore to make sure that our party got safely across the road. Woods had now brought the submarine to within three hundred yards of the beach. As I climbed into the rubber dinghy, he said to me: 'If anything goes wrong, give a series of signals with your torch and I'll come into shore until I ground. You can then swim for it.' In fact, nothing went wrong. We landed without incident and loaded up the gear in the shelter of the ruined house. We then slowly climbed the cliff-side path. There was no sign of life on the road and presently we found a broad track leading into the mountains beyond it. There I shook hands with my friends and wished them well.

Douglas Donne and I then scrambled back to the beach. The night was so dark that we thought for a moment *Triumph* had left the bay. It was not until we reached the ruined house that we could make out its silhouette. We paddled out to sea and were welcomed on board with a tot of rum and a cup of hot cocoa.

When I woke next morning we were off Dubrovnik. I went to look at its sea front through the periscope and was astonished to see less than a hundred yards away an open sailing boat, manned by a youth in bathing trunks and a very pretty blonde. It would have been fun to surface and carry off the blonde. For a moment I thought Woods was going to. Alas, more prudent if duller counsels prevailed.

I had done my job and, as far as I was concerned, the rest of the cruise was a holiday. I had plenty to read and good companions to talk to. I have always found the Navy the most considerate of the three Services towards strangers. The Army, even in the best regiments, are often suspicious of outsiders. Their experience of journalists and politicians has been too bitter. The Royal Air Force buy you a drink and leave you to your own devices. They are individuals first and only secondly members of a Service. But the Navy, perhaps because they are so very sure of their own superiority, have a greater sense of *noblesse oblige*. They are sorry for you, in the nicest possible way, for not being a sailor and try to make up for this by courtesy and kindness.

Within the Navy, the submariners are very much an élite. Every man in *Triumph* was a volunteer, and they were all very young. Woods was still in his thirties. The Chief Engineer 31, Janfryn 26, and Douglas Donne only 20. They accepted me without reserve and admitted me to the personal and professional confidences of their daily life as men only do when they spend days together in cramped and dangerous conditions. They told me about their past exploits, and their hopes for the future.

Woods' imagination had been fired by the job we had just done. He saw no difficulty in landing men and supplies in quantities of up to seventy tons. It was exciting work and called for very skilful navigation. The degree of risk was in his view acceptable and such landings could be combined, as we had seen off Crotone, with more routine submarine operations.

We had further proof of this last point two days later. We were lunching under water opposite Shibenik, near the head of the Adriatic. Suddenly the officer of the watch reported a 5,000 ton tanker in sight. Our first torpedo struck it clean amidships and by the time I got to the periscope from the wardroom, there was nothing to see but the ship's bows sticking out of the water and two lifeboats heading for the shore.

Just short of Pola, we cut across the Adriatic and turned south along the Italian Coast. Off Ortona we sighted a magnificent tanker deep in the water, and so presumably fully loaded. We had only three torpedoes left. The first struck the target with a resounding bang, which we heard quite plainly in the control room. But the tanker was far from sunk. Our next torpedo missed. So did our last. Woods, however, was determined not to let his prey escape. He gave the order to surface and to attack with the submarine's gun. As we surfaced, Douglas Donne, who was first on the ladder going up the conning tower, was blown through the hatch, like a rocket, by the change of pressure, and quite badly bruised. Woods asked me: 'Would you care for a shoot?' I followed him up to the conning tower, where someone handed me an old Lewis gun.

The sun was shining. It was the first time I had been in the sun since we had left Malta. We were in the centre of a flat bay, perhaps two miles from the fortress of Ortona. The crippled tanker was less than half a mile away. Donne, by now recovered from his spectacular exit, had trained his gun on to the tanker and was firing at regular intervals. My job was to act as anti-aircraft gunner but as no aircraft came in sight, I loosed off a few rounds of the Lewis gun at the tanker as well. Donne's fire was very accurate, and presently the tanker was ablaze. We had been firing away for about ten minutes when a column of water shot up about a hundred yards short of our bows. Then we heard a nasty whine and saw another column of water on the far side of the submarine. The guns of Ortona fortress were opening up on us. A third round came rather too close for comfort; and Woods led us back down the tower and gave the order to dive. Half an hour later an aircraft began dropping depth charges. But they were well wide of us.

We continued south and off Bari ran into a small fishing fleet. But we had no torpedoes and were almost out of ammunition for the gun. We accordingly stayed submerged and passed through the Otranto straits without difficulty.

Just off Ithaca, Woods received a signal forecasting a major Naval
engagement off Sardinia, and summoning any available ships to the area.
With no weapons left, we could make no contribution and so continued
on our course to Alexandria. But Woods' day was spoilt by the thought
of missing an action. He was due for promotion on our return and this
would be his last cruise in command of a submarine.

I rose early on 3 October and climbed to the conning tower to see
the dawn. We were now in friendly waters and would not be diving again.
Presently, out of the south-east, came the Mediterranean Fleet steaming
westward: mighty *Bahram, Queen Elizabeth,* half a dozen cruisers and a
pack of destroyers. We passed them within half-a-mile and exchanged
signals. A little later the palm trees and buildings of Alexandria came into
view and then the great mole of the harbour. The submarine's company
put on their smartest uniforms. My Army cap was discovered mildewed,
but swiftly furbished up. We entered the Grand Harbour about nine
o'clock in the morning. I stood with the officers on the conning tower.
The crew lined the casing. Above our heads flew the Jolly Roger with
three white bars for each of the tankers we had sunk and a dagger for
Operation Bullseye.

The crews of the ships in harbour, even those of the immobilised Vichy
French Fleet, stood to. The sun shone brightly. We stepped on board
Medway, the parent ship, and Woods took me at once to see Captain
S. He asked a few questions and stood us a round of 'horses' necks'—
brandy and ginger ale—as a pre-breakfast aperitif.

I reached Cairo in the evening and went at once to the office. The
first signal from the Bullseye party had arrived but was still being
deciphered. I saw the text an hour later. It reported that the mission had
made contact with a group of guerrillas and were moving into central
Montenegro.

Woods and his officers came and dined with me in Cairo some days
later. He was by now Commander S. in Alexandria, and I was to see
him on and off over the next few years in the Admiralty and later when he
became Commander-in-Chief of the Home Fleet. I did not meet his other
officers again. A few months later *Triumph* was reported 'overdue and
presumed lost'.

26

Mihailovitch and Tito

Operation Bullseye had been successfully completed. Hudson and his colleagues had established contact with a group of Tito's *Partisans* in Montenegro. A week or two later they reached Mihailovitch's headquarters. Hudson's early reports fully confirmed our assessment that most of Serbia, Bosnia and Montenegro was in insurgent hands.

Our plain duty was to send in further missions to try and co-ordinate insurgent operations with general allied strategy and to arrange supplies by sea or air. I hoped to be given command of one of these missions.

But it was by now mid-October. Two precious months had been lost; and, almost as soon as Hudson reached Mihailovitch's camp, the Germans launched a major punitive expedition designed to smash the revolt. Up to this time, there had been contact between Mihailovitch and Tito. Now, in the face of the German attack, Mihailovitch tried to force the *Partisans* to accept his leadership of the insurrection. Tito, likewise, sought to impose his authority upon Mihailovitch and the *Chetniks*. This led to armed clashes between the two sides.

Helped by these internal dissensions the German Army soon recovered control of most of the liberated territories. The civil population were cowed into submission by brutal reprisals. Mihailovitch dispersed the bulk of his forces to their homes and had himself to abandon his headquarters and take refuge in the Sanjak. The *Partisan* leaders were driven out of Serbia into the remoter parts of Bosnia and Montenegro.

In the course of the fighting Hudson became separated from Mihailovitch and, worse still, from his wireless set. We were thus cut off from any direct communication with the Yugoslav Resistance, apart from very occasional wireless messages from Mihailovitch to the Yugoslav Government picked up in Malta.

It was not, indeed, until the spring of 1942 that Hudson found his way to Mihailovitch's new Headquarters—and we again had reliable news of what was happening inside Yugoslavia. Even then, the omission of certain agreed code words in Hudson's messages aroused suspicions that he might be communicating with a German pistol in the small of his back.

Though badly mauled, both the *Chetnik* and the *Partisan* organisations survived the German offensive. But all through the winter relations between Mihailovitch and Tito deteriorated steadily until they came to regard each other as enemies. A civil war broke out between them and in many parts of the country this domestic struggle took priority over resistance to the Axis Powers. Worse still, Hudson had evidence that, in some districts, Mihailovitch's commanders had reached temporary accommodations with the Germans or at least with the 'Quisling' forces of General Neditch[1] so as to be free to concentrate their energies against the Partisans.

The fighting in 1941 had only accentuated the basic differences between the two movements. The failure of the insurrection and the violence of the reprisals seemed to many to confirm the wisdom of Mihailovitch's strategy of lying low in order to launch a general uprising when the Allies opened a front in the Balkans. Tito, on the other hand, could claim that, though the insurrection had failed, it had diverted several divisions of Axis troops to Yugoslavia thus increasing the pressure on the enemy and bringing some relief to the hard pressed Soviets. The price in terms of reprisals might be very high but the acceptance of such sacrifices was the best way of ensuring that Yugoslavia would be recognised, in the end, as one of the victorious powers.

Yugoslav opinion was sharply divided between these two views. A first cause of division was social and economic. The wealthier peasants and others with a stake in the country were more vulnerable to reprisals and so tended to side with Mihailovitch.

By contrast, the 'have nots', younger men without family ties—and many young women—and especially those Serbs who had escaped massacre by the *Ustachis* in Croatia, were attracted to Tito's flag and found in guerrilla life both a cause to serve and an exciting if dangerous way of life.

The other cause of division was regional and political. Mihailovitch was a Serb and a Monarchist. The exiled Government in London, indeed, appointed him Minister of War and Commander-in-Chief of Yugoslav forces in the Homeland. He was thus the embodiment of Yugoslav legality and stood for the restoration of the old establishment which had been predominantly Serb. His influence was thus paramount in Serbia and very strong in Montenegro and the Serbian districts of Bosnia.

Tito, by contrast, was a Communist and a Croat. He condemned the old régime both as a dictatorship and as responsible for the country's defeat. His influence was strongest in those regions such as Croatia, Dalmatia and Slovenia which had never taken the Serbian dynasty to their hearts. Beyond that he attracted the sympathies of left-wing elements

[1] General Neditch had been Minister of Defence before the coup d'état of 1941. After the outbreak of the Russo-German War and influenced by the massacres of Serbs in Croatia, Neditch was persuaded by the Germans to become Prime Minister of Serbia.

everywhere and of the strong pro-Russian and Pan-Slav sentiments which inspired so many Yugoslavs and especially Montenegrins.

It is very doubtful whether the basic antagonisms between *Chetniks* and *Partisans* could have been reconciled for any length of time. But there was one chance: and it was rejected. I was only marginally involved in the negotiations, but they are perhaps worth recording.

In the later part of July, as I have already related, Djonovitch had told us of the message he had received from Mihailovitch and Misitch describing the strength of their forces and the location of their Head-quarters. He had also informed the Soviet representative in Istanbul. After communicating with Moscow, the Soviets came back to Djonovitch and offered to provide an aircraft to fly in a mixed Yugoslav, British and Russian military mission to Mihailovitch's headquarters at Suvabor. If necessary, the aircraft would make a crash landing. Just before embarking on Operation Bullseye, I had been told that the aircraft would be available in a week to ten days. The offer seemed very attractive. It would commit the Soviets to work with us and with the Yugoslav Government in exile. It conformed exactly with the policy of co-operation with Moscow which Bailey had recommended immediately after the German attack on Russia and to which our London Office had agreed. It was accordingly arranged, just before I left for Malta, that John Bennett would recruit another Anglo-Yugoslav team in Cairo and take them to Leninakan in Soviet Armenia where the promised Soviet aircraft was expected. But, while I was cruising under the Adriatic, our Headquarters in Cairo changed their minds and decided to refuse the Soviet offer.

What happened was this. The Yugoslav Government in London were naturally suspicious of the Soviets. They hoped to exclude them from any contact with the Resistance movement or at any rate to establish close co-operation between Britain and Mihailovitch before bringing the Soviets into the picture. They, accordingly, instructed General Ilitch, their Chief-of-Staff in Cairo, to advise S.O.E. against the Soviet proposal. Masterson, who had just taken over the Balkan section from Bailey, was under instructions to work closely with Ilitch. He accepted Ilitch's advice and countermanded John Bennett's instructions. The Yugoslav Govern-ment had good reasons to fear the Soviets. Yet had the Soviet proposal been accepted, there would have been an Anglo-Russian military mission at Mihailovitch's headquarters before he and Tito finally fell out. This might have led Tito to adopt a more conciliatory attitude towards the *Chetniks* and might have made Mihailovitch less suspicious of Tito's intentions. At this stage of the war, moreover, when the Soviets were in full retreat before the German onslaught they might well have proved more amenable to British influence than they later became. The basic antagonism between Mihailovitch and Tito would not have been removed, but the conflict between them might well have been postponed, and what is postponed long enough is sometimes avoided altogether.

The Russians soon found out why the Yugoslav Government had opposed their offer and assumed from its rejection that the British too were determined to keep them out of the Balkans. The Soviet official who had been in touch with Djonovitch and Bennett was withdrawn from Istanbul. His successor was plainly under instructions not to do business with us. Both sides, thereafter, adopted increasingly rigid positions. The Soviet Radio gave its backing to Tito and presently began to attack Mihailovitch. The B.B.C. were instructed to support Mihailovitch and ignore the existence of the *Partisans*.

Through the winter of 1941/42 the issue between *Chetniks* and *Partisans* was for S.O.E. largely academic. In the absence of communication with Hudson, we did not know what was going on.

But once Hudson came on the air again, the situation changed. We now knew that there were two distinct Yugoslav Resistance movements and that they were fighting each other. What was to be our attitude towards them? The question was urgent since the resumption of wireless contact with Hudson meant that we could now hope to send in further liaison missions and military supplies.

To give our main support to Mihailovitch seemed to me the right policy for Britain. Mihailovitch represented the pro-British as distinct from the pro-Soviet forces in Yugoslavia. He would be a better friend to us than Tito after the war: and his *Chetnik* organisation would prove just as effective as the *Partisans* in the event of an Allied landing in the Balkans. Nevertheless, it seemed to me unrealistic to pretend that Tito did not exist. He was plainly a major factor on the Yugoslav scene; and his *Partisans* seemed readier than the *Chetniks* to carry out the kind of sabotage and terrorist operations which S.O.E. was designed to promote. The wise course, in my judgement, was to establish missions with both sides. This would enable us to know what was going on, to build up Mihailovich's forces for an eventual rising and meanwhile to make use of Tito's considerable military potential for sabotage and guerrilla raids. Our presence would also put us in a position to work for a reconciliation or at least a truce between the two sides.

I pressed this view on Masterson but without success. His policy was to give all-out support to Mihailovitch and have nothing to do with Tito. For the time being, this difference of opinion was not over-important. The practical difficulties of dropping men and stores from Egypt into the

Serbian mountains were very great. The R.A.F. had no aircraft to spare except in the intervals of operations in the Western Desert. They needed good weather but no moon to fly a sortie. At the other end, Hudson's wireless set was frequently out of order or German patrols prevented the *Chetniks* from lighting the necessary signal fires to guide the aircraft to the dropping grounds. Several sorties were attempted but it was not until August 1942, nearly a year after Operation Bullseye, that a further British mission was successfully dropped to Mihailovitch.

The feud between *Partisans* and *Chetniks* sent ripples as far as Cairo. Bailey, then in the United States, had come upon a certain Robertson. Robertson—I forget his real name[1]—had been a reserve officer in the Yugoslav Army but had become a Communist and fought in the International Brigade in Spain. His Spanish experiences, however, had produced a profound revulsion against Communism and he had emigrated to the United States to settle down as a wireless operator in the Merchant Navy. His proficiency in wireless transmission made him an obvious recruit for S.O.E. while his knowledge of both the Yugoslav Army and the Yugoslav Communist Party suggested that he might be of some use to us in unravelling the tangled skein of the *Chetnik-Partisan* feud. Bailey had accordingly sent him to us in Cairo dressed as a British captain, with a view to attaching him to one of our missions in Serbia. John Bennett and I were too busy to look after him during the weeks he would have to wait in Cairo. We accordingly asked that someone else be appointed to see to his needs, preferably someone who spoke Serbo-Croat.

In view of Robertson's antecedents, we also asked that an eye be kept on the people whom he saw. A few days later Robertson told us he was being followed and feared a Communist assault. We told our people, who said they had seen nothing suspicious. A day or two afterwards, however, Robertson was badly beaten up by a gang of Yugoslavs and Greeks and only rescued by military police. Our people, who arrived on the scene just afterwards, believed that Robertson's assailants had been right-wing Yugoslavs. Robertson, however, was quite clear that they had been Communists and suspected that he had been caught in a trap laid on information supplied by someone on our side. Following a natural British prejudice, we preferred not to believe him, foolishly as it proved.

Robertson was eventually dropped into Serbia, though only after several abortive attempts, some of them accompanied by nasty incidents which looking back suggest sabotage. He was attached to a *Chetnik* command but presently made contact with local *Partisan* forces. A few months later he was murdered, though by which side was not, to my knowledge, established.

Meanwhile, the person to whom suspicion pointed continued to flourish and it was only after the war that he emerged as a fully-fledged

Communist. No names, no pack drill; but Tito and Moscow were certainly kept very well informed of the fluctuations of British policy towards Yugoslavia and of the terms of the instructions given to the British missions with Mihailovitch and later Tito.

The clash between Mihailovitch and Tito opened up a wider issue. What was to be the fate of the Balkan peoples after the war? This was a problem of some practical importance for S.O.E. If we were to call on the different Balkan countries to rise against the Germans, we had to tell them not just what they were fighting against, but also what they were fighting for. Their peoples would not be easily brought to take up arms for their Governments in exile. The Yugoslav Government had been largely discredited by its failure to put up an effective resistance to the Germans. The Greek Government of General Metaxas had had a brilliant war record but Greek opinion was bitterly divided on the question of the Monarchy. In Bulgaria, Rumania and Hungary, the Governments had declared for the Germans. Communism would no doubt have a strong appeal for some sections of Balkan opinion, especially in the Slav countries. But the growth of Communism would tend of itself to drive anti-Communists into the arms of the Germans. In the longer run, moreover, the triumph of Communism in the Balkans would be contrary to Britain's interests in the Eastern Mediterranean.

One of my jobs in the winter of 1941 was to prepare a position paper setting out for S.O.E. a policy which would appeal to the potential forces of Resistance in the Balkans and still be consistent with British interests.

The Germans—and we suspected the Soviets—sought to dominate the Balkans. Independence—'the Balkans for the Balkan peoples'—was thus the first plank in the platform I recommended. German policy was to divide and rule. Our answer, therefore, had to be Balkan unity, whether on a federal or confederal basis. German—and for that matter Soviet—ideology was totalitarian. Ours, therefore, should be liberal and, in what were predominantly peasant countries, might best be based on peasant co-operatives. Our war aims for south-east Europe could thus be summed up in the slogan 'Balkan Unity on a basis of peasant democracy'.

Walter Monckton, the deputy Minister of State in the Middle East, gave this programme his support. So did my old friend, Milan Gavrilovitch, who came through Cairo at the beginning of 1942 on his way from the Soviet Union to join the Yugoslav Government in London. A few weeks later, largely at Gavrilovitch's instance, the Greek and Yugoslav Governments in London signed an agreement proposing an organic union between Greece and Yugoslavia as the nucleus of a wider Balkan grouping.

At my suggestion, Oliver Lyttelton, the Minister of State in the Middle

East telegraphed to Eden urging him to make a statement in the House of Commons welcoming the conception of a Balkan Union. On 4 February 1942, the following exchanges took place in the House of Commons:

ENEMY OCCUPIED COUNTRIES (ALLIES' AGREEMENTS).

Dr. Russell Thomas asked the Secretary of State for Foreign Affairs whether he has any information in regard to the Agreement made between the Governments of Greece and Yugoslavia, and the Agreement made between the Governments of Poland and Czechoslovakia which, among other matters, involves a common economic policy and the proposal for a Customs union?

Mr. Eden: As my hon. Friend is aware, the Agreement between Greece and Yugoslavia was signed in the Foreign Office on 15th January, and I am glad to have this opportunity of welcoming an Agreement which cements the friendly relations already existing between two Allied Governments and which affords a basis for a future Balkan Confederation. The text of the Agreement has already been published, and there is nothing that I can add to it.

The text of the Polish-Czechoslovak Agreement has also been published. In reply to a Question by the hon. Member for East Wolverhampton (*Mr. Mander*) on 26th November, 1940, the Prime Minister said that His Majesty's Government warmly welcomed the original Polish-Czechoslovak Declaration of 11th November, 1940. They equally welcome this new Agreement as marking a further important stage in the development of closer relations between these two Allies.

Dr. Thomas: Without attempting to make any difficulty for my right hon. Friend, may I ask whether he will be good enough, when he has consultations with the Allied Governments, to look at the point of view that economic blocks may be a hindrance to post-war trade and possibly sow the seeds of future European trouble?

Mr. Eden: It is difficult to pursue a counsel of perfection in these matters. I am convinced that the Greek–Yugoslav Agreement is very much a step in the right direction.

Mr. Noel-Baker: Are we right in thinking that it is the intention of the Governments which honour the Agreement that it shall be open to all other Balkan countries to adhere to it as soon as they have democratic and peace-loving Governments? Is it their intention that this should be an organisation within a wider framework for the suppression of aggression and the maintenance of peace?

Mr. Eden: It is difficult to answer for other Governments, but what I can say for sure is that this Greek–Yugoslav Treaty is definitely to form the basis of a Balkan Confederation.

This statement gave us, for a time, a firm basis for British propaganda to the Balkans and for negotiation with different Resistance leaders. But it was only a blue-print, and its fulfilment inevitably depended upon how the different Balkan countries were liberated.

Who would get there first? Soviet or British forces? At this time, the winter of 1941/42, the answer was far from clear. The Soviets had been driven out of the Crimea and back on to the Volga. The British forces by contrast had high hopes of clearing the Germans and Italians out of North Africa by the summer of 1942.

What would happen next was uncertain; but, if Turkey declared for us or if Italy collapsed, the Army in the Middle East might be in a position by early 1943 to open a front in Greece or in the Adriatic.

The fates decided otherwise. Auchinleck's Winter Operation 'Crusader' in the Western Desert failed to reach its objectives, instead by June 1942 Rommel had reached El Alamein, threatening Alexandria and Cairo. Many at G.H.Q. expected that Egypt would fall to the enemy. Essential records were evacuated to Palestine and orders given to burn the rest.

The prospect of the fall of Cairo presented S.O.E. with a number of problems. Our first duty was to make sure that our German, Italian and Balkan friends or agents did not fall into enemy hands. The key men were evacuated to Jerusalem. The others were embarked on a troop ship for South Africa. I dressed Jakob Altmaier up as a British Army Captain and got him on an aircraft to Lagos.

At five o'clock on the afternoon of 1 July, Maxwell sent for me. He had decided to send me to London to explain in detail to our London office his plans for the dispersal of S.O.E. Middle East and for its future operations. He had a passage for me on a Liberator bomber leaving for Britain next day. There was no time, he said, to prepare a full report. My job would be to spend the rest of the evening with him and other colleagues, making notes of their plans. I was then to commit these to memory.

I spent most of the night and the following morning at a series of meetings. Then on the afternoon of 2 July left Cairo for an aerodrome on the road to Alexandria. Within twenty-four hours I was back in the S.O.E. office in Baker Street. I was destined to stay there for more than a year.

The tide of war now turned in favour of the Allies. Rommel was defeated at El Alamein. Von Paulus capitulated at Stalingrad. British and American forces landed in North Africa.

Montgomery's victories in the Western Desert were partly due to the massive reinforcement of the Middle East Air Force. There were now four Liberator bombers available to parachute supplies into the Balkans on a regular if limited scale. Communications with General Mihailovitch's head-quarters had been restored and we now established liaison officers with his different commanders and began to drop arms and ammunition to them.

Chetniks and *Partisans* had largely recovered from the German attempt to crush them in the previous autumn. They tied down very substantial garrisons of Axis troops and were a constant threat to German communications with Greece and Bulgaria. Nevertheless their military value was seriously diminished by the open warfare which continued between them.

In these circumstances, it was decided to send a high-powered mission to Mihailovitch to assess the situation and to try and influence developments. The obvious man to lead the mission was Bill Bailey, my former chief. No other Englishman combined to anything like the same degree, fluent command of the Serbo-Croat language, knowledge of the political background, experience of clandestine operations and the necessary physical stamina.

Bailey had many critics in S.O.E. and in the Foreign Office, largely because of the rather radical policies he had advocated in 1940 and the disregard which he had occasionally shown for higher authority. But he was so plainly the right man for the job that his appointment was rapidly confirmed. Before leaving for Yugoslavia we agreed that he would send for me as soon as he had established himself at Mihailovitch's headquarters.

Bailey was parachuted into the mountains of Montenegro on Christmas Day 1942. In March he asked that I be sent to join him.

All organisations tend to develop cliques within them, and this is particularly true of Secret Services where security can always be invoked to stifle criticism. The group of men then in control of S.O.E. in Cairo did not like Bailey and did not like me. They maintained that I had been a bad influence on Bailey in 1940, and that I might again encourage him to advocate and even pursue policies different from their own. They bluntly refused Bailey's request. The London Office was not prepared to over-rule them. I accordingly continued in the Balkan Section of S.O.E. in London attending to routine business and making an occasional contribution to the debate on Tito and Mihailovitch.

My own proposal, which I had first made in Cairo and now repeated in London, was that we should give our main support to Mihailovitch but also seek to establish missions with Tito. This was turned down on the ground that it was inconsistent with our commitments to the Yugoslav Government. I accordingly conceived an alternative plan which might possibly prove more acceptable. This was to set up a joint Anglo-Yugoslav military staff in the Middle East. This would be responsible both to the King of Yugoslavia as Supreme Commander of the Royal Yugoslav armed forces and to the British Commander-in-Chief Middle East. British liaison officers would be attached to both Mihailovitch and to Tito and would receive their orders from the Joint Staff in Cairo. Both Mihailovitch and Tito would be invited to attach Liaison officers of their own to the Joint Staff and if they so wished to be represented on it. All supplies would be sent in the name of the Joint Staff; and, though Tito was unlikely to accept its authority, he would scarcely refuse its supplies. If British forces were to land in Yugoslavia, the Joint Staff would probably be the best instrument for exercising British influence and for trying to reconcile the contending forces in the country. Meanwhile, it might limit hostilities between them and perhaps even bring about a truce.

I discussed these ideas with Djonovitch, Gavrilovitch and other Yugoslav exiles whose judgement I valued. They had no more desire than I to encourage Tito's movement. But they recognised that the policy of ignoring Tito was becoming increasingly unrealistic and that some device such as I had proposed offered the best way of maintaining both Mihailo-vitch's influence and their own. They put the idea to King Peter, who accepted it with youthful enthusiasm. He proposed to go out to the Middle East himself and then return to Yugoslavia. He had learned to fly in England and spoke of leading a sortie in, piloting his own aircraft. He asked for me to go with him as a British liaison officer.

Lord Selborne, who had taken over ministerial responsibility for S.O.E. from Dr. Dalton in February 1942, supported the King's proposal. But the Foreign Office advised against appointing me as liaison officer apparently on the ground that I was too pro-Tito. In the light of their own subsequent change of view this was rather ironic. King Peter took the matter up with Churchill who decided to accept the Foreign Office advice. The King later told me that he had pressed the point. 'But,' he said, 'the old Bulldog was very firm.'

King Peter duly went to Cairo but was kept at arms length by S.O.E. and the Military Commands. Surprisingly, however, S.O.E. and the Foreign Office now accepted my proposal of establishing a mission with Tito. Our first liaison officer to *Partisan* headquarters was Bill Deakin, a history don at Wadham who had helped Churchill with his *Life of Marlborough* and other books. Deakin had originally been sent to Cairo to join Bailey, at the latter's special request. He was now sent to Tito. Thanks to Deakin, we soon had accurate information of the situation in the *Partisan* camp.[1] With Bailey at Mihailovitch's Headquarters and Deakin at Tito's we were well informed and well placed to exercise such influence and pressures as were open to us. In the event, we made little use of our opportunities.

---

[1] For a detailed account of the Deakin mission see his book *Embattled Mountain* (1971), Oxford University Press.

27

The Partition of the Balkans

S.O.E.'s refusal to let me join Bailey at Mihailovitch's Headquarters was a bitter blow. I had been connected with Yugoslav affairs since the outbreak of war. I had organised and accompanied the first mission to the Yugoslav insurgents as early as September 1941. I had confidently expected to be allowed to play a part either as Bailey's deputy or as an ordinary liaison officer with *Chetnik* or *Partisan* forces. I believed I understood the Yugoslav problem better than most people and that I had a contribution to make. Men like Bailey and Hanau who knew Yugoslavia best shared this view. On top of this, I had now been refused what seemed at least an interesting staff job with King Peter.

What made my sense of frustration worse was that subversive operations were the only form of warfare I knew about and the Balkans the only area where I could claim special knowledge. It was too late to think of returning to the R.A.F., and it began to look as if I would spend the rest of the war at an office desk in Baker Street.

Then in September 1943, Brigadier Eddie Myers arrived in London summoned by the Prime Minister. Myers was a regular Sapper officer and had been dropped into Greece to blow up the Gorgopotamos Bridge. He knew no modern Greek and nothing of modern Greek politics but he had a natural political flair. He had found the two main Greek resistance movements, the nationalist EDES commanded by Zervas and the Communist ELAS commanded by Sarafis, heading rapidly for a Civil War on the Yugoslav pattern. With a mixture of military bluntness and semitic flair, Myers had persuaded the rival factions to suspend their feuds and, nominally at least, to work together. He was, however, convinced that unless the Greek Government in exile was broadened to give more representation to the left-wing parties, his work of reconciliation would not last. He had accordingly come out of Greece to put his views and those of Zervas and Sarafis to the British and Greek Governments. He hoped then to return to Greece with a stronger mission and a clearer political directive.

Ian Pirie, who was then in charge of the Greek section in Baker Street, advised Myers to consult me about the very similar if even more acute problems of the Civil War in Yugoslavia. Myers was interested in these both because of the parallels with his own difficulties and because he looked forward to developing relations between the Greek Resistance Movements and their neighbours to the north. I took the opportunity to suggest that I might go back to Greece with him with the special task of establishing contact between his mission and the Resistance forces in Albania, Yugoslavia and Bulgaria. Myers was a man who liked new ideas, and, after a dinner at home where we discussed Balkan affairs late into the night, he invited me to join his staff. Lord Selborne gave his blessing and wrote me a kindly letter wishing me good luck. The Foreign Office, however, intervened and tried to stop me from going on the grounds that I was likely to encourage Myers to take a different line from Foreign Office policy. I was, apparently, regarded as a dangerous radical, presumably because of my earlier views on Prince Paul and King Boris. This was too much for Selborne. He seized the telephone and got through to Anthony Eden. I do not know exactly what passed between them. Pat Hornsby-Smith,[1] then Selborne's private secretary, afterwards told me that at one point my chief had said, 'Don't be silly, Anthony, keep your sense of humour.'

He followed up the conversation with a letter which was as generous to me as it was firm towards the Foreign Office. It was, he argued, absurd that I should be denied the opportunity to serve my country in a sphere for which I was well qualified just because I had gone against Foreign Office policy in 1940 and been proved right. Selborne had his way. But the matter seems to have created some stir in the political stratosphere. At a dinner in Wavell's honour a few days later, the Prime Minister wished me good luck in my new mission and then added with a smile: 'Don't get rid of the King of Greece just yet.' I have never ceased to be amazed that so much importance could have been attached to the opinions of a junior officer; and it shows how much damage a black mark in the Foreign Office books, however undeserved, can do to a young man's career. But for the exertions, first of Dr. Dalton and then of Lord Selborne, I should undoubtedly have spent the rest of the war as a clerk in an office. I was lucky to have two such chiefs.

Just before I left with Myers for Cairo my father took me to see Lloyd George at Churt. My childhood hero was showing his years, though there were some flashes of the old fire. He talked mainly about the urgency of opening a second front in France and seemed obsessed with the fear that, unless we did, the Soviets might make a separate peace with Germany. The only other person there was Miss Stevenson, his secretary, whom he was to marry a few months later. I had told Lloyd George about my mission to Greece and as we were leaving asked if he had any message

[1] Later Dame Patricia Hornsby-Smith, M.P.

for the Greeks. His answer came like a flash of lightning: 'Tell them to fight on and be worthy of their fathers.' My last sight of him was standing in the drive wrapped in a cloak against the chill of the autumn sunset.

The journey from London to Cairo proved uneventful. There was little risk of interception now over the Atlantic, and with North Africa and the south of Italy in allied hands, the flight along the Mediterranean presented no problems.

I spent the first few days in Cairo reading up the back-log of signals and reports about operations in Greece and learning about Greek affairs from Monty Woodhouse,[1] Francis Noel-Baker[2] and others with first-hand knowledge of them. After this, I went for three weeks on an intelligence course at Helwan just outside Cairo. This consisted of a detailed study of the German Army, and of guidance on the art of interrogating prisoners.

But, while I was on my course, the situation in Greece deteriorated sharply. The Communist-led guerrillas of ELAS clashed with the EDES supporters of Zervas. A British officer was killed. Anthony Eden flew to Cairo, and a firm decision was taken support the King of Greece against the Communists and, indeed, against the Republican parties. The Myers proposals for making the exiled Government more representative of the Resistance thus fell to the ground; and at the King's request it was decided that Myers should not go back to Greece.

I returned to Cairo to find myself once more without a job. But Cairo meanwhile had become the centre of the Allied world. The Cairo Conference was in full swing. Roosevelt, Chiang Kai-shek and Churchill were established in spacious villas. Their second elevens were accommodated in various comfortable houses. The lower echelons 'pigged it' in a makeshift camp. I took no part in the Conference, but Randolph Churchill was busy promoting the claims of the Fitzroy Maclean mission to Tito and we had several discussions about the Balkan situation.

Fitzroy Maclean had followed Bill Deakin to Tito's headquarters and had now come out to urge that we should abandon Mihailovitch and give our support exclusively to Tito. The future of the Balkans was very much on the agenda, but as yet no decisions were taken.

The President and the Prime Minister presently departed for Teheran to meet Marshal Stalin. The Prime Minister stopped in Cairo on his way back from Teheran and I saw him at a dinner at the Embassy. I described it to my father as follows:

[1] The Hon. C. M. Woodhouse, later Conservative M.P. for Oxford and Minister of State at the Home Office, author of *Apple of Discord*, a detailed account of his experiences in Greece.
[2] Francis Noel-Baker, later Labour M.P. for Swindon.

The major event for me was a dinner at the embassy with Winston, Smuts, Eden, Cadogan, Casey, the Killearns, and youth represented by Fitzroy Maclean, Randolph, George Jellicoe, David Wallace and Jannie Smuts. Winston was in grand form and had a good sparring match with Smuts. Smuts, alas, speaks too softly to get most of his points across the P.M.'s after dinner barrage. . . . Among his (the P.M.'s) better remarks was a reply to a question about his future plans—'I am the victim of caprice and travel on the wings of fancy.' And on France 'the destinies of a great people cannot be determined for all time by the temporary deficiencies of its technical apparatus.' He told us that he had been on the point of using this at Teheran and had only just remembered in time that it had originally been coined by Trotsky.

The younger members of the party were all concerned with Balkan Resistance and after dinner Churchill collected us in a corner. He told us that no final decisions had been taken, but that he was minded to support the King in Greece and Tito in Yugoslavia. I was frankly puzzled why he should be advocating completely different policies for two neighbouring countries when their circumstances were remarkably similar. Presently, he asked me what I thought. I questioned whether to support a King in Greece and a Communist dictator in Yugoslavia might not lead to difficulties especially in Macedonia where the populations were to some extent interlocked. To this, the great man replied: 'I see you think that what I am proposing is inconsistent. It may be. But it is my policy and I still have some influence here.' It was a crushing reply, though said with good humour, and admitted of no rejoinder. But I guessed that Churchill's refusal to explain his policy must conceal some major difficulty. It was some time before I discovered what this was.

Before leaving the dinner Churchill took me by the arm and, with a broad grin, said: 'You have backed the wrong horse in Greece' (meaning Myers) 'but I hope you will ride home on the Yugoslav one.'

In view of this remark and of Randolph's promptings, I went to see Fitzroy Maclean next day. He did not ask me to join his mission and I did not press him to do so. I had always advocated maintaining contact with Tito and sending him supplies. But I did not want to become involved in breaking with Mihailovitch and this had become Fitzroy Maclean's main objective. Indeed, the nearer we came to victory, the more important it seemed to me to support Mihailovitch. His movement might be less effective militarily than Tito's. But it was much more likely to conform to Britain's interests.

What were Churchill's motives in inclining towards Tito and away from Mihailovitch? It is clear that by the time of the Teheran Conference he had made up his mind that British influence should predominate in Greece. The Monarchy was to be restored if necessary by British arms

THE PARTITION OF THE BALKANS

and without regard to the wishes of the Communist *Partisans* of ELAS. The fact that the Communists had fought better than the Nationalists and even the charge that the Nationalists had made accommodations with the enemy were regarded as irrelevant. This was a firm, clear policy; and events would justify it.

Why then did Churchill take a different line over Yugoslavia? It is clear from his memoirs that he still hoped, even after the Teheran Conference, to persuade Roosevelt to launch the Army of Italy against Vienna through the Istrian gap at the head of the Adriatic. This would have involved the presence of British troops on Yugoslav soil and must have given Britain a considerable, perhaps a predominant influence upon developments inside Yugoslavia. But Roosevelt and Stalin were opposed to this strategy and suspected that Churchill's real motive was political rather than military—to reach the Danube before the Soviets and preserve some British influence in the Balkans. Was the new policy of supporting Tito, which began to develop after the Teheran Conference, a desperate attempt on Churchill's part to persuade Stalin and Roosevelt that the Istrian strategy was advanced on purely military grounds and without regard to ideological considerations? Or was it rather an increasing acceptance that the prospect of an Istrian strategy was steadily receding? Whatever the answer, all through the winter of 1943/44 British policy inclined increasingly towards Tito and away from Mihailovitch. It was not, however, until May 1944 that the decision was taken to break with Mihailovitch and withdraw the British missions attached to him. By this time all hope of an Istrian strategy had been abandoned. The Soviets would 'liberate' Yugoslavia and Tito's victory was assured. In the circumstances there was no longer any purpose in supporting Mihailovitch. The *Chetniks* would never rise to support a Soviet invasion of the Balkans, and any arms we sent them would only be used against Tito's Communist *Partisans*.

In these circumstances the British Government had no choice but to support Tito. But what was wrong and unworthy was to turn against Mihailovitch and denounce the *Chetnik* movement as 'collaborationists' because of occasional accommodations with the enemy to which we had turned a blind eye for two years and for which there were many parallels in Greece. The right thing would have been to tell Mihailovitch frankly that there was no longer any prospect of a British landing in Yugoslavia and to advise him and his principal colleagues either to come to terms with Tito or to join King Peter in honourable exile in London. Mihailovitch might well have declined such an offer; but at least it should have been made.

But there is in our national character a strong urge to find a moral justification for political decisions. Instead of admitting that we had

failed to get our strategy accepted and that it was therefore no longer
practical politics to support Mihailovitch, we made a virtue of necessity
and turned the man who had been our friend into a scapegoat for our
own impotence. This hypocrisy, and it was nothing less, was accepted
by British opinion while a more realistic admission of our true motives
would have been found profoundly shocking. But few people outside
were taken in. Mihailovitch was known to the world as Britain's friend in
Yugoslavia. The decision to abandon him and his pseudo-judicial murder
at Tito's hands after the war were great blows to British prestige. This
suffered not only among anti-Communists, but among the Communists
themselves. When Tito broke with Stalin in 1948, the British Government
of the day rightly decided to give him their support independent of all
ideological considerations. But when a neutral visitor told Tito at the time
that he could rely upon the British, Tito is said to have replied somewhat
caustically: 'They didn't do much for Mihailovitch.'

To condemn our denunciation of Mihailovitch is not to criticise our
support of Tito. The right course, as I had believed throughout, was to
support both at any rate until the Adriatic strategy of the Allies was
decided. Once the Western Powers decided not to land in Yugoslavia
support for Tito became the only practical course. We gave that support
belatedly but even so we drew an important military dividend from it. It
hastened the end of the war. It also contributed directly, by threatening
German communications, to the British liberation of Greece and the
restoration of the Greek monarchy. We also derived another and un-
covenanted advantage from it. Co-operation first with Deakin and later
with the high powered mission led by Fitzroy Maclean was a considerable
education for Tito. He owed his victory to British more than to Soviet
material support. He also found that the British were reasonable people
to work with. These things played their part in later years when the
Yugoslav Communist leaders had to decide whether to stand up to Stalin
or submit. They may yet bear still stranger fruit.

My brief interview with Fitzroy Maclean marked the end of four
years of personal involvement in Yugoslav affairs. I was now without a
job and saw little prospect of active service or even interesting staff work.
Cairo was a fascinating city. I had many friends there and remained on
the strength of S.O.E. But the winter of 1943/44 remains in my memory
as a period of deep depression verging at times on despair. It was not
long in fact before a golden and unexpected opportunity opened. But,
before describing it, I must go back and say something of my other and
more overt experiences in the Middle East.

VI

ORIENTATIONS

April 1941–December 1943

'The East is a university where the scholar never gets his degree.'
George Nathaniel Curzon

28

The Middle East Command

The reader may recall that, after the coup d'état against Prince Paul at the end of March 1941, Bailey had sent for me to join him in the Balkans. But, by the time I reached Cairo, Yugoslavia and Greece were already lost. The Battle of Crete had begun, but no-one had any confidence that we could hold the island. We had neither the air power nor the men. What would happen next?

I consulted Shearer, Wavell's Director of Intelligence. He admitted that the Greek campaign had left us desperately weak in the Western Desert, but he was also convinced that the Italians were in no position to take advantage of our weakness. He saw little danger of an Italian attack on Egypt in the month or two ahead.

The immediate danger came from the East and the North. Baghdad was in the hands of Rashid Ali Gailani and the pro-German officers of the 'Golden Square' conspiracy. Our garrison in Habbaniyah was besieged. German influence was growing daily in Syria; and a German mission was planning supply lines from the Balkans, through Crete and Vichy-held Syria, to Iraq. Turkish morale was very low. No doubt the Balkan campaign had strained German supplies and communications. The fact remained that the British Army of the Nile was temporarily a paper tiger and that we had virtually no forces north of the Suez Canal. Looking back it has often seemed to me that Hitler made his greatest mistake in not concentrating through the summer of 1941 on the conquest of the Middle East. His chances of success were high. The result would have made the Axis Powers supreme in the Mediterranean and prevented an Allied landing in North Africa. It would also, with the conquest of the Persian Gulf, have assured their oil supplies. Beyond that, possession of the Middle East would have enabled Hitler to outflank the Soviets to the south and so placed him in a far stronger strategic position for his final reckoning with Moscow. Fortunately for us, Hitler was essentially a continental animal. He never seems to have understood the crucial importance of the Middle East and the Mediterranean. Or else, he lacked the flexibility to postpone Operation Barbarossa against Russia and take full advantage instead of his victories in the Balkans and Crete.

In the spring of 1941 it seemed to me almost inevitable that the War would soon spread to the Middle East. If so, it would be a long time before Balkan Resistance became practical politics; and I began to wonder whether I might not find more opportunity for active service in the Arab countries than in the Balkans. I consulted Clayton, who was responsible for intelligence about the Middle East and was then forming an Arab bureau. He offered me a place in it, but advised me to stick to the Balkans. I knew about them, he said, and very few Englishmen did. This might give me a chance to influence events and make a serious contribution. The position in the Middle East was very different. He had many experienced officers who knew its languages and peoples, and, if I joined his Bureau, it would inevitably be in a very junior capacity.

At the same time, Clayton was anxious that a young Englishman with political ambitions should learn as much as possible about the Middle East. He asked me to consider myself as an honorary member of his team and to come and learn about their work and talk with him and his officers whenever I had time. I took full advantage of this invitation.

I carried letters from my father to Wavell and went to see him in his office in 'Grey Pillars' as the G.H.Q. was known. He seemed physically tired and fatalistic in his approach to his problems. Fresh from reading *War and Peace* I was at once reminded of Tolstoy's description of Kutusov —the one-eyed Russian Commander-in-Chief in the war against Napoleon —and his stubborn determination to let geography fight his battles rather than force an issue for which he lacked the means.

I asked Wavell whether he could have driven the Italians out of North Africa if he had not been ordered to divert forces to Greece. On balance he thought not. His stocks of petrol had been too low to push his offensive much further. The strain on his maintenance organisation had also been intense. The war in the desert was a war of movement and without more petrol there could be no final victory. Petrol, indeed, was the theme which dominated our talk, much as Tanks had been the dominant theme at our first meeting, the previous autumn. Wavell's chief anxiety, for instance, about developments in Iraq was that they might cut him off from his petrol supplies. When I asked him what S.O.E. could most usefully do, he answered that we should concentrate on the sabotage of petrol supplies to the Axis army in Libya. Their problem was the same as his. To deny them petrol was the next best thing to providing him with more. At the time, it all struck me as rather over-simplified. I would think differently a year later when Rommel's invasion of Egypt was checked more by the strain on his supplies than by our capacity to resist his armour.

Wavell was a hero to his staff and to his Armies. His victories in the

Western Desert and in Abyssinia had proved his genius as a strategist. The outcome of the operations in Iraq and Syria would soon confirm his wisdom in accumulating swollen staffs in Cairo. It was their task to prepare for the many contingencies for which he had few if any troops to spare. His one weakness was in council. He had no gift of exposition, and found it hard to share his vision with others. His visitors and his political chiefs were all too often left with the impression that he was tired and lacked resourcefulness. I must confess that, at this stage, I shared these misgivings. It was only later, after he had become Viceroy of India and I came to know him better, that I fully appreciated the greatness of the man.

Wavell's command stretched from the Turkish and Persian borders in the north to the Equator in the south. In this vast and turbulent area, he was the supreme British authority. Yet he never had a diplomatic staff to guide him through the cross currents of Middle Eastern politics, nor an economic staff to mobilise the resources of the area in support of his armies. As I wrote at the time:

> I do not think even in the history of Egypt anybody has been asked to make bricks with so little straw.[1]

It seemed clear to me, as, indeed, to many others, that a member of the War Cabinet should be stationed permanently in Cairo. I wrote to my father:

25 June 1941
I am convinced, along with most other people, that it is essential that the Government should send out here, at once, a Plenipotentiary Minister of Cabinet Status. More than three-quarters of the problems here are political and it is difficult for anyone with less than War Cabinet authority to get things done. In the first place there is the supply and shipping problem. This I am convinced is being handled less well than it might be. Then there is the political problem of our relations with the Arab World, and, now that Russia has come into the War, with the Russians and the Turks. These problems require the presence of a man who would command the respect of the heads of the three Services and who would really be listened to at home. He would only need a small staff. Probably just one liaison officer with each service and a few political and supply advisers.

Unless this is done, there is no reason whatever to believe that the present muddle, both of supplies and policy, will be discontinued. The problem, of course, is to find the right man. There are very few possible names. But I think the man who has created the best impression out here so far is Smuts. . . . It has always been obvious since the fall of France that the Government in London is too far away to settle problems here.

[1] Letter to my father 25 June 1941.

My father sent on my letter to the Prime Minister. The pressures making for the appointment of a Minister of State were already very strong and what I wrote can only have swollen the file. Still it was in the right sense.

I dined with the Wavells soon after returning to Cairo, and was at once impressed by the improvement in their table and the easier flow of the conversation. Something had happened to the household. The influence at work was that of Major Peter Coates, the General's new ADC. Coates was a man of great sensitivity and unusual social gifts. He had been quick to see the importance of providing better entertainment for the Commander-in-Chief's visitors. What was more, he had also discovered that, with adequate briefing and occasional prompting, Wavell could be a very engaging companion.

Wavell, indeed, was a man of wide culture as well as natural talent. But he had spent his life in a rather narrow circle and had never been encouraged to talk. Peter Coates who belonged to the sophisticated world of 'Chips' Channon and Lady Cunard now became, as it were, his impresario. He stimulated Wavell's interest or sense of fun; fed him the gossip of Cairo and brought people to his house whom he would never otherwise have seen, but whose talk influenced opinion. I do not know that Coates ever influenced Wavell's military or policy decisions but he did much to make his Chief's star shine brighter, and this was important at a time when it was passing behind a cloud and even seemed threatened with extinction.

When I left the Wavells after dinner, Coates asked me if there was anything I needed. I expected to spend some time in Cairo and said cheerfully that it would be a help to have a car and a flat with views on both the Nile and the Pyramids. It was like asking for the moon, and I never expected to be taken seriously. But a fortnight later I received a short note from Peter enclosing the keys of the car and the flat. The flat stood on the banks of the Nile. The bedroom window looked on to the Pyramids. The rent was just within the limits of a Captain's pay. It was some time, however, before I had much chance to enjoy them.

My first task on returning to the Middle East had been to go to Jerusalem to pick up the bits from the collapse of Yugoslavia. The Balkan section of S.O.E. had made their headquarters there, and I spent much of the summer in Jerusalem, living at the King David Hotel.

As it happened, the King David soon became the hub of the war in the Middle East. Among its new patrons were the Iraqi leaders just escaped from the rebels in Baghdad. There was King Feisal's uncle, the regent Abdulillah.[1] He looked a weak man but his looks belied unusual

[1] King Feisal II and Prince Abdulillah along with Nuri Said were murdered in Baghdad in the revolution of 1958.

courage and what would prove a fatal streak of obstinacy. Then there was Nuri Said, the Odysseus of the Arab World. I did not come to know him well till many years later but was struck even then by his total lack of pomposity and the way he came and went by taxi or on foot, when much lesser men never moved without a bodyguard and in large motor cars! With the Iraqi leaders were two remarkable British 'Arabists', Gerald de Gaury and Pat Domville. De Gaury was tall and could have been taken for a regular officer, except that his movements were too slow and his attitude seemed too detached. He introduced me to his Iraqi friends and to some of the Syrian refugees in Jerusalem. We also spent a day together riding with the Camel Corps at Beersheba. I found this an alarming experience. The camel is an unloveable beast and even at the age of twenty-two a short patrol left me uncomfortably stiff. De Gaury, though I could scarcely judge this at the time, combined a deep understanding of the Arab mind with a clear view of Britain's interests in the Middle East. But he was too much of a perfectionist in his work and too fastidious in his ways to exercise the full influence that could have been his.

Domville was very much his opposite. He was Irish and essentially a man of action. He spoke perfect Arabic and was equally at home in the Palace or the *Souk*. He had twice saved Nuri's life in Baghdad; and, if Rommel had taken Cairo, it was Domville who would have stayed in the city to command the Resistance network we planned to leave behind. British Intelligence lost one of its most penetrating eyes, when he was dropped shortly after the war. Even then, living on a pittance in a Cairo suburb, he secured the plans and names of the young officers plotting against King Farouk some months before they made their coup d'état in 1952. I put this information on the Foreign Secretary's desk but it was not believed.

The Iraqi leaders and their British advisers presently departed to settle accounts with the rebel officers of the 'Golden Square' in Baghdad. But the reception clerks at the King David were soon kept busy again by the approach of the Syrian campaign against the Vichy French.

Clayton and his staff were now in permanent residence in the King David. General Catroux, dark eyed and sallow even in the Levant, was a frequent visitor. Crown Prince Mohammed Ali of Egypt also came to stay. He was there, he said, to escape from the heat of Cairo. But others whispered that his purpose was to secure the crown of Syria for himself. The Emir Abdullah of Trans-Jordan was known to covet this prize as well. He remained in Amman, but Glubb Pasha[1] was often to be seen in Jerusalem pressing his master's claims. Another prominent hotel guest was Air Commodore Buss, an Englishman turned Moslem. He was

[1] General Sir John Glubb, Commander of the Arab Legion.

negotiating with the Druze leaders through the intermediary of the beautiful Princess Atrash, and, so the gossips said, had lost his heart to her.

The overture to the Syrian Campaign was the defection to our side of General Collet and his Circassian brigade. This was a regiment raised from descendants of Shamyl's followers, settled in Syria by the Sultan after the Russian conquest of the Caucasus. They were reputed good troops and certainly looked very dashing in their astrakhan caps and cossack type uniforms.

I saw a good deal of the General and his wife in the next few days. She was ambitious for him and had dashed off a book designed to make him popular with his British allies. One sentence in the typescript ran: 'A fox dashed across the road. Collet, always a sportsman, reached for his gun.' I remember suggesting that this might be counter-productive.

My only direct intervention in the Syrian campaign seems more important in retrospect than it did at the time. S.O.E. had organised a small group of Arabs to attack Vichy communications in Syria ahead of the Army's advance. Some of these defected at the last minute, and I was asked by our Arab section if I knew of any Balkan Moslems—Bosnians or Albanians—who spoke Arabic. The matter was urgent. The Allied advance was to begin in a few days and S.O.E. would lose all its credit with G.H.Q. if it failed to fulfil its sabotage commitments. None of our Balkan refugees had a word of Arabic. But I happened to be lunching that day with Moshe Shertok, the 'Foreign Secretary' of the Jewish Agency.[1] We were working closely together on operations into the Balkans; and, when our own business was done, I asked him whether he knew of any Palestine born Jews who could pass as Arabs and would be suitable for a sabotage job in Syria. He produced half-a-dozen young men the same evening and I introduced them to our Arab expert who took them on at once. That, as far as I was concerned, was that. I was afterwards told that they had carried out their mission successfully but did not go into detail. It was only years later that I learned that one of them had lost an eye in the process. His name was Moshe Dayan. It is a curious fact and perhaps a hopeful portent for the future that Israel's national hero should have lost an eye disguised as an Arab and in the service of Britain.

S.O.E. also worked closely during the Syrian campaign with Prince Aly Khan who was seeking to mobilise his father's Ismaili followers to cut communications between Damascus and Aleppo. Though best known as a playboy, Aly had a well-stocked and penetrating mind. When there was a serious job to do he could do it very well. His weakness, unusual in an Oriental, was that he had neither patience nor discretion.

When Damascus fell the weather was extremely hot. Aly was one of the first into the city and slept the night naked on top of his bed in the Orient

[1] Later to become Prime Minister of Israel as Moshe Sharett.

Palace Hotel. The Lebanon was still in Vichy hands and their Air Force made a rather half-hearted raid on Damascus. Two or three bombs were dropped and the air raid sirens blew. Aly got up, walked across the room to where his tin hat lay on a chair, picked it up, returned to his bed and placed the hat firmly over his private parts. He then went back to sleep satisfied that he had done all he could to protect what was most essential— a fine example of faith and works combined.

Collet was made Governor of Damascus and I spent some days as his guest exploring the city with one of his Circassian aides. It remains one of the world's most beautiful cities, fully living up to its description of 'a precious pearl set in an emerald ring'. The Vichy French had gone. The Arabs were demonstratively pro-British; and the chief peril in Damascus came from the Australian troops. They had been brought up on the legend of their fathers' toughness in the First World War and were determined to live up to it. One of their favourite pastimes was to break into the mosques and boot the faithful up the backside as they prostrated themselves in prayer. The Military Police had a difficult time in dealing with them and there were casualties on both sides. One story, then current, told of a British officer in the Military Police who had chanced on an Australian private playing with a group of Arab children. 'They seem to like you, Aussie' he said in an attempt to improve relations. 'Meaning you don't?' answered the Australian, and knocked him cold.

In the intervals of my work I tried to learn something of the Palestine problem. The High Commissioner, Sir Harold MacMichael, and his Chief Secretary, Jock Macpherson, though both over burdened with work, did their best to instruct me. Despite the strong pro-Zionist views held by Churchill and many of the Cabinet, British officialdom on the spot un-doubtedly favoured the Arabs rather than the Jews. In a sense this was natural. The Jews were already committed to the Allied cause by Hitler's anti-semitism. The danger to Britain at the time came from the Arab side and since we were in no position to cope with an Arab revolt, it was perhaps logical that we should try to appease potential opponents. While the tide of war was against us, the policy worked well enough. The Jews gave us unstinted support. The Arabs in Palestine remained calm and in Trans-Jordan proved themselves our friends. But the continuation of the policy, after the tide had turned, left a legacy of bitterness in the Jewish community for which we would pay dearly in the closing phase of the Mandate.

I worked closely with Shertok and Zaslani,[1] the heads of the foreign and clandestine sections of the Jewish Agency. We had many mutual interests

[1] Later known as Reuben Shiloah.

in the Balkans and were often able to help each other. I was impressed by their efficiency and by the originality of their operational thinking. They were quick to see our point of view but held tenaciously to their own. But when they made a deal they stuck to it. My experience of working with them in these early days has left me less surprised than some at the scale and speed of their victories in three Arab wars.

The Jewish leader who impressed me most was Pinhas Rutenberg, an old Russian Social Revolutionary, who looked rather like Ernest Bevin. As a young man, Rutenberg had strangled Father Gapon, the *Okhrana agent provocateur*, with his own hands; and his hands, when he told the story, looked like two bunches of bananas. He had been Kerensky's police chief in Petrograd and had then escaped to Palestine to become a capitalist and a strong supporter of the British Empire. He showed a greater understanding of Arab susceptibilities, if not of Arab interests, than most of his compatriots.

My work took me quite often to Haifa, Tel Aviv and various collective farms, mostly in search of Jews who knew Balkan languages or had links with the Balkans. In the process I had many strange talks with farmers and labourers who only a few years before had been teaching philosophy or playing in orchestras somewhere in Central Europe.

My education on the Arab side was undertaken by 'Michael' Stirling,[1] our Albanian adviser. Stirling had been Governor of Jaffa after the First World War and knew most of the Arab leaders in Palestine. He took me to the houses of the great Jerusalem families, Nashashibis, Husseinis and Khalidis and taught me to appreciate their generous hospitality and quick-witted conversation. We drove out together to farms in Nablus and consorted with the notables of Jaffa. Stirling brought me, too, into touch with the prophet of the Arab Awakening, George Antonius, and we had several talks in Jerusalem and later in Cairo. For all his passion and revolutionary talk, George Antonius was essentially a humanist and a liberal. He would have been the first to denounce the gangsterism of Nasser and the *Baathists* which has done so much to blacken the name of the true Arab Nationalism which he preached.

What I saw of the Zionist achievement impressed me profoundly, but I could also understand the fears and anxieties of the Arabs. Zionism for all its internal divisions was a highly organised modern movement. Arab nationalism by contrast was a retarded version of the romantic nationalism of the nineteenth century. Personal relations between individual Arabs and Jews of my acquaintance were very cordial. But with the influx of Jews resulting from Hitler's persecutions it was hard to see how a clash between the two communities could be avoided. My letters to my father show that I saw no solution except in some kind of partition, and that even this would

[1] Colonel Frank Stirling: see p. 162.

only succeed provided we maintained a British military presence in Haifa and Jerusalem to hold the ring. Looking back, I still believe this view was right. Both sides would have resented any partition. But Britain's name stood so high in the Middle East at the end of the war that our decision would have been accepted. It was our indecision which led on inexorably to tragedy.

Jerusalem itself, with its mixture of races and creeds, was one of my chief joys. Like many visitors before and since, I was rather shocked by the contrast between the anarchy of the Holy Sepulchre and the serenity of the Dome of the Rock. But I delighted in the community of Abyssinian monks nestling on the roof of the Holy Sepulchre and would sometimes share their simple hospitality.

Princess Peter of Greece—she was a Russian and highly intelligent as well as beautiful—had taken up residence in the Greek Patriarchate inside the Old City. She was deeply interested in the study of comparative religion. Thanks to her I was introduced to a little circle of Christians, Moslems, and Jews who used to meet in the house of Dr. Martin Buber, a well-known Jewish theologian. I sat at the feet of these learned men and soon found that the essential unity of outlook of the Peoples of the Book far outweighs their differences. Since Eton, I had been through phases of agnosticism but the talk of these wise men and my own wartime experiences went far to restore my faith.

In October 1941, after Operation Bullseye—the submarine mission to the Yugoslav Resistance—I returned to staff duties in Cairo. The situation at G.H.Q. was by then greatly changed. Wavell had gone to India as Commander-in-Chief and had handed over the Middle East Command to Auchinleck.[1]

Auchinleck sent for me soon after my return from Yugoslavia. He wanted a first-hand report of Operation Bullseye and the prospects ahead for Mihailovitch. To me, Auchinleck was the most impressive of all our wartime commanders. His square jaw, massive head and the steady gaze of his clear blue eyes proclaimed him a natural leader. He seemed completely relaxed and genuinely interested in whatever subject he was discussing. In marked contrast to Wavell he was easy to talk to and quick to express an opinion. I came away from this first meeting very much under his spell.

Wavell's G.H.Q. was reputed to be an Augean stable crammed with superfluous staff officers whose time was largely taken up by prolonged siestas and the Cairo social round. The 'Auk' determined to cleanse them. Several sections of the staff were moved out of Cairo to a camp in the

[1] Later Field Marshal Sir Claude Auchinleck.

desert. The siesta habit was discouraged. The wits even had it that an order
had gone forth proclaiming that 'no officer is entitled to a room in the
Headquarters unless he has a job'. These reforms were not, in practice,
very helpful. The siesta habit is a good one in hot weather; and in winter
the break in the middle of the day gave over-worked staff officers a chance
to take some exercise. Nor was the social life of Cairo only a distraction. It
was also a stimulant to intelligent and original thinking. Wavell, it is true,
had tended to hoard staff officers, in case they might come in useful. But
this, too, had its merits. If they were worthwhile men, and Wavell was a
good judge of men, they had a way of finding useful work to do and in so
vast a command there was much to be done.

Auchinleck brought with him a rising military star, Brigadier 'Chink'
Dorman Smith. Dorman Smith was an Irishman with a natural flair for
politics and a provocative and controversial turn of mind. He had some
original ideas about desert war and advocated new and unorthodox dispositions. Later on, these were much criticised and he was widely held to
have been a bad influence on the High Command. This is something I am
not competent to judge; but he was certainly a stimulating and persuasive
talker, who made us feel that the Germans had no monopoly of forward
military thinking.

Despite his dynamic personality, Auchinleck was very much a G.H.Q.
man. He did not show himself to the Army in the same way as Wavell had
done. He believed in delegating authority; and, at quite an early stage, I
began to hear doubts whether he delegated wisely or picked his subordinates well.

For my own part, I can only say that he always showed me great
kindness. He wanted me to go to the Staff College at Haifa and then to join
his personal staff. I was flattered by the invitation; but the lure of the
Balkans proved too strong and I declined. Besides, I had had enough staff
duty and wanted a job in the field; and I was only likely to get one in the
Balkans.

The Cabinet by this time had appointed a Minister of State to reside
permanently in the Middle East. Churchill's choice here fell on Oliver
Lyttelton[1]; and his gay and buccaneering personality had a tonic effect on a
rather discouraged G.H.Q. In addition to more serious qualities, Lyttelton
was a brilliant mimic; and his parodies of meetings with the top brass in
Cairo made strong men break down and giggle like schoolboys. Lyttelton
concentrated mainly on supply and economic questions delegating issues of
foreign policy to his deputy, Walter Monckton.[2]

My work on the Balkans often brought me in touch with Monckton and

---

[1] Later Lord Chandos.
[2] Later Lord Monckton of Brenchley and for a time Minister of Labour and then of
Defence.

with Anthony Greenwood,[1] then his private secretary. Monckton was very quick to take a point and amazingly skilful at reconciling seemingly incompatible points of view. Sometimes, indeed, he carried this virtuosity too far; and slower men became resentful when they found they had been charmed into making unintended concessions.

Cairo then was the cross roads of the Free World. You could not get from America or Britain to India, the Far East or, indeed, to Russia without passing through Cairo. It was the Clapham Junction of the war. There was thus a constant stream of V.I.Ps on their way to Moscow, Delhi, Chungking, Singapore or Canberra. Exiled Kings, Ministers, Commanders-in-Chief, Members of Parliament, high officials, journalists and important neutrals all came through. They were entertained according to their rank and function by the Embassy, the Commanders-in-Chief, or the Ministers of State. But they also wanted some relaxation and the chance to see their friends. For these things they went to 'Momo's'.

'Momo' Marriott was a daughter of the great American financier, Otto Kahn, and the wife of Major-General John Marriott of the Scots Guards. She was small and dark, with delicate semitic features and large brown eyes. She had the figure of a child rather than of a woman, and combined a capricious feminine character with an almost masculine intelligence. As a young woman she had decided to standardise her clothes and way of life. Her hats, shoes and bags were always the same. The colours and materials might change, but not the style. Her routine was the same whether she lived in London, New York, Paris or wartime Cairo. She never rose before lunch. She spent an hour and a half reading in the bath before dinner. She gave luncheons and dinners almost daily and saw a constant stream of visitors in between and well into the night. She was, as a result, exceptionally well-informed.

The first time I was asked to lunch with Momo, the other guests included an Egyptian Princess, well-known as a drug addict. At table she sat next to a British General, dressed in a bush shirt and shorts. In the middle of lunch the General let out a piercing scream. The Princess, had tried to give herself an injection under the table and had mistaken his bare leg for her own.

This was only the first of many lunches with Momo. We soon became close friends and I have valued few friendships more.

Momo's house was the social centre of Cairo. Friends came to it to relax, to exchange information; sometimes even to meet informally and settle some difficult business. If you wanted the latest news or the latest

[1] Later Lord Greenwood, Secretary of State for the Colonies and then Minister of Housing.

gossip, Momo had it. If you wanted the latest books, in a world tortured by censorship, somehow they were there. If some new star rose on the horizon, you would be sure to meet him at 'Momo's'. If a young officer wanted help to advance his career or to change his job, Momo could pull the necessary strings. English, Egyptians, French, Americans all thronged to her house. It was the most influential as well as the most entertaining salon I have known. Three things made it possible; the time—War; the place—Cairo; and the woman—Momo.

29

The Egypt of the Pashas

Napoleon once called Egypt 'The most important country in the world'. It is the ground where Europe, Asia and Africa come together and, as such, was for seventy years the hinge of Britain's Empire. Its people are the heirs to seven thousand years of continuous civilisation; and the monuments of the Nile Valley testify to the past glories of Pharaohs and Ptolemies, Caliphs and Khedives.

I spent much of the war in Egypt, and since war involves a prodigious amount of waiting, had ample opportunity to explore the wonders of the land and to get to know its people. The Pyramids at Mena and at Saqqara were in easy reach of Cairo and I passed many happy hours beside them. In the winter of 1941, I also took a few days off—my first leave of the war— to visit Luxor, Edfu and Aswan.

The days in Luxor remain among my brightest memories. I used to spend the mornings on the west bank, where the dead are buried, exploring the ruined temples and shattered colossi and marvelling at the freshness of the murals on the walls of the royal tombs. The people depicted on them or sculptured in the temple friezes had the same features as the *fellahin* who rowed me across the river or whom I saw working in the fields. Their crops, their cattle, even their boats had scarcely changed. Once, entering a temple, I saw a jackal poke its head round a column. It had been resting, appropriately enough, under the altar of Anubis, the jackal-headed god of the dead.

In the afternoons I used to ride along the east bank of the river, the bank of the living. There I would visit the splendid palaces of the Pharaohs and then go on to have tea or dinner with the hospitable Egyptian land-owners of the district. My constant companion was Billy Joseph, a Coptic guide full of the lore of ancient Egypt but equally knowledgeable about the customs and the gossip of contemporary Upper Egypt. For Billy, there was no clear-cut break between past and present. He was equally at home in both and would tell stories about Rameses or Akhnaton with the same wit and gusto as he would mock the heavy drinking of some British General or the greed of a well-known Pasha.

Most Moslem countries treat their dead with scant respect. They wrap the bodies in a sheet and place them in a shallow grave, crowned with a plain headstone. Occasionally an inscription is carved on the headstone. More often only the dead man's turban identifies his last resting place. Not so in Egypt. The tradition of the Pharaohs has lived on. There are two whole districts of Cairo which house only the dead. They consist of several streets and what from the outside look like ordinary houses. The streets have names, and the houses are numbered, but the only dwellers are the dead. There is no uniformity about the architecture. Some of the houses are grand, some mean, according to the wealth of the family buried there. The oldest are the great Mosques where the Fatimite Caliphs lie, but the bulk are nineteenth- and twentieth-century villas. On the feast of Bairam, in those days, many Egyptian families used to go out and spend a day or two with their dead, passing the time in feasting and recollection. For the rest of the year, the dead cities were deserted save for occasional watchmen or sorrowing relatives.

The Egyptian tradition from the time of the Pharaohs has been to try and preserve for the dead some of the splendour which they knew in life. I found a curious survival in the Coptic Church of the philosophy underlying this tradition. I was dining one night with a Coptic priest of considerable learning and intelligence. We talked about his Church and he invited me to come back a week or so later to attend a festival which he thought would interest me. It was just before Operation Bullseye and I accordingly excused myself pleading that I would have left Cairo. He took it that I was rejoining my regiment and begged me earnestly to avoid the battle zone. He spoke not as one anxious for my safety but as if warning me against a sin. His tone aroused my curiosity. Death, I answered, came to all of us one day and there could be many worse things than to die young in full possession of one's powers and senses. He put his hand on my shoulder and told me that I was very wrong to think such thoughts. The important thing, he went on, was to die 'full of years'. When a man was very old his memory faded so that he lost the power to remember yesterday or to worry about tomorrow. Memory was the essence of the soul. If a man died very old, with fading memory, his soul would soon be at peace. But if he died young, memory might continue for a full life span of seventy or eighty years, or even longer, and would be tortured by missed opportunities and unfulfilled desires. I asked if this teaching was in any way derived from the Pharaonic beliefs. He seemed embarrassed by the question but then said that the ancient Egyptians 'had understood the problem' even if they had failed to solve it. They had certainly tried to offset the haunting effects of memory by burying the dead with pictures or symbols of the good things they had enjoyed in life. He also claimed that they had taken much more trouble to embellish the tombs of those who died young than of those who died old.

I spent many hours in the old quarters of Cairo exploring the great Mosques, the Citadel, the tombs of the Caliphs, Mamelukes and Khedives, the scattered churches, and the maze of the *musky* or bazaar. Much of my work involved discussions with Balkan *émigrés*; and since these were usually prolonged and sometimes tedious, I tried, whenever possible, to hold our meetings in some vantage point of the old city. Recriminations between Serbs and Croats, or Greeks and Bulgars were much easier to endure on the battlements of the Citadel, under the shaded arcades of the Mosque of Ibn Tulun, or by the fountains and lotus pools of the dilapidated Palace at Shubra.

I would try during the *Ramadan* to be on the Citadel or the Mukattam cliff towards sunset. A gun was fired from the cliff just as the sun went down. Most of Cairo had been fasting since sunrise. In every house, the evening meal was cooked and stood ready. As the gun boomed, some two million people shook themselves out of their lethargy, praised God and fell upon their food. A noise like a great buzzing of bees drifted upwards from the city.

Cut in the face of the Mukattam was a *teke* or monastery belonging to the Bektashi order. Most of the dervishes there were Albanians and still received occasional news from monasteries in Albania. I went there originally to gather intelligence. But the place was so delightful that I made a habit of calling on the Abbot to sit among the bougainvilleas or in the cool cliffside caves and enjoy the *teke*'s simple hospitality. The Bektashis are fond of wine and kind to animals. They kept some tame gazelles; and sometimes these would nuzzle up to us as we were talking and gobble a sweetmeat from our plates or even take a surreptitious sip from our cups.

My work sometimes took me to Alexandria or to Ismailia and Port Said. But these were Levantine cities rather than Egyptian and made little appeal to me. It was Cairo and its people that I came increasingly to enjoy.

Much has been said of the cowardice, decadence and corruption of the Egyptians. And most of what has been said is true. And yet they are among the most agreeable people in the world. The women could be very beautiful especially those with some Circassian blood. The men of the ruling class mostly spoke three or four languages besides their own and were as familiar with the literatures of Britain and France as most of our own university graduates. Great wealth and the security offered by British protection might have sapped their sterner qualities, but it had also enlarged their scope for the appreciation and enjoyment of life. The middle-classes were solid and industrious folk. The poor—and they were very poor —accepted their misery with patience and even cheerfulness. All Egyptians seemed gifted with a rich sense of humour and there were few difficult situations which could not be overcome by a timely jest. Sometimes, admittedly, the humour was rather macabre. I shall never forget going to a friend's house by the Nile and finding his servant in fits of laughter. I asked the cause. He pointed to the river and, still shaking with mirth, said: 'Little schoolboy, he playing by the water, then he fall in. He no come back no more.'

The leaders of Egyptian society showed great kindness to the British officers and men serving in the Middle East. The wives and daughters of the Pashas joined with English officers' wives in running canteens and welfare centres. British officers were welcomed in Egyptian houses and lavishly entertained. The great Coptic families gave the lead in this; but Moslem financiers like Aboud Pasha and the rather exclusive Turco-Albanian aristocracy soon followed suit.

At an early stage in the War, Prince Mohammed Ali—the heir to the throne—invited a number of us to join the Mohammed Ali Club. This was the social centre of Cairo and in quietness, comfort and good cooking surpassed any club I have seen anywhere in any country. Its presiding genius was a portly Cypriot head waiter called Kosta. Kosta knew everything that was going on in Egypt and often seemed better informed about the battle in the Desert than G.H.Q. itself. He left Egypt soon after the Revolution and I saw him last as master of ceremonies to Archbishop Makarios.

The Pashas lived mostly in the garden suburbs of Zamalek, Giza and Gezirah, though there were still a few great houses in the older quarters of the City. Some had fine carpets and good furniture, though all too many favoured ornate and gilded chairs and sofas which were supposed to combine French fashion with English comfort. It was a style aptly described by an Egyptian friend who knew better as 'Louis XXIII'. Their wealth was vast and they had developed a form of hospitality which was both lavish and by European standards agreeably informal. Time was of no account and the nature of an evening's entertainment quite unpredictable. One hostess I knew never decided whether to serve dinner indoors or in the garden, at one big table or at several little ones, until an hour or so after her guests had come and she had assessed their mood. Since servants were legion, the logistics of last-minute decisions presented no problem. Everything possible was done to give a guest pleasure; and, since almost nothing was beyond their purse, it was thought a compliment to the host to ask for something difficult or unusual.

To satisfy a caprice, indeed, was regarded as a particular pleasure. One day I went to see the Saqqara Pyramids with a young Egyptian lady of great wealth. On our way back from one of the remoter monuments, we lost our way. Presently we came on a small bright-eyed urchin aged perhaps ten or twelve. He was in rags but quick to understand our problem, and jumped into the car to put us on the right road. Once in the car he begged us to take him to Cairo, which he had never seen. He had relations there, he said, who would look after him.

We agreed and his sharp and humorous questions and comments made the drive home seem short. He was clearly a boy of great intelligence and yet had no chance at all of education or advancement. My Egyptian friend had a very large income of her own. I asked her if, as a favour to me, she would educate the boy. She agreed at once and saw his parents next day to make the necessary arrangements. He is now, I believe, a leading doctor in Cairo.

Before the War most rich Egyptians spent several months of the year abroad. The War put a stop to foreign travel, and the weekend habit began to develop instead. As my circle of Egyptian friends grew I would spend occasional weekends on their estates and so saw something of Egyptian country life. Sometimes, too, when riding on the outskirts of Cairo, the Headman of a village would press me to stop for a cup of coffee at his house and some elder with a smattering of English would tell me of their problems.

At first, I was deeply shocked by the glaring contrast of wealth and poverty. I had never seen wealth so ostentatiously flaunted or poverty so patiently endured. There had been great wealth in England before the war and a good deal of poverty but the poverty had been much less stark and anyway the rich and the poor had lived very separate lives. I had seen great poverty in the Balkans and in Turkey, but there had been little display of wealth. In Egypt wealth and poverty were intermingled. Beggars sat at every rich man's gate and doubtless were often fed at his expense. Smart ladies in Paris fashions went shopping in the stench and rubble of the *musky* with a servant to clear their way through the jostling crowds of itinerant vendors, sweating porters and ordinary folk in ragged *galabias*.

My initial reactions were rather radical. I wrote to my father:

14 October 1941

After my last adventure (Operation Bullseye) I have settled down to a prosaic staff existence—lots of minutes, memoranda and red tape. Not really my sort of work, but perhaps it won't last—*en dépit* I have turned to the Egyptians and begun a study of their political, economic, religious, and social problems. Never did a country so richly deserve revolution. The average wage is a 1½d. a day; and three out of five Egyptians suffer from trachoma or bilharzia, usually both.

The contrasts of wealth and poverty in Cairo are probably the most glaring in the world. Twenty years ago the country was in the hands of a small Turkish aristocracy. Now the power has passed to the Egyptian middle-class and every day the *fellah* grows more aware of his abject condition. Islam is, of course, one of the principal factors in keeping him quiet. One has to see this in practice to understand Mustafa Kemal's attitude. George Lloyd I am told was greatly loved by the peasants as a protector against King and Pashas. All the same there is a lot of beauty in Cairo, and a lot to learn from their customs and ideas. Last night I went to the chamber of deputies, not a very inspiring experience.

The more I read of modern Egyptian history the more impressed I became by Cromer and Milner's work in Egypt. They had changed arbitrary rule and corruption into a semblance of law and order. They had introduced far reaching reforms in agriculture and secured to each peasant the inalienable ownership of some at least of his land. What was needed now, as I saw it, was a further industrial and social revolution. If Britain could set her hand to this task, she might leave an enduring monument behind her.

But the more I looked into the social and economic problems, the more baffling they became. I sought out Russell Pasha, the former Chief of Police, who had acquired international fame by his suppression of the drug traffic in Egypt. He confessed to me that he had the gravest doubts whether he had done more good or harm. The bulk of the *fellaheen*, he explained, suffered from bilharzia. Bilharzia is a disease caused by a parasite of water snails, which in its free-swimming form penetrates the human skin when immersed in water, and which matures within the body into a worm which attacks the internal organs. Common in the Nile, these parasites were spread throughout Egypt with the extension of irrigation which followed the building of the first Aswan Dam. The disease produces apathy and impotence in its early stages and considerable pain later on. It is curable, but peasants earning their livelihood working in fields irrigated by Nile water were and are constantly at risk. Hashish had at least offered some relief from bilharzia. Russell had cut the victims off from this relief. The doctors had failed to give them any compensating immunity from the illness.

I went on to consult Sir Robert Greig, who had been Chairman of the Ottoman Debt for close on a generation. He gave me a sketch of the economic history of Egypt between the wars. His conclusion was that the country had become much richer and the people much poorer. The explanation was simple. The paradox was not caused by the exploitation of one class by another. This was no more, if no less than before. It flowed from the grace of God and man's action. The richer the country grew, the more people it could support. Prosperity, law, and order had all combined to produce an explosion of population which exceeded the growth of the country's resources. I suggested compulsory birth control. Sir Robert laughed at me and pointed to an Egyptian workman who was very slowly piling stones into a wheelbarrow. 'That man,' he told me, 'is not working slowly because he is idle but to conserve his energy. He wants to make love tonight. It is probably the only pleasure he can afford.'

With my experience of peasant co-operatives in the Balkans, I naturally enquired about the possibilities of land reform. But Egypt's agriculture is one of the most artificial in the world. An efficient system of co-operatives could no doubt supply the tools, the fertilisers and the credit which in those days were provided by the landowner. But the difficulty is to find qualified people to administer a co-operative, as Colonel Nasser later found. And here I came on one of the fundamental weaknesses of the country.

Egypt was rich in talented men worth several thousand pounds a year. She also possessed an industrious and reasonably honest peasantry. But there was an acute shortage of reliable men to fill the intermediate posts— managers, country doctors, schoolmasters or civil engineers. This deficiency was to some extent made good, especially in business, by the employment of foreigners. But it set limits to the rate of economic expansion or social reform. There might be capital enough to build and equip a factory. It was not so easy to staff it. A fine modern hospital might be opened in Upper Egypt by the King himself, but it was difficult to find competent doctors prepared to leave Cairo or nurses who did not steal the drugs and sell them on the market. Centuries of despotism had bred out the sense of public service and the sense of pride in work. All this made it very difficult to by-pass the classical phase of rather crude capitalist development through which the country was passing.

30

The Egyptian Triangle

The political life of Egypt at this time revolved around three centres of power: the British Embassy, the Palace and the *Wafd*.

With a powerful British Army behind him, Sir Miles Lampson, the Ambassador, was the real ruler of Egypt. He was not a prepossessing man to meet. The bulky frame, coarse features and blotchy complexion seemed pure Falstaff. So did the taste for heavy pleasantries. On account of this, no doubt, there was a general prejudice against him in British military and business circles. More serious, it was widely known that King Farouk resented Lampson's rather avuncular manner and often referred to him as Gumus Pasha or Lord Waterbuffalo.

In fact the externals belied the real man. At heart, Lampson combined in a rare degree the essential features of the Achaean warrior or the Elizabethan buccaneer, the eye to size up a situation and the heart to act upon it. In 1927 when still quite a young man, he had persuaded Chiang Kai-shek to break with the Chinese Communists and to expel his Soviet mentor, Borodin. Later he had negotiated the 1936 Treaty which gave Egypt independence and yet allowed Britain to maintain bases there indefinitely. He was soon to take a decision which may well have saved us from defeat at El Alamein. But more of that later.

Lampson showed me great kindness. I was a frequent guest at the Embassy and went to several of his fabulous duck shoots. More important, he encouraged me to take an interest in Egyptian politics and arranged for me to meet leading Egyptian politicians. Many Ambassadors, in my experience, like to keep political contacts in their own hands. They are reluctant to bring in outsiders from a natural fear of crossing wires or encouraging unauthorised initiatives. Lampson was above such preoccupations. He knew I had political ambitions and wanted me to learn something about the personalities and problems of a country with which Britain's interests were so closely bound up.

At Lampson's elbow stood Walter Smart, the Oriental Secretary. No one could have looked less like a Pro-Consul. The long hair, the tapering fingers, the diffident manner and the rather *avant-garde* opinions all belonged to a literary salon or an Oxford Common Room. Yet Smart was the mainstay of British power in Egypt and throughout the Middle East for thirty years and more. No Englishman since Cromer did so much to uphold and broaden Britain's position in the Levant.

Smart combined a liberal and humanist outlook with a ruthless realism and iron determination. He knew and loved the cultures and peoples of the Middle East and could enter into the minds and hearts of its political leaders to an extent that sometimes made him suspect to British colleagues. But, unlike so many of our Arabists, he never allowed his sympathy for Arab causes to overshadow his commitment to British interests. He had the quality of being completely objective in judgement and yet strongly partisan in action. It is a quality sometimes found in the Church and can be intimidating. In Smart's case, it was saved from this by the breadth of his outlook. He was the last High Priest of British power in the Middle East. But he interpreted it as a very tolerant and humane religion. In this he was subtly helped by his Arab wife, Amy, whose quick sympathies and gifts as a hostess made their house a popular meeting place for Arabs and British.

The rest of Lampson's staff included such brilliant juniors as Bernard Burrows and Charles Johnston, both destined to make notable careers in the Foreign Service. But the Embassy suffered from one glaring if perhaps unavoidable weakness. It never succeeded in establishing good personal relations, at any level, with King Farouk.

I met Farouk several times, but apart from a talk about Tito and Mihailovitch, in which he showed keen interest, our exchanges were mostly trivial. He was already very fat, rather bald and, for a young man, strangely lethargic. He had a quick natural intelligence. But his education had been cut short and his conversation in those days jumped from the sophisticated to the naive. His early life had been passed entirely within his father's palaces. He once told me that, by the time he came to England as a boy of fifteen, he had not even been taken to see the Pyramids.

Unpunctuality is common in the East. But Farouk pushed it to absurd lengths. He would sometimes come to a dinner party as much as two or three hours late. This could be hard on other guests in a house where, out of respect for protocol, no drink was served before the King arrived. At one party, I remember, he suddenly asked towards midnight for a room where he could rest. Along with some other guests who did not depend on his favour I made my escape. But most of my Egyptian friends did not like to leave before the King. I heard next day that after two hours' rest he had emerged again in the best of spirits and kept everyone up until seven in the morning.

As a very young man he had sometimes gone out incognito in the tradition of Haroun al Rashid to sit in cafés and hear what people thought about the Government and the King. By this time he was too well-known among his own people for this particular sport. But he would sometimes go to a night club dressed in Air Force uniform and invite young English officers to his table. One night one of his guests mistook him for a Greek Air Marshal and Farouk gradually turned the conversation to Egypt and asked the young man what he thought of Egypt's King. Farouk was not a popular figure with the Allied armies and the young man produced a string of unflattering and rather obscene anecdotes about him. At two or three in the morning, Farouk offered him a lift back to his quarters, merely stipulating: 'Do you mind if my chauffeur drops me off first.' The car drove to the Abdin Palace where Farouk gave the astonished British officer his wrist watch as a souvenir of what he described as an 'enlightening conversation'.

One night, Farouk's father-in-law, Zulficar Pasha, gave a ball to celebrate Queen Farida's birthday. She was a woman of exceptional beauty but had failed to produce a son; and, for some time, there had been rumours of an impending divorce. All the grandees of Cairo were at the ball along with a few privileged diplomats and British officers. Towards midnight the King suddenly stopped the dancing and, standing in the middle of the floor, called Queen Farida over to him. She was dressed in white and wore a magnificent *parure* of diamonds. 'You are much too young to wear all that jewellery,' said the King. 'Take if off.' The Queen stood like a statue. He repeated the command: 'Take it off.' After a moment's hesitation she submitted, handing him the earrings, two bracelets and the necklace. He threw them on the floor. The atmosphere became electric. Everyone was convinced that the Queen's disgrace had come. Then Farouk slipped his hand into an inside pocket and handed her a red Morocco case. It held another and even finer *parure*. 'I thought it was time you had a better one,' he said. The tension snapped, and they went on with the dance.

The King's Chief Counsellor was Ahmed Pasha Hassanein, who was both Minister of Court and the Queen Mother's favourite. Hassanein had been educated at Balliol and at a first meeting seemed very westernised. At heart he was a true Oriental. Time meant nothing to him. And, although one of the busiest men in Egypt, he would sometimes spend five or six hours recounting his explorations of the Western Desert or telling me the details of some political intrigue. For Hassanein personal relations were everything. Affairs of State could always wait until tomorrow.

Hassanein was an idealist with a romantic vision of what Egypt might become. Yet at the same time he was a cynic, despising most of the people he had to work with. He believed sincerely in the Anglo-Egyptian treaty and yet lost no opportunity to denigrate Lampson or Nahas Pasha, the authors of the Treaty. It was not that he really disliked Lampson or Nahas; but they were more powerful than he was, and to run them down had become an instinctive, almost reflex action. Generally speaking,

Hassanein gave the King good advice. But he was too much of a courtier to criticise or to insist. The King, for his part, did not always understand the subtlety of Hassanein's arguments and was perhaps impatient of his prolixity. He was more inclined to listen to the bodyguards, secretaries, barbers and servants who formed his immediate entourage.

The heir to the throne was Prince Mohammed Ali. I had met the Prince on my first visit to Cairo in November 1940 and, in a rash moment, had forecast that Russia would be at war with Germany within a year. With truly royal memory he had remembered the prophecy and often asked me to call. He wore a white beard, a red *tarboosh* at a rather jaunty angle, and immaculate clothes. A big emerald cabochon ring obscured rather than adorned his hand. Despite his years, and he was then close on seventy, his conversation was spirited and often light hearted. His palace, the Koubbeh, had the finest garden in Cairo and a magnificent collection of Turkish, Egyptian and Russian *objets d'art*. He lived there alone with a French lady who had been his friend for many years, insisting, it was said, that she wore a different dress every night.

Prince Mohammed Ali had no illusions about King Farouk, and I shall always treasure his opening gambit when describing a talk with King Farouk and King Peter of Yugoslavia. 'These young Kings, you know, Mr. Amery, think they know everything. In fact, they know nothing; nothing at all; neither about politics nor even about manners.' He went on to speak at length about King Farouk's shortcomings and prophesied that he would lead Egypt to disaster.

The Prince was a Turkish gentleman of the old school and was convinced that his dynasty could only survive with British support. He would like to have been King, and would have made an excellent constitutional monarch. But his real ambition was to be remembered as a 'Grand Seigneur', known for his liberality, his patronage of the arts and his enlightened opinions. He had made a study, indeed, of what a prince should be and had written a short book entitled: *Princes I have known*. This relates a number of amusing anecdotes about the virtues and vices of different Imperial or Royal Highnesses of his acquaintance. But he evidently got bored with the business of writing, for the book ends abruptly with the words: 'It has also been my fate to meet a number of Maharajahs.'

When Nasser seized power, Prince Mohammed Ali retired into exile at Lausanne. Most of his wealth had been confiscated, but he bore the trials of poverty with the same serenity and even gaiety which he had always shown in Cairo. The last time I saw him, I asked what he thought of some piece of news from Egypt which I had seen in the previous day's *Times*. 'My dear fellow,' he replied, 'I know nothing about it. You see that blasted Nasser gives me such a small allowance, that I can't afford a

secretary any longer. And, really, how can you read *The Times* if you don't
have a secretary?'

Few of the Princes were allowed to play any part in public affairs. One
exception was Prince Ismail Daud, who had become a General in the Army.
One day, in a combined exercise with British troops in the desert, the
Prince turned up very late at the luncheon rendezvous with the British
G.O.C., General Stone. He apologised for his unpunctuality, explaining
that the young Egyptian officer in charge of his transport had somehow lost
his way. 'I expect you gave him hell,' said General Stone. 'What? and make
an enemy for life?' came the Prince's rather surprising reply. The British
officers present thought the Prince's attitude absurdly soft. It may well have
saved his life when the revolution came.

The Egyptian ruling class was divided into cliques on English eighteenth-
century lines rather than into modern political parties. Its leaders were, for
the most part, of mixed Egyptian and Turko/Albanian parentage. It had,
indeed, been the settled policy of Khedive Ismail to rally Egyptian opinion
to the throne by marrying promising young Egyptians to Albanian,
Turkish and Circassian girls. Some of these men were big landowners.
Others had become prominent as lawyers or in the world of business. They
had grown influential by making themselves useful to the Palace or to the
British Embassy.

The most impressive of them was Ismail Sidky, who had been virtually
dictator of Egypt in the 'thirties. Sidky understood economics and finance
and, unlike most of Egypt's political leaders, was a highly competent
administrator. Old, cynical, with a dry sense of humour, he was quick to
see the threat which Russia would present to the Middle East if the Allies
won the war. At our first meeting, indeed, he told me that, though he
despised Hitler and Mussolini as upstarts, he would welcome a compromise peace with them at the expense of the Soviets.

More in tune with Allied thinking were the Saadist leaders, Nokrashy
and Ahmed Maher. Both men had been implicated in the murder of the
Sirdar, General Lee Stack, after the First World War, but had since
become staunch supporters of the Anglo-Egyptian treaty. Ahmed Maher
was short, dynamic, loving the pleasures of the table. He had believed in a
British victory from the start and wanted to bring Egypt into the war so as
to be among the victors at the Peace Conference. British policy sought to
discourage such ideas from a fear that a declaration of war would split
Egyptian opinion and make the country a less secure base for our forces.
By a curious irony, Ahmed Maher's brother, Ali, was the leading pro-
German politician in Egypt; and the wits used to say that whoever won the
war, the Maher family would be all right. I learned much from Ahmed.
Nokrashy I only saw once. He was then Prime Minister and rather
reserved. Both men were destined to fall to the assassin's bullet.

The most picturesque of the political leaders was Abdurrahman Azzam Pasha. Azzam claimed pure Beduin descent and had fought in 1913 with the Senussi in their guerrilla war against the Italians. He was a romantic, lean and hollow-eyed, living on his nerves and spinning dreams of Arab unity late into the night. His pan-Arab views were unusual in the Cairo of those days. King Farouk occasionally flirted with the idea of reviving the Caliphate and proclaiming himself the spiritual leader of all Islam. But most Egyptian political leaders, even the leaders of the *Wafd*, saw Egypt's destiny in the Nile Valley. They coveted the Sudan. They were interested in Libya. But they had no wish to become embroiled in the quarrels of the Arab world. Indeed, when Eden first encouraged the formation of the Arab League, Egyptian politicians showed a marked reluctance to become involved.

My chief mentor in Egyptian politics was Hafiz Ramadan, the doyen of the Egyptian Nationalist movement and a friend and admirer of Mustafa Kemal. In public, Hafiz Pasha was an uncompromising opponent of any British military presence in Egypt, but, in private, he often told me that he thought it very much in Egypt's interest, as well as our own, that we should remain for many years to come. He taught me, indeed, that the public professions of Middle Eastern leaders often bear very little relation to their real intentions. 'Don't bother about what they say, my dear boy,' he would tell me, 'Try and find out where they think their interests lie.'

As a young man Hafiz had been something of an athlete but by this time his chief pleasure was talking. I have never known a man talk so much. I would often go to his house at about seven o'clock in the evening. He would put a bottle of whisky and some nuts before me. He would then begin talking and go on until, towards midnight, a servant would bring in some grilled meat or a chicken. I would get a few words in while he ate and then he would begin again letting me go towards three or four in the morning. Hafiz Pasha had lived at the centre of Egyptian politics for a generation. He knew the inside story of every political transaction of his time. He was also a mine of information on the financial or sexual aberrations of most of his contemporaries. Since his own hands were exceptionally clean and he no longer had hopes of office, he saw no reason to let discretion spoil a good story.

The great popular party of Egypt was the *Wafd*, founded by Zagloul Pasha and led at this time by Nahas Pasha. It represented the medium-sized and small landowners of purely Egyptian descent and the rising middle-class in the towns.

The *Wafd* were in power much of the time I was in Egypt. Its leaders were very busy and, inevitably, I saw less of them than of the Opposition.

I saw something, however, of Fuad Serageddin, the energetic Minister of Interior, and of Hamdi Seif El Nasri, the Minister of Defence, who had charged with Churchill at the Battle of Omdurman. Both men were responsible for co-operation between Egypt's armed forces and our own, and it was largely thanks to them that we never had to deploy any British troops on internal security duties even when our fortunes were at their lowest ebb.

I also had several talks with Amin Osman, the capable Coptic financier, who was the chief intermediary between Lampson and Nahas. When Amin Osman was murdered by the Moslem Brotherhood, Britain's relationship with the *Wafd* was weakened; and Nahas was led into courses of extravagance and extremism which would prove his undoing.

Nahas and his wife showed me great kindness. She was beautiful, if of rather ample proportions, and exercised a considerable and some thought dangerous influence over appointments. He was curiously incoherent in conversation and seemed to proceed by flair and instinct rather than by calculation. He was accessible to all comers, and people often brought disputes to him for judgement rather than have recourse to the Courts. But this was a risky proceeding, for, when angered, Nahas was known to beat importunate petitioners out of his office with his walking stick. But the real secret of his popularity lay in his power as an orator. His speeches were long rambling stuff combining parables and earthy anecdotes with bitter denunciation of opponents and very one-sided accounts of past events; but they made a strong appeal to the vast audiences that flocked to hear him. He spoke for Egypt like no-one else at this time; and when he died, after some fifteen years of virtual house arrest under Nasser's dictatorship, a quarter of a million people came out into the streets of Cairo to follow his coffin to the grave.

The more I saw of Egypt, the more I began to revise my original judgements. The country certainly cried out for social and economic reforms but it was forging ahead by comparison with any country in the Eastern Mediterranean or the Middle East. The rich might be very rich and the poor very poor. But the middle-classes, the lawyers, the doctors, the teachers, the clerks, and the shopkeepers were better off than their counterparts in Turkey, Greece or Yugoslavia. Their food was cheap, their rents were low. Direct taxation was negligible. Indirect taxation light. Even in wartime, there were no serious shortages. Britain was responsible for their external defence and paid for it. Public order was assured. Justice was even handed if slow. And, if there was corruption, it was little worse than elsewhere in the Eastern Mediterranean. By contrast, moreover, with other countries in the area, the Egyptian people enjoyed great political freedom.

There was a military censorship in time of war but it did not stop the press from criticising the Government freely. The Party in power might do its best to rig the elections but the result was by no means a foregone conclusion and the Opposition were always strongly represented in the Parliament. In cafés, clubs and private houses, freedom of speech was complete. Moreover, despite the inequalities of wealth, the tradition of the country was, when compared to Europe, very democratic. The ruling group had never been a closed caste. The caprice of a Minister or a great landowner could raise a man from the humblest circumstances to high office and great wealth; and many of the leading men were the descendants of peasants or even slaves. Nor were the differences of origin as obvious as sometimes in the West. With us civilisation is still only a veneer, and it takes time to polish up a self-made man. But every Egyptian was the heir to seven thousand years of civilisation and quickly adjusted himself to any improvement in his circumstances.

Egypt, by the end of the war, had become the unchallenged commercial and financial centre of the Middle East. Cairo was its cultural capital; and, since no-one thought of Egypt as an aggressive Power, Egyptian teachers, doctors and intellectuals were in demand throughout the Arab world. Whether Egypt could retain its pre-eminence without the backing of a British military presence, was not much discussed at the time. There was some talk after the allied victories in North Africa of withdrawing British forces from Cairo and Alexandria to forestall possible criticism. No-one ever seriously considered withdrawing them from the Suez Canal Zone. The British presence was regarded by Egyptians as much as by British statesmen as a guarantee that Egypt would go forward along evolutionary rather than revolutionary lines. So it might have been but for the follies of Farouk, the naive ambitions of the American State Department, and the weakness of post-war British Governments.

31

The Coup at Abdin

In February of 1942 Lampson asked me for the weekend to his villa in the Fayoum. We were a small house party; and, after a late lunch, where Duff Cooper had talked of the war in the Far East, Lampson took me down to the lake for a shot at duck. We had some brisk shooting at the start and then settled down to wait for the evening flight. An hour must have gone by and the daylight was fading when a servant waded out to my butt with a summons from the Ambassador. A despatch rider had just brought news of a Cabinet crisis in Cairo. Lampson had decided to return at once. He would leave his ADC to look after the other guests. Would I come with him instead?

We were alone in the car on the drive back to Cairo, and presently Lampson began to talk about his problem. It was not that he sought my views or felt under any obligation to explain. He simply wanted to clear his own mind.

Sirry Pasha, the Prime Minister, had decided to break off relations with Vichy France. King Farouk had refused to agree and Sirry had resigned. A new Government would have to be formed. But who was to lead it? There were several prominent politicians available. But they had little following in the country and so would be dependent on the King. And the King's sympathies were with the Axis. Here was the crunch. Did it matter, at this juncture, whether Egypt had a reliable Government?

Diplomats and soldiers often dwell in watertight compartments with little understanding of each other's problems. Not so Lampson. Auchinleck, he explained, was considering a major offensive in the Western Desert. If we won the battle, it didn't matter much who became Prime Minister of Egypt. But supposing his plans went wrong? Auchinleck's offensive could use up all his reserves. There was no chance of early British reinforcements. If the wide-ranging desert fighting went against us, we could easily face an Axis invasion of Egypt. Every available British soldier would then be needed to hold the front. But what would happen to the Army's communications with Alexandria and across the Delta to the Canal? Everything would depend on the attitude of the Egyptian Army and Police.

'I am no soldier,' said Lampson, 'but I have seen a lot of war and I wonder if the Auk isn't being a bit over confident.' The right course, he concluded, was to take out an insurance policy. He would so play the political hand in Cairo that, if Rommel beat us in the desert, we should still have the best chance of Egyptian co-operation in defending the Delta. How was this to be done? I asked. 'By bringing in Nahas.' Nahas was just then conducting an outspokenly anti-British campaign. Knowing nothing of Egyptian affairs, I was rather shocked at the idea. It was as if the Viceroy had proposed bringing Gandhi to power to help defend India against Japan. I showed surprise.

'You have been listening to the soldiers,' grunted Lampson. Nahas, he explained, would be our best friend while his Government remained strong. All Egyptian Governments were weakened in time by the wear and tear of power. That was when they turned anti-British. But for the first year or so Nahas would prove our staunchest ally. He had the people behind him. He was the architect of the Anglo-Egyptian treaty and would stand by it. Lampson's problem all along had been to judge when to play the *Wafdist* card. Now was the time.

Would King Farouk accept Nahas? He would not like it, was the reply; but most likely he could be persuaded. If not, Britain would have to choose between the King and Nahas. We might well do worse, Lampson hinted, than unfurl the Union Jack against the palace and on the side of the people.[1]

Next morning Lampson called on the King and urged him to entrust the Government to Nahas. The King, who disliked and resented Lampson, asked for time to reflect. In the afternoon, we learned that the King would not have Nahas. He talked, indeed, of recalling the pro-German leader, Ali Maher Pasha. Lampson accordingly conferred with the military commanders and with Oliver Lyttelton, the resident Minister of State. There was no time to consult London. A decision had to be taken on the spot. The military were prejudiced against Nahas. Lyttelton, though all for firm action, feared that to act against the King might provoke disorders. Nevertheless, all agreed that Lampson should present Farouk with an ultimatum to accept Nahas as Prime Minister or to abdicate. The ultimatum was to expire at five o'clock next day.

Drafting a Deed of Abdication at short notice presented no problem. Sir Walter Monckton, the Deputy Minister of State, had drafted the abdication of King Edward VIII and soon drew up the appropriate formula for King Farouk. It would hardly have done to present it on Embassy paper, and it was accordingly typed on ordinary foolscap, the only plain paper available. All was now settled except that Oliver Lyttelton, who

[1] Thus far the story is personal recollection. The rest of the chapter is based on talks with Lampson and Smart a few days later.

spoke with the authority of the Cabinet, urged that the King should be given every chance. Lampson, for his part, hoped to kill two birds with one stone, bringing Nahas to power and replacing the King by his pro-British uncle, Prince Mohammed Ali.

At the Abdin Palace, the King called a Crown Council. They proposed a National Government of all the Party leaders with Hassanein Pasha as Prime Minister. But this too would have been a King's Government; and, in any case, Nahas would not have joined it. Lampson firmly declined the offer.

Silence followed. Five o'clock came and went. Still there was no sign of compliance from the King. As darkness fell a brigade of British troops surrounded the Abdin Palace while armoured cars patrolled the approaches. When the cordon was drawn, Lampson, with General Stone, the General Officer Commanding British troops in Egypt, and Harry Legge-Bourke,[1] Lampson's ADC, drove to the palace. Behind them went an empty car intended to take King Farouk to a warship at Alexandria.

They found Farouk alone with Hassanein. The ultimatum, Lampson said, had expired; and he handed the Deed of Abdication to the King.

Farouk read it through and remarked, 'You might at least have made it out on decent paper.' Then he took up a pen and made as if to sign. At that moment Hassanein stepped forward and said: 'Your Majesty, for the sake of Egypt think again.' The King covered his face in his hands; then, turning to Lampson, said: 'Yes, Hassanein is right. I have been mistaken. I will send for Nahas if you will give me another chance.'

The King's *volte-face* put Lampson in a difficulty. He had gone to the palace determined to get rid of 'the young man'. But now that Farouk had given in, was it still reasonable to demand his abdication? And if he refused to sign the deed, were we to kidnap him? Lampson would have liked to go back to the Embassy to think things over. But this was the one thing he could not do. With the troops outside and the ultimatum on the King's desk, he had to take a decision before he left the room.

With his usual contempt for protocol, Lampson led Stone to the opposite corner of the room where they conferred in whispers on a sofa. Farouk watched them settling his fate. In the end Lyttelton's injunction to give Farouk every chance prevailed. Lampson took back the Deed of Abdication; and Hassanein summoned Nahas to the Palace.

There were still some hurdles. Nahas's hour had come. But the Palace was surrounded by British troops and the tribune of the Egyptian People was stopped at the main gate by a British N.C.O. 'Sorry,' he said 'no wogs in 'ere.' A hurried telephone call from a nearby café soon put matters right. The gates were opened and Nahas received the royal commission.

Meanwhile, at the Koubbeh Palace, Prince Mohammed Ali, warned of

[1] Later Sir Harry Legge-Bourke, M.P.

a. The plateau at Biza in Albania, where we landed.

b. Bill McLean *(right)* and the author.

a. Muharrem Bairaktar (in cloak) with his bodyguard.

b. Gani Kryeziu and his staff: from left to right in the front row: Said Kryeziu, Hassan Kryeziu, Lazar Fundo, Gani Kryeziu and Captain Hibberdine.

a. Smiley, the author and the Turkoman deserters.

b. An alfresco meal: Abas Kupi, Bill McLean and the author, with two bodyguards in the background.

a. Abas Kupi, a photograph taken at our last headquarters in the coastal plain, just before the end.

b. The author during the retreat to Mirdita

the ultimatum, awaited the summons to the throne. But in the confusion of the evening no-one remembered to tell him that it was all off. It is said that he waited up until the dawn dispelled his dreams.

The coup against Farouk was scarcely handled with finesse. Its basic flaw, so Lampson afterwards believed, was to leave Farouk on the throne. 'Kings are like snakes,' a Macedonian refugee told me at the time. 'You must admire them from a distance or kill them, but never tease them.' Farouk certainly never forgave and many of the powerful Egyptian families connected with the palace were alienated. Had a wiser sovereign taken his place, Egypt might have been spared the Nasserist revolution.

But Lampson's basic decision to bring Nahas to power was abundantly justified by events. Auchinleck's offensive was never launched. Rommel struck first. In one engagement we lost over a hundred tanks in under a quarter-of-an-hour. Tobruk fell, and by the end of May Rommel had crossed the border and was marching on Alexandria. Every man who could be spared was sent to the front. And the defence of our communications was left in the hands of the Egyptian Army and Police.

Seldom can an occupying power have presented a more tempting target. If ever there was a time to pay off old scores, this was it. And a powerful fifth column was straining at the leash in Cairo. In this supreme crisis of the Middle Eastern War, the *Wafdist* Government of Nahas stood loyally by the Anglo-Egyptian treaty. They gave us unstinted support. Not a man had to be diverted from the front for internal security. There was not a single case of sabotage or terrorism.

Suppose Lampson had not acted as he did. Suppose some King's man had become Prime Minister instead, leaving the real control in the hands of Farouk and the fifth column; Rommel's advance into Egypt might easily have touched off an explosion of anti-British violence in Cairo and Alexandria. The Army's communications could well have been disrupted. It is not too much to say that but for Nahas, Montgomery could never have conquered at Alamein; and but for Lampson's foresight and daring, Nahas would never have come to power.

32

Intervention in Higher Strategy
May 1942

As Rommel advanced into Egypt, S.O.E.'s work into the Balkans ground
to a halt. No aircraft or submarines could be spared for cloak and dagger
operations across the Mediterranean. Telephone lines were jammed with
priority calls in support of the battle. Even staff cars were commandeered.
With little work to do myself, I had plenty of time to keep in touch with
G.H.Q. and to talk with friends from the Eighth Army. Once or twice I
drove out to lunch with units encamped between El Alamein and Alexandria. It was soon clear to me that the Eighth Army had lost confidence in
its leaders. There was little criticism now of inferior equipment, such as I
had often heard in 1940 and 1941. The criticism was of the commanders in
the field and the strategists at G.H.Q. Junior officers said quite openly that
our top brass had no real grasp of the business of armoured warfare. They
might understand the theory but they had never led a troop or a squadron
themselves. How could they ever be a match for Rommel, Ravenstein and
Schmidt, all real professionals of the tank and the armoured car?

If morale was low at the front, there was something like panic at
G.H.Q. It was widely known that there could be no general evacuation of
the Delta. There was simply not enough rail or road transport to undertake
a retreat to Palestine or to the Sudan. Some units might fight their way out.
But if Auckinleck failed to stem the German advance, the bulk of the
Army and certainly the staffs and the maintenance units in Cairo would be
put 'in the bag'.

On the morning of 1 July, Rommel's advance guard came up against
our positions at El Alamein. El Alamein is not very far across the desert
from Cairo and German armoured patrols might reach the Pyramids at
any time and even try to cross the Nile and raid the defenceless city.
Such a raid might well be timed to coincide with an attempt at insurrection
by the Fifth Column inside Cairo. Orders were accordingly given to
evacuate essential records to Palestine and to burn the rest.

It is not so easy to burn several tons of documents in a hurry. There
was no proper furnace for disposing of secret files. The bulk were simply
burnt in the open. But then the wind got up and a mass of secret documents were blown away little more than scorched, rising like so many

phoenixes from their ashes and pursued all over the city by irate and frenzied officers. It all made us look rather ridiculous to the Egyptians, though the destruction of records doubtless made its contribution to our subsequent victory.

At five o'clock on the afternoon of 1 July Maxwell told me that I was to fly home next day to tell our London office about his plans for the dispersal of S.O.E. Middle East and for its future operations.

I spent most of the night and the following morning at a series of meetings. Then on the afternoon of 2 July I left Cairo for an aerodrome on the road to Alexandria. It was only twenty-seven kilometres away, but the journey took three-and-a-half-hours. The whole length of the road was jammed with convoys of Free French, West African, South African, New Zealand and British troops. They looked dejected and worn. The aerodrome had been a bomber base but the bombers had just been evacuated. Next morning fighter aircraft would take it over. That evening our Liberator was the only aircraft there.

The rest of the party consisted of Naval Intelligence officers and two captured German airmen. I was accommodated in the bomb bay of the Liberator, which would be very cold but where I could at least stretch out. It was a broiling Egyptian summer day but as the bomb bay seemed too cramped to move about in, I wrapped myself in a heavy fur coat before climbing in. I had expected that we would take off in a matter of minutes. In fact, there was a technical hitch, and I lay there for the best part of an hour too cramped to undress and sweating as if in a Turkish bath.

At about eight o'clock we at last took off heading for Gibraltar, fourteen hours flight away.

As I lay in the belly of the bomber, it dawned on me that I now had a responsibility beyond my mission for S.O.E. The last Liberator had left for England four days before. There would not be another direct flight for a week. My fellow passengers were all technicians or prisoners. For ten days, in fact, I would be the only officer in London with up-to-date first hand experience of the situation in Egypt. Was there anything I could do to influence the outcome of the battle? If so, it was plainly my duty to do it.

I was not qualified to suggest any last minute alteration in the disposition of forces or in our supply arrangements. Such factors, in any case, are not easily improvised. A new armoured division was on its way. It would reach the front as soon as the staffs could get it there and no sooner. The only factors that might be improvised were the imponderables. A gesture or a speech, for instance, or a new appointment might make all the difference to the Army's morale. I knew that many of the old hands wanted to bring Wavell back. But this would have been bitterly resented by

Auchinleck's friends and would only have added friction to demoralisation. The only way I could see of injecting new heart into officers and men at every level would be a personal visit from Churchill. If Churchill could go out to Egypt and show himself to the troops in the desert, it might give the Army just that extra stimulus to hold on until the reinforcements already on the way turned the scales back in our favour.

It would not be easy for a young officer, engaged in what regular soldiers regarded as the 'side show' of guerrilla war, to criticise the morale of a famous fighting force like the Eighth Army. What I had in mind to say would be resented in many quarters; perhaps by Churchill himself. And yet the more I revolved the idea, the more convinced I became that it was my duty to let him know what I thought. He presumably knew all the facts of the military situation. But who else would tell him of the state of morale? I could not expect him to act simply on my advice. But I might start a train of thought in his mind; and if I was right, others would probably nourish it.

We landed at Poole while the House of Commons was still debating the war in the desert on a vote of censure. To judge from the newspapers next morning, the Government had had a rough passage in the debate. The critics, I noticed, had said nothing about the Army's morale but attributed our reverses to inferior equipment. Worse still, from the point of view of what I had to say, they had been very critical of the Prime Minister's frequent journies away from home. He had been in Washington when Tobruk had fallen.

I went at once to the India Office and began to tell my father of my impressions. Before I even suggested seeing Churchill, he interrupted me and said: 'You must see the P.M. at once.'

He rang through to one of the private secretaries at 10 Downing Street, who suggested that I should write a short memorandum. My father thought it would be much more effective if I saw Churchill personally. He pressed the point and the secretary promised to call him back after speaking to Churchill. We lunched together at home along with Harold Macmillan. I told my story again for Macmillan's benefit. His reaction was the same as my father's. I must see the Prime Minister at once.

After lunch, the private secretary rang through from Downing Street to say that he had failed to catch Churchill before his afternoon siesta. Churchill was leaving for Chequers in the evening and there could scarcely be time for a meeting. Could I not write a short memorandum instead? Macmillan, who was then Under-Secretary for the Colonies, thought this would be a mistake. He was going back to his office and said he would call in at Number 10 and speak to the Private Secretary himself.

I went off to the S.O.E. office in Baker Street and was reporting on our plans for the future when a message came from Downing Street. The Prime

Minister wished to see me at five-thirty. My watch showed that there were four minutes to go. I ran downstairs and commandeered the first staff car I could see. A few minutes later I was shown into a narrow room furnished with a long table and some twenty chairs. The ceiling at one end was supported by white classical columns. This was my first sight of the Cabinet Room. Halfway down the table, with his back to the fireplace, sat the Prime Minister. At his right was the C.I.G.S., Sir Alan Brooke. With old-fashioned courtesy Churchill rose to greet me as I came in and introduced me to the C.I.G.S. He then motioned me to a chair immediately opposite him. He was dressed in an Air Force-blue siren suit, with a white silk shirt open at the neck. In one hand, he held a cigar and in front of him was a glass of rather pale whisky. His face seemed very white; the skin clear and firm but without colour; the eyes a watery blue. He had flashed a benevolent smile of welcome when I came in, but, as soon as I sat down, his expression became a mask. He asked one or two perfunctory questions. What was my job. Where had I been? When had I reached London? Then there was a pause and he puffed at his cigar. 'Now tell us what you have to say.' He looked for a moment at the C.I.G.S. and then added, 'Speak as freely as you wish.'

I told my story, explaining that I was reflecting the views of friends in the Eighth Army as well as on the staff in Cairo. Morale was low. The Army was looking over its shoulder. The armoured units, especially, had lost confidence in the Command. Churchill's face remained a mask. Alan Brooke frowned, as if resenting my comments on morale and, leaning across the table, asked me how I had reached these conclusions. My answers seemed to satisfy him; and he sat back, though still frowning.

I went on to say that, as far as I could judge, Auchinleck was doing all in his power to save the situation. But one extra thing could still be done to influence the outcome. This was to give a boost to the Army's morale; and the only way of doing this that I could see was for Churchill to go to Egypt himself.

'What should I do out there to improve morale?'

'Your presence among the troops in the battle area would be enough. It would have an electric effect.'

'You mean just go round and talk to them.'

'Yes, to the officers and to the men.'

There was a long pause. The Prime Minister sank down in his chair and gazed at the ceiling. The mask relaxed a little and he seemed to forget that the C.I.G.S. and I were still in the room. Perhaps he was trying to imagine himself with the soldiers in the desert. Then the mask froze on again.

'Yes, it might do good. But you know there are many other considerations.'

He then began to ask practical questions. How high had the Liberator

flown on the way home from Cairo? Had we used oxygen? How long had
it taken? Had it been very cold? Then he said: 'Thank you for coming.
What you say it very interesting. I will think about it. But there are many
other considerations.' He rose and walked over with me to the door. At
the door, I mentioned that I had seen Randolph, only two days before, and
told him something of Randolph's raid into occupied Benghazi. He asked
about Randolph's health and then said: 'Did you discuss all this with
Randolph?'

'Yes, I think he agrees with me.'

The interview had lasted just over twenty minutes. As far as I could
judge, Churchill had been attracted by my proposal. I was less sure of Alan
Brooke's reaction. Now was the time to reinforce success.

Back at home, I telephoned to Simon Wardell, then working on the
Daily Express, and asked him to arrange a meeting with Beaverbrook.
Beaverbrook was not in office at the time. But he was still very close to
Churchill. I saw him next afternoon, with Simon, at Brook House, where
he had an ultra-modern and rather tasteless flat. He looked sunburnt, his
eyes sparkled. He wore a shiny blue suit and brown shoes. For the next
three-quarters of an hour he cross-examined me until he had extracted the
whole of my story, meat, bones and marrow. Then: 'Have you spoken to
the Prime Minister about this?'

'Yes.'

'He'd like the idea. Did he say he liked it?'

'Well he looked as if he did. But of course he didn't commit himself.'

'I'm sure he'd like it. I'm seeing him tonight. I'll find out. I like the
idea. I'll put it to him again.'

I heard no more until, a few days later, my father told me that Churchill
with Alan Brooke had just left for Cairo. There, in the intervals of reorganising the High Command, he spent several days with the Eighth
Army inspecting units and talking to groups of officers and men. Friends
later said that his presence had a tonic effect on morale. Some even
claimed that it had turned the scales.

A few months afterwards, John Martin,[1] who was one of Churchill's
Private Secretaries at the time, told me that my intervention had been
in a sense decisive. Churchill and the C.I.G.S. had known, of course, all
the facts of the military situation. But my account of the state of morale
had come to them as a shock. This had made Churchill receptive to my
suggestion that he should go to Egypt. The idea had caught his imagination. It had taken root; and, despite the doubts of the C.I.G.S. and of
some of his colleagues, he would not let go of it. He had for some time
been toying with the idea of a visit to Moscow; and now seized on the opportunity to combine this with a personal intervention in the Desert War.

[1] Later Sir John Martin and High Commissioner, Malta.

33

Whitehall Warrior

After this brief intervention in the higher direction of the war, I spent the next few months attached to the Balkan section of S.O.E. in London. Most of my work, as I have described in an earlier chapter, was concerned with policy towards Yugoslavia. But other issues sometimes intruded.

Since the collapse of Yugoslavia in 1941, S.O.E. had altogether lost touch with Albania. In 1943, however, two British liaison officers, my old school friend Bill McLean and David Smiley, made their way across the Greek–Albanian border from one of our missions with the Greek guerrillas. They presently established contact with the Albanian Resistance movements which, as in Yugoslavia and Greece, were divided between Communists and Nationalists. McLean's reports and requests for supplies led S.O.E. in London to give new thought to Albanian affairs. As a result I was asked to go and see King Zog to sound out his views.

I had been impressed, when first involved in Albanian affairs in 1940, by the respect which the different groups of Albanian exiles seemed to share for Zog. Certainly his record as a ruler showed that he was both forceful and shrewd. He had also behaved with unusual dignity in exile. At a time when other exiled Kings patronised London's restaurants and night clubs, Zog seldom appeared in public. He lived either in a suite in the Ritz hotel or in a house in the country. He thought it inappropriate to be seen in places of public entertainment, while his country was under enemy occupation.

One incident from his earlier life struck me as especially to his credit. Political assassination is an occupational risk of monarchy; and some years before the War, an attempt had been made on Zog's life, as he entered the Opera House in Vienna. Some Kings have walked calmly on when shot at. Others have taken evasive action. Zog did neither. He drew his own gun and shot the would-be assassin. Such a man, I thought, deserved to be a King.

Nevertheless, there was a prejudice against Zog in British official circles. Though born of a distinguished highland clan, he was widely regarded as an upstart and an adventurer. I was curious to see for myself what the man was like.

He received me at Parmoor House in the hills above the Thames where he was living with Queen Geraldine, his numerous sisters and a fairly large retinue. I had imagined him to be short and dark. He was, in fact, a tall man with light eyes and a fair complexion. His hair was elaborately arranged to conceal premature baldness and he wore a rather melodramatic waxed moustache. I had expected a rough dynamic man of action and was surprised by his languid movements and the gentleness of his voice and gestures. He talked at length about the future of his country and of the Balkans and hoped that England would take the lead in setting up some kind of Balkan Union. He recommended that as a first step we should establish a bridgehead in Albania from the heel of Italy. With our naval and air supremacy in the area this should present little difficulty, while the Germans would find it difficult to reinforce their slender garrison in Albania. Once in control of Albania we could threaten German communications with Greece and give massive support to the Resistance Movements in Yugoslavia. The alternative he suggested, with gentle irony, was to hand over the whole peninsula to the Soviets. No doubt, Mr. Churchill would be the best judge of which course of action would suit British interests better. The more Zog spoke, the more I began to realise that his gentleness of tone concealed a coiled spring of ruthless determination.

Over a drink, after we had finished business, Zog told me an anecdote so improbable that it could hardly have been invented. A few days earlier he had been persuaded, much against his will, to go out with Queen Geraldine to one of the big London stores. From a prejudice against running up bills, he had put three hundred pounds in his breast pocket. The lift in the shop had been crowded and, going up to the third floor, he had developed an instinctive aversion to a little man standing just beside him. He had, however, thought no more about him until, putting his hand in his pocket to pay for one of the Queen's purchases, he found that his wallet had gone. He decided to go back to his hotel, but on the way out of the shop again saw the little man who had stood near him in the lift. He stopped to watch him more closely when suddenly another man came up and proceeded to pick the little man's pocket. To Zog's astonishment what the pickpocket picked from the little man's coat pocket was his own wallet. At this point he walked up and took the wallet himself while the two thieves scattered in opposite directions.

I came away convinced that this was a man of Odyssean proportions, brave, without illusions and of many devices. Closer acquaintance in later years would amply confirm this first impression.

One of our problems in S.O.E. was to recruit liaison officers for the Balkans who knew something of irregular warfare and, if possible, something about Communism. It occurred to me that there might be English-men who had fought in the International Brigade in Spain who would possess both qualifications. The Home Office and the security services seemed to have no lists of the individuals concerned. On Altmaier's advice, therefore, I consulted Ellen Wilkinson, then Under-Secretary for Educa-tion, who had been a leading supporter of the Spanish Republic.

Ellen Wilkinson was a diminutive red-head, with sharp features and unbounded courage. She could act like an angry fishwife on occasion but underneath there was a deep humanity. She had spent all her life on the left wing of the Labour movement and knew the British Communist Party and its fringes well. Having worked with it and against it, she had no illusions about it, or its Soviet masters. She was, indeed, one of the first members of the Government, of any Party, to recognise the threat which the Soviet Union would present to Europe after the War.

Ellen Wilkinson soon put me in touch with several old combatants of the International Brigade. Some were still dedicated Communists. Others were well known as outspokenly anti-Communist and would thus scarcely do as liaison officers with Communist-led Partisans. In the event nothing came of the exercise, but it was the beginning of a friendship with Ellen Wilkinson which lasted till her death.

The war against Hitler, indeed, purged the Labour movement for a time of much of the illusionism about foreign affairs and the consequent disregard of Britain's economic and strategic interests overseas which had been such a marked feature of its pre-war attitudes. I certainly found Labour Ministers like Dalton and Ellen Wilkinson just as concerned about Soviet ambitions in Europe as their Conservative colleagues. It was not, indeed, until the wartime Labour leaders had died or retired that the British Labour movement returned to less responsible courses.

But outside a limited circle there was very much of a taboo in London, even after Stalingrad and El Alamein, on the public and even the private discussion of the conflicts of interest that were bound to arise after the war between Britain and the Soviet Union and Britain and the United States. In the interest of the war effort the growing differences between us were cloaked by a conspiracy of silence. All this was, no doubt, necessary. Nevertheless, it was refreshing and healthy to listen to a man like Freddy Voigt, the brilliant editor of the *Nineteenth Century*, who held court most evenings in the Majorca Restaurant. Voigt was a liberal but he was also a realist. He saw that the war was won and was obsessed with the im-portance of not losing the peace. His aims were clear. To maintain a firm understanding with France. To keep the Soviets north of the Danube and to keep the Americans out of the Middle East. These were difficult goals but seemed to me worth trying for.

During these months in London I lived at home on terms of ever closer friendship and understanding with my father. He showed me many of the Cabinet papers and would often discuss with me the drafts of memoranda he was circulating to the Cabinet and to Cabinet Committees. I saw much too of his colleagues and of those Allied leaders who had made their homes in London or who came through it on business.

There was, of course, a steady flow of visitors concerned with Indian affairs. Their views varied widely. The Soviets, who had little idea how much the Viceroy depended on Indian goodwill, could not understand the kid-glove treatment we accorded to Gandhi and Nehru. One day, at lunch, Ambassador Maisky spoke very harshly of the way we were appeasing Indian opponents of the war effort. My mother asked him what he would have us do. 'Madam,' he replied, 'in the Soviet Union we have our methods.' And Madame Maisky nodded approvingly.

The Americans were even more naive. Ambassador Phillips came to lunch on his way out to India as the President's special emissary. To my father's surprise, Phillips kept asking where the Congress Building was situated? He was evidently under the impression that the Indian Congress was not a political party but like the American Congress, a parliament over which the British were riding roughshod.

The Americans were always ready to lecture us on Indian affairs. So were the Chinese, who, with American encouragement, saw themselves as the future leaders of Asia. Fortunately, the Chinese Ambassador, Dr. Wellington Koo, was a wise and polished diplomat and interpreted his instructions with discretion. At his suggestion a number of Indian officials visited Chungking. All returned even stronger pillars of the *Raj* than they went out.

The bombing of London had virtually ceased; and social life was stirring again. Lady Oxford, 'Margot,' gave lunches at her house in Blooms-bury for her granddaughter, Priscilla Bibesco, just married to Michael Padev, the former *Times* correspondent in Sofia. Lady Colefax held weekly buffet suppers. Above all, Lady Cunard had returned to London. Emerald, as her friends knew her, though she had been christened Maud, reminded me of some brightly coloured enamel bird in a Turkish jewel. Her face was a painted mask but her eyes sparkled with mischief, melted with sympathy or went dull if she was bored. Her little claw-like hands fluttered as she talked. Emerald had read everything, met everyone and knew all that was going on in London. She gave small dinner parties in her rooms at the Dorchester Hotel almost every night, mixing the young and the old, the grave and the gay. One of her favourite conversational gambits was to fire leading and, sometimes, slightly outrageous questions at one of her grander or more sedate guests. One night she turned to Wavell who had just been appointed Viceroy of India. 'What do you think about love, Field Marshal?' she asked. Knowing how tongue-tied Wavell could be, I feared the worst. To my astonishment, the great man replied, without a moment's hesitation: 'It is like a cigar. If it goes out you can light it again, but it never tastes quite the same.' It was game, set and match to the warrior.

Emerald knew her own world in every detail, but she had little idea how the mass of people lived outside it. One summer evening I went to the Dorchester to take her to a dinner at Claridges. The weather was very fine and, unexpectedly, she said she would like to walk. As we strolled down Park Lane, an elderly working man, unshaven and with a scarf round his neck, came up to us holding out his cap. 'I've had nothing to eat for three days,' he said. Emerald turned to him with a look of genuine concern and answered: 'But that's very wrong of you. It's very bad for your health. You must try. You must force yourself.' When I gave him some money, she looked at me in amazement and asked: 'Do you mean he really can't afford a meal?' For all that she had a quick sympathy, a generous heart and a much greater store of wisdom than many understood. To me, she was a true friend.

In the summer of 1942, Lord Moyne was appointed deputy Minister of State in the Middle East. Moyne combined great wealth with inexhaustible curiosity. He loved travel and had explored the remoter islands of the East Indies bringing back the first dragons from Komodo to the London Zoo. He had also discovered Pygmy tribes in the Congo hitherto unknown. He had tasted everything and, perhaps because of this, seemed strangely detached. It was said that he once asked his secretary, 'I want to give a party. Please type out a list of my friends.' When she asked who they were, he had replied: 'I don't really know, but have a look at my letters and diaries and invite the people you think I'd like to see.' For all this seeming impersonality, he cultivated the society of beautiful women, much as other rich men collect beautiful pictures. He also kept a monkey. I asked him once if he had become attached to it. 'Not very,' he answered. 'But it is a healthy reminder of what human nature is really like.'

Moyne's wife, who had died some years before, had loved the early Tudor period. It had amused Moyne to gratify her slightest wish and he had accordingly acquired the ruins of the abbey of Bailiffscourt in Sussex. With the help of experts he had built there an early Tudor mansion with some thirty bedrooms. Each of these, and this was his only departure from the Tudor style, had its own bathroom. For the rest, the furniture everywhere was either real or imitation Tudor. The plate and drinking vessels were of pewter or silver. The forks were two-pronged instruments, on which it was very difficult to eat green peas. The servants in pre-war days had all worn period costume and, even in wartime, the head parlourmaid still did so on more important occasions.

Moyne had known my father for many years and I suspect knew how slender were his means. At any rate, on his appointment to the Middle East, he lent us Bailiffscourt and insisted that we should live there as his guests. Thanks to this generous gesture we had a luxurious country house for the next two years. This was a great boon to our family and to many friends engaged in the higher direction of Indian policy or the more subterranean labyrinths of Balkan Resistance.

34

Arabian Nights

I returned to Cairo in September 1943, and there again was for a few days Moyne's guest. He had taken Momo Marriott's old house; and I had comfortable quarters with a blue tiled Roman bath just big enough to swim in. In the October heat, and October can be very hot in Cairo, this was a joy.

I have said something in an earlier chapter of the Cairo Conference between Churchill, Roosevelt and Chiang Kai-shek. This was Cairo's finest hour but, thereafter, the city became increasingly a backwater. The High Command moved to Algiers and then to Italy. Oliver Lyttelton and Monckton had gone home. Casey, who followed Lyttelton, would soon go on to govern Bengal. S.O.E. was still based on Cairo but already advance parties were being established in Bari where the Balkan Air Force had its headquarters.

Life in Cairo was also running down. French wine was unobtainable. Whisky was scarce, and Cyprus brandy and local gin became the standard drinks. We were still much better off than our brother officers at home, but the flesh pots of Egypt were not what they had been. With few exceptions, places of entertainment had become scruffy, though this too could provide amusement.

In Gizeh on the banks of the Nile was a garden restaurant known as the Casino des Pigeons. This sold nothing but grilled pigeons. They were plump and delicious, though there was a theory that to eat pigeon three days running was fatal. It was hard enough, however, to get through one meal in the garden of the Casino. The place was full of stray cats. If there were several customers in the restaurant all was well. The cats attached themselves to different tables. But I dined there once alone with two friends and we spent most of the evening fending off the cats.

Not far from Shepheard's Hotel was an Arab restaurant called Hatih with a roof garden. The food was good, but late in the evening, as the guests began to leave, rats used to come out to eat up bits of food from the floor. They were the biggest rats I have ever seen and quite tame. One evening I took an attractive but rather prim English girl to Hatih's and, when she was not looking, scattered bits of food around her chair. Presently three very large rats crept up to within a few inches of her feet. When I pointed out that we had company, she literally fell into my arms. It helped to break the ice.

Momo had gone back to New York and nothing could take her place. But a more exuberant if less sophisticated social centre had come into being. This was Tara. Tara was a large house in Gezirah which had been taken by an enterprising Polish lady, Countess Sophie Tarnowska. She ran it as a kind of club for a few young officers, mostly engaged in guerrilla operations. The members, at this time, included Bill McLean and David Smiley, just back from Albania, Xan Fielding, Paddy Leigh-Fermor, and Billy Moss who had just kidnapped the German Commander-in-Chief in Crete, in one of the most spectacular operations of the war,[1] and Rowland Winn.[2]

Rowland in those days sported an eye glass and an Edwardian Cavalry moustache. He had been a newspaper correspondent in the Spanish Civil War; but though he had a sound grasp of higher strategy, had repeatedly failed the elementary tests to qualify for a commission. After a boring spell in a training depot, he had somehow attached himself as an orderly to the Yugoslav General Staff in Cairo where he became a close friend of Colonel Popovitch, the Director of Intelligence. Rowland yearned to become a liaison officer with Mihailovitch; and, after some lobbying of myself and others concerned, this had been arranged. The night before he was to drop into Yugoslavia, he gave a small farewell party. One of the guests asked him what a parachute landing was like. 'It's about the same as jumping off this table,' he answered and proceeded to do so, only to break his leg. The aircraft and crew were waiting at Derna in Libya; and in the Serbian mountains the *Chetniks* were preparing to light up the dropping ground. It had not been easy to explain away the accident; but somehow a court-martial was avoided; and Rowland was now waiting to be dropped to the Communists in Albania. Next time there was no supper party, but he landed in Albania on a rock and broke his leg again. For several weeks he lay in a peasant's hovel with his leg in a rough splint constructed by an Italian veterinary. The Albanian *Partisans* then launched their attack on Tirana. Rowland was determined to take part. He had himself hoisted on to an Italian cavalry charger to accompany the advance. But the mountain paths were too steep for the heavy Lombard horse. It stumbled, fell, rolled on the leg and broke it again.

Rowland, indeed, has always been accident prone. One evening when I was driving him home from a dinner in Cairo and was expounding my

[1] For an account of this operation see *Ill-met by Moonlight* by William Moss.
[2] Later Lord St. Oswald and Parliamentary Secretary to the Ministry of Agriculture.

views on some topic of importance, I suddenly noticed that he was no longer in the car. I turned round and found him some five hundred yards further back sitting on the kerbstone and using rather obscene language. I remarked that to drop out of a conversation, without a word of warning, was rather ill-bred. He told me that he had failed to shut the door properly and had fallen out when I went round a corner rather quickly. This, no doubt, explained his behaviour but, at three o'clock in the morning, I was not sure that it altogether excused his discourtesy. He thought I was being over punctilious. Next day we both took a rather different view of the incident.

Life at Tara was luxurious rather than comfortable. Sometimes there were lavish dinners. Sometimes there was only bread and cheese. In principle, there were hot baths for all. But sometimes there were no baths at all because Vodka was being made in them. There were two kinds of Tara Vodka; Vodka and Old Vodka. Vodka took twenty-four hours to make; Old Vodka, three days.

Tara's evening parties were gay, but more surprising were its breakfasts. I went there once in the middle of the morning to find half a dozen young officers in dressing gowns breakfasting around Sophie's bed. She reclined on the pillows armed with a cavalry sword and used it to make sure they kept their distance.

Life in Cairo was never dull. But I was unemployed and saw no prospect of congenial work. Yugoslavia, Greece and Albania were in open revolt against the Germans. I knew I had a part to play; but no-one else seemed to think so. All this was frustrating and led me to one of the few spells of depression I have ever known. It was in this black mood that I accepted a kind invitation to stay from an old friend, Donald Mallett.

Mallett was an Irishman who had started life as a newspaper boy. He had graduated to become a crime reporter first in Glasgow and then on the *Daily Express*. We had met in 1940 when he had come to Belgrade to help set up the *Britanova* News Agency. In the crisis of Alamein, he had become press attaché at the Embassy in Cairo.

Like many Irishmen, Donald was a great talker, with a fund of stories dramatic and humorous. At a first meeting he seemed rather hard boiled. At heart he was an incurable romantic and idealist. This was the secret of his remarkable success as a propagandist. All of us have a streak of romance and idealism; and one of the arts of propaganda is to know how to awaken it and appeal to it. No-one can do this unless he has some genuine romance and idealism himself.

With Donald's help I enlarged my circle of Egyptian acquaintances, breaking through the upper crust of political leaders and penetrating the world of journalism and broadcasting.

On the surface, Middle Eastern politics seemed calm. But in the depths the seeds of extremism were beginning to sprout. Small groups of left-wing intellectuals were forming in Cairo. I met some of their members at the house of Mamdouh Riaz, whose beautiful and intelligent Rumanian wife had outspokenly left-wing leanings. Egypt and the Soviet Union had by now exchanged Ambassadors; and the first Soviet Ambassador created something of a stir by giving a garden party for the servants of other embassies and of the leading Pashas.

At the other end of the political spectrum were the right-wing Moslem Brotherhood centred mainly on the University of El Azhar. Sir Hassan Suhrawady, one of my father's Indian advisers, took me to meet the Rector of the Azhar, Sheikh El Maraghi. Maraghi was a kindly and learned man in the best traditions of Islam. He was of a liberal cast of mind and sought to widen the University's curriculum to embrace more humanist as well as theological studies. He gathered his sons and nephews to meet me. I made friends with the family and was often their guest.

The Maraghis were naturally suspicious of the Moslem Brotherhood, but soon put me in touch with some of their spokesmen. Nothing came of these talks. The Brotherhood were, at this time, sworn enemies of Britain and would soon gun down good friends like Amin Osman, Ahmed Maher and Nokrashy.

Terrorism, too, festered beneath the surface in Palestine and our kind friend Walter Moyne was soon to be murdered by two young men from the *Stern Gang* on the doorstep of the Gezirah house I had known so well.

But in the winter of 1943, these stirrings were still faint. Britain's influence reigned supreme from Tunis to Calcutta and from Teheran to Cape Town. British officers were made welcome in every part of the Middle East, even those least accessible to foreigners. One morning, walking down the Kasr el Nil, I ran into Sheikh Hafiz Wahba. Sheikh Hafiz was the Saudi Arabian Ambassador in London and one of my earliest mentors in Middle East affairs. We dined together that night and he brought me an invitation from Prince Feisal[1] to go to Jeddah with him two days later. They had, he explained, their own aeroplane and Prince Feisal would like me to be the guest of the King, the legendary Abdul Aziz Ibn Saud.

On my return, I sent my father this account of the visit:

7 January 1944
I am just back from ten days in Hejaz . . . as guest of King Ibn Saud. That I went at all is entirely thanks to Sheikh Hafiz Wabha, who showed himself a good friend.

I flew down to Jeddah by special plane with Amir Feisal—he looks like a Byzantine icon—and two of his brothers, Mansour and Khalid,

[1] Later King Feisal I of Saudi Arabia.

not to speak of their bodyguards, slaves and other entourage. When I was introduced to Feisal he said simply: 'We go to my father and shall be brothers on the way.' 'The way' led for five hours down the Red Sea; and we reached Jeddah about midday. The whole city had come out to greet us, all in Arab robes, and Feisal, the Foreign Minister and Viceroy of Hejaz, received the notables and diplomatic corps in a tent on the aerodrome, where we drank the bitter bedouin coffee poured into tiny cups by a Sudanese slave. Then Sheikh Yusuf Yassine, the King's secretary, as clever as a fox, and the only man in all Arabia I ever saw walk fast, came to greet me in the King's name and to call me to lunch at the Palace.

The Palace, a white building with crenellated walls is outside the city wall of Jeddah, furnished with carpets of incomparable beauty and furniture out of a Brighton hotel. I entered, passed a guard of honour—I wa-in uniform despite Arabia's neutrality—and was conducted to a large rectangular hall with chairs all round the walls. At one end, leaning on a stick, fully six foot five, stood the King, dressed in Arab robes. In no single item was he differently attired from his subjects, yet he was unmistakably the King.

His welcome came in deep-throated Arabic, praising God who had sent him a guest. He sat me at his right hand and we exchanged courtesies in a language straight from the Arabian Nights and, on his part, wholly unaffected. He is powerfully built with black beard and moustache, dark of skin but not at all semitic of feature. A cataract has destroyed the sight of one eye, but his smile is warming and friendly. He walks with a stick from rheumatism, for he has exchanged the camel for the motor car and so lost his exercise. He is wholly a nomad, never staying anywhere for more than a month and continually setting up his whole Government in camps in the desert.

We drank coffee; and the dignitaries of the court and the notables of Jeddah came to kiss hands. 'Friend, go up higher' is still the rule; and each man seeks the humblest place. The King's sons sit near the door, the lowest place of all. Presently the King took me by the hand and led me through white roofless corridors to what he apologetically termed a light lunch. We sat down fifty, and the table fairly groaned with food, all the courses, and they included sheep roasted whole, being on the table together. We ate with our hands, and twice the King gave me tit-bits from his own plate. When each guest had finished, he left without thanks or greeting. After lunch we rose to wash our hands in great ewers borne by slaves; and the King gave me to drink, from his own cup, the famous water of Djauran, beloved of the Prophet. As a final mark of favour he covered my hand with a perfume of musk and sandalwood. As he had told Bertram Thomas he shared the three tastes of the Prophet; prayer, perfume and women; and, despite his years, he still gives nightly satisfaction to the latter.

After lunch we returned to the reception hall for coffee and again the chiefs and notables came to kiss the King's hand, among them one of the few remaining Sharifs who was allowed to kiss the King's forehead and sat down at his left.

That afternoon the King left for Mecca, having first installed Sheikh Hafiz and me in a beautiful villa by the sea. For three days I was feasted by the notables of Jeddah and the King's Ministers. Then on Boxing Day, the King sent down from Mecca to invite me to dine with him along with Jordan, the (British) Minister (in Jeddah).

We dressed in Arab robes to go into the interior and drove out towards the Holy City. The King came out and met us in the way, pitching a camp just two hundred yards outside the city limits at a place called Chemezi, appropriately chosen for it was here that the Prophet signed his first treaty with the infidels. We arrived at sunset just in time to watch the King lead the evening prayer with his followers drawn up in a long line towards Mecca, hidden from sight and yet barely two miles away. (I never saw the Holy City but spoke to it on the 'phone.)

Dinner was the usual feast of twelve or more courses accompanied by flowery courtesies and proverbs from the Book; but, when it was done and we had talked a bit of current affairs, I asked the King to tell me, as a favour, the story of how he first seized the power in Nejd. He complied and we sat late into the night sipping little cups of tea and coffee while he talked of his early struggles in exile, his capture of Riyadh with forty men, his feud with Ibn Rashid and finally the war with the Sharifs which gave him the Holy Cities and finally made him Master of Arabia.

He left next day for Riyadh, 1,200 kilometres across the desert, with a fleet of six hundred cars.

Time was short so I paid a brief visit to Taif, the summer capital of Hejaz, 5,000 feet up and famous for its gardens which lie in an amphi-theatre of barren granite crags and tors. Here I lived in a huge white and blue palace with fountains playing day and night tended by an elderly gardener from Bokhara who looked like a figure of Chinese porcelain. I rode an Arab horse without stirrups, a difficult and stiffening process, and talked with the notables who included a most intelligent chief-of-police who had served with Lawrence. He showed me the Law Courts where the Sharia law still runs—hands are cut off for stealing and adultery is still punished with stoning unto death.

Back in Jeddah I was taken on a shooting expedition by some of the leading Jeddahis. We chased gazelles from motor cars travelling at 60 m.p.h. across rough country; and encamped for the night on the road to Medina where we sat talking to each other and to passing pilgrims. Soon after I returned to Cairo with Jordan, the Minister, who had meanwhile become my host. Before my departure, the King sent me a gold watch, a gold dagger and a set of Arab clothes.

My general conclusions on the country after a ten day visit are: There seems little doubt that the King is our sincere friend. He proved it at the time of Rashid Ali's rising and when the trouble comes again over Palestine he will be a counsellor of moderation in the Arab camp. It is, however, easy to exaggerate the influence of the 'desert' over the 'sown'.

The measure of the man's greatness is that he has united Arabia for the first time since the Caliphate transferred to Damascus, and that whereas twenty years ago it was not safe to go from Jeddah to Mecca alone, you can travel through the length and breadth of the land today as safely as in England.

The secrets of his power are: the wireless which makes centralised administration possible, the motor car with which he can pursue the raider or conspirator to the uttermost end of the desert and finally the fact that his revenue, whether subsidy, pilgrimage tax, or oil royalty, is not derived from his people but is, in part at least, spent on them.

The administration is mainly in the hands of Syrian adventurers or Nejdi warriors. There is much corruption and a good deal of misery from the drought, which has been broken this year for the first time for three years.

The succession is by no means assured, though no doubt it could be with British intervention. I did not see Saud, the heir, and I think you have met Faisal, the second son. The latter makes a most dignified impression, is said to be more international and has a great reputation for keeping his own counsel. Whether any of them could keep the power for long on a reduced revenue is uncertain. Certainly none enjoys anything like the King's prestige.

From a British point of view, it would seem important to prevent the country from lapsing into anarchy, both because of our Red Sea and Gulf interests and to prevent it becoming a breeding ground for agitators in Palestine, Syria and Iraq.

The King expressed the hope that you would one day visit Saudi Arabia and praised God that you were a good friend of the Muslims. I'm sure he would much appreciate a telegram from you—for the son was honoured for his father's sake, and honoured as a prince.

Oil had just been found in Saudi Arabia and the first oil revenues were coming into the royal treasury. But in 1943 the King still attached more importance to the £5m subsidy which Britain paid him annually and in gold.

VII

MISSION TO ALBANIA

April–November 1944

Land of Albania! where Iskander rose,
Theme of the young, and beacon of the wise,
And he his namesake, whose oft-baffled foes
Shrunk from his deeds of chivalrous emprise:
Land of Albania! let me bend mine eyes
On thee, thou rugged nurse of savage men!

Byron Childe Harold

Northern Albania and the activities of the McLean mission
April – November 1944

35

The Drop

I came back to Cairo from Jeddah to find in my mail a small but thick envelope heavily sealed. After breaking the seals and opening three inner envelopes marked respectively 'Personal', 'Secret', and 'For Amery Only', I came to the following text: 'Please call at my office as soon as you are back.' The signature was that of Philip Leake, the new head of the Albanian section of S.O.E.

I called on him, at once, in the garage block of the main S.O.E. building where he had established his office. Leake greeted me rather tensely, motioned me to a chair and said: 'Our set-up in North Albania has been badly knocked about by Davies'[1] capture. There are only two chaps now at the mission headquarters and one of them has got bad frost-bite. The other, between ourselves, seems a bit queer to judge from his telegrams, but that's hardly surprising seeing what they've been through. We wondered if you would care to join them.'

He paused, as if to savour the full horror of this invitation, and then added, almost as an afterthought: 'You know it isn't my idea, but Bill McLean is going in again—this time to reorganise the North—and he's asked for you as a sort of political officer. Smiley is going too.'

I had a passage booked to Algiers, where Duff Cooper had offered to see if he could find me employment, and Wavell had proposed staff work in India. But I knew at once that this was the job for me.

Ever since Operation Bullseye, in the autumn of 1941, I had dreamed of going back to the Balkans to play a part in the revolt of the Balkan peoples against the Germans. My ambition had been to join Bailey's mission to Mihailovitch. But this had been thwarted. Later I had tried to go to Greece with Myers but his mission had been cancelled. Albania was, of course, a much smaller country than Yugoslavia or Greece. But it was also much wilder and to go there at all would be something of an adventure.

On the political level, moreover, it offered a challenge. By the beginning of 1944, the British Government had accepted that Rumania, Hungary and

---

[1] Brigadier 'Trotsky' Davies, Commander of the British Missions in Albania, had been wounded and captured by Albanian collaborationists on 7 January 1944. His Chief of Staff, Colonel Nicholls, had died of exposure.

Bulgaria would be part of the Soviet sphere. With the withdrawal of our mission to Mihailovitch, we had, tacitly, agreed that Yugoslavia's fate should be the same. We seemed determined to keep Greece within our sphere of influence. But over Albania there hung a question mark.

The country was of some importance to us because of its strategic position commanding the entrance to the Adriatic. But there was no settled British policy towards it, and no decisions had been reached about its future at the different summit meetings of the Allies. Was there, then, a chance that Albania might still be saved for the West?

In any case, it seemed fitting that I should end my contribution to the European war in Albania. It was there after all that I had begun it in 1940. Besides there could be no better companions for such a tiger shoot than McLean and Smiley.

McLean was of highland stock, tall and fair-haired, disguising a hardness of steel beneath an elegant exterior and rather lackadaisical manner. He was a natural guerrilla leader, relying only on himself and gifted with a sure eye for ground and a sure insight into other men's intentions. Adventure was his mistress rather than ambition, and he delighted in all that was extravagant or strange. He was then just twenty-five, had joined the Scots Greys from Sandhurst and, as a subaltern in Palestine during the Arab rising of 1938 had first seen guerrilla war from the 'receiving end'. Later he had served with Wingate in Abyssinia and had captured Gondar at the head of an army of Amhara irregulars.

Smiley was in the 'Blues' but had also served with the guerrillas in Abyssinia. Of sturdier build than McLean, and a year or two older, there was no velvet glove over Smiley's claw. He knew his own mind and spoke it so as to leave little room for argument and none as to his intentions. He liked his friends and disliked his enemies, but otherwise was more interested in things than in people and found an unusual satisfaction in practical tasks like organising a camp or testing a weapon. McLean regarded action as only one of the ingredients of adventure. Smiley lived for action alone and was happiest on a dangerous reconnaissance or when 'blowing things up'.

When I left Leake's office, half-an-hour later, I was already signed on for Albania. A few days later I was on my way to the parachute training school in the plain of Esdraelon in Palestine. I went reluctantly but there was no other way of entering North Albania.

Parachuting is neither difficult nor very dangerous. Even, in those days, official statistics showed no more than one fatal accident in ten thousand jumps and one limb injury in six hundred. Yet it is undeniably contrary to every human instinct. From the start, indeed, the would-be parachutist is taught that to fall naturally is the surest way to break a leg. You have to learn to fall. For three days, therefore, I rolled and tumbled from varying heights and from stationary and moving platforms. By the end of it I was so stiff that I could hardly walk. But this hardly mattered. I knew how to fall. Then, soon after dawn, on the fourth morning I clambered into a lorry with ten other trainees, and drove out to board the aircraft for our first jump.

Later I was to treat parachutes without much respect, but that morning it seemed a matter of life and death that every strap should fit exactly. I had convinced myself intellectually that parachutes do open under perfect conditions but I felt that everyone who bumped into me in the changing room was reducing my already slender chances of survival.

Before emplaning each of us was allotted a number, thus discarding our personal identities. Then grinning nervously at each other we clambered into the belly of the bomber. As the roar of the engines drowned our talk each of us was left to his own thoughts and fears all too clearly mirrored in the tense features of his fellows. The engines sang furiously as we gained height. Then as we came over the dropping ground a circular trap door was opened in the floor of the 'plane. Through this Numbers One and Two disappeared with a sickening metallic crack as the automatic rip-cord of their parachutes whipped back against the bomber's underside. I was Number Three so it was my turn next.

I sat facing the tail of the aircraft with my legs dangling through the hole and watched the ground race by 2,000 ft. below. With an effort I looked up and surrendered my powers of decision to the instructor. The bulb above my head flashed red in warning and then green, the signal to jump. The instructor brought his hand down like the starter in a race; and I gently eased myself away from the edge of the hole. I passed through it and was caught at once in the slipstream of the 'plane and almost shaken apart. For a moment I knew the full horror of falling through space. Then the 'chute opened and suddenly all was still. A quite unknown sense of elation came over me, a feeling of almost god-like detachment from time and space. I felt myself drifting very slowly and gazed around me at the snow-covered summit of Mount Hermon and, to the west, at the sunlit blue of the sea. Then with a wrench I tore myself away from the sheer enjoyment of the descent and forced myself to damp down the oscillation of the parachute and to bring my feet together for the landing. I was only just in time. The ground which still looked a long way below, suddenly seemed to come up and hit me. I rolled over and standing up awkwardly in my harness began to haul in the silken 'chute. The sense of elation was gone. I had come down to earth with a bump.

McLean and Smiley were still in London when I got back to Cairo from my course. I accordingly spent the next few days reading reports and telegrams from Albania and talking to my friends in the Bektashi monastery. They gave me a stone from the martyr Hussein's tomb and a *tesbe* or rosary of olive wood: amulets from which I was never separated for the next eight months.

Gueffrey Boutros Ghali, a close Egyptian friend, also took away my pistol. When he brought it back two Arabic texts were engraved on either side of its butt. One from the Koran read: '*For when you shoot, it is not you but God who aims.*' The other, from one of the pre-Islamic poets ran: '*The ways are many but death is one. Wherefore then should you be afraid?*'

By this time 27 March had come round. This was the anniversary of the Yugoslav coup d'état in 1941 and incidentally my birthday. It seemed an occasion to entertain my Yugoslav and Bulgarian friends and those Englishmen in S.O.E. with whom I had worked most closely. It was a farewell to old comrades and in view of the company, the gastronomy was essentially Serbian. I managed to secure some bottles of plum brandy and Donald Mallett's servant brought in a live sheep which spent the day baaing rather pathetically in the kitchen. In the evening its throat was cut and it was skewered on a spit. By the time the guests arrived it was cooking slowly over a charcoal fire on the balcony of Donald's flat. Djonovitch and Tupanyanin wept like children at the sight of this homely Serbian meal. Several toasts were drunk; and we were just preparing for the feast when suddenly raindrops began to fall. This in Cairo was very unusual. Donald went to the window. He was only just in time to prevent the Cairo fire brigade from turning our barbecued sheep into boiled mutton. A neighbour had seen the flames on our balcony and had telephoned to raise the fire alarm.

Ten days later McLean, Smiley and I left Egypt for Bari in the heel of Italy. The next stage of our journey would be the jump into Albania. The situation in Albania at this time was, in its essentials, very similar to the one we knew in Yugoslavia and Greece. There were the occupying Power and its local 'collaborators'. There were Nationalist and Communist Resistance movements. Relations between the Nationalists and the Communists were bad; and the worse these grew, the more the Nationalists were driven to co-operate with the 'collaborators' in self-defence against a Communist take-over. By comparison, however, with Yugoslavia and Greece the Albanian situation was bewildering in its details. This arose from the complex social structure of the country.

The south of Albania, or Toskeria as it was called, had a largely feudal society consisting of Moslem landowners with a peasantry which was part

Moslem and part Greek Orthodox. The intellectuals and middle-class, and they were few, also came from the towns of Toskeria. There were two Resistance movements among the Tosks. There was the Communist LNC, started by my old friend, Mustafa Gjinishi, whom we had infiltrated into Albania during the Yugoslav War of 1941. It was now led by Enver Hodja, the present dictator of Albania. The other was a Nationalist and Republican Movement known as the *Balli Kombetar*. It consisted mainly of former opponents of King Zog and was led by a distinguished intellectual, Midhat Frasheri.

The northern part of the country, or Ghegeria, had a social system not so different from that of the Highlands in the late seventeenth and early eighteenth centuries. This consisted of clans and sub-clans, of which slightly more than half were Moslem, the balance Roman Catholic.

There was no Communist Resistance movement among the Ghegs. But Abas Kupi had been active in the mountains, on King Zog's behalf, since his return to Albania in 1941. Three other tribal leaders had also constituted centres of Resistance against the Italians. These were Fikri Dine in Dibra on the Yugoslav frontier, Muharrem Bairaktar in Liuma, the rugged valley of the Black Drin, and, after their escape from prison in Italy, the Kryezius in the Kossovo. Only the Catholic Mirdita and their 'Captain' Jon Marko Joni remained loyal to the Italian cause.

When Italy collapsed in the summer of 1943, there was a general rising throughout Albania. In the north, Abas Kupi seized his native city of Kruya; Fikri Dine and Muharrem Bairaktar took Dibra and Kukes; the Kryeziu brothers raised the flag of revolt throughout the Kossovo. In the south the Communists occupied Korcha, Gjinokastro and Elbasan; while the countryside around Valona declared for the *Balli Kombetar*. The Italian Army retained control of Tirana, Valona, Durazzo and Scutari. But they were on the defensive; and, after Marshal Badoglio, the Italian Commander-in-Chief, declared for the Allies, no longer had any cause to fight for. Some Italian units went over to the Resistance. Others disintegrated. Yet others held together and sought instructions from the German Command in Belgrade.

For some weeks Albania lay wide open to an Allied landing. But the Allies were concentrating all their energies on what they expected to be a 'quick kill' in Italy. The Americans, besides, were determined, for political as well as military reasons, to keep out of the Balkans. All S.O.E. could do in the circumstances was to send in more British liaison officers and to step up the airlift of war supplies.

The German High Command, for their part, were quick to appreciate the threat which an Allied landing in Albania would present to their communications with Greece. They reacted strongly, as they had done in Italy itself. A parachute division was flown to Tirana, and quickly dispersed the

Zogist guerrillas hanging on the fringes of the city. The Germans then marched against Abas Kupi and took Kruya by storm after a three day battle. Similar action followed against Fikri Dine, Muharrem Bairaktar and the Kryezius. Meanwhile, another German division was rushed to south Albania and methodically drove the Communist *Partisans* and the *Ballists* out of the towns. Within a fortnight the insurgents had been thrown back into the mountains and onto the defensive.

The Germans decided to limit their Albanian commitment to two-and-a-half divisions. These were deployed to defend the coast from invasion across the Adriatic and to guard the principal towns and the roads between them. They, prudently, determined to neutralise the rest of the country by policy rather than by force.

As a first step, they instituted a reign of terror, shooting hostages, burning houses and carrying off cattle, in those districts where the insurgents had been most active. In the process, they virtually destroyed the network of British missions in the north and centre of the country.

Having gained the respect of the population they proceeded to try and disarm their hostility. They released the bulk of political prisoners held by the Italians. They ended the union of Albania with Italy, and recognised Albania as an independent State. They invited the Albanians to set up a Council of Regency and an independent Government, and agreed that this Government should declare Albania's neutrality in the War. Albania, it was argued, could legitimately be neutral under German occupation just as Egypt remained neutral under British occupation.

These tactics paid off handsomely. A number of respectable Albanian notables joined the 'Collaborationist' Government. Others who had fought against the Italians found they could return to Tirana with impunity. The Germans kept a tight hold on the main roads, the airfields and the coast. But, for the rest, they left the Albanians very much to their own devices.

This produced a curious situation. In the south, the Communists, who had soon learned that the Germans were a much tougher proposition than the Italians, now turned their guns against the rival Resistance movement, the *Balli Kombetar*. Civil war broke out. The Communists got the better of the initial fighting; and the *Ballists* found themselves driven back into areas controlled by the Tirana Government and the Germans. With German connivance the Tirana Government now proceeded to rearm the *Ballists* and so enable them to strike back at the Communists. The pro-Allied *Balli Kombetar* was thus increasingly driven into the arms of the pro-German Tirana Government, until it became difficult to distinguish between them. The struggle against the occupying Power was thus superseded by the struggle between Nationalism and Communism. All this suited the Germans very well.

The situation in the north was rather different. There was no Civil War because there were virtually no Communists. Instead the country relapsed into its traditional state of anarchy. Blood feuds flourished; highwaymen multiplied; no taxes were collected. The only authority was that of the great tribal leaders, Abas Kupi, Fikri Dine, Muharrem Bairaktar and Jon Marko Joni; while, in the Kossovo, power was disputed between Jafer Deva, the pro-German leader, and our friend Gani Kryeziu.

Except for Marko Joni and Jafer Deva, the tribal leaders were pro-Allied. They welcomed British missions in their territories and gave them protection. They also looked after any Allied airmen or escaped prisoners of war who came into their hands and passed on to us any information they received about German movements or intentions. But they had suffered severely from German reprisals in the autumn of 1943 and were reluctant to take the offensive again. Their policy, instead, was to build up their own strength against the time when the Allies landed or the Germans began to evacuate. They could then fall upon an enemy no longer capable of inflicting reprisals, grab what loot they could and seize power in Tirana.

Here was the crunch. By the beginning of 1944 everyone in Albania assumed that it could only be a matter of months before the Germans were driven from Albania or left it of their own free will. For every Albanian, therefore, the main issue was: who would take over after the Germans? The Communists or the Nationalists? But for the Allied High Command in Caserta,[1] the main issue was: how to bring the Albanians to harass the German retreat most effectively? The best chance from Caserta's point of view lay in persuading the Albanian leaders that the road to political power lay in complying with British military directives. The greatest danger was that the different Albanian factions would waste their strength in Civil War and so allow the Germans to retire in good order.

We discussed all this at a conference in Bari. At the end of it the charter of our mission and our exact terms of reference were defined. We were:

(1) To reorganise and co-ordinate the activities of the British Missions in North and Central Albania;
(2) To raise the Ghegs in general and the *Zogist* forces of Abas Kupi in particular, against the Germans;
(3) To attempt to bring about co-operation between the *Zogist* Movement and the Communists of Enver Hodja.

We were to be responsible to the H.Q. Balkan Air Force, under the command of Air Marshal Elliott, and through him to General Wilson, the Supreme Allied Commander in the Mediterranean. Political matters were to be referred to the diplomatic staff of the Resident Minister of State, Harold Macmillan. But McLean had special authority to communi-

[1] The palace of Caserta outside Naples where the Allies had set up their Mediterranean G.H.Q. under General 'Jumbo' Wilson.

cate direct with Anthony Eden in cases of overriding importance or
urgency. We were authorised to promise arms to any group which would
fight against the Germans; but we were also told that no arms would be
sent until fighting had begun.

One question was raised but remained unanswered. Was our policy
to be determined exclusively by military considerations? Or were we
concerned to see that the post-war Albanian Government was friendly to
Britain? In Yugoslavia the former view had prevailed; in Greece the latter.
The leaders of S.O.E. saw themselves primarily in a military role. But a
final determination of policy towards Albania was to await our appreciation of the situation inside the country.

Once we had received our final instructions, there was no more to be
done until the remnant of our mission with Abas Kupi and the Balkan Air
Force could agree a date for our drop into Albania. They wasted no time.
On 17 April, we drove out along the road that follows the flat and dreary
Apulian shore to Brindisi, where an aircraft was waiting. We spent the
morning supervising the packing of our gear into steel containers and
watched them being loaded on to the 'plane. We had a bad lunch in the
station mess and for the rest of the day sought to kill time speculating on
the problems that lay ahead of us, reading papers, playing cards, or walking the chilly streets of Brindisi.

We took off half an hour before sunset. The aircraft was a United
States Air Force Dakota and through the big door in its flank, left open
for our jump, we watched the Italian coast recede while sea and sky
melted into one another as night drew on. Our pilot had to locate two
dropping-grounds; the first destined to receive our gear but judged too
rocky for our own descent; the second where we were to jump ourselves.
The flight across the Adriatic lasted perhaps three-quarters of an hour;
and we soon made out the signal fires of the first of our targets. Here the
American despatcher, assisted by my old friend Peter Kemp[1] who had come
with us for the ride, heaved the containers out into space. In twenty
minutes all our precious gear was scattered over the mountains of Albania,
to the sole profit, as it proved, of the rapacious mountaineers. Our pilot
then altered course to find the second target. He circled for nearly two
hours over the appointed area, but no trace of the signal fires could be
seen. At length the drone of our engines disturbed the enemy. Searchlights
swept the sky and just north of Tirana, we ran into anti-aircraft fire. Our
pilot now decided to give up the search; and at one o'clock in the morning
we were back in Brindisi. There was no accommodation to be had in
Brindisi and it was nearly dawn before we found a bed in Bari.

[1] See p. 95.

Two days later, we set out to make a second attempt. But, this time, we drove over to Lecce to avoid the depressing atmosphere of Brindisi. There we enjoyed a sumptuous meal in a small black market restaurant. The sun was shining when we came out and for a couple of hours we wandered through the streets of Lecce forgetting the sterner duties ahead of us in the enjoyment of its gorgeous baroque palaces and churches.

We were late returning to Brindisi and it was already night when we took off. The aircraft seemed cold and noisy; and I felt irritated and awkward, trussed in my parachute. I was fast asleep, however, when the despatcher woke me to say that we were over the target. We each took a gulp of *grappa*—the fiery Italian grape spirit—and formed up by the open door for the jump. Through it I could see the signal fires, set out in the form of a cross at the bottom of a snow-rimmed trough in the mountains. The surrounding ranges made the approach to the target difficult; and we could see that the pilot had overshot his mark when the bulb by the door flashed green—the signal to jump. I went out last, shrinking inwardly from the plunge, and was caught up in the slipstream of the 'plane and violently shaken. Then the parachute opened; the smell and vibration of the aircraft ceased; the tension went from me: and I felt suddenly warm. We must have jumped from near three thousand feet, for my arms soon grew tired of straining at the guiding ropes of the parachute to check its oscillation. I could see the mountains rising past me as I drifted down, but the ground was still hidden in the night.

Suddenly I was aware of something white. Then, without the slightest jar, I found myself sprawling on my face in a deep patch of snow. Luck was with me, for I had fallen in a forest and might well have been impaled on some jagged pine. McLean had come down perhaps a mile away, also unhurt; but Smiley, landing less than a hundred yards from me, bruised his back badly against a tree. Nor was this our only near escape, as we discovered next morning. McLean and I had, by some accident, been issued with cotton parachutes. These were of a type designed for dropping stores and, unlike the silk parachutes, frequently failed to open.

We had landed about half way up the side of the mountain trough and presently saw torches moving towards us through the trees below. In the distance wolves were howling; and I remember speculating which would reach us first. The torches seemed a long time in coming and we guided them with our own electric flashlights. But when they drew near, we placed our flashlights on suitable mounds and retired some twenty yards from them so as not to present a target, should the torch bearers prove unfriendly. Some of our colleagues had been trapped in such ambushes but we had fallen among friends; and the torch bearers turned out to be a *Zogist cheta*. There were a dozen of them, still shadowy figures in the night, save for their leader, Bairam, a former gendarme with a mighty moustache, who shook hands and greeted us in broken Italian.

Bairam led us downhill through the trackless forest for an hour or so until we came to a half open sheepfold in a clearing on the mountainside. There we sat round an open log fire and drank tea. Then, seeing it was late, I lay down warming one side of my body by the fire while the mountain wind chilled the other. All around the guerrillas sat cross-legged, bristling with bandoliers, pistols, and hand grenades; their unshaven faces sinister in the firelight. They showed no sign of sleeping and now and again spoke to one another in a whisper. For some time I watched them through the flames and smoke, seeking to measure the span, intangible and yet experienced, which separated this brigand encampment from the baroque splendours of Lecce and the bourgeois pleasures of its black market restaurant.

I woke at dawn and looking out saw that we were on the edge of a broad grassland plateau set in an amphitheatre of rock peaks. The snow was still thick on the higher slopes and in the ravines. The country here was under Abas Kupi's undisputed control; and we could move freely. A four hour walk across the plateau and downhill brought us to a prosperous Moslem village where we were hospitably entertained by the local *Zogist* leader. We lay up there for the rest of the day, for we were now on the edge of territory patrolled by the Germans and the Tirana Government. The people beyond were loyal to Abas Kupi but it was only safe to move there at night.

Our guides had procured ponies for us in the afternoon, but even so the next stage of the journey was a nightmare. It rained hard. The night was as black as pitch. Boulders and branches seemed to rush at me from the darkness, crushing my leg against the wooden saddle or dragging me almost bodily out of it. The paths were stony, steep and precipitous; blocked by snowdrifts on the heights, and in the valleys washed away by the thaw. A slip would often have meant a fall of fifty or a hundred feet.

In mountain country distance has little meaning; and the Albanians always calculated the length of a journey in terms of time. Our guides had told us that this journey would take four hours; but as was often the way, this estimate was given to encourage rather than to inform. We had, indeed, already ridden nine hours when, shortly after daybreak, we crossed a ridge and came down through a large and straggling orchard to the house which sheltered the remnant of the British mission. The door was opened before we had even knocked; and a peasant led us through a cowshed to a loft where Alan Hare and his colleagues worked and slept. Alan still limped from a frostbitten foot and looked pale from prolonged confinement indoors; but it was reassuring, if in this setting rather surprising, to hear his familiar voice which brought back memories of undergraduate dinners, a tour of Burgundy and heated political discussions in London night clubs.

36

With Abas Kupi

Our first task was to see Abas Kupi and form our own opinion of his strength and intentions. A few days later, therefore, I rode off with a small *Zogist* escort to the meeting place appointed by him.

We rode for some hours through forests of beech and pine and at length came to a grey stone keep, built on a jutting rib of the mountain range. The path leading to it was so narrow and precipitous that I had to send back my horse and make the last stage of the journey on foot. Abas Kupi came out to meet me, as I turned into the walled courtyard of the house, and welcomed me with the traditional greeting of *Tungyatyeta*—'May your life be prolonged.' He was dressed in riding breeches and a grey *redingote* which increased his resemblance to Napoleon; but he looked older and leaner than when I had known him in Belgrade.

He led the way up a flight of wooden steps, resting like a ladder against the wall of the house, and took me by the hand into a dark and dusty room, hung with rifles and sub-machine guns. It was thronged with *Zogist* notables and their bodyguards: wild and rugged men, corrugated with cartridge-belts, and festooned with pistols, daggers, and hand-grenades. Most of them were dressed in black, baggy Turkish breeches, braided homespun jackets of black or brown, with multi-coloured sashes wound about their waists, and white *fezes* or skull-caps on their heads. A few besides wore Albanian uniform, or leather jerkins.

We sat down cross-legged by the fire; and, while we drank coffee and exchanged greetings, the guerrillas milled around or sat together in small groups, whispering intently. To a stranger, this whispering seemed sinister and conspiratorial; but the others took no offence at it; and I soon got used to it myself. Of necessity the guerrillas lived a communal life, especially in winter; and it was only by whispering that any private discussion was possible at all. It was only on rare occasions—and this fortunately was one—that Abas Kupi would clear the room so that we could talk freely.

He began with the story of his trials and triumphs since our last meeting in Belgrade in 1940. It was like listening to the tale of some Homeric hero and, with interpretation, took a couple of hours. Then we got down to business.

The first duty with which we had been charged was to reorganise and regroup the British missions in north Albania. This presented no problem. We were welcome to establish ourselves in the territories under Abas Kupi's control and to move through them freely. He would provide bodyguards for us and would ensure our supplies. He would also try to collect any intelligence we wanted about the Germans.

I asked him next about the possibilities of co-operation between his movement and the Communists. He said that they had become his main enemies. He would like to have destroyed them before they grew too strong and had only held his hand because they had British officers with them. I put the case for reconciliation and joint action, and he answered, 'If you will impose friendship between us, I shall be glad. But I know these men and, *Vallahi!* they will not have it.'

I turned next to the question of fighting the Germans. Abas Kupi answered that he was already at war with them and pointed to the presence of British military missions on his territory as the proof. He had not, indeed, attacked them since the autumn; but the winter had been harsh, and all his energies had gone into preparing for a general rising when the time should come. The people, we must remember, had been demoralised by the failure of their revolt the year before. Then the British missions had incited them to action; but there had been no British landing. Instead, their homes had been burnt, their relatives interned, and their flocks carried off. The Germans were not as pestilential as the Italians, but they were more ruthless, and the tribesmen would hesitate to attack them again, at least until we sent them arms and ammunition.

There were besides political considerations. What was to be the future of Albania? What would be its frontiers? Had it been assigned to the Soviet sphere of influence, as the Germans maintained? 'We Albanians,' he went on, 'are few and poor. But in proportion to our strength we have made great efforts and great sacrifices in the common cause. So far we have received no encouragement nor recognition from the Great Allies. I still put my trust in Great Britain as I did in 1940. I have fought and I will continue to fight: but you must send me arms and make some gesture that you have our country's interests at heart. We are, after all, Albanian patriots not British agents.'

I did my best to put our side of the argument and told him how Mihailovitch's passivity had led to the withdrawal of British support. And Mihailovitch, after all, had been a Minister in an Allied Government. This made some impression on him but plainly it would take more than one talk to change his mind. I, accordingly, welcomed his suggestion that McLean and I should go with him to visit the *Zogist* strongholds of Mati and Kruya. This would give time for discussion in depth.

A few days later, McLean and I set out with Abas Kupi and his chief lieutenants. We marched escorted by a hundred picked *Zogist* guerrillas. This was a strong enough force to overawe any local opposition. It also meant that the Germans were unlikely to move against us with less than a battalion, and we should have ample warning of any such move. We had brought horses with us. But Abas Kupi always went on foot and as a mark of respect we followed his example, leaving our bodyguards to lead our beasts. My bodyguard was a lean and wolfish fellow, and a source of constant anxiety to my companions. He had started life as a brigand, but in Zog's time had turned gendarme, appreciating that under a strong government only the police can rob with impunity. When the Italians invaded Albania he had returned for a time to his earlier calling, but business had been slack and he had ended up with Abas Kupi's forces. He was attached to me at the beginning of our march but at an early stage was caught stealing. Abas Kupi wanted to have him shot, but I interceded for him and saved him from his deserts. Thereafter he protected my belongings as if they had been the Holy Grail, and looked after me with almost motherly devotion. Other people's property, however, he continued to regard as fair game; but, though he sometimes boasted to me of his plundering expeditions, he was careful for my sake to honour the eleventh commandment.

It was already May, but in the mountains we still lived amid the gales and snow of winter. On the second day's march, however, we came out of the swirling mountain mists into the sunlight and saw the broad Mati valley spread out below us like a promised land. Fat sheep and cattle grazed in the undulating pastures; whitewashed houses, the tallest in Albania, were scattered over the low, wooded hills; and beyond the sparkling river the ground rose steeply to the wild glens of Mirdita. The guerrillas had not left the mountains since autumn; and now, at the sight of the sunlit valley, the long line of men winding down the hillside broke into a strident song.

Mati was Zog's own country; and the King's first care had been for the people of his valley. Many of its chiefs, though they could not read nor write, had been given appointments in the civil service or commissions in the Army. The valley had benefited, moreover, from an ambitious pro-gramme of public works. A road and several bridges had been built; and Burrel had been made the model provincial capital of Albania. The men of Mati were thus staunch for Zog; we found his picture in most houses and at night, sitting round the fire, listened to tales of his adventures and even epic poems about them. This loyalty to the King was accompanied by a wholesome respect. As one cunning old warrior put it to me: 'I am a monarchist in case the King should come back.'

Our progress through the valley was leisurely and public, and, indeed, was intended by Abas Kupi as a demonstration to show the *Zogist* flag and to parade the new British mission—the outward and visible sign of Allied support. We marched most of the day through rolling fields and leafy forests; coming at evening to some new village where we spent the night and were feasted by the clans.

Albanian houses varied in size with the wealth of the owners; but all were essentially built for defence. As a rule, they were sited to command a good field of fire and were often surrounded by walled courtyards entered through heavy, wooden gates studded with iron. Most were built of rough stone and wood and consisted of two stories, joined by a narrow indoor staircase, or by a flight of wooden steps on the outside. The ground floor was the cattle and the women's quarters. Above was the guest-room. The guest-room was the heart of the house, and, except for a stout chest in which the family's valuables were stored, had no furniture at all. At one end of it was an open hearth from which the smoke escaped through a chink in the wall or, in statelier keeps, through a chimney. Narrow windows, usually without panes, served as a means of ventilation or, when required, as rifle slits: but they gave so little light that it was often difficult to read indoors, even at midday. At night the room would be lit by the glow of the fire, or sometimes by oil lamps or pinewood torches.

On entering a house we would take off our boots and give up our rifles to the host, though retaining our side-arms. As foreigners, we would then be led to the place of honour, on the right-hand of the hearth. Abas Kupi would sit with us or take the left-hand side; and the rest of the company, including bodyguards and orderlies, assembled in a horse-shoe round the fire. The youngest sat at the apex of the horse-shoe, and, since there were often a score of us, the evening would begin with much show of 'Friend, go up higher'.

We sat on carpets or sheepskin rugs, cross-legged or reclining against our saddle-bags. When all were seated, the host rolled cigarettes, which only non-smokers might refuse, and tossed them with unfailing accuracy to each guest. Presently a warm drink would be served, usually coffee, though in the poorer houses sweetened or salted milk was brought instead. As outlaws we sought to keep our movements secret and our arrival was, as a rule, the first warning of our visit which the host received. Custom demanded that he serve us meat; and since several hours must pass before the sheep or kid had been killed and made ready, it was often past midnight before we dined.

While the meal was cooking we variously slept or talked while the bodyguards dried damp clothes by the fire or massaged our weary limbs. Sometimes to beguile the time, one of the company would recite from the long epic poems in which the Albanians record the exploits of their heroes. These were weird, monotonous laments, sung in a high-pitched nasal voice to the accompaniment of a one-stringed mandolin.

An hour or so before the meal flasks of *raki* would be brought, accompanied by *mese* of onions, cheese, and sometimes hard-boiled eggs or lumps of grilled meat. *Raki* is a fiery, colourless spirit, made from the pulp of grapes, or sometimes, like *slivovitz*, from plums. Among the mountaineers it was usually home-brewed, and varied greatly in quality and strength. The principal guests would each receive a small flask, the shape of an old-fashioned burgundy flagon and holding perhaps half a pint. The rest of the company fared according to the resources of the host, sharing a flask between two or three. Toasts were drunk to the traditional greeting of *Tungyatyeta*—'May your life be prolonged'; and, though the mountaineers habitually drank to excess, they did so with grave, if sometimes mellowed, dignity.

When the cooking was done, the chief guest would be asked if the meal might be served. There was never conversation after meals; and so the greatest compliment which he could pay his host and the rest of the company was to ask for a postponement so that there could be further talk. As soon, however, as he had given his assent, a circular wooden table some five feet in diameter would be carried in, standing about six inches from the ground. Round this a dozen of us would gather, sitting cross-legged, but in a crocodile, each sideways on to the table so as to make room for as many as possible. A spoon was our only piece of cutlery and with this we helped ourselves to the more liquid dishes at the centre of the table. There were no plates, so that each spoon plied steadily backwards and forwards between the individual mouth and the communal dish. More solid foods, such as meat or rice, were eaten with the fingers; and, since each dish was communal, those who ate slowly went hungry.

In the nine months that our mission lasted we touched life at many angles and experienced extremes of poverty and plenty. Often we were lucky even to get a lump of cheese and maize bread, or a cup of unsweetened milk. At other times, as on our progress through Mati, we were surfeited by a wealthy host on successive dishes of eggs, boiled mutton, roast mutton, pilaf and luscious *halvas* and *baklavas*. But as a general rule, Albanian fare was lacking in variety and the average meal consisted of a soup of beans, a dish of boiled mutton, and a bowl of buttermilk or 'yoghourt'. The guest of honour was usually given the sheep's head. The brains and eyes were considered the greatest delicacies—or sometimes the kidneys and the tail. Fatness was the quality most admired in sheep, though, even with hard exercise, none of us except Smiley really took to lumps of hot boiled fat. Milk was the usual drink at meals, drunk like soup from a communal bowl and served as the last course. Water was also to be had, but only on request and there was seldom more than one glass or mug in the house. Before and after meals the host came round with a basin and ewer, and the guests washed their hands—a most necessary proceeding

seeing that these were used for eating. In the richer houses the washing
water was warmed and there was home-made soap. Each man left the table
when he had finished eating, without waiting for his fellows; and, when the
chief guests had done, there would be a 'second sitting' for the rest of the
company. The guests had the right, and often used it, to criticise any mean-
ness in their entertainment to their host's face. He, for his part, would never
sit at table or taste food until the last of the guests had eaten.

When all had done, mattresses and eiderdowns would be brought and
spread out on the floor for the half-dozen more important guests, while the
others made themselves as comfortable as they might with their overcoats
and jackets. It was considered indecent to undress, but, before the lights
were snuffed out, prudent men gathered their arms and effects about them
against the dangers and confusions of a night attack. In cold weather the
fire was kept in until morning. In summer the room would often become
intolerably stuffy from the accumulated animal warmth of a score of
snoring sleepers.

The Albanians like most mountaineers rose late; and, by a generous
convention, the younger were left sleeping till last. There was no breakfast; but in many houses the host would bring us a cup of coffee or of hot
sweetened milk when he saw us wake. Ablutions were perfunctory, each
man, or the host, pouring cold water from an ewer over his fellow's hands,
with which the latter seldom did more than dab his eyes. Moustaches were
de rigueur, though Abas Kupi was clean-shaven; but only priests or bandits
grew beards. Shaving, however, was most often a weekly affair and a
sufficiently rare occasion to warrant the valedictory greeting of *Meschnett*
—an equivalent of 'God bless you'—to the shaver.

Albanian sanitary arrangements were primitive but ingenious. The
closet, which adjoined the guest-room, projected, sometimes precariously,
from the first floor over the courtyard below. It consisted of a can of water
and a hole in the floor, often of impracticably narrow circumference.
Underneath, the thrifty mountaineers were wont to keep their poultry,
which gobbled up a strange diet with evident relish.

Women, among the clans, were but the slaves and chattels of their men.
In the mountains they were unveiled but almost all were prematurely aged
by hard work and child-bearing. Sometimes we saw one hurrying across a
courtyard or peering up at us from the kitchen fire; otherwise they had no
part in our lives.

Social distinctions among the guerrillas were subtle and changing;
the chieftains and their sons were treated with respect but never with
servility; the bodyguards, sometimes as poor relations, but always as
members of the same family. All ate and slept together, and, in so far as he
could, the host provided alike for all. Luxuries in the mountains were
inevitably scarce, but, if the choicest morsels went to the chiefs and elders,

the rest received their portion until the whole was finished. The Ghegs, indeed, regard hospitality as a sacred duty enjoined upon the host, never as a favour conferred upon the guest. To give of his best was a point of honour, and a tribesman would kill his last ewe lamb or even his milch goat, rather than fail to set meat before the meanest guest. In the old days, indeed, Albanians had been known to sell their wives or children into slavery to provide hospitality for a stranger.

As we progressed through Mati, Abas Kupi worked hard to strengthen his faction, rewarding friends and seeking to win over enemies by threats or cajolement. One of his chief problems was to call a halt to the blood feuds between clans which threatened the unity of the *Zogist* movement. The *hakmeria*, or blood feud, had its merits. It was a great teacher of manners and of respect for the dignity of the individual. No Albanian, indeed, could strike another with impunity; and even schoolmasters had been known to pay with their lives for a hasty cuff in class. But the feuds took a heavy toll of life and caused much suffering. We often met men from weak clans who had scarcely left their homes in twenty years for fear of neighbours with whom they were 'in blood'.

Zog had made some attempt to suppress the feuds; and they had begun to decline before the growing power of the Central Government. But, with the collapse of Italian rule, the mountaineers had returned to their former anarchy, and blood feuds flourished on every side. As foreigners we stood in no danger from them; but they were none the less an important factor in our daily life. A guide would take us several hours out of our way to avoid the territory of a clan with which he was 'in blood'. Chieftains would suddenly postpone a meeting, alarmed by rumours that their enemies were lying in wait. Once or twice at tribal gatherings we saw a man pass the coffee cup to his neighbour under his knee—the supreme mark of contempt for a man who had not even tried to avenge a wrong.

The blood feuds presented Abas Kupi with a serious problem, for every time he won a clan to his cause, their blood enemies would side automatically with his rivals. He, therefore, spent long hours trying to reconcile the contending parties, and invited them to submit their feuds to his arbitration. There was, besides, a tradition that a general truce, or *besa*, might be proclaimed, like the mediaeval 'Truce of God', if a region was in danger of foreign attack; and Abas Kupi worked hard to persuade the clans to accept such a *besa*.

Our progress through Mati was crowned by a grand gathering of the Mati Chiefs in the stronghold of Dule, head of the powerful Allemani clan. A score or so of notables had assembled to meet us, and their bodyguards encamped about the keep must have numbered close on a thousand men.

They had all taken part, that autumn, in the rising against the Italians, and many had seen their homes burnt and their livestock slaughtered in the subsequent reprisals. They had fought with spirit for they had been exasperated by Italian rule and had believed that the hour of liberation and of looting was at hand. But their revolt had been premature. The price had been heavy; and they intended to make doubly sure of the fruits of victory before they again exposed their families and property to the risks of war. The fear of reprisals, indeed, had become an obsession with them; and, when we urged them to take the field, they simply pointed to the ruins of Burrel—the provincial capital which had been their pride—and to the gutted houses which in every village recalled the passage of an Italian or German punitive expedition. They were our allies, they said, and would fight again but they would leave it to Abas Kupi to settle with us the exact terms on which they would take the field and the timing of the operation.

The Mati Chiefs made no attempt to conceal the fear and hatred which they felt towards the Communists. They reluctantly accepted our advice not to join the Tirana Government in an anti-Communist drive. But they made it clear that they would resist any attempt by the Communists to enter Mati.

Next day we forded the Mati river and climbed the great Skanderbeg range which divides Mati from Kruya. Four thousand feet below us lay the coastal plain, with its broad acres, turgid inland lagoons, and the wrinkled promontory of Rodonit crawling out into the glinting waters of the Adriatic. Tirana and Durazzo were wrapped in the evening haze while Kruya itself was masked by the massive Kruya Mountain. This was a flat-topped cliff honeycombed with caves—the legendary abode of Said Saltiq, the wizard of Albanian folklore.

In Mati, Abas Kupi had everywhere been received with the respect and honour due to a great guerrilla leader. In Kruya he was welcomed with devotion and enthusiasm, for there he was among his own people. He seemed to know each mountaineer we met and, for each, had a special word of greeting or enquiry. There could be no mistaking his popularity; and even in the poorest villages, the women would run out and kiss his hands or hold up their children to him.

The main Tirana-Scutari road passed close to Kruya, and this provided an opportunity for representatives of the *Zogist* Central Committee to come out from the city and meet us. They were Balkan politicians of the old school, steeped in the history of the Eastern Question, and frankly incredulous that any British Government could allow, let alone encourage, the spread of Russian influence to the Adriatic. They accepted that it would be their duty to take up arms again against the Germans, but they wanted first to be sure that we would not hand them over to the Communists.

The final stage of our tour was a visit to the *Zogist* General Staff in their mountain headquarters. The Staff proved to be a rather motley collection of Albanian officers and N.C.Os. Their real function was to man the mortars and field guns which Abas Kupi had captured from the Italians in the previous year. They gave us, however, an excellent lunch at which their Commandant toasted the guests in turn. Unfortunately, he had a very pronounced squint and every time he raised his glass two guests invariably replied.

We were now at the end of our tour of the *Zogist* strongholds, and it was time to take decisions. We accordingly put to Abas Kupi the two main issues we had discussed so often during our march. Was he prepared to work with the Communists? To our surprise he invited us to arrange for him to meet Enver Hodja or some other Communist leader as soon as possible. He would welcome a common front with them against the Germans, provided both movements kept their identity and independence. He laid down only one condition. This was that a British officer be present throughout their meetings. He wanted us to know where the responsibility lay if the talks broke down. Nothing could be fairer than this proposal and we agreed to pass it back at once to our headquarters.

We asked Abas Kupi next whether he was prepared to resume operations against the Germans. He answered frankly that his Central Committee were opposed to taking the offensive unless we sent them supplies and gave some assurance about the future of Albania. As a mere soldier, he did not feel that he could override their view on his own responsibility. But he would gladly do so if we could get him appropriate instructions from King Zog. 'Let the King send me a message through your mission, and if he tells me to fight with my bare hands, I will.' No question of official recognition was involved. All he asked for was a private directive from his King.

This too seemed a very reasonable solution; and I had little doubt that Zog would send a favourable answer. He was far too shrewd a man not to sieze the opportunity of establishing a new relationship with the British Government. Nevertheless, the proposal had its dangers. If Abas Kupi's request was refused, he could only conclude either that Zog was against a renewal of fighting or that the British Government was not even prepared to enlist his informal co-operation. The whole future of our relationship with Abas Kupi, or so it seemed to us, turned on accepting his request for a royal directive. McLean accordingly followed up our report to headquarters, with a personal message to Anthony Eden. This ended with the words: 'there is grave danger that without this measure of encouragement Abas Kupi will go the way of General Mihailovitch.'

The results of our talks exceeded our expectations; and we felt that we were well on the way to fulfilling our mission's three point charter. But several days must pass before we could expect replies to Abas Kupi's two proposals. McLean and I accordingly decided to make a quick reconnaissance of the situation in Dibra, Liuma, and the Kossovo. Abas Kupi was the most important of the Gheg guerrilla leaders. But he was not the only one. If we were to raise the whole of northern Albania against the Germans we should have to broaden the base of the revolt beyond the *Zogist* movement.

37

Raising the Clans

After two days at the base camp which Smiley had set up in a clearing in the mountains, McLean and I set out for Dibra. We put our trust in speed rather than strength and limited our party to our interpreter, Shaqir, three bodyguards and two mulemen to look after our animals and baggage.

Our headquarters had been studiously vague as to our position in international law. Some of our colleagues in other Balkan countries had been treated as prisoners of war. Others had been shot as spies. We thought it wiser, even if more conspicuous, to try and preserve our military status by wearing uniform. But, despite badges of rank and decorations, we seldom contrived to look anything but irregular. McLean wore light Albanian sandals, jodhpurs, and a heavy, green regimental tunic. My own clothes were a hard-wearing cord tunic and trousers, the latter tucked Russian fashion into soft knee-length field boots. These were heavy, but a great protection against rocks and thorns. We both wore a broad sash wound about the waist. This was a most necessary garment, protecting livers and kidneys from insidious changes of temperature and against the successive feasts and fasts of an outlaw's life. For arms each of us carried a Merlin sub-machine gun and a Colt 45 automatic. The sub-machine gun was accurate up to about two hundred yards and deadly in an ambush. Its moral effect, moreover, was great as its killing power; and an irresolute enemy was often driven back merely by its noise and rate of fire. The '45 Colt was very powerful at close range; and a single shot from it would knock a man down even if it only hit him in the hand. Later on, I also acquired a miniature pistol which I kept concealed as a last resort in the event of capture.

The Dibrans lived by the upper reaches of the Black Drin, and were much poorer than the men of Mati. They were a grim and calculating breed, a border people waging a ceaseless war with their Slav neighbours in Macedonia. Dibra itself had been a prosperous market town under the Ottoman Empire, but was now shrunk to a quarter of its former size. Its trade was gone but the enterprising Dibran chiefs had learned to make a living out of the Eastern Question. For close on a century the Powers had contended for the support of Dibra and had tried to outbid each other in giving subsidies and arms to the Dibran chiefs. The chiefs, on their side, had been quick to learn the technique of power politics and, at any time, the balance of power between the leading Dibran families reflected fairly accurately the balance of power between their foreign patrons. Nor were the Dibran leaders mere recipients of outside aid. On the contrary, they were adept at raising the price of their support by playing off the Powers against each other. Moreover, to avoid being left, by some miscalculation, on the losing side, they systematically placed a relative in each of the different political camps.

Dibra was said to hold five thousand rifles. But the Dibrans were so split by local blood feuds and foreign intrigues that no clan could raise more than five hundred. The most powerful man in the region was Fikri Dine, once a henchman of King Zog. Fikri had led the rising of the Dibran clans in 1943 and had driven the Italians out of Dibra. But he was at this time in Tirana negotiating with the Germans and we did not see him. His friends, however, assured us that this was a purely short-term policy. He was trying to get as much out of the Germans as he could to defend Dibra against the Communists. But, when the time came, we should find him on our side. There seemed no reason to doubt this. No man was ever less ideologically committed than Fikri. He drew his power, not from the number of his rifles, but from his personal ascendancy over the bigger chiefs who admired his statecraft; and wherever we went in Dibra we saw signs of his powerful influence.

Our first halt was at a granite keep four storeys high, situated near the banks of the river. Here we received striking confirmation of the importance of Abas Kupi's request for instructions from Zog. I was talking with Aqif Llesh, a grizzled old warrior, whom I had known in Belgrade in 1940, and who was a bitter enemy of Zog. I asked him whether he held a reconciliation between the Communists and Abas Kupi to be possible. 'Yes,' he replied, 'if they will fight the Germans.'

'Can they be persuaded to fight again?'

'I fear there is only one way. If Zog will come to the radio and tell them to fight then they will. You know I have worked against him all my life, but I tell you now that he is the only man who can raise the hegs and so prevent civil war.'

The Drin was in spate and the crossing guarded by a gendarmerie post. But it was past midnight when we reached it, and the aged ferryman, delighted by a proffered half sovereign, punted us over on a raft under the nose of the sleeping gendarmes. One of them woke up as we reached the other side and shouted after us, but by that time we had melted into the night.

At daybreak we reached the stronghold of the powerful Kalloshi clan. In our first talk with Ramadan Kalloshi I came across a fine example of the realism for which the Dibrans are famous. In the opening exchange of courtesies, we had enquired after different members of the family, and someone had asked:

'How is your cousin, Selim?'

'The dead one?' Ramadan queried.

'Forgive me,' said the questioner 'I didn't know that he had died.'

'Well, he's not dead yet,' came the reply, 'but the doctors say there is little hope, so we call him "the Dead One" and are dividing up his property!'

His words shocked by their heartlessness but on reflection it struck me that they were symbolic of the Albanian attitude towards the War. In their eyes the Germans, like the unfortunate Selim, were 'dead' because past hope of recovery. In such a situation there was no point in indulging in sentiment. All that mattered was to make sure that the right people got the inheritance and not the wrong ones. Whether the end came a few weeks sooner or later was neither here nor there.

From the Kalloshis, we passed to the strongholds of their principal rivals, the Elezis. The Elezis had a foot in every camp. The head of the clan had just gone to Tirana to receive the title and salary of a colonel from the 'Collaborationist' Government and to collect a grant of four thousand gold *napoléons*. His brother and nephew held high positions in the Communist movement. His two sons, Gani and Islam, who received us, worked with Abas Kupi. Both spoke good English having studied at the American College in Tirana. They expressed strong sympathy for the Allies but were frankly puzzled by the support we were giving the Communists.

'As you know,' said Islam, 'there are three parties in Albania: the agents of Germany, the agents of Russia, and the agents of England. That is quite natural. But what none of us can understand is why the agents of Russia are paid in English gold.'

'Perhaps it's what they mean by "lease-lend,"' muttered his brother.

This starkly realistic approach was later followed up by a sharp reminder that generosity and readiness to make concessions for the sake of agreement is the privilege of the strong. McLean had spoken reprovingly of the spirit of faction which rent the Albanian clans and of how much they stood to gain by sinking their differences to fight the common enemy. Islam heard him in silence and replied:

'All that you say is true, Mr. Colonel, but you must remember that we Albanians are everything that is wicked: we are poor; we are ignorant; we are small.'

Towards evening we left the Dibra lowlands and climbed into rugged glens where the snow was not yet wholly melted. Our way led up a stony gully which ended in a long slope of shifting scree. It was steep, and the going treacherous; so we dismounted, leading our ponies for the last few hundred feet.

Heavy thunder-clouds were billowing up at the head of the gully, and on the crest stood a square, stone barrack, grim and windswept—the lair of Osman Lita, the Black Douglas of the Dibran march. Dark, cruel, and grasping, Osman was growing old, not with the dignity which years can bring, but with a thickening of the body and wandering of the mind. He received us, indeed, with traditional hospitality; but I slept little that night. It was a house of fear.

In the morning we conferred with his son, Sherif, a lean and hungry man with cold, light eyes, who had spied on Mihailovitch for the Italians. He listened impassively while I explained our policy, but when he saw that he could hope for neither arms nor subsidies in advance of attacking the Germans, he brought the conversation abruptly to an end, saying quietly: 'Words without gold are to us like chaff without corn.'

Our talks in Dibra convinced us that none of the Dibran chiefs would start a rising on his own, but that they were likely to follow if some greater chieftain such as Abas Kupi or Muharrem Bairaktar gave the lead. We were impressed, too, by a suggestion of Ramadan Kalloshi's that we should call the Gheg leaders to a conference to settle the terms on which they would take up arms again. 'They'll give each other courage,' he had said, 'and with so many competing for Allied support, you'll get them all cheaper!' This seemed sound advice, and showed an instinctive grasp of political realities.

To a stranger, the Dibrans seemed soulless mercenaries. But this was to misjudge them. They had the same aims as other more enlightened polities; to keep their freedom and increase their wealth. And they had learned that these goals could only be attained by the exercise of power, eked out where power was lacking by diplomacy. What was different about them was that they were entirely uninhibited by any consideration of religion, morality, ideology, convention, or even superstition. They were solely concerned with the stark realities of power. This might not be very admirable but to see them at work was an education. I had been reading Professor Laski on our journey, but I now put his book away. Four days in Dibra had taught me more about the essentials of politics than all the books on constitutional theory and political economy I had ever read at Oxford.

We had heard much of Muharrem Bairaktar in Dibra, and so pressed on northwards to meet him. Muharrem was the Lord of Liuma, the high mountain country to the east of the Black Drin between Dibra and

Kukes, and was reputed worth more than 1,000 rifles. He had helped Zog to power but later had turned against him and gone into exile. After the Italian annexation he had come back to Liuma, but remained in his castle refusing all contact with the Italians. We had been in touch with him in 1940 from Belgrade; and in 1941 he had mobilised to support the rising attempted by Abas Kupi and Gani Kryeziu. Thereafter he had lain low, though we knew he had been in touch with Mihailovitch. When Italy collapsed Muharrem had raised his clan and captured Kukes. Kukes commands the vital bridges on the road from Prizren to Scutari and the Germans had sent a strong force to drive him out. Muharrem saw that resistance was hopeless and agreed to retire without fighting, on the condition that no German troops should enter Liuma. The Germans had kept to the agreement, and Muharrem had sheltered a British mission through the winter.

Our way to Liuma followed the eastern wall of the Drin gorges. The powerful river lay two thousand feet below us, narrowly compressed between smooth black cliffs, through which its deep and swirling waters ran a vivid blue. Beyond us, the jagged peaks towered into the sky. We followed a narrow path scratched in the face of the cliff above the river, and now and then passed little stone cairns beside it. Each marked the grave of some traveller who had fallen to a blood enemy, lying in wait. The dead were buried where they had been killed; for the path was too steep and the way too long to bring their bodies home.

At nightfall we came on a cluster of buildings, surrounded by a high crenellated wall. This was Muharrem's castle. Our guards called out and beat upon the gates; and, after an exchange of shouts with shadowy figures on the battlements, we were admitted to a wide courtyard. In front of us was a stone keep built on a rock; and, on the steps leading up to it, stood the Lord of Liuma, flanked by a bodyguard holding a torch of blazing pinewood. He led the way indoors to a room furnished with tables and upholstered chairs, the first I had seen in Albania.

Muharrem was of stocky build, dressed in a plain grey uniform with a lumberjack's leather cap on his head. He looked rather like photographs I had seen of Kaiser William with the same iron-grey hair and waxed moustache, loose mouth, and small piercing eyes. When at rest there was an almost abnormal concentration in his gaze, and sometimes a sly smile would cross his face, as if prompted by his inward thoughts. He was reserved of speech and his delivery rapid and jerky, but he had picked up a working knowledge of French and German; and we were spared the boredom of badly interpreted conversation.

The evening meal was served towards midnight in a separate dining room and was distinguished by excellent Turkish dishes and a coarse local red wine. We were waited on at table by Muharrem's two sons, who stood guard behind our chairs while we ate. Both were grown men, but treated their father with almost servile respect.

Muharrem laid before us his plans for raising the Gheg tribes against the Germans. He was not against the Communists. Indeed, he had sheltered some of them through the winter. But he was determined to prevent the establishment of a Communist régime in Albania, and assumed that we should feel the same way. The right course in his view was to build up a strong Albanian Nationalist Movement, which would attack the Germans and take over political power in the hour of victory. They would work with the Communists, but as senior partners.

To achieve all this, Muharrem asked us for arms and cash on a grand scale. But when we told him that our headquarters would not send him supplies until he had attacked the enemy, he said, with some plausibility: 'I have fought against the Italians and I intend to fight against the Germans. If you will send me arms I will fight when and where you tell me; if not, then I will choose my own time and place for action.'

Muharrem cherished great ambitions but he also wanted to work closely with other Nationalist leaders, like Abas Kupi. He took the initiative, indeed, in proposing that we should set out together to talk matters over with Gani Kryeziu in the Kossovo.

We were roused at first .ight and soon after sunrise rode out through the castle gate, still deep in the shadow of the eastern mountains. Muharrem was wrapped in a dark-blue cloak and sat a milk-white but frisky mule, caparisoned with a Kilim carpet of red and green design. Some forty well armed tribesmen marched in our train; big, bony fellows, dressed in brown jackets and close-fitting white breeches, braided with black.

We climbed all morning and, in the afternoon came out on to the grassy uplands of Teya, in parts still deep in snow. Teya is a plateau over eight thousand feet high, with stretches so broad and smooth that they might almost have made a landing-ground for aircraft. The day was cloudless and we turned aside from the path to scale a pyramid-shaped knoll for the view. All Albania was spread out at our feet, convulsed into a chaos of broken valleys and intersecting ranges. To the north the wavy, jagged chain of the Albanian Alps rose to its climax in the tooth-like, snow-covered peak of Shkelzen. Westwards, the rolling highlands of Mirdita ran down to the sea. To the east Korab towered immediately above us, shutting out any view of the Vardar valley; and in the south the snowy summit of Tomori hung above the haze.

We marched all that day and the next; and towards evening reached the crossing of the White Drin just east of Kukes. The ferry was moored some forty yards from the main road and Muharrem posted two machine-guns to protect our crossing. The ferry was a broad punt attached to an iron hawser slung across the river. It could carry ten men at a time and took a quarter of an hour to cross and return. Meanwhile, the rest of the men lay down in the long grass to wait. The first ferry load had just pushed off from the south bank when a German convoy thundered past, escorted by two armoured cars. Fortunately, they failed to see us, for, with our backs to the river, it would have been an uncomfortable fight. As it was, we crossed without incident and after an hour's climb spent the night in a wood alive with nightingales.

Another day's march brought us to the tall stone keep of Mehmet Ali, the Bairaktar of Hass, an excellent host but reputed the most prudent man in Albania. He had persistently refused to give the name of the friend who had sheltered him in the Balkan wars thirty years before.

'You never know,' he would say, 'when I may need to hide with his family again!'

Towards midnight the sudden barking of the watch-dogs warned us that strangers were at the gate. Mehmet Ali went out to meet them and presently returned, ushering two men into the room. The first was Said Kryeziu, a sub-machine gun slung across his shoulder and two hand-grenades dangling from his belt. Prison had left its mark on him, and his face was thin and drawn. He shook hands gravely with the assembled company and was just murmuring some formal greeting to me when a flash of recognition crossed his face and we fell into each other's arms. He had no idea until that moment that I was in Albania.

Said brought us the best news since our landing. His brother, Gani, had just fought an engagement against a German patrol, the third in recent weeks. So at last we had found a Gheg leader who was fighting. Nor was this all; Gani had firmly refused to join the Communists, but he was on good terms with them and provided them in his district with shelter and food.

We were now on the edge of the Kossovo, a region where German influence was strong. We accordingly spent the day indoors and set out at nightfall with a hundred men to guard us. Our way led through fields and woods; and the level going seemed strange after long weeks of climbing in the mountains. Just before the dawn it grew very cold; then, as the sun rose, we entered a dense forest where we soon came on one of Gani's sentries who led us to where he was encamped. The hardships of internment had aged him but they had also given him strength, and there was now a more determined look in his eyes than I had seen in Belgrade.

With Gani were representatives of the *Kosmet Partisans*,[1] a Com-

---

[1] *Kosmet* was an abbreviation for Kossovo and Metohya, two provinces of Yugoslavia with a largely Albanian population.

munist group working with Tito, and a number of Moslem chiefs from Kossovo and the mountains to the west. Gani led us to the shade of a clump of trees where carpets had been spread for our conference. Said, who spoke perfect French, acted as interpreter. Meanwhile, the other chiefs rested around us in a semi-circle, listening. Our first instinct had been to bid them withdraw, that we might talk in privacy. But Said had dissuaded us from this, arguing that nothing would impress the chiefs so much as to see us reach agreement in public.

Gani told us of his recent fights with the Germans and stressed that only lack of arms and ammunition had stopped him from undertaking larger scale operations. He said his say, and then added: 'I have come to receive your orders.'

We answered along familiar lines that the time had now come for an all-out effort against the Germans. We congratulated him on his actions but stressed that we could only send him arms in proportion to the scale of the operations he undertook. He spoke of the advantages of building up a reserve of weapons before taking the offensive, but then said:

'Since first we worked together in 1940, I have regarded myself as a soldier of the Allies. You represent the Allied Commander-in-Chief, and I must obey your orders. I have told you my objections, now I will do my duty. In ten days from now we will attack the Germans wherever we can. Give me such help as you think right and send me a British officer, trained in sabotage. I promise you that he will have work enough!'

Such complete and unconditional agreement surpassed our wildest hopes and we at once arranged to attach one of our officers, Major Tony Simcox, to his forces. In return, Gani invited us to take his brother, Said, with us to help in our negotiations with Abas Kupi. 'Let him be the pledge of my good faith,' he said. He then addressed the assembled chiefs, explaining the terms of our agreement, and adding: 'I put my trust in Great Britain, but my efforts alone will not be enough. If Albania is to be saved, you must all play your part.' They shook their heads, a disconcerting gesture but one which, among Albanians, signified approval. We sensed, however, that they would wait and see how our alliance with Gani developed before taking up arms themselves.

Our meeting with Gani Kryeziu had taken us further north than we had at first intended. It was already 6 June, and we were due back at base next day for a meeting with Abas Kupi. To return by the way we had come would take perhaps ten days, but the only short cut—and this would take at least four days—lay through the wild highlands of Mirdita. This was the most primitive region in all Albania and firmly in the grip of Jon Marko Joni, still very much the ally of the Germans. Gani and Muharrem begged us not to attempt the crossing of Mirdita; but we judged that a decision was urgent in our relations with Abas Kupi and decided to take the risk.

We rested, through the morning and afternoon of 6 June, and set out at sunset with Said and Muharrem Bairaktar. The nights are short at this season, but we planned to cross both the Great Drin and the Scutari-Kukes road before dawn. The river was too deep and swift to ford, and there was no alternative but to cross by the ferry. This was guarded, however, by a gendarmerie post under a new commandant, and his attitude was still unknown to the local chieftains. Muharrem accordingly deployed his men so as to surround the gendarmes and if necessary overpower them. He then sent for the commandant and exhorted him as a patriotic Albanian to help our forces over the Drin. Intimidated by our array, and encouraged by a handful of gold, the commandant soon decided that his sympathies had always lain with the Allies. The necessary orders were issued to the ferryman; and within half an hour our forces were across the river.

An hour beyond the Drin our paths divided. Muharrem turned eastwards to go back to Liuma. The rest of us, now reduced to fifteen men, continued south, still hoping to reach the Kukes–Scutari road before it was light. But our parley with the gendarme officer had taken time; and the sun was already up when we crossed the motor road and entered the great beech forests of Mirdita. As we learned later, a German patrol caught sight of us as we crossed the road. Had they pursued us we must have been overtaken; for once in Mirdita we dropped to a leisurely climbing pace. Instead they sought to lay an ambush for us by taking a short cut; but the forests of Mirdita are dark and trackless and we passed like ships in the night.

We too soon lost our way in these forests and were forced to climb some five thousand feet to a rocky summit to take our bearings. We sat there for a time, but hunger, as well as prudence, led us to press on. Our ponies were by now too lame and galled to ride; and we had been marching seventeen hours, when towards three o'clock in the afternoon we reached the house of a certain Gyok Bairaktar, who had been recommended by Muharrem. Gyok, however, had fallen on evil times. His home was a wooden hut, divided into two rooms, one of which housed his goats and his womenfolk, while the other was kept for his guests, himself, and his sons. 'That's a funny sort of Bairaktar,' said Shaqir, our interpreter, 'he hasn't even got any trousers.'

Poor Gyok indeed was dressed in nothing but a dirty white shirt and long cotton drawers, having thriftily put away his one pair of breeches for the summer. He gave us a light meal of eggs and milk, for he had no flocks or cattle, and offered us a pinkish *raki* which I could scarcely stomach, even after the fatigues of the march.

More serious, we soon discovered that Gyok was very much a

liegeman of Jon Marko Joni and was certain to report our presence to him. We, accordingly, resumed our journey stiffened rather than refreshed by the halt, and after another five hours' march emerged from Mirdita and crawled painfully into a low stone fortress belonging to one of Abas Kupi's supporters. We had marched for twenty-two hours out of the previous twenty-four and were glad to relax among friends and sleep in safety.

We were now in *Zogist* country and the rest of our march was accomplished without incident and cheered by good news. On the way to Mati, we stopped by the side of the path to smoke and chat with a farmer returning from market. He spoke for some time of local politics and then added as an afterthought:

'They were saying, in the market, that Rome has fallen and that the English have landed in France.'

Our bodyguards greeted the news with wild shouts and fired their rifles into the air. The old man was embraced by all and sundry; and we left him sitting by the roadside, bewildered that anyone should be so excited by news of these distant events.

Twenty-four hours later we were back at our base camp where Abas Kupi and his leading supporters were already awaiting us. We had hoped, by this time, to have good news for him from our headquarters. But the telegrams from Bari were discouraging.

The Foreign Office were still considering whether to seek private instructions for Abas Kupi from King Zog, and were plainly hesitant to be committed to the King in any way. Pending a decision they advised us to 'keep the pot boiling', an operation, I ruefully reflected, which in politics, as in physics, leads to the eventual evaporation of the contents.

Abas Kupi's offer, however, to negotiate with Enver Hodja had been taken seriously in Bari; and Philip Leake, the head of the Albanian section, had dropped to *Partisan* headquarters to secure Hodja's agreement. In this he had failed. Hodja was adamant. He would not work with Abas Kupi. There was a telegram from Leake proposing that he and I should meet in the neighbourhood of Tirana to try and resolve the situation. But a little later in the file was another telegram reporting that Leake had been killed in a German air strike on *Partisan* headquarters.

Hodja's refusal to meet Abas Kupi convinced us that he would soon attack the *Zogists*. In the circumstances, Abas Kupi's best course was to attack the Germans before Enver Hodja attacked him. If he did this there was at least a chance that our headquarters would regard him as an ally and find ways of imposing a settlement between him and the Communists.

But, even with Said's powerful advocacy, it was not easy to persuade Abas Kupi of this. He had offered to meet Enver Hodja. We had failed to persuade Hodja to meet him. He had asked for a directive from his King. We had failed to get it. We now asked him to fight but refused to send him the arms he needed. His position, he felt, was honourable. Ours struck him as unreasonable.

All the same, he understood the danger of his situation, and, just as a cornered chess player tests every possible move, so he probed each of our arguments in turn. To attack the Communists was to break off relations with the British. To remain neutral was to expose himself to a Communist attack without hope of British support. To attack the Germans might seem to be the only course left open, but would the tribesmen follow? And if they did, had they enough rifles and ammunition to hold the field until the British sent supplies?

Our talks lasted two days; and on the morning of the second day we faced a complete deadlock. Abas Kupi even spoke of escorting us to the coast so that our headquarters could evacuate us to Italy. But in the end, wiser counsels prevailed. When he joined us again he said, 'Very well; you shall have action. Let Major Smiley come to me tomorrow and I will choose him a bridge. If he will bring the dynamite, I will provide the men. Then you can tell your headquarters that Abas Kupi is fighting again.'

Smiley who had been bored and depressed by 'all this politics' let out a whoop of joy at the prospect of 'blowing something up', and produced a bottle of cherry brandy to celebrate the occasion.

Abas Kupi was as good as his word. The target he chose for us was the bridge of Gyoles. This was one of the biggest bridges in Albania, on the main road from Scutari to Tirana and Durazzo. Its destruction would paralyse all German traffic through north Albania for several days and impede it for much longer.

Smiley, accordingly, set out with a picked *cheta* of a dozen *Zogists* and, after a hairbreadth escape from detection managed to pack charges of dynamite into the demolition chambers which the Germans, with typical thoroughness, had already prepared. The bridge was utterly destroyed; and it was six weeks before the Germans put up even a temporary wooden structure in its place. During these six weeks all traffic from Tirana and Durazzo to the north was diverted along a narrow dust track. This involved a detour of ten miles and became impassable every time it rained.

The destruction of the bridge at Gyoles meant that the *Zogists* had resumed active operations. We, accordingly, sat down again with Abas Kupi to settle the type and quality of supplies he would need for large-scale operations.

After two days' discussion we advised our Headquarters to supply him with enough mortars, bren-guns, heavy machine-guns, and anti-tank rifles to equip on an agreed scale, eight *chetas*, each of two hundred and fifty men. These were to form the shock troops of a revolt and the nucleus around which the tribes might gather.

Within three days our Headquarters accepted this proposal and told us that six aircraft loads of war material had been earmarked for Abas Kupi and were being held for him in the hangars in Brindisi.

Meanwhile, a letter reached us from Simcox, confirming that Gani Kryeziu was actively engaging the Germans and requesting supplies. These our Headquarters agreed to send.

We reckoned that Abas Kupi could mobilise between 5,000 and 10,000 rifles. Gani Kryeziu could raise at least 2,000 to 3,000. We were also convinced that once they saw that these two men enjoyed serious British support, Muharram Bairaktar and most of the other Gheg chiefs would also take up arms.

Their combined forces would total at least 15,000 at the start of a revolt, and with British support might well rise to 25,000 or more. They could harass German communications and isolate their garrisons; and it was by now very doubtful whether the Germans still had the energy or could spare the troops to suppress a revolt on this scale. In any case, the combined territories of the Gheg chiefs would provide an almost impenetrable 'safe harbour' where the non-combatants could withdraw with their flocks and moveable property beyond reach of reprisals.

With Abas Kupi and Said Kryeziu's agreement we accordingly summoned the Gheg chiefs to meet us in Lura, two days' march away. Our purpose was to proclaim a general rising, to set up a council to lead it and to determine a plan of action. Only Jon Marko Joni and Fikri Dine declined the invitation.

Thus by the end of June, there was every prospect that most of north Albania would soon be up in arms. The German retreat would be seriously threatened, perhaps paralysed. Moreover, by building up the authority of the Gheg leaders we should prevent a Communist takeover of the eastern shore of the Straits of Otranto.

38

Civil War

The mountains are a whispering gallery, and Enver Hodja soon learned that we had reached agreement with Abas Kupi and called a congress to raise the Gheg tribes in revolt. He saw in these things a direct challenge to himself and his movement. A Nationalist revolt supported by the British would defeat his aim of setting up a Communist régime after the Germans withdrew. He, therefore, decided to attack the Nationalists at once in the hope of defeating them before they could mobilise and receive British supplies on any scale. A civil war would allow the Germans to withdraw unmolested. But if he won it, Enver Hodja would also win the monopoly of post-war power.

Accordingly, Communist forces began to concentrate along the borders of the *Zogist* areas, and reports came in of sporadic clashes between *Zogist* and Communist patrols. We kept our Headquarters informed and stressed that civil war must disrupt our plans for a northern revolt. Their reply was short and robust. It stated categorically that Bari would cut off supplies to the Communists if they attacked the *Zogists*.

This was reassuring news and, despite the growing tension, we set out for the Lura Congress in a mood of cautious optimism. Abas Kupi had gone ahead of us; and after a two days' march we joined him at the appointed meeting place.

This was the glade of Zogolli—or the Birds—a strip of grassland not more than a hundred yards broad, but running for some miles through the Lura forests. The *Zogist* notables and several of the Dibran chiefs were already awaiting us. Fires had been lit, and the men were roasting whole sheep over the glowing embers. We sat down with Abas Kupi on a log near one of the fires; bottles of *raki* were produced; and, while the spits were turning, one of the older chiefs told stories.

We slept that night under the trees; but I was woken early by the sound of voices raised in heated discussion. Abas Kupi was already up and sitting among his chiefs dictating orders to a secretary. A few of the men still slept, but most of them milled around talking in little groups. I roused McLean and we walked over to where Abas Kupi was sitting. He told us that a courier had arrived an hour before with news that the Communists had attacked in strength and overrun his Headquarters. The Civil War had begun in earnest.

All through the morning more chiefs kept coming in mostly from the north. Muharrem Bairaktar rode in on his white mule with a strong body-guard of well-armed Liuman tribesmen. Even the mercenary Sherif Lita joined us, apparently convinced that we were now the winning side.

In the afternoon, we sat down for a formal discussion beneath a tall and spreading oak. The chiefs reiterated their determination to fight the Germans. But, plainly, they could not fight on two fronts, and there could be no general revolt unless Britain could restrain the Communists and bring about a truce. In mid debate a wireless message came in from our Headquarters. This told us that a Major Smith would be dropped to us that same night with proposals for ending the Civil War.

'The plot is just about ripe for a *deus ex machina*,' McLean remarked drily.

We told the leaders the news; and their spirits rose at the prospect of this dramatic, last-minute intervention. The meeting adjourned, and all decided to stay the night to hear what Smith had to propose.

We lit the signal fires at midnight, and in the moonlight, saw the aircraft almost as soon as we heard the drone of its engines. It circled once over the camp, then flew straight across the fires. Two parachutes opened and Smith and his wireless operator swung safely down to earth.

Smith proved to be a solid young man with a shock of fair hair and a jutting chin. His manner was brisk and he looked very boyish, dressed in shorts and a thick pullover. He had spent some months as a liaison officer with the Communist forces and claimed to be on good terms with most of the Communist leaders. His instructions were to propose an immediate armistice between the *Zogists* and the Communists, and to invite both sides to send delegates to confer with General Wilson in Italy. 'There,' so he said, 'we can knock their heads together and make them see sense.'

Smith was not very clear just how Enver Hodja would be brought to 'see sense', but brushed aside our suggestion that the Communists were acting only too sensibly from their own point of view. It all seemed a trifle amateurish, but Smith's instructions were confirmed in writing over the signature of Air-Marshal Elliot, and he told us that a similar conference had just brought about an armistice between the Nationalist and the Communist forces in Greece. We concluded, therefore, that our Head-quarters meant business.

Abas Kupi welcomed the idea of an armistice and at once accepted the invitation to meet the Communist leaders in Italy. He would go himself and take Said with him. We applauded this suggestion; for Said was a personal friend of many of the Communist leaders and genuinely anxious to come to terms with them. He was empowered, moreover, to represent his brother,

Gani, and Muharrem Bairaktar. Any agreement reached would thus cover the main centres of Resistance in north Albania.

Smith had secured Abas Kupi's assent to his proposals in less than half an hour, and had thus completed half his mission. The next step was to bring him safely to the Communists. But we thought it prudent that he should first have a talk with Hare at our base. Hare had been watching the fighting and would know best where to cross the lines. We, accordingly, set out with Smith towards our base while Abas Kupi and the other chiefs moved off to organise the defence of their territories.

As we crossed the Mati Valley we passed several groups of armed *Zogists* taking up defensive positions. Towards noon, we began to hear the sound of sporadic rifle fire. But it was still some way off, and we halted to bathe in the river. Another hour's walk brought us to the foot of the mountains, where we stopped for the midday meal and sent out spies to report on the course of the battle.

Sporadic rifle and machine-gun fire continued throughout the afternoon, and our spies returned with news that the Communists were not more than half an hour away. They put the Communist strength at between one and two thousand men, and seemed impressed by what they had seen of their British equipment. As yet there had been no serious engagement. The *Zogists* were still fighting a rear-guard action, while the Mati Chiefs concentrated their forces for a counter attack.

We now climbed into the mountains on the last stage of the journey to our base. The light was beginning to fail and looking back, we could see tall pillars of smoke, shot with flame, rising from the far side of the valley. We trained our glasses on them and saw that they were houses on fire. The Communists were burning down the strongholds of the Mati Chiefs.

As we sat watching the flames we speculated on what kind of reception we might expect from the Communists. At this point, Smith casually remarked that our Headquarters had accepted a proposal of Enver Hodja's that the Communists should take any British officers they might 'meet' in *Zogist* territory under their 'protection'. This was the first we had heard of this agreement and we cursed Smith roundly for his reticence. It meant, of course, that if we fell into Communist hands our Headquarters would be cut off from Abas Kupi and their efforts to end the Civil War would be gravely prejudiced.

Our base was less than two hours' march away, and for all we knew might already be occupied by the *Partisans*. We accordingly stopped in our tracks and sent a scout to reconnoitre the situation and ask Hare to join us if he was still free.

Our scout returned next morning and reported the Communists had overrun our base two days before. They had looted our stores, seized our wireless and marched off Hare and his wireless operator. They were also said to be sending out patrols to track us down. The poor man wept with indignation as he told his tale and finally burst out:

'But you don't yet know the worst. Your *Zogist* guards were disarmed and your officers led away by women!—By what they call anti-Fascist women!'

We now realised that the Communists had advanced along the Shupal and Mati valleys which ran roughly parallel. We were on the range of mountains between and, in effect, surrounded. We accordingly bade Smith farewell. He climbed on alone to find the Communists. We moved off into the forests in search of a 'hide-out' where we might set up our wireless and await the outcome of his efforts to secure an armistice.

All day we marched and counter-marched along the mountainside, searching for a gap in the Communist lines; but in vain. We spent a cold and hungry night on a wind-swept ridge; but, in the morning, came on a deep depression in the forest, sunk like a crater behind a projecting rib of the range. It was sheltered by trees and dense undergrowth and carpeted with fallen leaves, under which we found a spring of clear water. There was no sign that man or beast ever passed that way. There, for six days, we hid from our Communist allies.

Food was our first problem. We were a dozen strong and it is no easy task to keep a dozen men alive in a forest when every village is in hostile hands. Gold, however, corrodes most obstacles in time; and, after two days' fast, we won over a young shepherd who brought us a daily sheep from his father's flocks and an occasional loaf of bread or lump of cheese.

The sunless days passed slowly, enlivened only by the distant crackle of rifle fire, the stuttering of machine-guns and the histrionic bursts of mortar bombs. The nights were cold, especially in the hour before dawn.

There are few contrasts so sharp as those produced by the loss of power. So long as Abas Kupi had swayed the valley, the men of Mati had treated us as honoured guests. But now the Communists were the masters. They had burned down the homes of men who had befriended us. They denounced us in the villages as 'agents of foreign reaction'. They even talked of bringing us to trial before a court-martial. One day, they captured a young mule-man whom we had sent out to look for food, and beat him unmercifully to make him disclose our hideout. The youth refused to betray us and managed to escape from his guards. But this treatment of one of our men was a shock to the confidence of the others. In these depressing circumstances, we experienced all the dissolving influences of adversity. Food prices rose, the surest indication of our distress; and the price of a sheep jumped from one to four *napoléons*. Fear overtook our escort, and, skulking in the forest, their morale ebbed away. Couriers we sent out did not always return. One of our bodyguards deserted. Others refused duties assigned to them. The wonder is only that we were not betrayed.

All this time our main hope and interest was in Smith's progress. We followed this closely in the situation reports from our Headquarters. Smith had been well received by the Communists but none of their Commanders whom he met would take the responsibility of accepting an armistice. He was thus escorted from one headquarters to another until finally he was brought to Enver Hodja at Berat in the south. On the sixth day of our sojourn in the forest, we learned that Enver Hodja had rejected out of hand all proposals for an armistice or for negotiations with Abas Kupi.

The Smith mission had clearly failed, and there was no chance now of an early cease fire. We, accordingly, made up our minds to escape from a dangerous and uncomfortable isolation in which we could neither influence events nor even observe them.

But to escape from the forest was no easy matter seeing that we were surrounded on all sides. In the end, we decided to divide our forces. McLean would stay in our hideout with the wireless set. Smiley would try to escape to the north to join one of our missions on the other side of the Mati. Said and I would try to join Abas Kupi near Kruya.

We accordingly slipped out of our hideout accompanied each by a single bodyguard, and halted an hour before sunset, judging that the front line was near. We sent a scout ahead to reconnoitre the Communist positions and rested meanwhile in a meadow full of wild strawberries.

Our scout returned at nightfall and reported that he had found what seemed to be a gap in the Communist lines. The night was black as pitch. There was no path and the ground was in places impassable for our horses and forced us to make lengthy detours. By daylight, however, we were well clear of the Communist positions and a few hours later came on a *Zogist* patrol. They led us to Abas Kupi who was encamped with a force of about 1,000 men. In the distance we could hear the sound of rifle and machine-gun fire. The *Zogist* counter-offensive had begun that morning.

Despite the failure of the Smith mission, Abas Kupi's morale seemed high. He had mobilised 4,000 men in two days and was confident of driving the Communists out of Mati. But on one score he showed concern. He had reliable reports that arms had been dropped to the Communists in the Mati Valley while they had been engaged against his forces. I said this was impossible. Our Headquarters had given us the most categorical assurances that no arms would be dropped to either side so long as the Civil War continued. I promised, however, to make enquiries.

I now set out with Abas Kupi to observe the course of his counter-offensive. On the second day of the advance, however, I went down with a fever and so temporarily lost touch with his Headquarters. When I was fit to ride again I came on one of the *Zogist* leaders, Hamsa Drini, seated on the steps of a village mosque, arranging a distribution of bread to his troops.

I asked him for guides to Abas Kupi, and he offered to take me himself. We waited until it was dark, since the paths leading down to Mati were still under fire from the Communists, and then set out along a broken mountain track with a force of some three hundred men. An hour's trudge brought us to the main road, cut, for a stretch, along the face of a cliff and offering neither cover nor escape. We marched, I thought rather imprudently, at the head of the column. Hamsa was expatiating volubly on the future of Anglo-Russian relations, when suddenly a challenge rang out. He seemed not to hear it, and continued developing his argument. The sentry's voice sounded again. This time Hamsa stopped and, scratching his head, muttered: 'My God, I've forgotten the password!'

Almost at once there was a burst of sub-machine gun fire, at perhaps forty yards' range. We flattened ourselves on the road, or scrabbled vainly for protection against the cliff. Meanwhile a hail of bullets, some of them tracer, whined past our heads and ricochetted against the rocks. We guessed that the fire came from a *Zogist* patrol; but it was some minutes before we managed to identify ourselves. By a miracle only one man was wounded. The leader of the *Zogist* patrol now courteously reminded us of the password, and we were allowed to resume our march.

A man's courage varies with the nature as much as the extent of danger; and I noticed that night that some of our Albanian bodyguards who had literally turned grey with fear at the prospect of creeping through the Communist lines a few days before, remained perfectly calm in what, to me, seemed far more trying circumstances.

I reached Abas Kupi's headquarters towards midnight and found him just going to bed in a room crowded with sleeping *Zogist* chieftains, many of them lying half-naked in the stifling summer night. I slept soundly myself, though not for long. Soon after daybreak, I was roused by the rattle of machine-gun fire, punctuated by the occasional slap of a bullet against the stone wall of the house.

The guest-room was empty, and, going downstairs to investigate, I found an officer who took me round the *Zogist* positions and explained the situation. The *Zogist* forces were concentrated in the groves and orchards of Fshat, a village separated only by the breadth of the River Mati from Klos, another village where the Communists had their headquarters. Neither side was strong enough to attempt a frontal attack across the river. Instead, both had settled down to a quite useless long-range machine-gun duel.

I completed my inspection of the *Zogist* positions and then retired to await developments in a nearby orchard. There I feasted on red mulberries until spent shots, one of which wounded a fellow fruitpicker—the only casualty of the day—drove me to look for a safer resting place. I walked towards the river and, during a lull in the firing, came on Murad Basha, the

Zogist Chief-of-Staff, seated on a low mound. He was nursing an upset stomach and treated me to a lucid and comprehensive description of his symptoms and to a rather less coherent explanation of the *Zogist* fire-plan. This briefing was presently interrupted by the resumption of the machine-gun duel and the discovery that, though masked from the enemy by a clump of bushes, we were sitting in the direct line of fire.

I slept through the afternoon, and, waking towards six o'clock, found the rival machine-gunners still busy wasting ammunition. I went out again and in the garden found Abas Kupi, sitting cross-legged under a tree while a secretary read him letters and reports. He handed me a sheaf of German newspapers containing the official account of the attempt on Hitler's life. 'For me he has already been dead a long time,' was his only comment.

That night the Communists withdrew from Klos and by the following evening had evacuated the whole of Mati. Abas Kupi thus recovered the full extent of his territories. That night, his men lit beacons to announce the liberation of the valley and roasted sheep to celebrate their victory. Abas Kupi, however, had no illusions that he had won more than a breathing space, and while his men were still celebrating, he took me aside to urge that we should now renew our efforts to stop the Civil War. He had no intention he said of pursuing the Communists beyond his own borders and, in spite of their unprovoked attack, was still prepared to join hands with them to fight against the Germans. It was up to us to take advantage of his victory to persuade Enver Hodja to come to terms.

But at our Headquarters, the will to impose a settlement had wilted with the failure of the Smith mission. Pro-Communist sympathies were again in the ascendant and were fortified by appeals for arms from British liaison officers with the Communists, each of whom was naturally anxious to make a success of his mission. Unknown to us, and despite repeated assurances to the contrary, the Communists were again receiving regular supplies of arms from Italy. These had been dropped, among other units, to the Communist forces in Mati, who were thus reinforced with British weapons at the height of their operations against the *Zogists*.

No word of this important decision had reached us at the time, and it was only now, more than a fortnight after the event, and then only in reply to our own pressing enquiries, that our Headquarters admitted the facts. We protested vigorously that they had put us in a false position and asked for some explanation. Why had they gone back on their word and abandoned the policy of mediation so dramatically initiated by Smith? Their replies showed only too clearly that they had no settled plan but were drifting before events and Communist pressures. We decided, therefore, to make a last bid to save the situation by putting alternative but definite policies before them.

In a long telegram we urged them to stand by the Smith proposals, stressing that it was still possible to stop the Civil War if only they were prepared to put the necessary pressures on Enver Hodja. This would involve cutting off all supplies to the Communists and all propaganda in their favour. This, in our view, was the course best calculated to promote our military, as well as our political interests. But if this course was no longer acceptable, then we saw only one alternative. This was to evacuate Abas Kupi and other pro-Allied Nationalist leaders to Italy and to transfer our entire support to the Communists. We could not recommend such a policy since it meant handing over Albania to the Soviets. But it would put an end to the Civil War and enable us to cut our losses with the least dishonour.

In their reply, our Headquarters agreed that these alternatives were the only courses of action still open to us. The issues involved, however, were too big for them to settle and they were therefore referring our proposals to London for decision. This they warned might take some time.

Our position as a mission to the *Zogists* had now become acutely embarrassing. We could not explain away the fact that arms were again being dropped to the Communists. We could no longer claim that our Headquarters were working to end the Civil War. Nor could we, in reason, press Abas Kupi to attack the Germans when the Communists might attack him again at any moment. In the circumstances, we judged it wiser to withdraw from Abas Kupi's Headquarters, and to keep to ourselves until we had fresh instructions. We accordingly pitched a camp in a grove of olive trees. This stood on a broad ledge, some 2,000 ft. above sea level near the northern horn of the crescent of mountains which lies about Tirana. The approaches to the grove were steep and guarded by friendly villagers, while a cleft in the rocks above, tapering into a narrow 'chimney', offered a strenuous but secure line of retreat. Tirana itself was only three hours' march away and, from our camp, we commanded an uninterrupted view of the city and its airfield. On our first evening, we saw a German bomber crash in the take-off, to enrich the night with a glory of red and golden flame. We stayed in this camp for nearly a fortnight, and still there were no instructions from Headquarters.

In the early hours of 11 August, I felt a hand on my shoulder and woke to hear McLean saying: 'Tell me what you make of this: it sounds like trouble for someone.'

I propped myself up on my elbow and listened to the unmistakeable sound of firing on the mountainside below. Presently, we saw a spray of tracer bullets flash across a ravine barely an hour's climb away. The rattle of machine-guns and the occasional burst of a mortar bomb showed that this was no ordinary tribal feud. The Germans or the Communists must be attacking the *Zogist* garrison in the village below. Our mission might well be the objective of the attacking force and we judged it prudent to withdraw. We roused our guards; and in a few minutes the wireless equipment was loaded up and our mounts were saddled. Most of our pack-animals, however, had been sent down to the plain to graze, and we had to leave them behind with the bulk of our stores and kit.

We were on the run again; and once again our pursuers proved to be the Communists. We caught sight of their scouts that evening on the crest of the ridge above, but before they saw us, we hurried down towards the plain and marching along the bed of a shallow water course presently came to a small clearing in a wood made otherwise impenetrable by a dense growth of brambles and thorns.

As a camping-site, the place was wretched. The ground was swampy; and men and beasts soon turned it into a morass of black mud. The stagnant waters smelt foul and exuded a chilling ground mist at night. Clouds of malarial mosquitoes tormented our sleep; and McLean and I both found small scorpions in our clothes. This was no place to stay but we judged it a safe 'hideout' from the Communists on the mountains above and from the Germans in the plain below. We accordingly endured it for four days while we communicated with our Headquarters and determined our next move.

39

Tirana

Meanwhile, the war in the Balkans moved towards its climax. The Red Army was advancing into Rumania. Bucharest lay in the grip of a political crisis; and the leaders of Bulgaria prepared to abandon a lost cause.

In Albania, the Communists renewed the offensive against Abas Kupi and re-occupied the Mati Valley. This time, they came in strength and there could be no question of a *Zogist* counter-attack. Abas Kupi was thus deprived of half his territories and thrown back on to Kruya and the tangled range of low hills along the coast.

Fikri Dine had long hesitated between the Allies and the Germans. But when he learned that the Smith mission had failed and that the British had supplied the Communists during their attack on Abas Kupi, he came down on the German side and agreed to become Prime Minister. From this shaky vantage point, he tried hard to form an anti-Communist front with the *Ballists* and Abas Kupi. But Abas Kupi refused to commit himself; and Fikri knew well enough that the Germans were preparing to withdraw and would prove a broken reed.

All this time British policy towards Albania remained undecided and our Headquarters continued drifting before events. We pointed out that unless something was done the Germans would withdraw unimpeded through north Albania. They acknowledged the truth of this and said that they were still prepared to send Abas Kupi supplies in proportion to his actions. Presently, they also told us that though they had little confidence in Fikri Dine or the *Ballist* leaders, the British Government would reconsider its attitude towards these men, if they now joined Abas Kupi to attack the Germans.

This gave us some straw, though not much, with which to make bricks; and we accordingly left our stinking 'hideout' and headed north to find Abas Kupi.

We came on him in the foothills of Mount Kruya, and at once put our cards on the table. We had failed to secure a directive for him from Zog. We had failed to restrain the Communists from attacking him. Our interest, however, was still to harass the German retreat when it came. As his friends we could only advise that this was his best interest too. We were authorised to offer him arms in proportion to his actions; and action remained the only way in which he could still gain some influence with the Allies. It was true that he had lost half his territories and was much weaker than a month before. But Fikri Dine, the *Ballist* leaders and even Jon Marko Joni must now see that they had nothing to hope for from the Germans. The time had come for them to leave Tirana and rally to Abas Kupi. If they did so, he would still be at the head of a formidable guerrilla force.

This was bitter medicine for a man who regarded himself as Britain's friend. But he saw the strength of the argument and sent that night to Tirana to invite Fikri Dine to come and confer with him. Fikri came two days later bringing with him the Commander-in-Chief of the 'Collaborationist' Albanian Army, General Previsi. They were obviously attracted by Abas Kupi's proposal but wanted confirmation that it really had British backing. This was already waiting for them when they got back to Tirana.

After leaving Abas Kupi, McLean and I had pushed on through the night to Ihsan Toptani's farm, some ten miles from Tirana. Ihsan was a landowner and the head of one of the greatest families in Central Albania. He had always kept aloof from politics but his private sympathies were unreservedly pro-British and he had run considerable risks to rescue British officers left wounded or sick after the punitive operations of 1943. We had found him a wise and impartial adviser and he had acted more than once as our intermediary to frustrate German plans for strengthening the 'Collaborationist' régime in Tirana.

We reached Ihsan's house before dawn and looked forward eagerly to the unwonted comforts of real beds, clean sheets and hot baths. Before retiring, however, we asked Ihsan to try and arrange a meeting with Nureddin Vlora. Nureddin was a great landowner from the Valona area and one of the most respected men in Tirana. His pro-British sympathies were well-known but the Germans had nothing against him and, indeed, had sought to persuade him to take office as Prime Minister or Regent. Nureddin had kept us informed of these offers and had followed our advice in rejecting them. There could be no better intermediary with Fikri Dine and the *Ballist* leaders and no more understanding advocate of our cause.

Ihsan went into Tirana while we slept off the night's march but returned at lunch with disappointing news. The Germans had started a reign of terror in the capital. They had arrested a number of Albanians on the mere suspicion of favouring the Allies and shot some of them without trial. Nureddin did not want to attract attention by leaving Tirana at such a moment and suggested that we postpone our meeting until the 'terror' had subsided. We thought the situation too urgent for delay and, in view of the

German 'terror', judged that a dramatic gesture on our part was just what was needed to impress the leaders in Tirana.

If Nureddin could not come out to see us, then one of us must go into Tirana and see him. Ihsan agreed to make the necessary arrangements; and since McLean was too tall and fair to pass as an Albanian, we decided that I should go.

Next morning, I dressed in a grey suit of Ihsan's and so laid aside any claim to military status. I am dark enough to pass as an Albanian, but I had no identity papers and little fluency in the language. Ihsan, however, had not been challenged for his identity card for some weeks; so we decided to leave this problem to chance. As to language, we agreed that I should pose as a German if stopped by the Albanian gendarmes and as an Albanian if stopped by the Germans. Each of us besides 'packed' a gun and a bag of gold to buy or shoot our way out of any tight corners.

We left the farm towards ten in the morning in a carriage, driven by an old and trusted coachman of the Toptanis. With petrol rationing, horse-drawn vehicles had again become common in Tirana; and Ihsan considered that a carriage, although slower, would be less likely to attract attention than a car. We rumbled on over dusty country lanes, stopping once for Ihsan to greet some neighbours. He told them that I was a sick relation on the way to the doctor.

After an hour or so we joined the main road and drove along the edge of the airfield, littered with scrap heaps of twisted fuselages, blitzed by the R.A.F. Beyond the airfield we came to the 'check-point' marking the entrance to the city. The barrier was up and a group of Albanian gendarmes lounged and smoked in the sun some ten yards back from the road. Behind them through the window of a little wooden hut, I could see two German military policemen writing at a desk. Our coachman shouted a greeting to the gendarmes, and one of them beckoned us on with a lordly gesture. The two Germans looked up for a moment and then went back to their work. The coachman cracked his whip, and we rolled into Tirana.

Tirana was to us what Damascus had once been to Lawrence; the goal of all our efforts. We had imagined it in our dreams, scanned it through our field-glasses and made its capture the climax to which we strained. Now, at last, I had entered it, though in disguise and not in triumph.

The streets down which we drove from the 'check-point' were dirty, and presented the usual Balkan contrast of cheap modern structures, interspersed with hovels. Towards the centre of the city, however, the hovels ceased, and the buildings became more substantial. Presently we emerged into a broad and pleasing square which was the heart of the city. At one end of it stood a painted mosque with broad dome and slender minarets. At the other an ornamental clock-tower rose above a small public garden, flanked by open-air cafés and gay-looking shops. Beyond the city's heart was its head—a wide crescent of well-proportioned buildings of Italian design. These were the government offices; and, as we passed them, Ihsan pointed out the windows of the Council Chamber, whence Fikri Dine and his colleagues still issued their vain decrees. A few moments later the coachman pulled up in a narrow street at the entrance to Ihsan's Tirana home. Immediately opposite stood a German sentry on duty outside the Hotel Metropole. This was *Gestapo* Headquarters.

We went upstairs and were presently joined first by a friend of Ihsan, who knew that I was coming, and then by an agent of Abas Kupi who had recognised us as we drove into the town. They told us of the latest arrests made by the *Gestapo*, and also brought us a summary of an important speech by the Bulgarian Prime Minister foreshadowing the rupture of relations between Bulgaria and Germany. We sat talking for perhaps half an hour, and then climbed back into the carriage. We passed the ultra-modern Hotel Daiti, the centre of 'Collaborationist' intrigue, and then King Zog's palace, a tall, yellow building set in a wooded park. Beyond, we entered the smart residential quarter of the town. For some minutes our coachman followed a broad shady avenue and then, turning into a side road, pulled up outside a modern villa standing in a well-kept garden. I got down from the carriage and saw two armed German soldiers standing at the entrance. For a moment I feared a trap. But Ihsan quickly explained that they were only guarding the German Minister's residence. We were to lunch in the villa opposite.

This villa belonged to a friend of Nureddin, and we might well have been in France from the taste and style of its decoration. Our charming, French speaking hostess let us in herself, and we stayed talking while Ihsan and her husband went to fetch Nureddin. Suddenly, there was a knock at the door, and I was dismissed to the dining room while she went out to answer it. She was back in a few moments and told me with a smile that the visitor had been a young German attaché who had come to ask permission to retrieve the German Minister's dog from her garden.

Our host and Ihsan presently returned with Nureddin; and we sat down to an excellent lunch of delicious Turkish dishes, good Italian wine, and genuine Benedictine. Our hostess had given her maid the day off for greater safety, and served us herself.

Nureddin was resplendent in white ducks and a white silk bush shirt and seemed completely relaxed. He began by describing the extent of German demoralisation. Their strength was running down, their friends were deserting, and they were vainly trying to stop the rot by a reign of terror. They had shot the *Ballist* leader, Skender Mucho, without trial, but on the suspicion—so *Gestapo* headquarters had put it out—that he had been in touch with the British. Since then they had arrested some forty prominent *Ballists* and *Zogists* and deported them to the notorious concentration camp at Zemun, in Yugoslavia. Meanwhile, their relations with the Tirana Government were close to breakdown. They had no confidence in Fikri Dine and were withholding the arms and funds which they had promised him. They were haunted by the fear of revolt, and started even at their own shadows. Nor was there much loyalty among them. Indeed, the S.S. General Vistun, who had taken over command in Albania after the attempt on Hitler's life, had arrested several of his own officers on grounds of political unreliability.

Nureddin then turned to the prospect before Albania. The Communists already hung on the fringes of Tirana, and there was scarcely a night when they did not raid into its suburbs. Unless some other authority was created to take over the city when the Germans left, they would break in and, as he tactfully put it:

'I dread to think what may happen, for life in the mountains has made some of these boys rather rough.'

He went on to speak of the danger of violent revolution and the destruction of the 'cultured classes' which it would involve. As he saw it, the situation was desperate, and, unless the British could restrain the Communists, the Albanian Nationalists were politically doomed and most of them personally as well. He paused a moment and added:

'If there is anything we can still do to gain your help, tell me. You may be sure that I will do everything in my power to see that the Nationalist leaders follow your advice.'

I had been waiting for such an opening and answered:

'It is already the eleventh hour and I can promise you nothing. But if all of you will now turn on the Germans and attack them with all your forces, perhaps something can still be saved.'

The news from Rumania and Bulgaria underlined my argument and Nureddin only asked:

'To whom should we rally?'

'You will find us with Abas Kupi,' I answered; and he signified that he understood.

We were still talking when a middle-aged man of heavy build with close-cropped grey hair and vinous countenance came into the room. He greeted me in fluent, rather clipped English; and but for the suspicion of a foreign accent, I would have taken him for a retired cavalry colonel. This was Nureddin's brother, Jemaleddin Vlora Pasha, the last Albanian to bear the title. Jemaleddin had been a dignitary at the court of the Sultan and had married a daughter of the Khedive of Egypt. After the downfall of the Ottoman Empire he had lived for some years in Cairo, where he had known Lord Lloyd and other leading Englishmen. Unlike his brother, he played little part in politics, but he remembered the strong anti-Communist prejudice of his English friends and simply could not believe that we would ever abandon Albania to 'the Reds'. Revolution was spreading over the Balkans like a flood; kings, statesmen, and generals were engulfed in a common ruin; but, as the Communists hammered at the gates of Tirana, the last Pasha of Albania turned to me and said:

'You really must do something, my dear fellow, or we shall have a lot of trouble with these rotters in the mountains.'

From these conversations we walked back through Tirana towards Ihsan's flat. The sun shone, and the crowd in the streets reproduced all the contrasts of Albanian life. Ragged peasants in white caps and baggy breeches rubbed shoulders with smart, Italianised young officials. There were old-fashioned Balkan merchants, some still wearing the red *fez* of Turkish times; down-at-heel soldiers of the regular army; and *Ballist* irregulars, armed to the teeth and swathed in bandoliers.

Every now and then we passed small groups of German officers and soldiers, hurrying to their offices with bulging brief-cases, or strolling towards the shops and cafés. Boyish in their tropical kit, pestered by pedlars and jostled by the oriental throng, they reminded me irresistibly of British troops in the Middle East. It was a new and perhaps healthy experience to see an army of occupation from the native's point of view.

Ihsan had arranged for me to meet two other political leaders and I spent the next hour or so in his house, answering their questions and giving them advice. I then went out again to reconnoitre the *Wehrmacht, Luft-waffe,* and *Gestapo* headquarters. I wanted to check up on rumours that the Germans had begun to evacuate them, and also to find out how they were defended in case we should ever have a chance to seize Tirana. We were thus engaged when suddenly an open carriage pulled up beside us, and one of Abas Kupi's officers jumped out and shook me warmly by the hand. He, too, was on a reconnaissance mission and I trusted his discretion as well as his goodwill. But it was the second time I had been recognised that day, and an ominous reminder that Tirana was little more than a village.

By this time, the day's work was done, and there was nothing to be gained by prolonging our visit. We stopped to buy a filigree cigarette case as a souvenir and then returned to Ihsan's house to pick up the carriage. We drove back along the same dirty streets by which we had entered the city and reached the check-point half an hour before sunset. A convoy of some thirty trucks was waiting for the night when it could leave for Scutari without fear of attack by the R.A.F. A company or so of German soldiers sat smoking by the roadside. The gendarmes were checking the papers of two young Albanians driving a small car. One of them asked to see ours. But the other recognised Ihsan's coachman and waved us on with a friendly smile.

We returned from Ihsan's farm to find Abas Kupi concentrating his forces in the coastal range. His plan was to attack and take Durazzo, the second city of Albania. This was a bold design and clearly aimed at creating a bridgehead on the coast which the British could reinforce from Italy. Smiley went off with some of Abas Kupi's staff to reconnoitre the prospect. He concluded that Abas Kupi might capture Durazzo from its present garrison but could never hold it against a determined German counter-attack.

The Germans were sure to react vigorously; and unless the *Zogists* were reinforced by sea, they would be cut off from all hope of retreat and utterly destroyed. Everything turned, therefore, on the chances of British backing for the operation; and our Headquarters could hold out no hope of this. Abas Kupi was very reluctant to abandon an attack on Durazzo but, in the end, accepted our advice and agreed to concentrate instead on cutting the Tirana–Scutari road.

Nureddin Vlora, meanwhile, had seen Fikri Dine and the *Ballist* leaders; and told them of his talks with me. They decided to accept the advice I offered and to rally to Abas Kupi. On 28 August, Fikri Dine and General Previsi came out to the *Zogist* Headquarters. Their talks with Abas Kupi lasted through the night but before dawn the die was cast. They went back to Tirana and, at noon, next day Fikri Dine announced the resignation of his Government, declaring that his efforts to save Albania from Communism had been frustrated by the total absence of German support.

The Germans reacted sharply, but when they struck the birds had already flown. Fikri Dine was on his way to Dibra to raise the remnant of his supporters. General Previsi had left for Kurbenesh. The *Ballist* leaders went into hiding near Tirana and summoned their forces from the south. Muharrem Bairaktar mobilised the tribes of Liuma. Only Jon Marko Joni still hesitated to join Abas Kupi, but even he left Tirana to be among his own people.

The scene was thus set once more for a general rising of north Albania. Gani Kryeziu was in action in Kossovo and had already received some 'plane loads of supplies. On 1 September a first 'plane load was at last dropped to Abas Kupi. The other Northern Chiefs, except for Marko Joni, had all declared against the Germans and were mobilising. Between them, they could put at least twelve thousand rifles into the field.

Had the Nationalists and the Communists now joined hands, they might, with British supplies, and British officers trained in sabotage, have closed all the roads leading out of the country. The Germans would have had to abandon their heavy material and fight their way through the mountain passes on foot. It would have been a grim retreat; and beyond the Albanian border Tito's *Partisans* were waiting for them.

But Enver Hodja was no longer interested in destroying the Germans. His sole concern was to destroy the Nationalists. He showed this plainly enough when he learned that we had persuaded Abas Kupi to take the field again and brought Fikri Dine to desert the Germans. He sent, at once, for the British liaison officer at his headquarters and delivered an ultimatum demanding the immediate withdrawal of our mission. This stated that we were working with 'Abas Kupi and other traitors' and that he no longer regarded us as Allied officers but as 'agents of foreign re-action'. Unless we were withdrawn from Albania within five days, he would send out patrols to capture us and bring us to trial before a court-martial.

Our Headquarters naturally rejected this ultimatum. Yet it had a powerful effect on them. They were negotiating a formal military agreement with Enver Hodja, and, once this was confirmed, would become increasingly reluctant to do anything which might offend or upset him. But this was still some days off.

40

Into Battle

With Abas Kupi's help we had succeeded in penetrating the mind of the German Command. A young German officer, working in the Operations Bureau of the Corps Headquarters in Tirana, confided in an Albanian friend that he did not mean to trust his life to the hazards of a retreat through the Balkans. He wanted to stay in Albania and asked where he could hide. His friend was a *Zogist*, and, after devious negotiations, the German offered to supply us with full details of the German Order of Battle and with advance copies of all Operational Orders. In return he asked for a safe conduct, so that, when the Corps Headquarters were withdrawn, he might join our mission and be sent home as soon as the war was over. We accepted his terms at once, and for the next two months were able to inform our Headquarters and through them the R.A.F. of the intentions and daily movements of every company of German troops throughout Albania.

Among these troops were three battalions of Soviet soldiers, mostly Tajiks, Kazaks, and Uzbegs from Central Asia. They had either deserted to the Germans or been captured by them and then enlisted in the German Army for duties in occupied territories. One of these battalions was in the area of Cape Rodonit, north of Durazzo, and we sent them messages through a Turkish-speaking Albanian *hodja*, urging them to kill their German officers and come over to us.

On 3 September while we were at Abas Kupi's Headquarters, a *Zogist* patrol brought in two Tajik deserters. They told us that one company had already taken to the woods, and that the whole of their battalion was on the verge of mutiny. I left *Zogist* Headquarters at once with Abas Kupi's son, Petrit, and hurried towards Cape Rodonit. My plan was to round up the deserters, and organise them into a striking force under our Mission's command.

Our Zogist guides led me to a village where I stayed with a venerable *haji*[1]—the only one I met in Albania—whose living room was decorated with scrolls and crude lithographs brought back from the Pilgrimage. The deserters were said to be hiding in the forest nearby but it was past six

A Moslem who has performed the pilgrimage to Mecca.

o'clock in the evening before our scouts returned with four of their spokesmen.

They were dressed in German uniform but had torn off their regimental badges and demonstrated their hatred of the Germans in a fearsome pantomime.

They were gay, fiery people—horsemen from the Steppe and high-landers from the Pamir—and spoke a dialect of Persian. One of them, indeed, a youth called Achmet, might have stepped straight out of a Persian painting with his ruddy cheeks and thick arched eyebrows meeting over black almond-shaped eyes.

Language was our first difficulty, as their knowledge of Russian was almost as slender as my own. By dint, however, of patience, sign language, and the free interpolation of Albanian, Italian, Serbian and German words, we ended by making each other understood. The four were Tajiks from a Central Asian battalion consisting of one Tajik and three Kazak companies. They had been in touch with our Turkish speaking agent and the night before had killed their German officers and taken to the woods. They readily agreed to join us and, by next morning, I had some thirty Tajiks in my camp.

McLean and Smiley joined me in the evening with a force of a hundred and fifty *Zogists*, under the command of Ndue Palli, a Catholic chieftain and former Captain of Gendarmerie. We held a council of war, and decided to attack a German Battery Headquarters, the nearest worthwhile target.

We slept perhaps four hours, and then with a small bodyguard set out into the night to reconnoitre the German position. After an hour's march through the woods our guide turned aside from the path and led us uphill to a rounded summit tufted with a clump of trees. As the night faded out of the sky we saw that we were standing on a range of barren hills, running roughly north and south. Beyond us to the west, and perhaps two thousand yards away, ran another range parallel to our own, but lower and thickly wooded. The fold of ground between lay under a blanket of mist, through which gleamed a single light—the duty office of the enemy's camp. Taking advantage of the obscurity we now crawled some five hundred yards down-hill to a projecting knoll, where we crouched in the bracken and waited, chilled and cramped, to watch the Germans awake.

After what seemed an age the sun rose behind us and, as the mists parted, we saw that a road ran along the bottom between the two ranges. Beside the road, and perhaps four hundred feet below us, stood a wooden hut, where the solitary light still burned. Beyond, in the wooded hillside opposite, we presently made out three or four barracks or store-houses. As

yet, no-one stirred; but towards six o'clock a German soldier emerged
from the lighted hut and stamped up and down on the road, blowing on his
hands. Presently, he turned into the wood, and a few minutes later a bugle
sounded the *reveille*. This was the moment we had waited for in the hope
that the movements of the men as they went to work would reveal the
dispositions of the camp. We therefore searched the wood closely through
our glasses, and, as the soldiers woke up and set about their several
routines, we began to distinguish a number of camouflaged tents and dug-
outs which until then had escaped our notice.

At seven o'clock six lorries drove in from the south and were loaded up
from what we guessed to be a storehouse by a working party of Italians,
supervised by a German N.C.O. The drivers manoeuvred clumsily on the
narrow road, and once one of them backed his lorry into the ditch. His
angry shouts reached us on the hillside, but, with the help of the Italians,
his vehicle was presently righted; and by eight o'clock the convoy had
driven away.

Each of us drew a rough sketch of what he saw, and tried to count the
number of the enemy. This proved a harder task, for the soldiers were
continually disappearing and reappearing among the trees. Towards nine
o'clock the activity of the camp subsided; and we crawled back infinitely
slowly to the shelter of the clump of trees on the ridge above. There, with
the enemy positions still in full view, we sat down to concert our plan of
attack.

We decided to assemble our forces behind the eastern range two hours
before dark, and, to develop a pincer movement against the Battery Headquarters. McLean, with Petrit Kupi, Ndue Palli, and a hundred *Zogists*
would cross the bottom to the north of the German positions and approach
them from the flank. I would take our thirty Tajiks as the other arm of the
pincer and carry out a similar manoeuvre, but from the south. McLean
would start the attack with the Albanians and, once the Germans were
fully engaged, I was to fall on them from behind with the Tajiks. Smiley,
meanwhile, would remain on the eastern range with a reserve of some forty
Albanians and three machine-guns. With these he would keep the road
covered and try to cut off any retreat to the east. Finally a small group of
Albanians were to burn down a wooden bridge on the road, three kilometres from the camp, to prevent reinforcements from reaching the enemy.

We had planned to spend the day resting in preparation for the attack.
But Abas Kupi arrived unexpectedly to discuss his general plan of campaign. We were thus engaged when two of the Tajiks formed up to us and
complained that their N.C.O. or *Maréchal* as they called him had used them
badly when they were serving with the Germans. We sent them away,
saying that we would hear their complaints after our conference. They
saluted and marched off. But an hour or so later, while we were still

discussing plans, a shot rang out, and we heard the sound of rhythmic hand-clapping and of a song of triumph. An Albanian guard ran up shouting: *Ka Vdek, Ka Vdek*—'There is killing'—and, hurrying to the camp, we found the Tajiks standing in a ring, singing and clapping their hands while the handsome Achmet danced a dance of victory round the corpse of the murdered *Maréchal*. As a ballet it was splendid, but as discipline? and here I saw Sergeant Jones look meaningly at Sergeant Jenkins; for N.C.Os are also an international fraternity. Our own reaction was simple. It was useless to investigate the murder. What mattered was to commit the Tajiks to the discipline of fighting before they got into the habit of taking the law into their own hands. If we had not already planned an attack for that evening, we should have had to improvise one.

In the morning I had agreed with a light heart to take command of the Tajiks but, as we marched off to the attack, I was oppressed by sombre reflections. I knew nothing of their training or their ways, and had besides so little common language with them that I could only hope to give the simplest orders. Then there suddenly came back to me a fragment from a long-forgotten conversation with John Marriott,[1] who had then commanded an Indian brigade.

'It doesn't matter what you say to native troops,' he had told me, 'because they won't understand you. What matters is what you do. March in front of them and they'll do whatever you do; and if you don't run away, they'll be as good as the Guards.' I had been in Cairo at the time, ill with jaundice, and had forgotten his words with the next glass of medicine. Now, by some trick of memory, the sick-bed talk became a counsel of action. I went, therefore, to the head of the column, though with some apprehension. The danger from the Germans in front was part of the day's work. My worry was about my own men. The Tajiks had probably killed their Soviet officers to desert to the Germans. They had killed their German officers to desert to us; only that morning they had murdered their N.C.O. As we moved forward, I reflected that I was now their officer and had to steel myself not to look back too often over my shoulder.

We crossed the low ground, where a tongue of woodland stretched out from the western range, and, hurrying over the road leading to the camp, climbed on to the crest of the range behind it. There I turned northwards, and, devoutly hoping that the Germans were off their guard, moved silently towards them through the trees. Presently we came to a low thorn fence, broken only by a stile. On the far side was a clearing perhaps fifty yards wide. Beyond, the woods sloped steeply down to the camp itself. I decided that we should cross the clearing and lie up in the fringes of the wood beyond until McLean should start to attack.

[1] General Sir John Marriott, Scots Guards and later G.O.C. London District.

I led the way, therefore, over the stile and had gone perhaps ten yards beyond it when a machine-gun opened up on me from a clump of trees some forty yards away. I looked round to see how many of the Tajiks were already across the fence, and, as I turned my head, somehow lost my balance and fell down. I thought at first that I had only slipped. In fact a bullet had nicked me under the chin. The wound was little worse than a deep shaving cut, and caused me neither pain nor serious loss of blood. But it had thrown me to the ground.

When the Tajiks saw me fall, they ran back; and I lay in the clearing alone. The machine-gun was silent, the gunner taking me perhaps for dead. I waited a moment, then jumped to my feet and ran for the fence. The German opened up again, and bullets hissed round me, like furious hornets, as I vaulted the stile and made for the shelter of the trees. The Tajiks rallied when they saw me safe and, gathering round me, opened a blind and ragged fire in the direction of the machine-gun.

I checked them, as soon as I had recovered my breath and my wits, and, more by instinct than by reasoning, worked my way round the flank of the machine-gun post. When I judged that we were well past it, I lay down, and while the Tajiks got into position, tried to decide what to do next. It is sometimes a weakness to see things from the other man's point of view; but, as I imagined myself among the German defenders, I knew they were beaten. After months of inactivity they had been startled from rest, perhaps from sleep, by our approach. Their machine-gunner had seen a few Turkoman deserters, but, in the darkness of the wood, he could not possibly tell how many or where the attack would come from next. The alarm had been given, but while the Germans would soon recover from the initial confusion, they might collapse altogether if I pressed home the attack. I therefore decided not to wait for McLean's signal but to go in at once.

For a few seconds I racked my brain for orders which the men would understand. Then, on a sudden inspiration, I stood up, and hoisting my astrakhan cap on the muzzle of my sub-machine gun, ran forward shouting 'Hurrah'. The Tajiks understood and, fanning out on either side of me, charged through the trees, shoulders hunched and eyes glinting. The machine-gunners fled; we dropped over the crest of the ridge, and saw the huts and dug-outs of the enemy less than fifty feet below. I shouted 'Hurrah' again; and the Tajiks bounded down the hill like wolves, letting out blood-curdling yells and pouring a blind but withering fire into the camp. As we carried the first buildings I saw a German standing twenty yards from me, stripped to the waist, with a *Schmeizer* pistol in his hand. For a moment we looked at each other without moving, and I wondered which of us would shoot first. Suddenly he crumpled to the ground, pressing his hands to his naked stomach. I had not heard the shot, but

looked round to see Achmet standing just behind me grinning from ear to
ear. We pressed forward, and, as I passed the dying German, I noticed that
he was still a boy, with straight, fair hair and blue, staring eyes. His hands
were clasped over his wound as if in prayer, and the blood was oozing
quietly away through his fingers. Looking back a moment later, I saw
another of the Tajiks stripping off his boots.

The Germans now returned a ragged fire; but we had taken them by
surprise; and they could not see us clearly for the trees. Several were shot
down; and, as we came to close quarters, the rest broke and fled towards
the road. There they ran into Smiley's machine-guns and were driven back
leaving more casualties. We were by now masters of their camp; and the
survivors fled along the range towards the south.

McLean and the Albanians had arrived on the scene just as we had
gone in to the assault and at once advanced to join in the attack. The first
dead German, indeed, had fallen to Petrit Kupi's rifle. But, somehow, the
main body of Albanians failed to follow; and, when we took the camp,
only McLean, Petrit and three of their bodyguards were with us. The rest
of the *Zogist* forces now surrounded us, and, not realising that the Germans
had fled, poured volley after volley into the camp. Nothing could stop
them; and the victorious Tajiks were forced to take cover from their
Albanian allies in the German slit trenches and dug-outs. All attempts to
make ourselves heard above the firing failed; McLean and I sat behind a
clump of trees and despondently surveyed the battle-field. A few yards
away a Tajik was dying in the arms of one of his comrades. Several dead
Germans lay outside the tents and huts; and a group of Italian prisoners
huddled behind a heap of rubble under a Tajik's watchful eye. Spent shots
whined around us, and it was beginning to grow dark. I felt suddenly tired
and intolerably thirsty.

After half an hour Petrit somehow managed to persuade the *Zogists* to
cease fire. Night had already fallen, and it was too dark to plunder the
camp systematically. We told the men, therefore, to take away such
supplies as they could carry and retired across the road and up towards
the eastern range. There we found Smiley and Ndue Palli, who produced
a most welcome flask of *raki*. We sat down to enjoy it, and were discussing
the next move, when suddenly a flare burst in the sky above us, casting a
lurid metallic light over the hillside. A moment later two mortar bombs
fell quite close, followed by a burst of tracer bullets. German reinforcements had arrived; but we could not judge their strength and, having
secured our objective, we withdrew to the range, and trekked back to the
village of Kurat where we had encamped.

We had at last drawn blood; and a *Zogist* officer with a Tajik lay among
the dead to show the Germans who had been their enemies. Most of the
German garrison had been killed or seriously wounded and we had

captured twelve Italians. One Tajik and one Albanian had also been wounded. The honours of the day went to the Tajiks; and, now that we had seen them in action, we felt convinced of their military qualities, and confident of their loyalty. The Albanians had made a poorer showing but the fight had raised their spirits; and that evening both Petrit Kupi and Ndue Palli eagerly discussed plans for the next attack.

We went early to bed; but, while it was still night, I was startled from a fathomless sleep by the wail and burst of a mortar bomb. It was 3.0 a.m. The guest-room was already empty, save for Kolaver, who sat cross-legged in a corner watching over me.

'That was already the third bomb,' he said with a smile. 'It is good to sleep so soundly.'

I dressed hurriedly, and, going out to where the Tajiks were encamped, found McLean and Smiley walking up and down in the moonlight. They reckoned that the Germans would counter-attack at first light and were discussing whether to resist or to retire. Kurat stood on high ground and the Tajiks had already taken up defensive positions. The village elders, however, feared that a battle must lead to savage reprisals from the Germans and begged us to go. Petrit tried to give them courage, but in vain. We accordingly struck camp, and retired into the hills. Our discretion, however, did not save the village; and, looking back an hour later, we saw several houses on fire. Ndue Palli pointed towards them and said quietly:

'That is the price of the Germans we killed yesterday. Was it worth it? For us, perhaps; but hardly for the poor farmers who are paying it.'

As yet only one Tajik company had come over to us. The Tajiks, however, were convinced that the three Kazak companies in their battalion were also ripe for revolt. Accordingly, while McLean and Smiley went off to join Abas Kupi, I stayed behind in the hills to try to organise this additional subversion. I had Achmet dress in Albanian clothes and sent him to stir up the nearest Kazak company to kill their officers and join the Tajiks. He fulfilled his mission with conspicuous success. Two days later I was awakened by my bodyguards who led in a group of small Mongol looking men in German uniforms. Their leader knelt down before me and untied a big green handkerchief which he spread out on the ground. In it were six ears. 'Our German officers,' he said, and smiling, drew a finger across his throat.

After the mutiny of the Kazaks, the Germans disarmed the other Central Asian battalions in Albania and rounded up a number of the deserters. We succeeded, however, in forming a striking force about a hundred strong, organised into three squadrons, one of Tajiks and two of

Kazaks. They came to us fully armed and equipped; and the Tajiks brought with them two light machine-guns.

Since schooldays I had felt the lure of Central Asia, pored over the exploits of Genghiz Khan and Tamerlane, and dreamed of the glories of Samarkand and Bokhara. McLean shared this romanticism; and now, by a freak of war, the day-dreams of boyhood came true and we rode at the head of a Turkoman horde.

Sometimes at night, when they gathered round their fires to roast or boil their evening sheep, the Turkomans would sing and dance for us. At first they sang shyly and only Red Army marching songs. Later, when they came to trust us, they threw off the mask and sang their own songs and danced their own dances. The Kazaks made the best choir with sad laments of the steppe which sounded both of Asia and of Europe. There was also an Uzbeg among them; an ugly fellow, but perhaps the best singer of them all. Uzbeg songs were like Turkish, but simpler, with the crystal purity of a mountain stream. Tajik songs had a wild gaiety; and the Tajik highlanders from the Pamir were the best dancers, with their whirling reels and triumphant sword-dances. It was *Prince Igor* with the Kruya mountains for a backcloth, and lit only by the campfires and the moon.

41

War on Two Fronts

While we were organising our Central Asian striking force, Abas Kupi had concentrated his forces in the Kruya area and surrounded the city which was still defended by a German garrison. He had intelligence that the garrison was being run down and was preparing to attack and overpower the remnant. But, on the same day as I joined McLean and Smiley at his Headquarters, the Communists crossed the Skanderbeg range and attacked the *Zogist* forces on Mount Kruya in strength. Abas Kupi had accordingly marched off with the bulk of his forces to defend his home base.

All day long a battle raged on the face of the mountain; and, looking out across the plain, we could see the little white puffs of smoke which flowered where the shells were falling. The mountainside was too far away for us to follow the fortunes of the battle, but towards evening Petrit showed us a large building burning on the outskirts of Kruya. It was his father's house. More than five years had passed since Abas Kupi had crossed its threshold, and now on the eve of the liberation for which he had fought since Good Friday of 1939, Britain's Communist 'friends' were burning down his home.

Darkness brought no peace to the combatants, and for a long time we watched the blaze of burning houses, the flash of the guns, and the sprays of tracer bullets. At last the noise of battle died away, and later in the night a courier came with news that *Zogists* and Communists had joined forces and captured Kruya from the Germans. The news caused a great stir in our camp. But the morning showed that the report was false. Abas Kupi had, indeed, wiped out a German patrol which threatened his communications; but this had been only an incident in the day's fighting. The real battle had been between *Zogists* and Communists with the Germans looking on, as amused spectators, from the ramparts of Kruya citadel. The struggle had been bitter; but the Communists held the higher ground and in the end had driven the *Zogists* down to the plain where they had no protection from a German attack. Abas Kupi had thus lost his home base, and, under cover of night, had withdrawn his forces across the plain to Preza.

Preza was a rich and scattered village, boasting two white-washed mosques with stocky minarets and several solid houses attractively painted in pink, green or brown. It was perched right on the edge of an escarpment, fifteen hundred feet sheer above the plain, and looking down on the main Tirana–Scutari road. The accustomed calm of village life was broken by the arrival of some three thousand guerrillas, and the best houses were commandeered by the chiefs and their bodyguards. The villagers, however, did not grumble; and Abas Kupi preserved their natural *Zogist* sympathies by paying for his wants in hard cash. A wooden house, painted dark green, had been reserved for our mission.

We were joined in Preza by Midhat Frasheri and Abas Ermenye, the political and military leaders of the *Balli Kombetar*. Midhat came on a mule; Abas Ermenye rode a coal-black charger, and, in his blue-green uniform and flat, old-fashioned *képi*, looked like a hero from the Carlist wars or the Risorgimento. They had come to tell us that the *Ballist* central committee was now in the mountains, and that they had decided to begin operations against the Germans next day. Abas Ermenye planned to open his campaign with an ambush on the Tirana–Scutari road, and asked for a British officer to watch the conduct of his men, and certify the results of the action. We agreed at once.

Abas Ermenye duly laid his ambush, and with a force of two hundred men, surprised a German convoy of forty trucks. Three trucks were burned out, eighteen damaged and looted; eight motor cycles were destroyed and more than thirty Germans killed.

Abas Kupi's position was now precarious but he showed no signs of despair and eagerly discussed his requirements of arms and ammunition and our plans for cutting the road. The *Zogist* forces were still resting from their defeat in Kruya but he called for a few volunteers and these went off with Sergeant Jenkins and sowed mines on the road, destroying three German trucks. On the next evening, Smiley, with a mixed force of *Zogists* and Tajiks, blew up a bridge on the road, forcing a strong enemy convoy escorted by armoured cars to turn back to Tirana.

The Germans knew, of course, that we were in Preza, but the village was impregnable from the road, and to attack it from the rear would involve at least two battalions. Their communications with Scutari, however, had now been cut for three successive nights; and they could no longer ignore an enemy who was effectively blocking their retreat. General Vistun, accordingly, gave orders for our expulsion from the escarpment; and, on the morning of 12 September, our spy in his Operations Bureau warned us to expect a punitive expedition within forty-eight hours.

Guerrillas are not trained to hold prepared positions, and there could be no question of defending Preza against a German attack. Retreat was inevitable. But where should we go? The main *Zogist* areas of Mati and Kruya were already lost to the Communists. The coastal hills were still

loyal to Abas Kupi but if we retired into them we could no longer attack
the road and should cut ourselves off from the north. Abas Kupi now took
a brave but desperate step. He decided to march north, to Kurbenesh, a
Catholic region bordering on Mirdita where General Previsi's influence
would assure him the support of the local population. From Kurbenesh he
could keep up his attacks on the Tirana–Scutari road. Kurbenesh, moreover, marched with Mirdita; and the Agha hoped that with British
support he might still rally the Northern chiefs around him, and make
Kurbenesh a new centre of Nationalist resistance. But to abandon his
regions was a council of despair, and only three hundred *Zogists* and a
hundred and fifty *Ballists* agreed to follow. The remainder retired into the
coastal hills or melted away to their homes.

We, accordingly, struck camp and headed north; a rabble army of
Zogist tribesmen, *Ballist* irregulars, and Turkoman deserters. Abas Kupi
led the van at a good round pace, with McLean and myself close behind
him, while Abas Ermenye on his black charger caracoled up and down the
column in a cloud of dust. At nightfall, Abas Kupi called a halt in a field
close to the main road. There the leaders gathered round him to plan an
ambush, while, contrary to the best military practice, the men puffed away
contentedly at their cigarettes—five hundred glowing points of fire less
than five hundred yards from the road. No-one seemed to know the region,
and no reconnaissance was attempted. But at last, when everyone had said
his say, Abas Kupi set off towards the road with McLean and myself
following.

Our path ran through a narrow stretch of woodland, and we somehow
became separated from the main body, remaining with only ten men.
Suddenly, we heard the noise of vehicles just ahead. McLean cursed our
unpreparedness. But Abas Kupi's blood was up. Regardless of the fact
that we were almost alone, he ran nimbly forward as if intending to engage
the convoy single-handed. I feared a tragedy, and was greatly relieved to
see the last truck thunder by just as we broke out of the undergrowth.

A few minutes later the main body caught up with us, and, for nearly
half an hour the men milled around on the road, while the leaders discussed
where best to lay the ambush. At last a decision was reached, and the
guerrillas took up positions along a steep-banked S-bend in the road, with
orders to attack the first strong convoy that should pass.

Half an hour must have gone by, when we became aware of lights
moving towards us from the direction of Tirana. There was a succession of
metallic clicks as each man slipped a cartridge into the breech of his rifle.
But we soon saw that only two vehicles were approaching; and Abas Kupi
decided that so small a target was not worth attacking. The order not to
fire was passed down the line; and, a few minutes later, the Germans drove
by, unconscious of the danger they so closely shaved.

I now lay down with my back to a tree, prepared for an indefinite wait. But it was not long before reflections on the northern horizon announced that something more substantial was moving along the road from Scutari. We strained into the darkness and suddenly caught a glimpse of the white glare of headlights, still several miles away. This disappeared almost at once, but presently came into sight again on a straight stretch of road. We counted and recounted the lights anxiously. It was a convoy of nine trucks. This time Abas Kupi gave the order to attack, and the men crawled into position, grinning nervously at each other. For a long time we saw only the headlights, but presently we began to hear the throb of the engines and the rumble of the wheels which grew to a roar as the convoy turned into the S-bend.

The guerrillas held their fire until all the trucks were inside the trap. Then, at a given signal, they discharged all their bullets into the leading truck. It swerved, skidded, and, as the bullets crunched up the windscreen, jolted to rest, blocking the road. With a screech of brakes, each driver pulled up in turn, his truck floodlit in the headlights of the one behind. For a split second there was silence; and then all hell was let loose as machine-guns, rifles, and hand-grenades tore the life out of the convoy. Blinded by their own headlights and puzzled by the surrounding darkness, the Germans were doomed from the start. A few tried to shoot back but they could not see us in the dark; and, in less than a quarter of an hour, the convoy was silent. For some minutes longer the guerrillas worried only the dead. Then the shooting stuttered to a stop and one by one the Albanians stepped on to the road. At first they moved cautiously, but soon closed round the trucks, seeing that the massacre was complete.

There were only two survivors. One was a trooper whom we took prisoner; the other a young Austrian lieutenant. He was too badly wounded to move, and we left him by the roadside to tell the tale if he should live till morning. Meanwhile, the guerrillas fell upon the trucks to loot their contents and to rob the corpses. In twenty minutes the whole convoy was picked clean, and each truck was set on fire.

'It's just bloody murder,' said Jenkins as we turned into the hills.

By good luck one of our victims had been a courier, and we captured intact the 'bag' from Divisional Headquarters in Scutari to the Corps Commander in Tirana. This gave us the names of Albanians spying for the Germans on Gani Kryeziu and Muharrem Bairaktar. It also enabled us to check the reliability of our spy in the Corps Headquarters. But what interested us most were two appreciations of the guerrilla problem. These showed clearly that Abas Kupi had never reached any accommodation with the Germans. They presented him, along with Gani Kryeziu and Muharrem Bairaktar, as an inveterate enemy and a serious threat to their retreat. The tone of the appreciations showed that the Germans were

losing their nerve; and we derived considerable amusement from the
Machiavellian designs and almost Satanic influence which they attributed
to our Mission. If nothing else, we had at least been a bogy to the German
Staff.

Our next attempt to cut the road was less successful. We set out towards
evening with a mixed force of some two hundred *Ballists* and *Zogists* and
some fifty Turkomans to lay an ambush at a point where the road curved
sharply to avoid a wooded spur of the mountain. McLean took up position
on the spur itself with the main body of Albanians, while I advanced down
it towards the road with the Turkomans and some thirty *Zogists* under
Petrit. We were moving in single file along a narrow track when suddenly I
saw a light fifty yards ahead and heard voices talking in German. They
were just to the south of the bend. We therefore left the path and moved
down to the road just north of the bend. We then sent two Albanians to
creep up to the corner and see how strong the Germans were. A few
moments later our two scouts ran back and reported that there were two
armoured cars and a group of soldiers seventy yards away. I at once
suggested that we should withdraw on to the spur and join up with McLean
to attack them. Petrit agreed but some of his lieutenants began to argue
and a heated debate began in the middle of the road. Suddenly I saw a dark
shape nose round the corner. I leapt into the undergrowth; and in the same
second the armoured car opened fire. It pulled up where we had stood and
raked the hillside with its guns while I lay in a hollow with the Turkomans
scarcely ten yards away. The Albanians scattered in all directions, and we
too ran back to the shelter of the trees in the first lull in the firing. Meanwhile, from round the bend the German troops loosed off their mortars
blindly into the night. They must have had warning of our plans to lay an
ambush and had prepared a counter-ambush for us. Luckily, we had
sprung their trap, but in the process our own plans had been foiled. By a
miracle we suffered no casualities, though McLean had a narrow escape
on the return march. His bodyguard dropped a loaded sub-machine gun.
It went off; and a bullet ricochetting from a rock grazed his cheek just
below the eye.
      Smiley, meanwhile, had been away with a few guards to ambush
another reach of the road. At first all went well. Then came news that the
Communists were approaching. His bodyguards deserted, making off with
his mule and all his kit, leaving him only the shirt and trousers in which he
stood. The villagers had everywhere refused him shelter and even guides,
explaining that the Communists had announced that they would shoot 'the
rebel English' with Abas Kupi, and any Albanians who should shelter
them.

The same evening that Smiley returned we received warning that
Communist patrols had been seen only an hour away. We accordingly
resumed our retreat northward halting after a day's march at a poor and
straggling village called Malibardhe set on a bluff above a sea of undulating,
wooded hills. There we were received by the headman of the village, a
fierce old mountaineer whose only son had been killed in an R.A.F. raid.
The tradition of hospitality, however, proved stronger than a father's
resentment. He feasted us on sucking pig and grapes; and placed his house
at our disposal. There we were presently joined by Abas Kupi. He was
accompanied by the Central Committee of the *Balli Kombetar* and by
Fikri Dine and General Previsi.

Fikri was stocky and dark, with grey, rather lifeless eyes and a greedy
mouth. He looked tough; his speech was blunt; his manner arrogant,
though redeemed by a sense of humour. He sought neither to explain nor
to excuse his 'collaboration' with the enemy. He had tried, he said, to use
the Germans. In fact, he admitted wryly, they had used him. His only
comment on British policy came close to the mark. 'I know,' he said, 'that
you English have an interest in our country because we have a sea coast
and you are a sea power. Many of us count on that; but I have learnt from
bitter experience that, in politics, little interests are often sacrificed to
greater ones.'

General Previsi, the Commander-in-Chief of the Albanian Army, was a
dark, rather weak-faced man, and wore a blue-green field uniform with
red facings and highly polished riding-boots. We thought him a comic
opera general, but he would prove himself a loyal friend and would show
great dignity in defeat.

The *Zogist* forces and their various allies had been in action for a fortnight, and Abas Kupi waited with growing concern for the aircraft which
should bring him supplies from Italy. So far he had received only one of the
six aircraft loads of arms and ammunition our Headquarters had promised.
His war-chest was empty. His men were down to their last cartridge and his
geographical room for manoeuvre was now closely confined. With the
Ballist leaders and Fikri Dine he was now on his way to Mirdita. They
hoped to persuade Jon Marko Joni to raise 3,000 rifles in their support and
open his mountain fastnesses to them as a new base for Nationalist
Resistance. They seemed hopeful of winning over the wily Catholic
chieftain. But, as Abas Kupi frankly told us, they were playing their last
card.

McLean and I stayed on in Malibardhe to wait for Abas Kupi's return
from Mirdita. Abas Ermenye, meanwhile, continued to harass the German
retreat with a mixed force of Zogists and Ballists; and Smiley blew up

another bridge. The weather was fine, but the days were drawing in, and the nights were cold. The Turkomans grumbled, for they had only summer uniforms, and two men sold their rifles to buy warm clothes. The rank and file of the Albanians seemed to sense that the end was near, and they no longer even asked when supply drops from Italy would come. Every night, indeed, they gathered round to listen to the Albanian service of the B.B.C. or Radio Bari, but their despondency only grew as every broadcast poured out news of Communist operations and made no mention of their own fight against the Germans; or worse still attributed Abas Kupi's actions to the Communists. Food supplies began to fail; and every morning we woke to find that another contingent of tribesmen had deserted. The situation was tense and desperate.

The death blow to our hopes was delivered by our own Headquarters. A message from Bari ordered McLean to return to Italy 'to report'. Smiley, with Sergeants Jenkins and Jones, our team of saboteurs, were to go with him. I was to stay with Abas Kupi. But I was not to encourage him to attack the Germans, nor to hold out any hope of British support for him if he did. My role was textually defined as that of 'a neutral observer'.

These orders sealed the fate of the *Zogist* movement and the Nationalist revolt. Without supplies, Abas Kupi could not wage war. Without British support he could not hold his own against the Communists. On our Headquarters instructions we had promised arms to Abas Kupi if he attacked the Germans. He had fought; but now there were to be no arms. We were to go back on our word. The guilt of this betrayal was not ours, but we were the men who would be dishonoured in the eyes of the Albanians; and we felt as if we had been stabbed in the back. We contested these new orders fiercely; but in vain. The exchange of telegrams with Bari showed that our Headquarters were adamant in their decision to withdraw support from Abas Kupi. I was only to stay with him because there were no Communist forces in the north and the military wanted someone to watch the German retreat.

At nightfall on 20 September Abas Kupi returned from Mirdita with his own staff and the *Ballist* leaders. Neither Fikri Dine nor General Previsi were with him. The evening was still warm, and for some time we sat together in the courtyard of the house. But little was said: and, before dinner, Abas Kupi retired pleading fatigue from the march. The guerrillas gathered round when they saw him going into the house, and he stopped and made them a short speech. I could not understand what he said, but it made them laugh and seemed to raise their spirits.

In the morning we assembled in the small bare guest-room which served as our headquarters. Two tattered rugs had been spread for us on the floor, and some bunches of black grapes were laid out on a faded red handkerchief. Through the narrow, barred window a pale ray of sunlight fell on a

crude lithograph of the Virgin and Child. McLean, Smiley and I sat under
the window. On our left was Abas Kupi, smiling wearily with two of his
lieutenants beside him. On our right were the *Ballist* leaders, Abas Ermenye
plucking nervously at the rug, Midhat Frasheri erect and expressionless,
like some eastern ascetic, and Ali Klissura lounging against the wall.

Ali was their spokesman; and, for sheer eloquence, his speech surpassed
any I heard during the Albanian revolt. He began by recalling that the
Zogists and *Ballists* had been in action against the Germans for a month
without any encouragement from the British. Neither the B.B.C. nor Radio
Bari had even reported their actions and, apart from a single 'plane load of
supplies, they had waited in vain for the arms which we had promised
Abas Kupi. Their forces were still nearly a thousand strong, but their funds
were exhausted and they had scarcely enough ammunition for one more
action. They were hemmed in, besides, between the Communists to the
south and the Germans to the west.

With immediate British backing they could still win over Mirdita and
give a good account of themselves. But if it was delayed any longer they
must admit defeat.

There was nothing we could say, and indeed the *Ballist* leaders did not
stay for an answer. They left the room and we remained alone with Abas
Kupi.

'Ali Bey speaks well,' he said, 'but it is too late for words.'

Then in quiet, matter-of-fact tones, he told of his meeting with the
captain of Mirdita. Jon Marko Joni had asked how many cartridges and
how many sovereigns Abas Kupi had received from the British. He had
answered that as yet he had only promises; and the cynical old chieftain
had replied: 'The Germans have been my friends. To betray friends is
immoral and to betray them for nothing is foolish. Let us meet again when
you have something more solid from the British than promises.'

Mirdita was thus denied to us; and this meant that further retreat to the
north was closed. For a few minutes Abas Kupi talked of breaking through
to the coast to establish a bridgehead where the British could land. Then,
all of a sudden, he stopped and asked quietly:

'Tell me, have you still any hope that arms will come for me?'

I exchanged a glance and a nod with McLean; and we told Abas Kupi
of our latest instructions. The Nationalist revolt was over.

42

Defeat in Victory

When Abas Kupi saw that all was lost he wasted no time in vain regrets or feeble reproaches but manfully resolved to bring his affairs to an honourable conclusion. As a patriot he decided to spare his countrymen from further useless bloodshed, and, as a prudent man, prepared to make good his own escape. He left us, therefore, to disband the *Zogist* forces to their homes. After that he would come back and seek our help to leave Albania and join his King.

In Abas Kupi's absence we were committed to the care of General Previsi who lodged us in a lonely stone house, deep in the forests of Kurbenesh. We remained there a week watching the summer fade out of the year. The leaves were already turning and almost every day there were showers of rain. The evenings set in colder; and the General had a fire lit in front of the house so that we might enjoy the last hours of daylight in its warmth. We passed the time in anecdote and speculation, and I took lessons in Italian from Mario, a Neapolitan officer who had been for some months with our mission. Sometimes, Mario would sing for us, or we would call on the Turkomans to dance. Once Smiley raided down into the plain with a mixed force of *Zogists* and *Ballists* and blew up a bridge. But this was our last attack.

Meanwhile, the tragedy of the Nationalist leaders moved swiftly to its appointed end. Muharrem Bairaktar had driven in the German outposts around Kukes and was threatening the town itself, when he learned that the Communists had entered Liuma. He went to meet their commanders and proposed a close alliance. They offered him a choice of joining their movement or of death. Muharrem was heavily outnumbered in the Conference Room and made a show of yielding. The Communist leaders relaxed and the talk took a friendlier turn. This was Muharrem's opportunity. Choosing his moment carefully, he drew his gun and shot his way out of the room to rejoin his troops.

Muharrem was free; but he could not fight on two fronts. He raised the siege of Kukes and drove the Communists back into Dibra. But his supplies were exhausted by the battle while the Communists' were soon replenished from British sources. They attacked again; and this time

Muharrem was defeated, escaping to Mirdita. He stayed in hiding for many months to make his way to Greece after the war was over.

While Muharrem wrestled in the toils, Gani Kryeziu had mobilised 3,000 men and prepared to storm Jakova. Simcox, his British liaison officer, afterwards described the action as 'very brave'. Gani captured all the villages in the plain. His forward troops stormed the German barracks on the outskirts of Jakova and fired their petrol dumps. But the Germans remained masters of the city. Gani, accordingly, fell back and prepared for a second attack. A strong force of Communists now arrived at Gani's Headquarters. Gani was away with the main body of his men; but the Communists kidnapped Simcox and Gani's brother, Said, and carried them off to the south along with Gani's political adviser, an ex-Communist called Fundo.

The Communists beat Fundo to death on the way. We were soon apprised of his murder and feared for Said's life. From our hideout in the forest we begged Headquarters to intervene on his behalf. For once, they reacted honourably and, after a fortnight of negotiations, Said was handed over to the British mission at Communist Headquarters and evacuated to Italy.

Gani held his forces together for some days hoping that our Headquarters might still keep their promise to 'take a strong line' with the Communists on his behalf. But there was no British reaction and, rather than call his forces to civil war, Gani, too, disbanded them and took to the mountains with his brother Hassan. Both men were eventually captured by Tito's *Partisans*. They murdered Hassan. Gani was brought to Belgrade to perish some years later in one of Tito's jails. All this time the German retreat through north Albania continued unmolested.

It was not yet October but there was frost now at night and heavy rains fell from an angry sky. The locals warned us that the waters of the Mati and Fani rivers were rising fast and would soon become impassable. There was nothing for it but to cross them while this was still possible. The two rivers, indeed, were already breast high at the fords. But we consoled ourselves for our soaking with the thought that they would rise still further behind us and bar the way to any pursuers.

We were now in Mirdita; and, though our Turkoman force would protect us from attack, we could no longer count on the support of the local population. After a long and frustrating march we halted on the last evening of September in a small village set on the southern shoulder of Mount Velyes, the broad grey pyramid of rock which rises five thousand feet above the ancient city of Llesh. Llesh itself was hidden from us by a fold in the ground, but we could see the ruins of the castle where Skanderbeg expired, brooding over the defection of his Western Allies and the triumph of the Crescent. Beyond, the broad belt of the coastal plain dissolved through stagnant lagoons into the living sea.

Our host in Velyes was the village priest, a kindly fellow who placed his rambling house at our disposal and tolerantly invited our Moslem Turko-mans to sleep and shelter in his church. One Sunday I attended a service in this church; a low, stone barn, decorated only by a crude, wooden cross, erected on a bare altar of rough stones. At the door one of the congregation collected our rifles and stood guard over them, but each of us retained his pistol or his knife.

McLean had proposed that he and Smiley should be evacuated by boat from the coast between the estuaries of the Mati and the Drin. Our Head-quarters, however, refused this request. They sent orders instead for him and Smiley to hand themselves over to the Communists for evacuation through southern Albania. In explanation, they alleged difficulties with the Navy; but, as we later discovered, their real and puerile purpose was to prove to Enver Hodja that the mission had really been withdrawn. For McLean and Smiley to cross over to the Communist camp would certainly be dangerous for them and an intolerable humiliation for Abas Kupi. They therefore multiplied excuses for delay, making much of the difficulties of travel with the rivers in spate, and discovering objections to each rendez-vous proposed by our Headquarters. It was lucky that they did. In a drunken moment, one of the Communist leaders let out that the Com-munist plan was to march McLean and Smiley south as prisoners to show the people Enver Hodja's power. The previous order was now counter-manded; and our Headquarters signalled that the whole Mission, myself included, would now be withdrawn by sea.

Since our whole mission was now to be withdrawn, we assumed that Abas Kupi would be evacuated with us and included his name in the list of those we proposed to embark. To their shame, our Headquarters categori-cally forbade us to bring out Abas Kupi, lest his presence in Italy should damage their relations with Enver Hodja.

In the kaleidoscope of politics all alliances and relationships are subject to change. Interests converge only to separate again; ideologies and principles serve their turn in the unending struggle for power. It is, there-fore, often necessary and—since in the anarchy of international affairs, necessity is law—legitimate to abandon causes long supported and to dissolve the pledged bonds of alliance. But it is always wrong to abandon men who have been friends to their fate. We may have to jettison their interests, but we should leave no stone unturned to save at least their lives.

We were not prepared to abandon Abas Kupi; and, since our Head-quarters would not bring him out, we sent off Petrit to advise him to charter an Albanian craft. Then we could all cross to Italy together. Three days later Abas Kupi joined us at Velyes with the last remnant of the *Zogist* forces. He had marched for twenty-seven hours, fighting two actions against the Germans on the way. His guards were worn out and in rags. He himself looked grey and old.

The British Command's refusal to evacuate him with our mission was a bitter blow to his pride. But he understood our shame and was touched by our decision to come out with him rather than leave in a British ship. 'It is better this way,' he said 'for it is my duty as your host to escort you to safety.'

That same afternoon, therefore, he despatched agents to find a boat; and we remained together on Mount Velyes.

The weather had broken now, and the first snow fell. The days passed slowly, for it was too cold and damp to sit outside and too dark to read indoors. One day the Germans, fearing an attack on the road, sent a patrol to dislodge us from Mount Velyes. Abas Kupi seized his rifle and set out to meet them. We hurried after him with the Albanians and Turkomans, and took up defensive positions on the crest of a ridge below the church. The ground in front of us was wooded, but though we could see the Germans working their way through the trees, Abas Kupi told the men to hold their fire. When they were quite close he gave a shout and a single volley crashed through the branches. The Germans hesitated; then, as the guerrillas began firing in their own time, turned and fled back towards the plain. They left three dead and did not come again.

Abas Kupi's agents were sanguine about the prospects of a boat, and we accordingly decided to move down to the coastal plain. Before striking camp, however, we climbed with Abas Kupi to the rocky summit of Mount Velyes to look for a last time on the hills and valleys where we had toiled and fought. Looking south I recognized the rocky peaks and the plateau of Biza, where, seven months before, we had swung down out of the night. From there I followed the path which had led us to the *Zogist* strongholds of Mati, Kruya and Tirana, whose rich valleys and barren ranges were of variously pleasant but equally familiar memory. Tirana was concealed by its guardian crescent of mountains, but across the plain, beyond the minarets of Preza, I could just make out the outlines of Durazzo, where Abas Kupi had first raised the standard of Albanian resistance. To the east lay the rolling forests of Mirdita—'the land of happy days'—which we had crossed as outlaws but had never known as friends. Beyond them towered the jagged peaks of Liuma, over which we had toiled with Muharrem Bairaktar; and to the north the view was blocked by the dark massif of the Jakova Mountains, where the indomitable Kryezius had waged their lonely war. The course of the Drin was masked by the Liuman gorges, but beyond Kukes, where the Black and White streams mingle, I could see the river flowing northwards to sweep round the base of the Procletiya Alps and return south to join the sea five thousand feet below the summit where we stood. To the north, beyond the river, rose the red towers and minarets of fanatical Scutari; and, between the grey waters of its lake and the glinting Adriatic, the skyline was broken by the black mountain bastion of Montenegro. All around us lay the prize which we had lost; and, as we sat there gazing down on it, I heard Abas Kupi say almost to himself: 'If only Mirdita had been with us. . . .'

Next evening, 14 October, we abandoned Velyes and marched down rough and rocky paths towards the plain. Below the ruins of Skanderbeg's castle we came out on to the road within a few yards of the gendarmerie post which guarded the entrance to Llesh. A sentry stood outside, but he ran indoors when he saw us; and the gendarmes literally turned a blind eye slamming their doors and shutters as we passed. Two hundred yards separated us from the turning into the plain, and we were still on the road when a German armoured car drove up behind us. We were an easy target, but the German crew, like the gendarmes, favoured the better part of valour. They ducked down inside the turret, and drove past at top speed.

We now turned off into the coastal fens, a tangle of swamp and forest with occasional water-logged pastures, intersected by canals and high thorn fences. By sunrise, we had already marched fourteen hours, and soon afterwards halted in a wood to lie up and rest through the day. Towards evening we resumed the march, and came by devious ways through the fens to the lonely farmhouse which was to be our last Headquarters. It was a strong, square building, painted white, and stood two hours' march from the sea. Its owners, by a strange coincidence, had sheltered Abas Kupi from the Austrians during the First World War.

Our forces now consisted of a hundred or so of Abas Kupi's stalwarts, nearly as many Turkomans, and some fifty Albanian, Italian and other camp followers of our mission. Guarded by these faithful few, we were confined within an area of some five square miles. Germans and Communists surrounded us to landward; and, though the swamps and canals might afford us some hope of resistance, our only line of retreat lay across the sea.

Despite encouraging messages there was still no sign of Abas Kupi's boat; and it was in vain that our patrols lit fires each night on the beach. In despair, we sent Ihsan to Scutari to discover the cause of the delay. He returned on 23 October to say that the boat, a pilot launch, was lying up in the River Boyana. Her skipper planned to slip down the estuary on the first dark night. This was good news as far as it went; but as Smiley commented in his diary: 'all is arranged except when to pick us up, the date and the signals!' Meanwhile, our Headquarters had signalled that a boat would be sent for us on the night of 24 October. But our orders were badly drafted and this gave us a last pretext to delay. We agreed, indeed, that Smiley should keep the rendezvous with the rest of the mission. But McLean and I decided to stay behind with our wireless operator, Corporal Davies.

The two motor torpedo boats which evacuated Smiley and his party also landed a British patrol. Their task was to reconnoitre and harass the enemy's retreat; and, at our request, Abas Kupi gave them food and guides. But with the patrol were also two officers of the *Balli Kombetar*, who had escaped to Italy a few days before. No suspicion of 'collaboration' with the enemy attached to either of them; but, despite their protests, they had been sent back to face almost certain death, lest their presence in Italy should embarrass our relations with Enver Hodja. Their story spread consternation through the camp; and that night Abas Kupi talked of suicide.

On the morning of 25 October, the B.B.C. announced that Anthony Eden, the Foreign Secretary, had arrived in Italy. His intervention might offer a last hope, and we sent him an urgent appeal to order Abas Kupi's evacuation. The same night there was a brush between our sentries and a Communist patrol. The net was closing round us.

Next day, 26 October, a bodyguard roused me to say that two Montenegrins were in the camp and wanted to speak with us. Both belonged to General Mihailovitch's *Chetnik* movement. The spokesman of the two was a Major Vukadinovitch, a dark and determined looking, regular officer, whom I knew by repute. They laid before us a proposal from Mihailovitch to attack the German Army in Montenegro with all his forces in return for British protection against Tito. We agreed to pass on the proposal but could hold out no hope of its acceptance. Nor, perhaps, did the two Serbs expect that we should. I felt, indeed, that they had only come to satisfy themselves and their followers that they had done all that was humanly possible for their cause.

We set food and drink before them, and, as we discussed their country's fate, I reflected that these were the men who had made the coup d'état against Prince Paul when 'Yugoslavia had found her soul'. They had been our allies then, and, when the Germans had occupied their country, they had been the first in all Europe to organise an armed resistance. Civil war had diminished their ardour and worn away their strength until, in self-defence, they had been forced into accommodations with the enemy. In the dark days we had admired them as heroes; now in the hour of victory they were reviled as traitors; truly 'treason is a matter of dates.'

We were still in discussion when Davis came into the room with an urgent signal. It told us that a boat would be sent for us that night, and ordered us to be at the *rendezvous* without fail. We now bade the two Serbs farewell and faced up to the most unpleasant decision I have ever taken. We were quite prepared to disobey orders and our every instinct was to stay with Abas Kupi. And yet there was a doubt in our minds. We had delayed our departure nearly a month to give Abas Kupi time to find a boat. There had been hopeful news from Scutari; but of the boat itself there was still no sign; and we began to despair that it would ever come. In Albania we were powerless to influence events. In Italy we might still persuade the Supreme Command that Abas Kupi must be saved. In the end, therefore, we decided to go, resolved that, if Abas Kupi did not follow on his own, we should somehow get authority to come back and rescue him. It was a hard decision; for if we failed we should reproach ourselves all our lives with deserting a friend.

Presently Abas Kupi joined us and challenged me to a game of chess. The three of us were alone, and it was between moves on the board that McLean and I concerted our decision. At last Abas Kupi checkmated my king; and, as I put away the pieces, we told him we must leave that night. He heard us calmly and approved our reasons. Then, tapping the chess-board he said:

'*Inshallah!* We shall play the next game in Italy!'

When our Headquarters had first ordered our withdrawal we had asked to bring out our Turkoman troops, and our three faithful Albanian inter-preters. This had been agreed but now even that decision was reversed. It was argued, with some plausibility, that to take 100 Turkomans would dangerously prolong the time of embarkation. The three interpreters were excluded for fear of complications with the Communists.

We burnt our papers that afternoon and sought to put our affairs in order. It was several weeks since our Headquarters had been able to renew our funds; and our war-chest was now reduced to 7 sovereigns. Our body-guards had not been paid for a month, and we owed considerable sums besides for the upkeep of our mission and the feeding of the Turkomans. To have left the farmers unpaid would have been to plumb new depths of dishonour; and we accepted a loan of 50 gold sovereigns from Abas Kupi, to pay our debts.

At nightfall, while the Turkomans sang round their fires, we sat with Abas Kupi for the last of many conferences. He seemed confident that his boat would come, and we helped him draft a farewell proclamation to the Albanian people. When all that there was to say had been said, we drank the Albanian toast of *Tungyatyeta* and took our last meal together in silence. Outside, the camp already slept, and towards ten o'clock we gave orders for the ponies to be saddled. The day had been grey and wet, but there had been a rainbow in the evening, and now there was a full moon to light our way. I embraced Abas Kupi, swung into the saddle, and without turning back rode away between the groups of sleeping men huddled round the dying camp-fires.

All Lost Save Honour

Our way led from the forest through marshes and across a broad lagoon where the water was often up to my pony's girths. At first only the sound of splashing disturbed the night, but soon we began to distinguish the deeper murmur of sea water lapping the sandy shore. Beyond the lagoon we climbed on to a dune and, threading our way through a German mine-field, rode down on to the beach. The sea was calm as a lake, and a full moon hung just above the horizon. There was a German blockhouse a mile away to the north, but we judged that its garrison was too demoralised to disturb us.

When the moon was down we lit a fire of brushwood and, wrapped in our overcoats, sat down to wait for the boat. Two hours must have passed, and I had given up straining into the darkness, when McLean pointed to a dark shape out at sea. It seemed about a hundred yards away and it surprised me that I had not noticed it before. Presently, a smaller shape was detached from it, and, as the waves washed it up on to the beach, we saw that it was a flat-bottomed landing craft. It was paddled by two sailors with an officer who stepped out and saluted us. He belonged to 'Security' and had been sent to make sure that we did not embark Abas Kupi.

I now bade farewell to our interpreters and gave the faithful Kolaver my horse and saddlebags with a handful of gold. That lean and hardened brigand kissed me on the face and hands and burst into tears like a child. We climbed into the landing craft and pushed off to shouts of *Tungyatyeta* from the Albanians. In a few minutes we were alongside the motor-boat, a M.A.S., manned by an Italian crew. I clambered up on to the deck and sat down dejectedly on a coil of rope. The M.A.S. was comfortless and impersonal, like the aircraft from which we had jumped eight months before.

When all were safe on board, the landing craft was hoisted over the side. Then, with her engines barely turning over, the M.A.S. slipped quietly out to sea. As we cleared Cape Rodonit, her captain ordered full speed ahead; and we shot forward in a cloud of spray. Looking back into the fading darkness I could just make out the low Albanian shore and the black mountains of Montenegro running down to the sea.

At dawn the Balkan coast was lost to sight, and we cruised alone between sea and sky. The autumn night had been cold, but the wind and the spray dropped with the morning; and the M.A.S. made good headway through an oily swell. McLean joined me on deck and presently we saw the fortifications of Brindisi rising above the flat Apulian plain. We ran our course between the minefields which guarded the harbour approaches and, an hour later, were cutting the calm waters in the lee of the granite mole. The roar of the engines sank to a hum, and the M.A.S. nosed gently up against the quayside at the foot of the old castle.

Ashore, a squad of sailors were changing guard, while a few naval and army officers stood talking outside the Harbour Control. Their spotless uniforms made a striking contrast to our distinctly irregular appearance; and McLean justly observed that we could scarcely be mistaken for officers or gentlemen. McLean was dressed in sandals and torn jodhpurs, a faded green tunic swathed in bandoliers, and a white Kruya skull-cap on his head. My own headgear was a black, sheep-skin *shubara*; my field boots were cracked and coming apart at the heels; and my once smart cord uniform was soiled and stained from seven months' continual wear. I had let my beard grow, since the flesh wound under my chin; and it was several months since either of us had had a haircut.

Amid the hardships of guerrilla life I had sometimes looked forward to those creature comforts we might hope to find if we ever came out of Albania alive. The Hotel Imperiale, in Bari, however, was full to overflowing; and that night and the next we were lodged in a flat requisitioned by our Headquarters. It was entirely unfurnished, save for a single wooden chair, and had neither hot water nor electric light. We were, indeed, accustomed to sleeping on the floor, but, in Albania, there had usually been a mattress or at least a heap of ferns. No such luxuries obtained in our flat. There were army blankets and a hard parquet floor. Nevertheless, I slept heavily; for it was forty-eight hours since I had been to bed.

I woke soon after eight next morning and put on a battle-dress provided by Headquarters. It fitted well enough and only lacked badges of rank. McLean was still asleep, but I felt hungry and made my way to the Hotel Imperiale in search of breakfast and of a barber. The dining-room was crowded with staff officers munching their bacon and eggs; but a scruffy waiter barred the way in. Breakfast, he explained, could not be served after nine o'clock and I was already six minutes late. Baulked by this irksome regulation, I wandered off despondently to the hotel snack-bar, and, fighting my way through the crowd, grabbed a cup of coffee and a sardine sandwich. I had scarcely attacked this unappetising repast when an unknown officer curtly reminded me that it was contrary to King's

Regulations to wear a beard. At first I thought him drunk, despite the early hour, and offered him a chair. My courtesy, however, only aroused his wrath and he went red in the face, spluttering that he was the Provost Marshal. I rose to explain my situation; but, as I did so, his eagle eye observed that I wore no badges of rank. From red he turned purple, and hissed:

'What are you doing here anyway? Don't you know that this hotel is out of bounds to Other Ranks?'

My explanation drew a decent apology, but I already began to wish I was back in the mountains.

The rhythm of our lives in Albania had been among the healthiest of our circumstances. In the mountains, events could move no faster than a man might walk. Allies, neutrals or enemies approached alike on foot, and since no man can run for long uphill, retreat or attack proceeded at the same easy pace as the simplest errand. The march gave ample time for meditation; the camp for detailed discussion. The conduct of negotiations was likewise seldom hurried. Every meeting was preceded by a journey of hours or even days and so inevitably involved staying the night or at least sharing a meal. Each word could thus be weighed; and, since the necessary interludes for food or rest automatically divided each meeting into two or more sessions, there was always time to review conclusions or advance new arguments. Nor was this even tenor of our work distracted by unnecessary routines or interviews. Our way of life tended to eliminate all that was superfluous and no-one ran the risk of coming to see us unless they had important business to discuss. Above all, nothing was decided in a hurry, for we lived in a world where it was not unusual to be a day or more late for an appointment. Each of our problems was thus revolved in meditation and debate; and we had the satisfaction of knowing that our advice and decisions, whether right or wrong, were the soundest of which we were capable.

In Bari, this wholesome rhythm of life was rudely shattered. Staff cars rushed us from one office to another. Harassed officials plied us with superficial questions. Memoranda on the most intricate problems were required at half an hour's notice. Interviews were continually disturbed by the ring of the telephone; and conversations were brought to an end, not by exhaustion of the subject but by the approach of the next appointment. At first I was bewildered; then repelled; and, within a week, the three of us had agreed to return to the mountains as soon as we could.

Life in Bari was disagreeable; but more alarming was the distortion of men's minds. Never had there been so many British observers in the Balkans; yet never can so many responsible Englishmen have cherished so many illusions about that bloodstained region. It was perhaps inevitable that we should give exclusive support to the Communists in Yugoslavia and Albania. But such a policy involved the sacrifice of significant British interests; and, though Englishmen might be obliged to contribute to its success, it seemed natural to expect that they should do so in a mood of sober reluctance. Instead a genuine enthusiasm for the Communists and their works infected our Headquarters; and responsible staff officers revelled with indecent and almost masochistic glee in the destruction of *Chetniks* and *Zogists* who, whatever their shortcomings, were at least our friends. Tito and Hodja, it seemed, could do no wrong. Their wildest claims were accepted at face value. Their opponents—Socialists and Peasant Party included—were incongruously branded as 'Fascists' or 'Reactionaries' by Englishmen who would never have voted anything but Conservative at home.

Our Headquarters were strongly opposed to rescuing Abas Kupi and some officers went so far as to say that his sacrifice was necessary to a good understanding with Hodja. But our telegram to Eden had raised the issue to a higher level; and McLean and I were summoned to the palace of Caserta, the Allied headquarters outside Naples, to put our case to General Wilson, the Supreme Allied Commander.

We lodged in the Kennels where King Bomba had kept his hounds and, on our first night, dined with Harold Macmillan, then Resident Minister-of-State. His advice might well decide the issue and we accordingly sought to enlist his support. He heard us impassively, staring straight in front of him from the depths of his armchair, his attention apparently centred on his pipe. Then, with disconcerting detachment, he raised every possible objection to our arguments. Our answers, however, seemed to accord with his own inner thoughts; and at length he dismissed the subject saying:

'Of course we must save Abas Kupi. Personally I'd be all for bringing Mihailovitch out as well!' This robust attitude was a welcome contrast to the appeasing climate of Bari, and it was in a mood of confidence that we made our way next morning to the Supreme Commander's office. An orderly directed us to the General's ante-room, where an ADC was busy on the telephone, arranging an air passage to Cairo for a lady friend's pekinese. He offered us a drink, and, while we waited, showed us the signed photographs of wartime celebrities with which the walls were covered. Presently, a group of staff officers emerged from the adjoining room, a sign that the General's morning meeting was over. It was now our turn.

The Supreme Allied Commander, or 'Jumbo' as the British Army knew him, stood in the middle of the room, his bulky person clad in corduroy trousers and a thick, khaki pullover. He welcomed us with fatherly kindness and led us to a corner where half a dozen deep armchairs had been set

in a semi-circle like an Arab *majlis*. He sat us down on either side of him
and asked us to point out on a map of Albania the dispositions of Germans,
Zogists, and *Partisans*. He followed our explanations closely, peering over
narrow, horn-rimmed glasses, and then began to ply us with curiously
disconnected questions, taking rough notes in pencil of our replies.
Presently, he put down his writing-pad and, after a moment's pause,
announced:

'Yes, I agree with you, the fellow's been our friend and we must get him
out. We'll do it quite openly; and we'll tell Hodja too, but—' and here his
beady eyes twinkled, 'not until your man's safe in Italy.'

He then heaved himself out of his armchair, and, walking over to his
desk, called down the telephone for his Chief-of-Staff. A moment later we
were joined by General Gammel, who was asked to prepare orders for
Abas Kupi's rescue. McLean was put in charge of the operation. We had
won.

It was too late to travel back to Bari that day, and so we drove out to
spend the afternoon among the ruins of Pompeii. We had scarcely returned
to the Kennels when the telephone rang. It was Smiley. He told us that
Abas Kupi, with five companions, had landed at Brindisi that morning in
his own boat. Our sense of relief was overwhelming; and yet both of us
were disappointed that we had been denied the chance to go back to
Albania and rescue Abas Kupi in a British ship.

Enver Hodja duly demanded that Abas Kupi be sent back to Albania
for trial and there were some at our Headquarters who favoured the idea.
But Caserta stood by Wilson's decision and Abas Kupi's status as our
friend was confirmed. He and two of his sons were accordingly lodged with
Said and Ihsan in a villa above the little town of Rutigliano.

Our work was done now, but, before leaving for London, we paid a last
visit to Abas Kupi and his companions. The day was cold and wet; and the
armed sentries patrolling the grounds made the house look like a prison.
Indoors the rooms were dark and cheerless, furnished with a few wooden
chairs and army beds. It was a drab end to all our dreams. Yet, despite the
ruin of his hopes and the personal tragedy of exile—and exile is doubly
hard for an old man who can neither read, nor write, nor speak a foreign
language—Abas Kupi displayed his old steadfastness.

'I still put my trust in England,' he told us. 'The future is dark, but one
day you will be strong again. As for me, I shall live for the time when we
return together to the mountains to take up again the unending battle for
freedom.'

There was one last debt of honour to be paid.

Smiley had managed to evacuate two of our Turkoman soldiers. They
had begged to be sent to England, or at any rate not repatriated to the
Soviet Union. I understood their fears; and, indeed, it was widely known

that deserters from the Soviet Army or prisoners of war who had been in prolonged contact with foreigners, were liable to be shot or sent to concentration camps. I accordingly called at the camp where these two were held and secured permission to take them out to lunch. I was due to leave for London next day, and saw no reason to take them back to camp. Instead, I gave them each a small sum of money and turned them loose in Bari.

One of them opened a café near Naples and until quite recently used to send me a Christmas card. I never heard what became of the other.

Our mission to Albania ended in utter failure. We had, indeed, carried out our original instructions to the letter. We had reorganised the scattered British missions, covering the whole Gheg territory with an extensive network of liaison officers, saboteurs and wireless stations. We had persuaded Abas Kupi to agree to negotiations with Enver Hodja and even to accept our proposal for an armistice after the Civil War had started. We had brought Abas Kupi and other Nationalist leaders back into the field and, but for the Civil War, could have played havoc with the German withdrawal. It had all been in vain. Our Headquarters had altogether failed to exercise a corresponding influence on the Albanian Communists and, indeed, had become an instrument of Enver Hodja in the British camp. Nor were our military authorities prepared to risk committing British troops to operations in Albania.

Yet, in another sense, our work bore fruit. Our intervention with Macmillan and Wilson to save Abas Kupi opened the eyes of Caserta to the true nature of Communist policies in the Balkans. In the same way, our report to Lord Selborne, the Cabinet Minister responsible for S.O.E., helped to strengthen Churchill's resolve to maintain Western influence in Greece, even if this meant turning British arms against the Communist guerrillas we had previously supported.

Soon after our return to London, the Greek situation reached crisis point. The British Army working in partnership with the Greek Government of M. Papandreou took active steps to prevent a Communist takeover of Athens and Attica. I went with McLean to hear the debate on Greece in the House of Commons. Speaker after speaker rose from the left-wing benches, to denounce Papandreou as 'a Fascist' whereas his political position, then as always, was well left of centre. It was all so absurd that we had some difficulty in observing the rules and not jumping up to tell the House what was really happening in the Balkans.

A week later, Simon Wardell, then working on the *Daily Express*, got me into the Labour Party Conference on a press card. Once again Greece was the central issue and the Government's policy came under fierce attack. Ernest Bevin gave a courageous, if at times incoherent, defence of Government policy. Aneurin Bevan made an eloquent reply but it was made for Labour Party consumption and showed little understanding of Balkan realities. I could not help reflecting that, had Bevan been a Greek, he might well have joined the Communist led ELAS but would almost certainly have been shot as a deviationist long before the end of the war.

But the tide of illusionism which had set in after the Teheran Conference was beginning to turn in London if not yet in Washington. A reaction was setting in. It came too late to save the cause of freedom in Albania, Yugoslavia and Bulgaria—the Balkan countries where I had worked most. It was just in time to save Greece.

VIII

MISSION TO CHINA

December 1944 – May 1945

44

With Carton to Chungking

There was nothing more I could usefully do in the Balkans: and I accordingly began to cast around for other work. There were plenty of openings in the civil administration of Italy and Germany, and they would have brought promotion. But I had no ambition to become a policeman hunting down defeated enemies. Nor did I feel a call to re-educate Italians and Germans to Democracy.

The only thing I knew about was Resistance and, in particular, the pattern of antagonism between Communists and Nationalists which developed inexorably with the approach of Allied victory. Where could this expertise, such as it was, be best employed?

It was by now December 1944. The end of the war in Europe could not long be delayed despite the German offensive in the Ardennes. The centre of gravity in the struggle must soon move to the Far East. No doubt the Americans would take the lead in the war against Japan. But Britain with her vast interests in India, South-East Asia and China was vitally concerned. And what would be the attitude of the Soviets? If they came into the war against Japan, China could well become the cockpit of a clash between Soviet, American and British interests. It did not need much imagination to foresee the uneasy truce between Chiang Kai-shek and Mao Tse-tung developing into a gigantic Far Eastern version of the struggle between Mihailovitch and Tito or Abas Kupi and Enver Hodja.

My enquiries at Baker Street showed that the S.O.E. representation in Chungking was little more than a liaison office. I accordingly embraced an ambitious design. I would go to Chungking, and if possible also to Yenan, the Communist Headquarters, to see how the land lay. Then, if the Chinese authorities agreed, I would form a special S.O.E. mission combining the guerrilla experience of Bill McLean, Alan Hare and David Smiley with such experts on China as I might recruit on the spot. Our purpose would be to support Chinese resistance against Japan, especially in the areas around Hong Kong and Shanghai where Britain had important interests, and to keep a watching brief on Communist and Soviet activities.

Lord Selborne had received McLean and me with great kindness on our return from Albania. He had read our report carefully and was very much

in sympathy with our views on the triangular struggle between the Western
Powers, the Axis and the Soviets. I accordingly put to him the idea that we
might form the nucleus of a mission to China and apply to the largest
country in the world some of the lessons we had learnt in the smallest. His
reaction was very favourable. Like most people he expected the war in the
Far East to be a long-drawn affair. He wanted S.O.E. to get away to a good
start, and avoid some of the mistakes that had been made from inexperience in Europe. A good deal, he explained, was already in preparation
in Malaya, Thailand and Burma. China, however, was still almost virgin
territory from an S.O.E. point of view and he welcomed the idea that I
should reconnoitre the possibilities. He, accordingly, instructed the office
in Baker Street to give me every facility.

C'est le premier pas qui coûte. If I were to go to Chungking to look
round, I must go under respectable auspices, so that doors would be
opened and people would talk to me. It so happened, just then, that
General Carton de Wiart arrived in London from Chungking. Carton de
Wiart was Churchill's personal representative on the staff of Generalissimo
Chiang Kai-shek. My father asked him to dinner, along with the Secretary
of State for War, P. J. Grigg. I had been reading up the office files on
China, and, after dinner, drew Carton out on the subject. He was surprised
that I knew anything about it and said rather bitterly that I was the first
person he had met in London to show any interest in his work. I then told
him something of my experiences in the Balkans and explained that I
wanted to come out to China to explore the possibilities of organising
Resistance behind the Japanese lines. He seemed to like the idea and said
that he was flying back to Chungking in his own aeroplane ten days later.
He would be glad to give me a lift. I accepted at once and then decided to
follow up my advantage. Would he let me come out nominally as a member
of his staff? He replied that he had no work for me to do, but, if all I
wanted was to use his name as cover, he would have no objection. Then, as
an after thought, he added that he had drunk a good deal at dinner, and
would I confirm this arrangement with him in the morning. He was, he
said, an early riser, and asked me to call on him at eight o'clock.

This was a small price to pay for a first-class ticket to Chungking and
the best possible cover when I got there. I repaired at the appointed hour
to the small furnished flat off Piccadilly where Carton was staying. He
seemed, understandably, rather less genial than on the previous evening,
but he stood firmly by his promise. 'I said I would take you and I will.' I
should be nominally a member of his staff. He would introduce me to
Chinese generals and Ministers. I must make the rest of the running
myself.

I breakfasted off fried goose eggs with McLean at Claridges and we
then called together on Lord Selborne to tell him of Carton's offer. He was

delighted and told me to write out my own terms of reference. He would talk to the Foreign Secretary meanwhile and make sure the Embassy in Chungking were asked to give any help I needed. This time there were no difficulties from the Foreign Office. I had evidently worked my passage home where they were concerned.

I flew from London in Carton de Wiart's Dakota on 18 January 1945. My fellow passengers included Lady Seymour, the kind and vivacious wife of our Ambassador in Chungking, and Archie John Wavell, the Viceroy's son.[1] Archie John had lost a hand, and Carton had lost an arm and an eye; but I was to be continually embarrassed throughout the journey by how much nimbler and quicker they were in handling luggage or opening doors than I was. We spent a day in Cairo and, looking in at the Mohammed Ali Club, I ran into Sidky Pasha and Sirry Pasha. They argued earnestly that the time had come for Britain to withdraw her troops from Cairo and Alexandria. If we made the gesture now, there would be much less likelihood of a challenge to our base in the Suez Canal Zone. I thought there was some force in this and said so that evening at a dinner with Lampson, Smart and Ned Grigg,[2] who had become Minister of State after Moyne's murder. Smart was inclined to agree. But Cairo and Alexandria were very comfortable, and a victorious British Army was understandably reluctant to move to more austere surroundings. Nor, indeed, did the Egyptians press us very hard. They were disturbed by the growth of Soviet influence. They mistrusted the Americans. Above all, they were concerned that we should honour our war debts which stood at nearly £500m. As Sidky had said to me: 'We are tied to you by your debts to us.'

We staged through Aden which I had never seen and I stayed in a bungalow in the Government House compound. Aden in those days was very underdeveloped. There was neither electric light nor modern sanitation even in Government House. The town itself was little more than a village with a main street of dingy and ramshackle shops. British influence extended to Lahej; but in the tangled mountains beyond our writ scarcely ran at all. When I went back fourteen years later, it had grown beyond all recognition. So by then had its problems.

From Aden we flew to Karachi, stopping for lunch on the island of Masirah. Masirah was a barren air-strip in the Arabian sea, which we then held on a four-year lease. It subsequently became of considerable importance to our East of Suez strategy, and I negotiated a ninety-nine year lease of it from the Sultan of Muscat.[3] But my first impressions of it were

[1] Killed in action during the Mau Mau revolt in Kenya.
[2] Sir Edward Grigg a former Governor of Kenya, later Lord Altrincham.
[3] 1959.

unfavourable and showed no appreciation of its military significance. 'This', I wrote, 'is the most God-forsaken desert island.'

From Karachi we flew to Bombay and then to Ceylon where we stayed at Admiral Mountbatten's headquarters in Kandy. Mountbatten, then Allied Supremo in South East Asia, was younger than many of the senior officers under his command; and there was some resentment against him. But he had a fine presence, and always seemed extremely well briefed. His headquarters combined the luxury of a palace with the clockwork efficiency of the Royal Navy. The atmosphere, too, was enlivened by the company, in the intervals of business, of young officers and pretty girls. Carton, who was rather austere in such matters, scoffed at it as 'a court' and nicknamed Mountbatten 'The Archduke Charles' after Napoleon's unhappy opponent. Thanks to the atom bomb, the military efficiency of the Supremo and his staff were never fully tested, but as a centre of British influence and power it was an impressive headquarters.

While Carton conferred with Mountbatten and other brass hats, I was given intensive briefings, military and political, on our relations with China. I also managed to see something of the beauties of Kandy, which has been well described as 'an ideal place for a honeymoon'. I visited the Temple of the Tooth and prayed for guidance on my mission to Cathay, but the Buddha remained inscrutable.

From Kandy, a ten-hour flight over the Bay of Bengal brought us to Calcutta where I stayed with my father's old friend, Dick Casey, the Governor of Bengal.[1] Government House was a copy of Kedleston Hall, Lord Curzon's house, but had been painted purple to camouflage it from Japanese bombers. This gave it a rather surrealist quality. Casey was an outstandingly successful Governor; and I have often thought it a pity that we did not draw more often on statesmen from the Dominions to fill pro-consular appointments in India and the Crown Colonies. It might have strengthened the cohesion of the self-governing and the dependent parts of the old Commonwealth and Empire.

There were, at this time, only two ways of getting to China from India. You could go by yak through Tibet. This took the best part of three months. Or you could fly in a few hours 'over the hump', as the eastern ranges of the Himalayas were known. The flight over 'the hump' was still something of an adventure. Part of the flight path went over Japanese held territory. A DC 3 with a full load could only just clear the mountains and even then had to fly round rather than over some of the peaks. This called for accurate navigation and good luck.

We took off from the steamy, sultry heat of Dum Dum Airport. The Himalayas were ominously wrapped in clouds. The flight was cold, dull and bumpy. I felt rather sick until someone told me to suck oxygen. Then

[1] Later Governor-General of Australia, 1965-9.

after five-and-a-half hours' flight, we came out of the clouds into a world of red and purple mountains. They looked exactly like the mountains I had seen depicted on Chinese scrolls and porcelain and showed me that Chinese art is much more naturalistic than most Westerners realise. As we came down towards the great lake of Kunming, I fully expected to see dragons playing on the hillsides.

Kunming Airport was vast, dry and dusty. American and Chinese air crews were moving briskly in different directions. Hundreds of Chinese coolies, in Prussian blue denims and jackets, were carrying loads of earth, water or stones hanging from either end of a pole balanced across the shoulder. There were long trains of them moving like ants according to some preordained by but no means obvious plan.

We were welcomed on landing by General Chennault, a tall, dark man with hawk-like features, and, so it was said, a strong strain of Red Indian blood. He had left the United States Air Force in 1936 to fight for Chiang Kai-shek, and was still the effective though not the nominal commander of both the Chinese Air Force and the American squadrons serving in China. But the American military establishment looked on him as a soldier of fortune, and both Stilwell and Wedemeyer had done their best, so Carton told me, to have him removed from the Chinese theatre. Chennault, however, enjoyed the confidence of the Generalissimo, and stayed on till the end. Chennault was a natural leader who knew his own mind and spoke it fearlessly. He understood war in the air. He also knew both the strength and the weakness of the Chinese.

Kunming was the capital of the opium province of Yunnan; and, after lunch, we paid a courtesy call on its warlord and ruler, General Lung Yun. Lung Yun derived his private income and his provincial revenue largely from the opium trade. Thanks to this source of wealth and to the tangled mountains of Yunnan, he was virtually independent of the Chungking Government. His main problem was the growth of Kunming airport. This brought in new wealth but it might also help the Generalissimo extend his control over Yunnan province.

The General received us in a pleasant office, decorated with traditional Chinese furniture. He was short, rather squat, and dressed in a simple khaki uniform. He had no English; and the conversation was limited to a ritual exchange of compliments and the drinking of tea.

I spent the rest of the afternoon wandering around Kunming. It was a strange mixture of modern concrete buildings interspersed with charming old Chinese houses with curling eaves and ornamental doorways. Big American cars and jeeps mingled with rickshaws and sedan chairs. The streets were thronged with soldiers, merchants, coolies and beggars. A few of the older people were dressed in flowing robes; and I saw one or two old women hobbling down the pavement—survivors from the days when girls had their feet bound in childhood. A few people wore European clothes. But the vast majority wore some variant of what seemed to be the national uniform—a pair of trousers and a simple tunic, most often of faded blue, though sometimes black or khaki.

We set out next morning for Chungking and, soon after take-off, were again enveloped in clouds. When we came out of them, the scenery had changed completely. The light was soft and grey rather like the North-West of England. The ground was very green and the paddy fields full of water. The hills were rounded and terraced with little paddocks of every conceivable size and shape. There seemed to be few villages, but several large, rambling farm houses standing by themselves. Our aircraft flew between the hills along the valley of the Jaling which runs into the Yangtze at Chungking. The river waters looked grey and oily. Grey water buffaloes with curling horns stood belly deep in the pools that spread on either side of it.

We came in towards an alarmingly narrow airstrip cut out of the side of a hill on the very edge of the river. It was a difficult approach and the pilot made three passes at it before we finally touched down. A light rain was falling.

Our aircraft was soon surrounded by a milling crowd of Chinese generals and officials as well as representatives of our own and other Allied missions. There was no waiting room and no formalities. But as I stepped on to the tarmac, a smiling Chinese official offered me a large and welcome glass of brandy.

Chungking stands on three hills looking down on the confluence of the Yangtze and the Jaling. When Chiang Kai-shek retreated there after the fall of Nanking, it was still a medieval walled city, with a population of some two hundred thousand. This had grown to over two million, and the overcrowding was indescribable. Quite senior government officials lived in dormitories. Even generals shared rooms or slept in their offices. There were a few pleasant villas on the hill tops. For the rest, there were houses made of mud and bamboo and a mushroom growth of shanties: new slums, and old slums, repaired bomb damage and unrepaired bomb damage. At least a quarter of a million people had no home at all. They lived in the streets. They slept in the streets. They gave birth in the streets. They died in the streets. During the winter months there was an almost daily rain and the streets were covered in a thin layer of squelchy mud. There were no drains or sewers and the night soil was still carried away by coolies in great earthenware jars.

Transport was desperately short; inevitably since it had to be flown across the Himalayas or smuggled through the Japanese lines. As a result,

I was to do a lot of walking; a frustrating business since the streets, even in the less frequented parts of the town, were far more crowded than Oxford Street at Christmas time. Walking was an endless process of jostling, waiting and queuing, relieved only by the extraordinary patience and cheerfulness of the Chinese. When the distances were too long for walking, you could hire a rickshaw easily enough. These were comfortable and quite swift, but not without risk. Going down the steep hills of Chungking, the rickshaw boys would rest upon the shafts and touch the ground about once every twenty feet. The rickshaw would get up alarming speed; and broken bones and even fatal accidents were quite common.

The Government officially discouraged the sedan chair as a relic of feudalism. But it was still very much in use, especially on the steep steps leading from the heights of the city down to the river bank. The sedan chair was very comfortable. But it, too, could be alarming, when one of the porters slipped or stumbled in the mud.

I stayed at first with Captain Billiard Leek, the naval attaché, and then in turn with the British Ambassador, Sir Horace Seymour, and the Australian Ambassador, Keith Officer. Eventually I took a room in the house of Alan Bell, the representative of the Peking Syndicate. Bell was a man of very formal manner, but probably the best informed British businessman in China, and with a very wide range of Chinese acquaintance. So great was the inflation at the time that even the very modest monthly rent he agreed to accept from me filled a suitcase. It totalled several million Chinese dollars but was worth, I think, twenty five-pounds.

The military and political situation in China seemed as depressing as the damp, cold climate of Chungking. The Japanese had been for many years in occupation of all the most developed provinces of the country. Apart from Szechuan which was agriculturally rich if backward, Chiang Kai-shek held only the wild if extensive provinces of the north and the south-west. It was as if a British Government had lost all of Britain south of Perth and Aberdeen.

The nearest Japanese troops were a little over a hundred miles away. They had recently launched what proved to be their last major offensive of the War, and this was finally halted just as we arrived.

This particular battle was typical of the War. When the Japanese attacked, the Generalissimo ordered the three armies opposing them to fall back and cover Chungking. But two of the commanders concerned were local war lords and drew their strength from the region in which they were stationed. If they withdrew, therefore, many of their troops would desert and they would lose their private sources of revenue. Accordingly, instead of falling back to protect Chungking, they retired into the hills on either side, leaving the road to the capital open to the enemy. It looked for a moment as if a serious crisis might develop and Chiang Kai-shek was forced to throw in his crack units. These, though well trained, were primarily intended as a Praetorian Guard to defend the régime rather than fight the enemy. Their intervention however saved the city. The Japanese had outrun their communications and, on meeting serious resistance, halted and then fell back.

Chiang's problem was how to discipline the generals who had disobeyed orders. They were invited to a conference in Chungking. Both made excuses and proposed instead a meeting at their own Headquarters where they would be protected by their own troops. For several weeks nothing happened. It was then announced in the official gazette that one of the generals had been decorated. A few days later came a further announcement that the other had died suddenly. I never discovered exactly what happened. Apparently, it was thought expedient to forgive the one's insubordination and to make this clear by an award. Poison was slipped into the other's tea.

The *Kuomintang*, or governing party, was much more a coalition of interests than a totalitarian dictatorship. The official structure of single party government was in fact little more than a façade behind which different business groups, military cliques and secret societies struggled for power. There were the war lords with their own armies and in some cases their own revenues. There were the landowners who dominated the provincial government of Szechuan, and controlled its powerful secret societies or *mafias*. There were the regular officers. There was the Civil Service, drawn from all classes of the community and the traditional avenue to wealth and power. There were also the businessmen, bankers and industrialists, mostly from Canton and Shanghai. They were the chief channel of American aid and planned, with American help, to run China once the Japanese had been driven out. Above them all stood Chiang Kai-shek playing one faction off against the other and holding a balance as best he might. This was no easy task and it was primarily achieved by distributing or withholding supplies of arms and money.

Chiang and his family have often been accused of corruption. This is a misuse of the term. They certainly accumulated large sums of money but this was not primarily for their personal satisfaction. Their object was to have a larger private war chest than anyone else. With it, they subsidised a particular war lord or retained the loyalty of some important official who might otherwise have deviated from their policies. It was thanks to the power of the purse combined with the loyalty of certain selected regiments and of the secret police that Chiang was able for some twenty years to hold the Chinese State together and maintain resistance to Japan.

The joker in the pack was the Yenan Provincial Government, or, in other words, the Communist Army of Mao Tse-tung. Chiang and Mao had not fought against each other for some time, though Chiang still maintained a strict blockade of Yenan. The Americans had established a mission there and were trying to bring about a reconciliation between the Liberal Wing of the *Kuomintang* and the Communists. The Communist Army was still fairly small but well trained and well equipped. The Communists, moreover, were organising substantial guerrilla forces behind the Japanese lines north of the Yellow River. If the Soviets should enter the war against Japan, the Red Army advancing into Manchuria would come into contact with Communist guerrillas and with Mao's forces before they linked up with those of Chiang Kai-shek.

I summed up views on the problem presented by the Communists in a letter to my father:

28 March 1945
I do not personally believe there is much chance of a settlement between *Kuomintang* and Communists as, in fact, what each is asking of the other, under the façade of democratic verbiage, is not far from unconditional surrender. I believe the only possibilities of avoiding civil war or partition lie either in Moscow telling the Communists to climb down or in Chiang Kai-shek finding that he can't carry the country behind him to civil war.

The decisive factor is going to be the attitude of the great powers. The U.S.A. seem set on building an economic empire in China and tend to support the liberal capitalist elements in the régime—T. V. Soong, etc. They have infiltrated their advisors and technicians all over the place and are now busy reorganising Chiang's army which *may* play a part against the Japanese but *will* certainly be an important post-war political factor.

The Russians, for their part, have not yet shown their hand; though, if they come into the war, their troops will almost immediately come into touch with the Communist guerrillas whom they could hardly allow Chiang to attack at least while their own troops were there. It seems, moreover, to be a very open question how much the Russians would want to see a strong, united, American-industrialised, *Kuomintang* China growing up along their frontier.

The Allied representatives in Chungking included several remarkable men; none more so than my nominal chief, Carton de Wiart. With one eye, one arm, and seventeen different wound scars—as I saw for myself when we shared a tent in Assam—he must have been the most mutilated soldier on active service in any army. Carton was the son of a Belgian lawyer and had been brought up in Cairo. He had joined the British Army in the South African War to escape from Oxford and thereafter had given blood and limb for England in over forty years of service. Yet his outlook remained essentially gallic, and he once told me that he still thought in French more often than in English.

Until he knew you, he was rather reserved. But once you gained his

confidence, he spoke his mind and without fear of God or devil. He gave
me his confidence in the course of our journey out to China, and from
then on he spoke with utter frankness on every subject, official and
personal. I once asked him a question which he evidently resented. He
first answered it in detail and then rebuked me for asking it. He kept no
secrets from those he worked with. But this was a quality perhaps of
comradeship more than friendship, for once out of sight you were out of
mind, and he seldom bothered to answer letters. Carton's wounds caused
him a good deal of pain and sometimes led him to lose his temper. His
language when he did was the most violent and most varied I have ever
heard. Fortunately, he never lost his temper with me.

Carton's record and appearance caught the imagination of the Chinese
and, at parties, they used to enjoy touching him as if he were some fierce
dragon and to do so proved their courage. One Chinese General, it was
said, asked a colleague, 'What's Carton de Wiart like?' 'He's very fierce,'
came the reply, 'and over a hundred-and-fifty-years old.'

By a curious coincidence, de Gaulle's representative in Chungking was
General Pechkoff. Pechkoff, like Carton de Wiart, was a soldier of fortune.
He was a Russian, a son, it was said, of Maxim Gorki, but had served a life-
time in the French Army. Like Carton, too, Pechkoff had lost an arm in
the service of his adopted country. Both men had a keen political as well as
military sense and were inseparable companions.

Another close friend of Carton's was Doctor Lovink, the Dutch
Ambassador. Lovink, a tall, quiet man of wide culture, had been for
several years Governor of the Dutch East Indies. These three along with
Keith Officer, the shrewd and energetic Australian Ambassador, were
often together; and, though I was very much their junior, they very kindly
admitted me to their circle. We would lunch or dine together or go for
long walks, escaping from the squalor of Chungking into the three
mountain ranges beyond the river. There was said to be tigers in the third
range, but though I saw their skins in the Chungking market we never were
lucky enough to meet a live one.

Carton and his friends saw the Communist danger in China in much
the same perspective as I had expected. But they opened my eyes to
another and more immediate threat. This was the unconcealed hostility of
the United States to European interests in the Far East. Listening to these
wise and experienced men exchanging information on the latest trends of
American policy whether towards Indo China, the East Indies, or India, I
began to discern a clear pattern of American policy. It was Washington's
firm intention to break down the Colonial system throughout the Far East
so as to open the area to American trade and investment.

When I first heard these views, I was reluctant to accept them and sought the opinion of our Ambassador as a check. At a first meeting, Sir Horace Seymour seemed courteous and rather cautious. In fact he had an irrepressible sense of the ridiculous and seldom missed the comical side of any development. He knew from long experience the futility of most human endeavour and when decisions had to be taken took them unexpectedly light heartedly. When I first asked him about American policy in the Far East, he had replied with the usual platitudes about co-operation. But later on, when I had gained his confidence, he showed me the draft of a despatch he was preparing for the Foreign Office which fully confirmed what I had learned from Carton and Pechkoff. This, I remember, made the additional point that, if the Americans were to bring the rice bowl of South East Asia into China's sphere of influence, the problem of feeding India would become increasingly difficult, perhaps insoluble.

But perhaps the most conclusive evidence came from the Americans themselves. In Europe and the Middle East, I had always found American diplomats and officers eager to share information and ideas. In Chungking they showed the greatest reserve in their dealings with the British and other Europeans.

The American Ambassador, General Patrick Hurley, was a blunt, outspoken man, whose favourite parlour trick was a blood-curdling Indian war cry. But a more powerful figure was General Wedemeyer, who was Chiang Kai-shek's Chief-of-Staff and at the same time commanded all American forces in China. Wedemeyer was less openly anti-British than 'Vinegar Joe' Stilwell had been, but he was no less intent on building something like an American empire in China. There were American officers at every level in the General Staff. Chinese factories were largely staffed with American technicians. A visit to the front revealed a surprising number of American liaison officers with units in the field. I had not seen much of India; but a senior Indian official who came to Chungking told me that the American grip on the Chinese economy and the Chinese military machine was at least as strong as the British grip on India, probably stronger.

The Soviet Embassy retained its customary reserve. Russia was still neutral in the Far Eastern War, and Soviet diplomats did not normally attend Allied parties. But there were exceptions, as the following letter shows:

21 March 1945

Another week has gone by in which the highlight was a dinner given by one of our Embassy secretaries for the Reverend Woods, M.P., to meet Russian diplomats. The tactical plan of the dinner was to defeat the Russians at their own game, and the victory was so complete that about 1.0 a.m. I retired in fairly good order down the dark alleyways of Chungking, with two dead-drunk Russians draped round my neck lustily singing *Stenka Razin* They were both very nice really and not as cagey as the usual run.

45

Failure of a Mission

At lunch one day Pechkoff asked Carton de Wiart what my functions were. Carton tapped the black patch over his empty socket and replied, 'He's my missing eye.' It was quite untrue, as I did not work for him at all. But it was a good phrase and caught on. The Embassy also gave it out that in addition to my duties on Carton's staff, I was likely to enter Parliament at the next election and might be a useful friend to the Chinese. Interest was aroused and presently doors began to open.

The first leading man in the *Kuomintang* establishment to recognise my existence was Doctor Wang Chung-Hui, a delightfully frail old gentleman who wore blue silken robes, lined with fur. He had taken Law degrees in London, Harvard and Paris, and had been Foreign Minister. At this time he was Chairman of the Legislative *Yuan*—the Council which examined and finalised the texts of laws—but he was also one of the country's elder statesmen and a strong influence behind the scenes. We had two or three talks, but, though he answered my more serious questions courteously, he showed a marked preference for discussing birds, pictures, and the merits of different schools of Chinese cooking.

Then there was Doctor Wang Shih-Chieh, who sent for me as soon as he learned of my interest in the problem of Yenan. Doctor Wang was nominally Minister of Information, but as was often the case in China, his title concealed rather than explained his position. He was in fact one of the Generalissimo's chief advisers on foreign affairs and in charge of relations with the Chinese Communists. He was small in stature and possessed in full measure the delicacy and urbanity which are the essence of Chinese courtesy. At our first meeting he talked about his relations with the Communists in terms of platitudinous optimism. Later on, after I had told him something of our experiences in the Balkans, he opened up and admitted frankly that he did not see how American efforts to reconcile the two sides could succeed unless the Soviets put pressure on Mao to accept a permanently subordinate position.

Very close to Dr. Wang was Mr. Han Li Wu, nominally Minister of Education, but in fact the Generalissimo's chief adviser on relations with Britain, especially in connection with Hong Kong, the Treaties, and the future of South East Asia and India. In public pronouncements, the

Chinese Government liked to pose as the leaders of the new Asia and adopted a stridently anti-Colonialist line. But, in private, a more realistic view prevailed. The Chinese hoped to become a great Power with American help. But they knew the process would take time and they were very conscious of the potential threat from the Soviet side. Nor did they want to be wholly in American hands. In the circumstances, they wanted to see Britain retain some influence and interests in China, at any rate in the short term. We were likely to hear a good deal about their claims against us and their ambitions in Indochina and Burma, but they were unlikely to press these until China had grown stronger.

Conversations with these senior Chinese officials were by Western standards formal and by Balkan or Middle Eastern standards brief. Where time was concerned, there was a well established protocol. Tea would be served at an early stage of any interview. It would be served again a second time and this was often a sign that any further business should be raised. The appearance of a third cup indicated that it was time to bring the conversation to an end.

In point of form, I noticed one major difference between talks with Chinese leaders and with those of Europe or the Middle East. The Western and, for that matter, the Semitic mind, is either shocked or amused by glaring contradictions between profession and practice. Not so the Chinese. In Chungking the discrepancy between the ideal and the real was taken for granted and it was thought rather indelicate to discuss the real implications of a policy without first showing recognition of the ideal which inspired it. Thus General Wu Teh-chen, the Secretary General of the *Kuomintang*, felt no hesitation in saying to me: 'You will appreciate, Mr. Amery, that our party is essentially a proletarian party.' He knew it wasn't true and he knew that I knew it wasn't true. But he said it neither to amuse nor to deceive. He was simply making an obeisance to the ideal which Sun Yat-sen had set before the *Kuomintang* a generation before. Once this ritual bow had been performed, it was quite natural to discuss how, in the stage of transition through which China was passing and more particularly in the backward provinces of the south-west, the Government had to take more account of the interests of local war lords and landowners than they would, in theory, like to have done. It was hypocrisy, no doubt, but in La Rochefoucauld's sense of being the homage vice pays to virtue.

The military leaders were less approachable than the politicians. Few of them spoke English or any other foreign language; and most of them looked on contact with foreigners, except at dinner parties, as dangerous. The General who impressed me most was Pai Chung Shi, a Moslem war lord from Kwangsi, who gave an impression of quiet strength and determination, very different from most of his colleagues, who seemed to be either bland officials or picturesque thugs. The General I came to know best was General Yu ta Wei, then Under-Secretary for War. General Yu spoke perfect English and was a scholar too; but he was no more a regular officer than I was. I asked him once where he had made his military studies. He seemed at first not to grasp my meaning, but, when I repeated the question, he answered with a delightful smile: 'In Shanghai. You see before I was a General I was a banker.'

The naval leaders were more polished than the military and had mostly studied in England, America or Japan. I received much kindness from the Commander-in-Chief of the Navy, Admiral Shen Shao Kwan. The Admiral had no navy, but he had the prettiest garden in Chungking, and the best cooks. He delighted in giving lunch parties of eight where we would be feasted on such delicacies as carp's stomach, river slugs or live new born mice which the more squeamish drown in hot honey before eating.

At Admiral Shen's house I met Admiral Yang Suen Cheng. Admiral Yang was well over six foot tall, with a long drooping moustache and a shaven head. He had been for several years Director of Intelligence. Then one day he had been suddenly dismissed and, so it was said, sentenced to death at a secret court-martial. No-one seemed to know the nature of the charge against him, but by 1945 he was again a free man and a member of the National Military Council. His job was purely nominal; but he had an office and encouraged me to come and talk to him. He was a mine of information on Chinese relations with Japan and Russia and sometimes would lift the veil on the struggle for power within the *Kuomintang*. In the event his reprieve proved ephemeral and he was executed in mysterious circumstances in Formosa soon after the War.

The most remarkable of the Chinese leaders I came to know at all well was Chen Li Fu, then head of the *Kuomintang* party organisation and reputed by the liberal press in the West as the evil genius of the General-issimo. Chen Li Fu was very short with incredibly delicate hands, grey slightly wavy hair, unusual in Chinese, and a face that might have been made of alabaster. He was the head of what was known as the C.C. clique and had more patronage in his gift than anyone besides the General-issimo. He spoke atrocious English, but with great fluency, and convinced me of his sincere belief in the totalitarian policies which he thought necessary for the resurrection of China. He might well have been a Jesuit missionary, with a ruthless approach to means and a passionate faith in his end. I dined with him alone several times at his heavily guarded but modest house. His food was excellent, but instead of the hot rice wine that was usually served at Chinese dinners, we drank the *maotai*, a neat white spirit made of rice. This was inordinately strong but, despite his ascetic appearance, Chen Li Fu managed to put away substantial quantities of it without the slightest visible effect.

Chen Li Fu knew the Communists well and had no illusions about them. He watched what was happening in Eastern Europe closely, fearful of what it might portend for China, if sometimes hoping that it might keep the Soviets busy. But his main anxiety was over the encouragement which the Americans were giving to the more liberal elements in the *Kuomintang*. He believed, rightly as it proved, that this would undermine the régime and open the way to Mao.

I did not meet Dai Li, the notorious head of the secret service, but at an early stage he attached a General S. K. Yee to me. Yee was a handsome and Westernised officer, who looked much younger than his years and spoke fluent English or rather American. Like the good intelligence officer he was, he used to feed me tit-bits of information and expected me to repay him in kind.

With General Yee keeping an eye on me, I judged it wiser to avoid left-wing circles. Courtesy, as well as inclination, however, made it natural that I should call on Madame Sun Yat-sen, the widow of the father of the Republic, and Madame Chiang Kai-shek's youngest sister. Madame Sun lived in a modest bamboo and mud house some way back from the main road. The house was small and indifferently furnished, but Madame Sun had the kind of personality that shines through in any setting. At the beginning of a conversation, she seemed rather shy but as she warmed to her theme she showed all the fire and enthusiasm of the young rebel student which must have appealed to Sun Yat-sen.

Her theme at this time was the urgent need to try and bridge the gulf between Chungking and Yenan. She felt passionately on the subject, though her ideas for bringing it about were patently impractical. Perhaps she knew this herself and so devoted much of her argument to denouncing the weakness and corruption of her brother-in-law's Government. Her name and family connections made her immune from the authorities, and she took full advantage of this to say exactly what she thought of the leading men in the land. I went several times to see her in her house where she would dispense coffee, ham sandwiches and sweet liqueurs in the middle of the afternoon. The more I saw of her, the more I admired her as a woman and the more impractical I thought her as a politician. Sometimes, too, we would meet at dinner parties. There she would be received like royalty, and usually maintained an icy reserve broken only by an occasional acid thrust against the Government.

Madame Sun arranged for me to meet her stepson, Dr. Sun Fo, the son of Sun Yat-sen. Sun Fo was known as 'the man with the iron neck', because anyone else would have had his head cut off long before for daring to attack the Government so freely. I saw him several times in his large house on the Djaling Hill, which was filled with bad oil paintings and one very fine bust of his father. The more he talked of the need for an agreement with the Communists, the more I realised that he had no very clear idea how to bring it about. He knew the Communists and had little confidence in their willingness to compromise. But he thought it just possible that American and Russian pressures might impose a coalition between the *Kuomintang* and the Communists. If so, he was well fitted by his name and liberal opinions to emerge as its potential leader. It was a long shot but he saw no other role for himself in Chinese politics; and certainly some Americans in Chungking were grooming him for it.

Occasionally, at official receptions I met Chou En Lai, who was Mao's delegate in Chungking. On one occasion, I went to a party at his house. He seemed a man of considerable distinction but very reserved and I did not get to know him.[1]

By the end of February, I had come to the conclusion that my first objective should be to visit Yenan to meet the Communist leaders personally. I thought it unlikely that anything very constructive would emerge from the visit, but at least it would enable me to speak with some authority on what was clearly the central issue in internal Chinese politics. Most probably my visit would only provide further confirmation of the hard line favoured by the Generalissimo's advisers. But even this might have its uses. For a British officer to support the *Kuomintang*, at a time when the Americans were already looking for some compromise with the Communists, might be helpful both to S.O.E. and, in the longer term, to British interests at any rate in South China.

I, accordingly, went to see Wang Shih-Chieh and Chen Li Fu and put to them the idea that I should go to Yenan to see the Chinese Communists. They knew by this time from our talks that I had no illusions about Communism and they seemed to think that my visit might provide a corrective to the rather optimistic reports Wedemeyer was receiving from the American mission in Yenan. They, accordingly, agreed to put my proposal to the Generalissimo.

A few days later Dr. Wang sent for me and said with a sad smile that it had been decided that 'The journey to Yenan would not be worth your while'. His tone and expression admitted of no argument. He offered no explanation and he quickly changed the subject. When I next saw Chen Li Fu, I expressed regret at the decision. He answered bluntly that the Generalissimo had wanted me to go but that his American Chief of Staff, General Wedemeyer, had opposed the idea. In Chen Li Fu's opinion Wedemeyer regarded the proposal as the thin end of the wedge for establishing a British mission in Yenan and, thus, as an unwelcome

[1] Others were luckier. For an account of Chou En-Lai's views on this, see *La Chute de Chiang Kai-Shek* by Robert Rothschild.

extension of British influence in China. In the circumstances Chiang Kai-shek had decided that the issue was not important enough to justify a quarrel with his American allies. I found it very hard to believe that a man in Wedemeyer's position could have taken up such a position without first talking to Carton de Wiart. I, accordingly asked Carton if he believed what Chen Li Fu had told me. His reaction was the same as mine. But a few days later he told me that he was satisfied that Chen Li Fu was right.

With a visit to Yenan excluded, my next objective became the development of S.O.E. missions in South China and especially around Hong Kong. We already had a remarkably effective organisation in the area for helping prisoners of war to escape. A study of it convinced me that, given some air and sea support, it would not be difficult to organise sabotage and guerrilla activities against the Japanese on a substantial scale. I was satisfied, too, from my talks that the Chinese would welcome a British contribution of this kind, if only as a counterweight to American influence. But this time the refusal came not from the Chinese or the American side but from the British. Mountbatten's Headquarters in Kandy had proposed and London had agreed to concentrate S.O.E.'s efforts in South East Asia. China would be left to the Americans. The reasons for this were, I believe, primarily logistic. It was one thing to support operations in South East Asia from bases in Ceylon or Bengal; quite another to develop a new British base on the far side of the Himalayas where the Americans were already deployed in strength.

My mission to China had thus proved abortive. I was, however, ordered to stay on in Chungking 'pending further instructions'.

In the weeks that followed, I visited factories, was shown over welfare centres, and went once or twice to the front. My last visit to the front was towards the end of April when the weather was already turning warm. The General in command asked me what I would like to drink, and, when I suggested beer, at once produced it. I was thirsty and drank the bottle quickly, and he asked me if I would like another. I accepted the offer and he gave the order to his ADC. An hour went by and nothing happened. He made some enquiries and then turning to me with a bland smile said: 'We get our beer from the Japanese headquarters opposite in exchange for the chickens we send them. There seems to have been some interruption in the traffic. I'm so very sorry. Will you have a little whisky instead?'

I made friends, too, with a number of younger officers and junior officials and would sometimes go with them to the theatre to watch the delightful traditional Chinese plays. Once we went to the circus, and when the show was over, my companion, a Chinese lieutenant-colonel, intro-

A.M.—P

duced me to the circus manager. I congratulated him on the performance. He thanked me with a self-deprecating smile but said that it had been much better six weeks ago. At that time the circus had been performing behind the Japanese lines, and they had had elephants. Alas, they had had to leave the elephants behind. You could smuggle most things through the two front lines, but not elephants!

The squalor and discomfort of Chungking was fortunately relieved by frequent luncheon and dinner parties. Rice wine may not be the noblest of drinks, but Chinese cooking in its range and delicacy has no superior anywhere and no rival outside France. The explanation is, I believe, the same. Both countries have been over-populated in relation to their agricultural resources and have had to learn the art of making succulent dishes out of improbable material. This is as true of the France of Louis XIV as of the Ming dynasty.

Gastronomy apart, Chinese dinner parties have certain distinct advantages over our own. In those days, at least, the Chinese held that the basis of a lunch or dinner party was a round table of eight. You could have several tables if you wanted to entertain more than eight people, or you could have less than eight at table if you wanted to talk business. Otherwise, eight was the rule. It was a good rule too. Eight at a round table ensures a general conversation and one at least of the guests is likely to be interesting or fun. I have often sighed for the Chinese system at Western official dinners where twenty or thirty people sit down together but each is, in fact, the prisoner of his immediate neighbours.

Another sad feature of Western official entertaining is that, more often than not, our women have lost their looks by the time their husbands become prominent. Here the Chinese are luckier. The Chinese bone structure is such that Chinese women are spared bags under the eyes, double chins, pouches, and many of the other less attractive aspects of middle-age. This, too, helps to make Chinese entertaining a more graceful and decorative affair than it sometimes is in the West.

Chinese men enjoy the same advantage in bone structure as their women, and, throughout my stay in China, I had to make a conscious effort not to treat as my own contemporaries, men who were in fact at least twenty years my seniors. There are, of course, exceptions to every rule. But broadly speaking the Chinese seem, at least to Western eyes, to keep their looks much longer than we do. When they do look old, they look very old indeed. But perhaps that is as it should be.

Like many Europeans before me, I was delighted by the grace and lightness of touch of Chinese life, and found my tastes insensibly influenced by it. Walking through the streets of Chungking and seeing thousands upon thousands of Chinese faces every day, I suddenly realised how coarse European features can be. But though it is easy enough for a

European to lose his own standards in China, he very seldom succeeds in acquiring Chinese standards. These may perhaps be gained by long experience, but, at the end of my short stay, I still found that the pictures I liked, the ladies I admired, the dishes that pleased me, were seldom those that my Chinese friends thought the best.

Stronger even than this barrier of taste was the barrier of culture. Europe and the Middle East are essentially one world, sprung from the cultures of Egypt, Mesopotamia and Greece, united by centuries of Roman rule and by their essentially similar Semitic religions. An Englishman can travel the length and breadth of Europe, the Middle East, Africa, South America, North America and Australia, and find a common background of history, religion and literature. India has her own great cultural heritage. But there, too, centuries of Moslem and European rule have meant that most educated Indians are as much at home in the cultures of the West and of Islam as in their own. But China is another world, and only a handful of Europeans or Chinese, outside academic circles, have even a superficial knowledge of each others' history, philosophy, literature, or art. This limits conversation. There is no problem about the practical discussion of material issues. But it is difficult to enter the realms of speculation or theory without illustrating a point by historical or literary allusions. Once in a talk with a Chinese diplomat of some standing I referred to Julius Caesar as an example of a good dictator. 'Caesar?, Caesar?' he said, 'Ah yes, I think I saw a film about him once in Chicago.' Needless to say, I would have been equally in the dark had he referred to one of the Ming Emperors.

The fighting ceased in Europe. I was still without 'further instructions' and glady accepted an invitation from Carton de Wiart to go with him to Delhi and then to see something of the operations in Burma.

After the squalor and discomfort of Chungking, the grandeur and luxury of New Delhi was a tonic. The Viceroy was in London for discussions, but his regent, the Governor of Bombay, Sir John Colville, very kindly put me up at Vice-Regal Lodge. There and Government House, Calcutta, are the only two houses where I have been shaved in bed and dressed by servants.

Hugh Euston and Peter Coates were on the Viceroy's staff and, thanks to them, I saw as much of Delhi as time allowed. I visited the abandoned cities; revelled in the glories of the Red Fort with its crenellated walls and marble pavilions; meditated at the Great Mosque and stood in wonder before the grave of Humayun. The Moghul monuments stand out in my memory. But in their own way Baker and Lutyens' work at Vice-Regal Lodge and at the Secretariat seemed worthy of what had gone before.

Dinner at Vice-Regal Lodge was very much a ceremony, with a servant standing behind every chair. But to set an example, for the country was just recovering from famine, the meal itself was spartan in the extreme. I reflected that in Chungking the only comparable measure had been the issue of an edict forbidding the serving of more than twenty-one courses at any dinner.

We had planned to visit the Burma front, but Carton de Wiart was recalled unexpectedly to Chungking and we flew back together 'over the hump'.

Spring had come at last to China; my suits and my soul had been ironed out in India; and in the continuing absence of 'further instructions' I cast about for opportunities of fresh employment.

It so happened that the third secretary at the Embassy, Gordon Etherington-Smith, had just been appointed Consul to Kashgar in Sinkiang, or Chinese Turkistan. It was a lonely but romantic post and could only be reached by yak over the high passes of the Himalayas and the Kara Koram. Sinkiang covered a vast area and had been for many years under Soviet influence. Chiang had recovered control of it during the war when the Soviets had to concentrate all their forces against Hitler; but the Government of India was concerned about its future. In the circumstances, Gordon Etherington-Smith was authorised to take a military adviser with him. He offered me the job. I was all for going. I would have crossed the highest ranges in the world, gone riding with the Kazakh horsemen and hunted not with hawks but with black eagles. The project appealed to me all the more because of my association with the Turkoman soldiers in Albania. But before Etherington-Smith could secure formal permission to take me with him, a telegram came from my father warning me that the General Election was near and urging me to return to London. I was pledged to stand for Preston and had no choice but to obey the summons. Yet to have said 'no' to the chance of a year in Sinkiang remains a lasting regret.

Before leaving Chunking I went to say goodbye to the Generalissimo. Carton de Wiart had presented me to him when I first arrived and I had seen him at ceremonies and conferences. But this was the only time I saw him alone.

He received me in his office, a modest room furnished in European style in a heavily guarded concrete house. He was dressed in a plain khaki uniform without decorations or badges of rank. There was nothing Westernised about him. On the contrary, his ritual bow and unchanging smile conformed entirely to the traditional pattern of Chinese courtesy. Yet there was something distinctive about the man. His movements were a little more deliberate than is usual in China. His shaven head had a strangely luminous quality, as if made of alabaster. The eyes were very dark and sometimes sparkled. Madame Chiang, who was reputed to be much his best interpreter, was unfortunately in America. We had to make do instead with a young officer who seemed ill at ease and spoke very uncertain English.

I had been warned not to raise the subject of my proposed visit to Yenan, as he had been embarrassed at having to refuse it. Nor did he refer to it except to say that he had been interested to hear from Chen Li Fu of my experience of Communism in the Balkans and hoped this would help me to understand his problems. He asked me my impressions of China, talked a little of the future of South East Asia and then, to my surprise, asked if I had any advice to give him on the conduct of the war or the administration of the country. It is not every day that one is invited to lecture to a dictator, but I resisted the temptation and contented myself with a few suggestions about the need to develop Resistance and not leave this field entirely to the Communists. This seemed to meet with his approval and after a few more rather formal exchanges he wished me well at the election and urged me to come back to Chungking afterwards to take part in the victory over Japan.

Two days later I flew 'over the hump' to Calcutta in an American troop transport. I stayed once again with the Caseys and spent much of my time, while waiting for a passage home, writing a report on China for S.O.E. Smiley was also in Calcutta and we dined together the night before he was dropped into Thailand. McLean was in Delhi and I arranged for him to take on the job in Sinkiang which I had so reluctantly refused.

As often happened in wartime, my aircraft was repeatedly delayed. The hot weather came on; and the Caseys departed for Darjeeling, leaving me alone in Government House. I mostly ate my meals out with friends; but on my last evening I dined alone at Government House.

Following the example of Vice-Regal Lodge, the dinner was spartan, consisting of a thin soup, a fish the size of a sardine, a single cutlet and a little fruit salad. It was served, however, with due ceremony. There were, I think, four servants standing on each side of the room, and when I had finished eating, the butler poured me out a glass of port and invited me to drink the loyal toast. I rose in solitary state and raised my glass to the King Emperor. It is my last memory of British India. Three days later I was back in London.

46

Proud Preston

For most of the War, an electoral truce prevailed in the constituencies. The three main parties agreed not to oppose each other at by-elections. Sometimes an independent candidate might provoke a contest. Otherwise, the party holding a seat simply selected a new member when the previous incumbent died or retired. Members of Parliament were authorised to hold commissions in the armed forces but, unlike other mortals, they had the right to resign these at any time and go back to the House of Commons. In practice, too, they were often given leave to return to Westminster for important debates.

My early differences with the Foreign Office over Balkan policy encouraged me to think that it might be useful to combine my work in S.O.E. with a seat in the House of Commons. Accordingly, when I came back to London in the autumn of 1940, I asked to be put on the Conservative Central Office list of candidates. The odds against my being adopted were long. I was only twenty-one and, since I was likely to be overseas for most of the War, would be unable to give much time to any constituency. Nevertheless, on two or three occasions, I was interviewed by selection committees.

One of these consisted of half a dozen ladies and gentlemen gathered round a green baize-covered table in the local Conservative Club. The Chairman gave a necessarily short description of my qualifications and asked the committee if they had any questions to put to me. A long pause followed. Then, after some preliminary clearing of the throat, one gentleman enquired: 'Mr. Amery, would you say you were interested in politics?' This seemed to me a silly question to put to a budding statesman. But I seized the opportunity to make a short, crisp and, needless to say, carefully prepared statement of my political views. It was rather good stuff, but I could see that it was water off a duck's back as far as this particular audience was concerned. The Chairman then enquired if there were any further questions. Someone asked if I was married or engaged. I admitted that I was still a bachelor but at twenty-one there was still time to correct this defect. Why, I might even find my soul mate in the confines of the constituency. This went down rather well.

Nevertheless, a few days later I heard from the Chairman that his committee had decided against me, because they felt they really must have a married man. This rather presumptuous insistence on marriage was destined to be punished. The man selected instead of me turned out to be a bigamist. A scandal was only narrowly averted and the Association had to go through the whole process of selection once again.

One morning in the autumn of 1943 I walked into the bar of the Mohammed Ali Club in Cairo to find Randolph Churchill. On the table in front of him was a pile of letters from home. He handed one of them to me. It was from the Chairman of the Preston Conservative Association. Randolph was at this time one of the two members of Parliament for Preston, and the letter stated that the other member, Captain Cobb, disapproved of Randolph so strongly 'on personal and public grounds' that he was not prepared to stand again for Preston as his running mate. The Chairman went on to explain that the Association would accordingly have to select another candidate. They were naturally anxious to avoid further quarrels, and wondered whether Randolph could possibly think of anyone with whom he could work in harness and in harmony.

'Would you like to have a go?' Randolph asked. My mind, at the time, was wholly concentrated on the Balkans. The General Election seemed a long way off and I was not very sure where Preston was. Randolph, however, seemed to think it would help; so I light-heartedly agreed.

A few weeks later Randolph left for Yugoslavia with Fitzroy Maclean. Not long afterwards I jumped into Albania. I had heard nothing meanwhile from Preston and concluded that Randolph had forgotten to write or that the Preston people had chosen someone else.

In September 1944, when Bill McLean and I were in the Albanian mountains, we received a parachute drop of explosives and other supplies from Italy. These included a packet of mail. In this was a letter from Sir Norman Seddon-Brown, Chairman of the Preston Conservative Association, inviting me to stand as candidate in the room of Captain Cobb. The letter was nearly ten months old, and had been misdirected round most of the Mediterranean.

It is easy enough to drop mail by parachute but there is no comparable method of catapulting back replies. Two months later, however, I was back in Italy and wrote to my father to ask for his advice. I added that I was anxious to get out to the Far East as soon as possible and that my inclination was to miss the next Parliament. He replied that he had spoken to Seddon-Brown and that there was no need for an immediate decision. The Preston people were prepared to wait until I came back to London.

Back in London, I had first to decide whether to stand at the next election at all. I felt out of sympathy with much contemporary Conservative thinking and especially with the tendency to appease the Soviets and the growing demand for a return to *laissez-faire* economics. I put these objections to my father who argued cogently that the sooner I got into Parliament, the sooner I could hope to influence the Party's policies. I consulted Duncan Sandys and Duff Cooper. They gave me the same advice. Finally, to get a balanced view I went to see Hugh Dalton. He said that of course I must stand. He hoped that I might one day become a good Socialist; but as my father's son, the right thing for me to do was to enter Parliament as a Conservative. Where my political pilgrimage would ultimately lead, no one could tell.

I accordingly decided to stand and cast around to see if there were any safer seats in the market than Preston. I was thus engaged when General Carton de Wiart offered me a lift to China in his aircraft. We were to leave in ten days; and it seemed a clear case of 'better the bird in the hand . . .'.

I, accordingly, rang up Seddon-Brown and asked if he still wanted me to be the candidate. He did, and then and there fixed a date for me to meet his Committee.

On 16 January 1945, two days before leaving for China, I arrived in Preston for the first time in my life. It was a cold and wet winter afternoon. There was no-one to meet me at the station. The town looked grim in the blackout. Eventually, I found my way to a Conservative Club. It proved to be the wrong one; but I presently discovered another where Seddon-Brown and the agent, Fred Gray, were waiting.

Seddon-Brown was a textile industrialist of rather striking appearance. He had white hair, a pink complexion and shrewd eyes. He wore a blue suit with a rather loud chalk stripe in it, and had an orchid in his buttonhole. He gave me a drink, introduced me to one or two members of the club, and then took me aside for a private discussion.

In those days, candidates were supposed to make a contribution to party funds and to Election expenses. The amount varied with the safety of the seat. Preston was a marginal constituency, and I was asked to contribute £250 a year and half the Election expenses, which meant a sum of about £450. By the standards of the day, this was reasonable. I asked whether I would be expected to live in the constituency. 'Live in Preston? Good God, no!' came the reply. 'It's a very marginal seat. You're a young man. You're bound to sow some wild oats, and it would never do to sow them in the constituency.' I then asked how often I would be expected to come to the constituency. Seddon-Brown answered that regularity was the important thing. He wanted me to come once a month. If I came more often my visits would cease to be news. If I came less often there would be criticism. It was a very sensible approach.

I then asked about selection procedure. He expected no difficulty. One or two members of the Committee had asked if they could interview two or three people before making up their minds, but, 'I told them I would rather resign than ask a gentleman to submit to that sort of practice; and I've been Chairman here for twenty-five years.' He then gave me another drink and disappeared saying: 'I will go down and tell them you'll do. I will send for you in a few minutes.'

Some ten minutes later I went down to a small room where some ten people were sitting round a table. Despite coal rationing a fire was blazing generously. At Seddon-Brown's invitation, I made a short statement of my principles, stressing the importance of the Commonwealth, National Defence, and overseas trade. I was asked if I would make a study of the problems of the cotton industry and gave the necessary assurance. There were no other questions. The Committee then rose and went out to report to the General Council next door.

Presently a dark man, in his early forties, came into the room and introduced himself as Ron Gray. He was, he said, the Chairman of the Juniors, and the agent's elder brother. Seddon-Brown, he went on, would be glad if I would now come and say a few words to the General Council. Gray seemed shrewd and friendly, and I asked him what line he thought I should take in my speech. He seemed puzzled at first; then a flash of understanding lit up his eyes. 'Don't worry,' he said, 'you haven't got to win them over. We've already adopted you and just want a few words of thanks.' This was a great relief and I, accordingly, followed Gray into a larger room where nearly a hundred people were gathered. Seddon-Brown informed me that I had been adopted as their candidate and I made a ten minute speech of thanks for the honour they had done me. There were no questions. Seddon-Brown then wound up the proceedings and took me off to dine at the Park Hotel before I caught my train. He tried hard to raise a bottle of champagne to celebrate the occasion, but the best the hotel could do, at that stage of the war, was some Australian burgundy. I had failed to secure a sleeper on the train, but I slept soundly in the knowledge that I now had every chance of a seat in Parliament.

Parliament was dissolved on 15 June 1945, and, a day or two later, I reached London from Calcutta. I got in touch with Randolph at once and we began to concoct plans for our campaign. We listened together to Churchill's first election broadcast and I remember my misgivings about the violence of his invective which seemed out of tune with the country's mood. The Coalition Government had been popular, and I sensed that the public would not easily understand how Churchill could turn and rend his old colleagues in this way. Attlee's broadcast which I listened to two days later seemed much more statesmanlike. It was not our business, however, to decide the Party's strategy at the election. We had our own corner to fight. Randolph and I accordingly drove north in a large open car, which he had borrowed from King Peter of Yugoslavia. Ralph Assheton[1] kindly lent us his house a few miles out of Preston. Randolph had brought several cases of champagne from France, and Bob Boothby[2] sent us a barrel of herrings from Aberdeen. I took up our excellent cook, Mrs. Wills. Ian Pirie, who had been head of the Greek section of S.O.E., took leave to come and act as our campaign manager. Jane Wilson who had worked with me in S.O.E. now became my private secretary.

Preston is one of the oldest parliamentary boroughs in England. It has returned two members to Westminster since 1297 and has long been regarded as one of the barometer towns of England. It swings from one party to another with the political pendulum. Dickens' famous description of the Eatanswill election was, I believe, based on factual accounts of a Preston contest. Others were even more packed with incident. In 1768, indeed, when General Burgoyne was elected:

> Two thousand six hundred men, collected from twenty miles around, were brought into the town, armed with clubs, pickaxes and other destructive weapons. They were joined by some of the Militia, who marched with colours flying through the streets and ultimately wrecked the house where the Tory supporters met. The following day, the Mayor's house was gutted, and the Mayor himself was seized and put under the pump.

Preston was what was known in those days as 'a double-barrelled seat'. Each elector had two votes and the constituency of something over 100,000 electors returned two members. Sometimes, the electors split their votes casting one, for instance, for the Conservative and one for the Socialist. Sometimes they 'plumped' using only one vote. More often they cast both votes for the same party. Apart from Randolph and myself, the other candidates were two Socialists, a Liberal and a Communist. The town was wholly industrial and mainly concerned with textiles, engineering, and tank and aircraft construction. As I saw it for the first time in daylight I reflected that I knew much less about its economic and social problems than about those of Albania, Yugoslavia, Egypt or even China. But an election campaign is a great education, and I would soon learn.

We opened our campaign with an enthusiastic adoption meeting. Randolph made a brilliant, wholly unprepared speech. At the end of my own effort he turned to me and said in a hoarse whisper, 'Well, thank God

---

[1] Financial Secretary to the Treasury and later Lord Clitheroe.
[2] M.P. for Aberdeenshire East and later Lord Boothby.

for that, at least you know how to speak.' The roughness of the compliment seemed a gauge of its sincerity and I was duly impressed. So, for that matter, were the audience; for Randolph had forgotten that the microphone was still switched on.

The next task was to produce a joint election address. I tried my hand at a draft, and rather to my surprise, Randolph accepted it with very few amendments. It was printed in red and blue; and since it was the basis of all our campaign speeches, I reproduce it here:

Ladies and Gentlemen.
WHY AN ELECTION?
The country is faced with a General Election because the Socialists and Sinclair Liberals refused to accept Mr. Winston Churchill's proposal to remain in the Coalition Government and help him finish the job. The responsibility for the Election rests squarely on the Socialists and Sinclair Liberals.
MR. CHURCHILL'S NEW NATIONAL GOVERNMENT
We are standing as the Conservative candidates in support of the new National Government which Mr. Churchill formed when the Socialists and Liberals left the Coalition. This Government, though predominantly Conservative in character, includes many able men of goodwill of other parties or of no party who have proved their fitness for office by their successful achievements in the late administration. These are such men as Sir James Grigg, Sir Andrew Duncan, Lord Woolton, Lord Leathers, Major Gwilym Lloyd George and Mr. Hore Belisha. They, together with Mr. Churchill and the Conservative Ministers, are now tackling the job which the Socialists abandoned.
WHAT IS THE JOB?
These are the main tasks which will confront whatever Government is returned to power:
First: to defeat Japan as we have defeated Germany; to end the long agony of China and free the enslaved peoples of Asia from the Japanese; to bring home victorious our troops and prisoners-of-war in the Far East.
Second: To set up, together with the United States of America and the Soviet Union, a world order under which peace may be preserved and democracy may flourish.
Third: To provide for the British people full employment, good homes, education, health services and a more comprehensive system of national insurance.
Fourth: To change over from war production to peace production so that industry may satisfy the needs of the comsumers and provide the revenue necessary for policies of social reform.
That is the job. You, the electors, have to decide who shall tackle it:—
Winston Churchill or Clement Attlee?
OUR PROGRAMME
The following are the principles on which we take our stand as supporters of Mr. Winston Churchill and of the National Government.

DEFENCE

We believe that Great Britain must maintain a strong Navy, Army and Air Force to beat the Japanese, to preserve peace and to guard the fruits of victory.

THE BRITISH COMMONWEALTH & EMPIRE

We believe that the destiny of Great Britain is inseparably bound up with that of the Dominions, India and the Crown Colonies. Political and economic collaboration with the nations of the Empire is the surest road to peace and prosperity.

FOREIGN POLICY

The problems of the world can best be solved through the closest co-operation between the British Empire, the United States of America and the Soviet Union. We believe, in particular, that the main purposes of our foreign policy should be the maintenance of peace, the defence of our vital interests and the restoration of the Christendom of Europe.

The Prime Minister, Mr. Churchill, was the architect of the Grand Alliance which defeated Germany and which will surely bring down Japan.

We submit to you that in the difficult years that lie ahead Mr. Churchill and our Foreign Secretary, Mr. Anthony Eden, are the men best qualified by their experience, their intellect and their prestige to speak for England and pursue in peace the diplomacy which has triumphed so signally in war.

DEMOCRATIC RIGHTS

We believe that every Englishman has the birth-right of freedom of speech, freedom of thought and conscience and what Kipling called 'leave to live by no man's leave underneath the law'. The Institution of Parliament, which rests on the traditions of a thousand years, is the sovereign guarantee of these rights. Democracy is threatened from many quarters. We shall only preserve our British democracy if every citizen regards it as his duty to play his full part in the political life of the nation.

SOCIAL JUSTICE

We believe that every Englishman has the right to a good home, sufficient food, education, a health service and full employment. We believe that Mr. Churchill's Four-Year Plan provides the best way to realise these aims. The main features of this plan are the Butler Education Act, the White Papers on Full Employment and on National Insurance, the system of Family Allowances and the Housing Programme.

INDUSTRY AND AGRICULTURE

A strong and enterprising British industry, balanced by a stable agriculture, is essential to the achievement of all our aims. We believe that the Government must increasingly concern itself with the economic well-being of the nation, and that it is for that reason all the more vital to revive at the earliest possible moment a widespread, healthy and vigorous private enterprise. Without it, we shall never be able to provide the employment and standard of living which our people deserve. It is the duty of the Government to provide industry with guidance; but those war-time controls which threaten to stifle enterprise should be removed. The Socialists would cling to war-time controls for their own sake. It is our policy to lift them as soon as possible. So long as there is scarcity we must ration such things as food and clothing to ensure fair distribution; but the Conservative plan is to end the scarcity, not to perpetuate the controls.

WIN THE PEACE

We have won the war in Europe, soon we will defeat the Japanese. But victory will not solve all our problems. Unceasing vigilance will be needed to ensure that all we have gained by victory is not muddled away. The National Government has deserved your confidence on the proved record of its members. No Government which the Socialists can offer would have comparable authority in the world. And we must have a Government which can speak for England.

We therefore confidently appeal to you to send us to Westminster to fight under the leadership of Winston Churchill for EMPIRE, DEMOCRACY and SOCIAL JUSTICE.

Times have changed, but, in the light of circumstances as they then were, I see nothing to regret in these words.

Randolph was very keen that we should have a campaign song, and had some reason to believe that 'Lily of Laguna' was a Lancashire tune. We accordingly asked Ian Pirie to write some suitable lyrics. This was the result:

> Churchill and Amery,
> We're backing Churchill and Amery,
> They're the pair that Preston needs today
> They're the pair we'll vote for on Polling Day.
> Our votes they won't lack,
> We want them both back,
> We'll get them both back.
> Good old Winston wants them with him—
> And that's what Preston wants today!
>
> Winston for Premier,
> We're backing Winston for Premier.
> He's the one to make a Conference go
> He's the one who's known to Uncle Joe.
> A true friend of Truman.
> D'you want a new man?
> Some Laski crew man?
> No! We want Winston for our Premier—
> That's what Preston wants today!

We had gramophone records made of it, and played it both on the canvass and at evening meetings. Some of our supporters thought it in bad taste. The tune is admittedly rather dreary, but the general public seemed to enjoy it. At any rate, it helped to raise the temperature and this we thought good tactics.

Every morning and afternoon we spent a couple of hours doing a personal canvass in the wards. I used to begin by playing the gramophone record and so bring people to their doors. I would then make a short speech and go round and shake hands. The overwhelming majority were friendly, even when they were on the other side. Old Age Pensions were a problem, and there was a good deal of anxiety about the effect of the Butler Education Act on the church schools. But much the biggest issue was housing. No new houses had been built since the war; and there was fearful over-crowding. It was quite common to find eleven or twelve people sleeping in a single room, and in many of the slum districts there was virtually no sanitation.

I was immensely encouraged by the large numbers of Conservative supporters I met, even in the poorest streets. I shall never forget one old lady, an old-age pensioner, standing at the door of her slum home. I shook hands with her and asked if I could count on her support. The expression on her face never changed, and she answered: 'Well, ah'll think abaht it.' I did my best to charm and to convince, then she winked at me and said: 'Cum in 'ere, luv, yer don't ave ter worry abaht this 'ouse,' and she pointed to an almost life-size lithograph of Disraeli hanging above the fireplace.

After five years of war, the Election was looked on as something of a sporting event and aroused far more interest than any election campaign I have fought since. One day when I canvassed the Plungington Road, one of Preston's main thoroughfares, virtually the whole population of the road and of the side streets leading off it turned out to watch. I was surrounded by a crowd of thirty or forty children, singing our campaign song and must have shaken hands with well over a thousand people in less than an hour.

After the afternoon canvass we used to meet deputations representing different interests such as teachers, doctors, shopkeepers or religious denominations. Preston has one of the largest Roman Catholic popula-tions in the country—at least a third of the population. Some of the Preston Catholics were Irish but the majority belonged to the old English Catholic Community which had stood out against the Reformation; and religious divisions remained very strong in the town. It was the accepted view in those days that no Catholic was likely to be elected for Preston but that no one could hope to be elected without strong Catholic support.

Every evening we held two meetings; one in one part of the town, and one in another. Each of us addressed both and would meet at some half-way pub to compare notes. Randolph was a provocative speaker and often reduced his meetings to a state of pandemonium. One one occasion, as we crossed over, Randolph asked me how things were at my meeting. I answered: 'Very quiet; you could hear a pin drop.' 'Oh,' he said. 'Well you wouldn't hear an elephant drop in the one you're going to.'

There was no television in those days and meetings were livelier and better attended than they have since become. There was usually standing room only by the time the candidate arrived and volleys of heckling continued all through his speech. At first I was rather baffled by the Lancashire dialect, and made some silly mistakes. One questioner asked me: 'Wot does the Cundidayte think abaht the rahshuns?' I replied with a suitable statement of Conservative policy on relations with Russia. 'I didn't mean that,' came the rejoinder, 'I meant the baycun rahshuns.'

I seldom had much difficulty in getting a hearing at indoor meetings and found that even the rowdiest audiences will listen if you start by asking for questions. Outdoor meetings could be more difficult. Towards the end of the campaign, I went to speak outside the English Electric Works during their lunch break. I set up my loudspeaker opposite the factory gates, and used the roof of a supporter's car as a platform. In a few minutes I had a crowd of three or four thousand people surging round me. They barracked a good deal, but my loudspeaker was powerful and they could not drown my speech. Perhaps rashly, I launched into a tirade against the Labour Party's record on rearmament before the War and made some fairly savage jibes at individual Labour leaders. The crowd got very excited, but, thanks to my loud speaker, I could still make myself heard above the shouting and booing. At last it became too much for the left-wingers in the audience and someone raised the cry: 'Let's turn over the bloody car.' I only had two or three supporters with me; and it was not long before they were pushed out of the way and several pairs of willing hands fastened on the running board of the car. But it takes quite an effort to turn a car over. I got the timing right, and was able to bring my remarks to a dignified conclusion before jumping into the crowd just as the car went over. I wondered for a moment what would happen next. But the crowd were obviously shaken by what they had done. No-one tried to attack me. More remarkable still, the car was somehow put back on its wheels still in working order.

We had our share of distinguished guest speakers, though Lord Woolton, soon to be Chairman of the Tory Party, declined to come. He excused himself on the rather curious ground that he had never allowed his employees to take part in elections, and felt he could not set a bad example himself. My father, however, made a powerful speech for us in the Football Ground; and we called in such war heroes as Sheamie Lovat,[1] and Bob Laycock.[2] But a warning note was struck by the total failure of a meeting for Oliver Stanley. The house of Stanley was still believed to have great influence in Preston; and Oliver was a very popular figure in the country.

[1] Lord Lovat, D.S.O., M.C., then Under-Secretary for Foreign Affairs.
[2] General Laycock, later Governor of Malta.

With some difficulty Randolph and I persuaded him to fit a meeting in Preston into an already crowded programme of speeches. The meeting was well advertised and the press were present in force. But there were only six people in the audience.

Our spirits, however, were soon revived by the size and enthusiasm of the crowd that gathered to welcome the Prime Minister. Preston was to be his last meeting at the end of a tour of the North-West. Randolph and I went to meet him at Blackburn, where he was already running an hour and a half behind schedule. We found him wearing his old-fashioned bowler hat and wrapped in a light grey overcoat. He had been speaking since ten o'clock in the morning and was plainly exhausted. At Blackburn we trans-ferred him into a colossal battleship of an open car lent and driven by one of our supporters. Churchill insisted on standing and Randolph and I sat on the folded hood holding him up. Even in the country districts little crowds had gathered at every cross-roads. People rushed out of their houses as we approached. Cripples waved their crutches, and old women who looked as if they had not left their houses for years hung out of the windows screaming 'Good old Winnie,' at the top of their lungs. Once Churchill stopped the car to talk to a crippled child and reminded him of Roosevelt's example. Whenever we passed a group of people, he would ask the driver to slow down. 'Give them a chance,' he would say. 'They've come here to see me.'

We made our first stop in Preston at the Conservative Bowling Club, so that Churchill could have a drink before the meeting. We had not publicised this stop at all, but the word had got around and at least three thousand people of all ages had gathered on the green. Churchill gave them a short speech and we then took him into the Club house for refreshment and a few minutes' rest. There was little enough rest, in fact, as all our leading supporters insisted on coming in and shaking hands with him.

We then drove on through packed streets to the open air meeting in the Town Hall square. The meeting had begun at half past five, and it was by this time nearly eight o'clock. But the crowd had been kept together by candidates from the neighbouring constituencies. They had made good use of their opportunity to address a captive audience of certainly more than twenty thousand people.

Our platform was the balcony of the Public Library, a fine building in the classical style. Churchill spoke for about twenty minutes. He sounded very tired at the start but the voice regained its old resonance as he warmed to his subject. Randolph and I stood on either side of him, and then moved and seconded a vote of thanks. It was the biggest meeting I have ever seen in Britain. Churchill left the Public Library with difficulty. He seemed almost too tired to walk. All the same, he insisted on standing and giving the V sign as we drove off through cheering streets where enthusiasm was

a. The author in China.

b. General Chiang Kai-shek and his wife.

a. Randolph Churchill and the author during the Preston election in 1945.

b. Winston Churchill visits Preston during the campaign: with him in the car are his wife, the author and Randolph Churchill.

a. Mrs Julian Amery.

b. The author with his father at Lord Moyne's House, Bailiffs-court at Littlehampton in Sussex.

The wedding day.

mingled with gratitude. When at last we had left every vestige of human habitation behind, the Prime Minister fell back into the seat of the car and launched out at once into a diatribe against Herbert Morrison who had ventured to criticise him in a speech the previous day. 'That squealing pig; why, his chief joys were 18B and the blackout. Now that he hasn't got them any more he doesn't know what to do with himself. I'll go down and speak against him in his constituency.' Randolph, in an attempt to calm him down, questioned whether this would be thought wise or statesman-like. The effect was the reverse of that intended. 'What you say is very grandfatherly,' said the old man to his son. 'You're always giving me grandfatherly advice. You're not my grandfather, you know.'

A special train was waiting at a siding out in the country. As he got out of the car Churchill asked at once whether there was any news. One of the secretaries said, 'No.' He replied rather petulantly, 'Why not?' But his last words when he said goodbye to us were on a higher plane. 'We have got to work damned hard to repay these people.'

Many friends had warned me against the perils of trying to work in harness with Randolph. They told me that I would find him quarrelsome, overbearing and selfish. They begged me to stand almost anywhere but Preston. I am very glad I did not believe them.

I had liked Randolph from the moment of our first meeting at the Oxford Union, and we had become friends during the War. He had a lively intelligence, an astonishing memory and was a very stimulating companion. He liked to have his say at some length, but I soon discovered that pro-vided you first let him talk himself out, he was perfectly ready to listen to you afterwards. He liked a conversation to be a series of speeches like a debate in Parliament, rather than a rally of comments and interruptions. He was, besides, very quick to see a new idea and had no hesitation in changing his mind if he was once convinced that there were strong argu-ments for doing so.

I had feared a quarrel with him over the election address to which, as always to the written word, I attached perhaps excessive importance. In fact, he was very conciliatory, and accepted several points I wanted to make but with which he did not altogether agree. In fact, we only had one cross word in the whole campaign. My speech at our adoption meeting had been carefully prepared and I had read it out from a typescript. I prepared my speech for our next meeting in the same way, and, just before the meeting, Randolph asked if he might look at it. I took the text from my pocket and gave it to him. He tore it up, explaining that platform speeches were far more effective if made without notes. We were in a crowded hotel bar full of constituents, otherwise I would certainly have struck him. But he was, of course, quite right, and from then on I spoke with only the briefest notes or no notes at all.

I shall always be grateful that I fought my first election with Randolph. Most candidates have no-one with personal experience of electioneering to guide them. Agents and Chairmen may have views on how candidates should fight a campaign but they have never done the thing themselves. They are critics not authors, producers not actors. Randolph, however, had made a close study of electioneering and had considerable experience of it. He was bold in canvassing; stopping people in the street and making himself known to them. He was also very skilful at handling deputations. When he knew that he could not hope to satisfy them, as with the doctors in the 1945 campaign, he had an uncanny way of luring them into quarrelling among themselves and then urging on them the importance of reaching an agreed view before troubling busy candidates. He was an outstanding platform speaker, and if the meat he served up was sometimes a bit strong for the floating voter, his supporters revelled in it. He had, besides, a great gift of phrase and was adept at thinking out a point for the newspapers. Above all he had absorbed most of his father's and his grandfather's political maxims; and, since politics are continually repeating themselves, he was seldom at a loss for a formula for dealing with any challenge however unexpected.

Winston Churchill once said to me: 'Randolph has big guns but not enough ammunition.' Randolph certainly had a greater facility for speech and writing than his father. But this facility was a dangerous gift. He could dictate a good article in twenty minutes and make a good speech wholly unprepared. As a result, he seldom took enough pains to write a very good article or make a very good speech. It was a case, with him, of the good being the enemy of the best.

People often said that Randolph was overshadowed by his father. I do not believe that this was so. His difficulty, psychologically, was that the world did not accept him at his father's valuation. Churchill had always taken Randolph into his confidence and treated him more as a colleague than a son. So, in consequence, had Churchill's intimate circle. Randolph had learnt much in the process but, as he grew older, he found it increasingly difficult to speak his mind freely to his father and his father's intimates and yet to show proper respect for the views of lesser mortals. I am thinking, for instance, of Ministers and Commanders-in-Chief whom Churchill in private no doubt dismissed as 'boobies' but who were nevertheless Randolph's 'betters' in status or achievement.

My father, too, had taken me into his confidence; but I was several years younger than Randolph and my secret service experience had accustomed me to living my life in compartments. I might spend the evening discussing a coup d'état against King Boris, but, in the office next morning, I was careful to be only the keen, young, assistant press attaché. Randolph's experience had been the opposite. He had made a name as a journalist largely by writing for the public exactly what he said in private. With years the habit grew on him and, by the time of the 1945 General Election, he said what he thought quite bluntly without regard for the self-esteem of the great or indeed the self-respect of the lowly. This made him a host of enemies.

This lack of self-restraint emerged at an early stage of our campaign. Randolph decided that there was too much apathy among the voters and that we must do something to raise the temperature. We discussed different ways of doing this, but there were powerful objections to each. Then suddenly he hit on an idea. He and I would parade down the main street on two elephants. Our *howdahs* would be draped with placards or party favours, and we would address the passers by through loud hailers as the pachyderms ambled along Fishergate. Someone raised the question of cost. He took this as a valid point and at once got on to the Manchester Zoo to find that elephants could be hired for as little as £20 a day. He warmed to the idea and duly booked the elephants. It was, I still think, a good idea, but it had an exotic quality which shocked the officers of our association. 'We don't like stunts in Preston,' they said and went on to argue that in any case we could not afford the money. Randolph as a concession, offered to make do with only one elephant. He and I would share the *howdah*. But when this was refused he became very angry and told the committee that they were narrow-minded, middle-class provincials with no imagination and no guts. They never forgave him.

It was hard to fault Randolph in public; and at meetings or with deputations he was invariably courteous. But his private relations with his supporters were too often marred by scenes like the one I have described. Coming away from another angry confrontation with our Chairman, he turned to me and said with a smile: 'You know, Julian, I ought never to be allowed out in private.'

It was a true saying and an epitaph on the failure of his political career. And yet, though Randolph often showed lack of judgement in handling his own affairs, I have seldom known a man who gave sounder advice to others. Our partnership that summer formed the basis of a friendship that would endure until his death. I have never known a friend more loyal or more ready to help in time of trouble.

To return to Preston, our campaign reached its climax with the end of June. I was exhausted but exhilarated. The weather was fine. Electioneering was all new to me. There was real enthusiasm on our side and, as far as we could judge, very little on the other. We took a theatre for the eve of Poll;

and when the curtain went up, Randolph and I marched on to the platform, through a Moorish arch, to the strains of 'Land of Hope and Glory'. There were nearly three thousand people in the audience, and the stage effects and lights helped to convince the audience that they had come there to enjoy themselves. They cheered our speeches to the echo. Then, when the meeting was over, we were literally carried off by our supporters who chaired us—no easy task where Randolph was concerned—from the theatre down the main street to the Conservative Club.

On Polling Day we drove from nine in the morning until nine at night visiting the Committee rooms and polling stations. We went in a cavalcade of open cars preceded by a loudspeaker van which blared out slogans and played our campaign song. Our reception was lyrical. People cheered and waved their handkerchiefs. Even our opponents smiled. In the centre of town, barmaids came out into the streets proffering trays of drinks. At almost every polling station the policemen on duty wished us good luck. I was sure we had won; and, indeed, according to the canvass we had a majority of five thousand. As the stations closed, everyone forecast an easy victory for the 'lively lads' or 'terrible twins' as we were variously known.

There followed three weeks of suspense while the votes of the men overseas were collected and brought home. There were seven thousand Prestonians among them.

Randolph and I travelled back to Preston on the night train arriving on the morning of 26 July for the declaration of the Poll. The enthusiasm of the campaign had evaporated. Life had returned to normal. The count was held in the Town Hall. The results were:

Segal (Labour)	33,053
Sunderland (Labour)	32,889
Churchill (Conservative)	29,129
Amery (Conservative)	27,885
Toulmin (Liberal)	8,521
Devine (Communist)	5,168

The combined Labour vote was thus 8,928 ahead of the combined Conservative vote. Dr. Segal's majority over me was 5,168. Oddly enough, some six hundred people cast one vote for me and one vote for the Communist candidate. We were both young. We both had black hair. I could find no other common denominator between us.

After the count we retired to the Bull and Royal Hotel to give lunch to the officers of our association and to listen to the other results as they came in. We were deeply depressed by our own result and felt that we had let our side down. But, as the news of the landslide against the Conservatives came in, we soon began to realise that we were not alone. One after another, the great names in the party—my father among them—went down to defeat. It was soon clear that our result was considerably better than the average. We had been beaten sure enough but there was nothing to be ashamed of. By the evening, indeed, we had already received several telegrams of congratulations.

That night we went round the clubs to thank our supporters. There were half a dozen such meetings and, at each, the Chairman made a short speech, mostly in praise of Randolph and myself. But there was one Chairman, a staunch supporter of Captain Cobb, who hated Randolph and regarded me as an interloper. He spoke his regret at the defeat of our party, and talked of the country's ingratitude to the Prime Minister. But he made no reference at all to Randolph's efforts or my own. Randolph replied for both of us. I did not take a note of his speech, but it was on the following lines.

> I have been more touched than I can well say, and so I'm sure has Julian Amery, by the glowing tribute which Mr. X has just paid to our work at this Election. What he said about our eloquence was far too generous. What he said about our assiduity in canvassing touched me to the heart. What he said about the punctuality with which we discharged our many obligations was something I can never forget. I know how bitterly he shared my disappointment at our personal defeat, but the memory of his loyalty to me and to Julian is one that will encourage us through the years ahead.

The poor man blushed crimson. The audience roared their heads off with laughter; and for a moment, the bitterness of defeat was forgotten in the general mirth.

The election had been a stimulating and exhilarating experience. It had called for quite different skills from those I had learned in the War. It had carried me into the homes, the pubs, and the factories of industrial Britain and given me a first-hand understanding of its problems. I had enjoyed the fight and had a warm feeling for Preston and its hospitable, outspoken and down-to-earth people. I made no commitment that night, but, in my heart, I looked forward eagerly to the next round.

In the early summer of 1947, Mr. Charles Holt, then Chairman of the Preston Conservative Association, asked me to meet him at Crewe. He wanted to know in confidence if I would stand for Preston again. I agreed at once and was unanimously readopted a few days later without even the formality of an interview.

But Parliament still had nearly three years to run, and it was not until January 1950 that Mr. Attlee decided to go to the country.

Meanwhile, I had taken a crucial decision.

In the spring of 1949, I had telephoned Maurice Macmillan to ask him to lunch. His sister, Catherine, answered and said that he was out. So I asked her to lunch instead. She accepted. In the weeks that followed we were constant companions. At the end of the summer, I visited Delphi, and consulted the Oracle. The answer seemed clear and favourable and on my return I asked her to marry me. It was scarcely a responsible decision, as I had no income and no job. But I reflected that de Gaulle's maxim 'L'intendance suit' is applicable to love as to war.

We were married on 26 January 1950 in St. Margaret's, Westminster. Bill McLean was my best man. Parliament had already been dissolved, but, for that afternoon at least, there was a political truce and many of my Labour friends came to the wedding. S.O.E., the Balkans, the Middle East and Preston were also well represented.

We had three days to ourselves in Paris. But the rest of our honeymoon was spent in the rain and snow of a February election campaign.

Since 1945, Preston had been split into two constituencies. Randolph would not stand again; but I was lucky enough to secure the adoption of Bill McLean as my running mate. Our partnership begun in Albania was thus resumed among the dark, satanic mills of the North-West.

My Chairman this time was Ron Gray, a jeweller by trade but by vocation a showman. His oft repeated maxim was 'First you've got to be known. Then, if you're worth it, you'll be respected. If you're lucky you'll end up by being loved.' At this stage the job was to get me known: and Ron made sure that within two minutes of entering a pub, a shop or some function, everyone knew that I was there. He saw to it, too, that I met all the right people and then took me away from them so that I never had to break off a conversation myself.

Ron was also a brilliant critic. He would spot any weakness in a speech, an article, or an election address in a moment. He might not know at once how to put it right; but we would gnaw away at the problem together until he was satisfied. I have never known a better or more stimulating Chairman.

The campaign itself was much quieter than in 1945 but very tense. We saw from the start that it would be a close run thing. But all the world loves a young couple; and Catherine's presence on my platform swung many votes to me. At one meeting, in our worst ward, an old-fashioned type of working man, unshaven and wearing a scarf and cloth cap, asked me what time I got up in the morning. I answered that I rose at eight. He shouted back, 'Eight! You lazy bastard. Why I get up at five every morning.' Another man of much the same type got up two rows behind. He turned to his mate, and, pointing at Catherine, said to him, 'Yer wouldn't if yer went to bed with yon.' The hall collapsed with laughter and we must have turned a dozen votes that night.

My father, Harold Macmillan, and Maurice all came and spoke for us;

and the campaign became something of a family party. The results were:

Amery (Conservative)	21,888
Segal (Labour)	20,950
Hemelryk (Liberal)	2,012
Devine (Communist)	366

[Conservative majority 938.]

I had scraped in. Bill McLean was defeated by fourteen votes after three recounts. The Labour Government remained in power, but with a majority reduced to six seats.

As we travelled south, I looked back on the past and forward to the future. I had grown up in a closely-knit and understanding family. I had received as good an education as the world could offer; and war, too, is a great university. If the proper study of mankind is man, then Spain, the Balkans, the Middle East and China had been matchless courses in the subject. I had been lucky in my opportunities. I had tried to make the most of them.

After the War, I had expected to enter politics as my father's lieutenant. But by 1950, it was clear that his active political career was over. He was still at hand to encourage and advise, but the task of defending his causes would fall increasingly on me.

I was now thirty years old. I had a seat in Parliament. I had found a wife. We had not had much of a honeymoon; but the years to follow would take care of that.

Index

Compiled by F. D. Buck

Resistance, 233–72, 240, 361
  Albanian, 17, 228, 268, 330
  Balkan, 17, 232, 270, 276, 316
  Bulgarian, 268
  Greek, 267, 268
  groups, 235
  movements, 159, 222, 331, 332
  Yugoslav, 244, 245, 260, 268, 312
Reynaud, Paul, 170
Rhodes, Cecil, 75
Riaz, Mamdouh, 320
Ribbentrop, Joachim von, 128, 193
Ribbentrop-Molotov Agreement, 183
Ribnikar, Vlada, 140
Richelieu, Cardinal, 30
riding, 33
Rivera, Pilar Primo de, 99
Robertson, Grant, 127, 261
Robespierre, Maximilien, 161
Robles, Gil, 108
Rodney, Mrs. Sadie, 26, 32, 33, 66
Rodney, Simon, 26, 32
Rommel, General Erwin, 264, 303, 305, 306
  advance into Egypt, 306
  invasion of Egypt, 276
Roosevelt, Franklin D., 269, 271, 317, 440
Ross, Colonel Alec, 184
Routh, Dick, 54, 55, 56, 59
Rowse, A. L., 75
Royal Air Force, return to, 215–21
Royal Air Force Volunteer Reserve, 119
Rudolf, Archduke, 69
Ruff, Marcel, 56
Russell, Bertrand, 81, 292
Russia, Battle of, 245
Russian Revolution, 58
Russian War, 190, 243
Rutenberg, Pinhas, 282

Saar plebiscite, 61
Said, Nuri, 279
St. Hubert's rite, 64
Salamanca, 99, 111
Salonika, 163, 247
San Sebastian, 88, 89, 109
Sandys, Diana, 223
Sandys, Duncan, 219, 432
Sandys, Julian, 223
Santini, Madame, 81, 82
Saragossa, 91, 93, 97, 98
Sauerwein, Jerome, 78, 118
Schmidt, Ernst, 306
Schmidt, Guido, 70
Schratt, Frau, 70
Secret Intelligence Service, 159, 188
Seddon-Brown, Norman, 431, 432, 433
Seldon, Lord, 266, 268, 405, 409
Serageddin, Fuad, 300
Seton-Watson, Hugh, 195, 196, 197
Seville, 98, 99
Seymour, Lady, 411
Seymour, Sir Horace, 415

Sforza, Count, 81, 82
Shanghai, 409
Sharett, Moshe, 280 fn
Shaw, George Bernard, 42, 54, 78
Shean, Dr., 89
Shearer, Sir John, 204, 205, 206, 207, 275
Shebab, Emir Farid, 203
Shen Shao Kwan, 422
Shertok, Moshe, 280, 281
Shiloah, Reuben (see Zaslani)
Shone, Terence, 138
Sidky Pasha, Ismail, 298, 411
Simcox, Major Tony, 354, 358, 393
Simon, Sir John, 75, 121
Simovitch, General, 227, 236, 237, 238, 239
Singh, Ranbir, 77
Sino-Japanese War, 75
Sirry Pasha, Hussein, 302, 411
Sitwell, Sir Osbert, 61
skiing, 61, 109
Skoplye, 161, 163, 174, 189
Slovene Irridentist Movement, 168, 171
Smart, Walter, 232, 294, 295, 303, 411
Smiley, Major David D.S.O., M.C., 311, 318, 327, 328, 330, 335, 347, 357, 377, 381, 382, 384, 385, 389, 390, 391, 393, 396, 397, 409
Smith, Major Victor, 360, 361, 362, 363, 365
Smuts, Jan, 270, 277
SOE, 15, 159, 160, 162, 227, 228, 235, 238–40, 244, 247, 248, 250, 260, 261, 262, 264, 266, 267, 272, 276, 280, 307, 311, 330, 331, 405, 409, 410, 424, 425, 429, 430, 434, 446
  Albania, 327
  Balkan, 244, 265, 278, 306, 311
  Cairo, 244, 265, 317
  critics, 265
  'D' Section, 174, 178, 180, 181, 184, 188, 189, 190, 193, 195, 204, 205, 212, 220, 222, 223, 224
    London, 198, 207, 222
    Yugoslavia, 247
  Greek, 434
  joins, 160
  leaders of, 334
  London, 307, 308, 311, 409
  Middle East, 244, 307
  problems in, 312
  Sofia, 226
Sofia, 226
Sokitch brothers, 140
Soong, T. V., 417
Spanish Civil War, 17, 87–112, 147, 158, 234, 318
  articles, 102
  speaking engagements, 102
  war correspondent, 102–12
Spanish Foreign Legion (Tercio), 90, 105, 106
special service, 186–92